Dead
Wrong

Dead Wrong

Straight Facts on the Country's Most
Controversial Cover-Ups

Richard Belzer and
David Wayne

Afterword by **Jesse Ventura**

✳   ✳   ✳

Skyhorse Publishing

Skyhorse Publishing books may be purchased in bulk at special discounts for sales promotion, corporate gifts, fund-raising, or educational purposes. Special editions can also be created to specifications. For details, contact the Special Sales Department, Skyhorse Publishing, 307 West 36th Street, 11th Floor, New York, NY 10018 or info@skyhorsepublishing.com.

Skyhorse® and Skyhorse Publishing® are registered trademarks of Skyhorse Publishing, Inc.®, a Delaware corporation.

Visit our website at www.skyhorsepublishing.com.

10 9 8 7 6 5 4 3 2

Library of Congress Cataloging-in-Publication Data

Belzer, Richard.
 Dead wrong : straight facts on the country's most controversial cover-ups / Richard Belzer and David Wayne ; afterword by Jesse Ventura.
    p. cm.
 ISBN 978-1-61608-673-2 (hardcover : alk. paper)
1. Conspiracies--United States--Case studies. 2. Disinformation--United States--Case studies. 3. Political corruption--United States--Case studies. 4. Press and politics--United States--Case studies. I. Wayne, David. II. Title.
 HV6285.B45 2012
 364.1520973--dc23

2012019836

Printed in the United States of America

This book is dedicated to all those who defend the increasingly rare proposition that this country belongs to The People (not corporations, military contractors or "the best politicians that money can buy") and it's still up to The People to determine how it should be governed.

"History is the version of past events that people have decided to agree upon."

—Napoleon Bonaparte

TABLE OF CONTENTS

WARNING

There are those in positions of power who malign the pursuit of justice by intentionally associating the word "conspiracy" with the delirious hallucinations of unbalanced minds.

They're wrong.

The real-world definition of conspiracy is simply; two or more persons agreeing to commit a crime. In short, they are *everywhere*, a constant component of daily events throughout our history, and are by no means the restless imaginings of an over-attentive audience.

Most Americans are completely unaware that a jury in Tennessee in 1999 reached the verdict that a conspiracy involving agencies of the U.S. government was responsible for the assassination of Dr. Martin Luther King. In some of the most important court testimony in American history (which was completely ignored by mainstream media), in one of the most important trials in American history—the extent of media manipulation in the United States was clearly delineated by William Schaap, an attorney and professor who has testified as an expert witness in the areas of intelligence and governmental use of media for disinformation and propaganda:

- The reason that there was no mainstream media coverage of the trial resulting in a conspiracy verdict in the King assassination in 1999 is directly linked to governmental control of the media in the United States.
- "Disinformation is not only getting certain things to appear in print, it's also getting certain things not to appear in print. I mean, the first thing I would say as a way of explanation is, the incredibly powerful effect of disinformation over a long period of time that I mentioned before. For thirty years, the official line has been that James Earl Ray killed Martin Luther King and he did it all by himself. ... And when that is imprinted in the minds of the general public for thirty years, if somebody stood up and confessed and said: I did it. Ray didn't do it, I did it ... it just wouldn't click in their minds."[1]
- About a third of the CIA's budget is for its media operations, which includes <u>domestic use of propaganda</u>, such as solidifying and continuing the public perception that there were <u>no conspiracies</u> in the murders of

---

[1] William Schaap, "Testimony of Mr. William Schaap on the role of the U.S. Government in the assassination of Martin Luther Ling," The King Center, 30 November, 1999, http://www.ratical.org/ratville/JFK/MLKv9Schaap.html (accessed 22 Oct., 2011)

President Kennedy, Senator Robert F. Kennedy, and Dr. Martin Luther King. Their budget is secret (it's kept "classified" because you don't *tell* people that they are being intentionally misinformed); but at least a *billion dollars* per year goes to media propaganda operations, and much of it is *in* the United States.

- There is still an *active focus* on media propaganda in the U.S. by Intelligence agencies to discredit conspiracy theories and solidify the official version of historical events. Americans are particularly vulnerable to intentional misinformation as a result of the way that the notion of conspiracy has been so maligned by the press:

> **"I mean, after all, 'conspiracy' just means, you know, more than one person being involved in something. And if you stop and think about it, almost everything significant that happens anywhere involves more than one person. Yet here there is a – not a myth really, but there's just an underlying assumption that most things are not conspiracies. And when you have that, it enables a government which has a propaganda program, has a disinformation program, to be relatively successful in—in having its disinformation accepted."[2]**

You are certainly correct in assuming that not each death of a celebrity or public official signifies a conspiracy. You are also correct in assuming that, in some cases, the death of a famous person *was* the result of a conspiracy.

A more simplistic argument that's often heard is, "Too many people would have known, someone would have talked"—simply doesn't stand up to reason. To *whom* would they have talked?—try getting a story like *that* published in mainstream media. *Why* would they have talked?—wasn't keeping them quiet the whole *point*? And, in point of fact, some actually *have* talked—for example, longtime undercover operative William Plumlee, whose official Affidavit on the JFK assassination appears in our chapter on that subject.

Another common misconception conveyed in the mainstream media is that in order for a government cover-up to occur, numerous members of various agencies necessarily must *conspire* to commit that act. Nothing could be further from the truth. All that's necessary for a cover-up is a government deciding what's in its own best interest and acting accordingly—utilizing whatever method (often deemed "national security interests") that best achieves their predetermined destination.

Picture a high-level FBI executive "explaining" to an underling, the need to follow the White House's intervention in an investigation on the pretext of the highest levels of the nation's security. An average agent in the field is just going to go along. It's not a matter of *conspiracy*; it's simply the realities of the situation. "Your country needs you" is a very strong argument and more than sufficient for most people. So one is very inclined to just shut up and do their job. *Realistically*, the President of the United States is your Commander-in-Chief. Most

---

[2] William Schaap, "Testimony of Mr. William Schaap on the role of the U.S. Government in the assassination of Martin Luther Ling," The King Center, 30 November, 1999, http://www.ratical.org/ratville/JFK/MLKv9Schaap.html (accessed 22 Oct. 2011)

people in general, and most law enforcement officials in particular, would be happy, even *honored*, to participate in what they perceive as the official objectives and best interests of their nation.

Miguel Rodriguez was a heroic prosecutor who realized that Vince Foster's civil rights had been violated by a cover-up of the true circumstances of his death and he attempted to prosecute those who obstructed justice—he was forced to resign as a result. He responded eloquently to the argument of:

"How could so many people be involved in the cover-up?"

"Rodriguez replied that the evidence did not suggest that all the officials conspired together, just that everyone did what they were told to do, with a number of people fibbing about small matters that together added up to something far greater."[3]

It also bears noting that those who *cover up* a crime are not necessarily those who commit it. When issues perceived to be affecting "national security" arise, cover-ups tend to follow. Cover-ups are not the realm of "conspiracy-mongers" with overactive imaginations. They are very real and have taken place on a regular basis throughout history.

So, the scenario typically presented in major media is that as soon as someone famous dies, then the crazy conspiracy theorists start coming out of the woodwork with the "usual stories" that sensationalize the situation. Sometimes that may be true; on other occasions, it is preposterously inappropriate.

For example, when White House Counsel Vince Foster turned up dead in the park one Tuesday afternoon, mainstream media again blamed those "conspiracy kooks" for all the nutty stories circulating. That could not have been further from an accurate appraisal of the circumstances. The "nuttiest" story of all, in fact, was the official version that immediately placed the official stamp of suicide (contrary to established police procedure in any violent death) amidst a plethora of contradictory evidence which was highly indicative of foul play.

The actual *facts* of the matter indicate:

- The gunpowder burns on Foster's hands were ***defensive***—they were in a region where he could only have had his hands placed on the front of the gun barrel, i.e., in a position defensive to his assailant;
- Foster's fingerprints were nowhere on the gun even though it was a hot and humid day, which would increase the likelihood of leaving fingerprints on the weapon, as would the heavy perspiration that would be expected from a person seriously considering suicide;
- Police said they found a .38 caliber Colt revolver with high-velocity ammo in his hand, and the Government alleges that it was the murder weapon. But there was virtually no blowback. That is not possible. Any homicide investigator will tell you that a .38 fired directly into the mouth leaves a bloodbath all other the place, especially on the victim, their

---

[3] Christopher Ruddy, *The Strange Death of Vincent Foster* (New York: THE FREE PRESS, 1997), 213.

clothing, the gun itself, and anything nearby—it's everywhere, and it's a mess; yet the victim's clothing—even his white shirtsleeve and cuff—were in practically pristine condition. So was the gun. Not possible.

The above are certainly not minor concerns, by any stretch of the imagination, nor are they misplaced theories. And those are just three of the inconsistencies—there are dozens more. In such a matter it is clearly not a bunch of nuts expounding crazy conspiracy theories. It is a case where the official version is so full of gaping holes and inaccuracies that something is seriously amiss. And if the facts are fairly examined, one cannot help but conclude that the official version is the craziest theory out there!

To sum it up simply, unlike many of the authors and investigators whom we studied for this book, we didn't have any pre-formulated agenda: We just followed the evidence ...

Introduction By Richard Belzer

Defaming History or, Who Didn't Kill JFK

> *"President Kennedy's assassination was the work of magicians. It was a stage trick, complete with accessories and fake mirrors, and when the curtain fell, the actors, and even the scenery, disappeared. ... The plotters were correct when they guessed that their crime would be concealed by shadows and silences, that it would be blamed on a madman and negligence."*
>
> **—James Hepburn,** *Farewell America*

"It's pretty heavy, huh?"—Lyndon Johnson, after being presented with the hefty Warren Commission Report by Chief Justice Earl Warren

When I came across prosecutor Vincent Bugliosi's, *Reclaiming History*, I said to the salesperson who guided me to the tome, "It's pretty heavy, huh?" The clerk smiled knowingly as if to get my reference, I hope ... I thought to myself why would Vinnie (Bugliosi) spend, as he claims, five plus years writing a book that after 1600 some pages triumphantly declares, "Oswald did it!!!" In his increasingly testy and defensive style he boldly, if not patronizingly, announces that he is in fact reclaiming history, and in the bargain, he absurdly and summarily dismisses a virtual library of meticulous and overwhelmingly compelling research by the most serious and sober scholars, authors, journalists, archivists, historians, scientists ... who just happen to have come to radically different conclusions than the esteemed prosecutor.

Upon turning to virtually any page of his "history," one major glaring reality becomes more than clear: Mr. Bugliosi is a prosecutor first and foremost ... presenting his "case" ... which should in any reasonable reader's mind disqualify him as a true, let alone objective historian.

Even to the masses of us who are not lawyers, it is almost jokingly obvious that in the classic technique of his trade, there is a torrent of evidence ignored, ridiculed, distorted, reinterpreted, and when needed, he laughingly draws the most ludicrous conclusions and makes mindless ill-informed guesses about the who, what, and whys of Lee Harvey Oswald.

The so-called "mainstream media" in general and depressingly predicable fashion, of course embraced Bugliosi's assault on reason with the glee of ancient archbishops reviewing 1600 pages of a book verifying their "belief" that the world is indeed flat!

So what are we to make of the thousands of pages of theories, counter-theories ... facts chasing facts, a Japanese beetle jar ... that jug of motor oil filled with bugs ... a physicist's nightmare of neutrinos in a rodeo in the fifth dimension ... I sift through those pages and I begin to feel like Boo Radley watching Two and Half Men in Esperanto. It's like watching a David Lynch film projected on rain clouds in a Tasaday village.

I was taught the truth will set you free ... unless of course you want the truth about who killed JFK.

Like all of you, I have a beautiful wife, a house in France, and a career in show business. You might know me from the critically acclaimed and therefore doomed series Homicide: Life on the Street or from one of my television specials, or Law and Order: SVU, or perhaps my political commentary, or one of my books, or one of my personal appearances in a nightclub near you ... I don't know! Just leave me alone! But anyway, just like you, I would rather live my life than sit around thinking nasty thoughts about who killed JFK.

So it behooves me to settle one irrefutable reality about the "crime of the century": IT WAS PHYSICALLY IMPOSSIBLE FOR OSWALD TO HAVE SHOT PRESIDENT KENNEDY!!! There I said it: with no apologies to the likes of prosecutor Bugliosi. Let me explain this pesky fact once and for all. The prosecutor likes to boast that he is virtually the only person on earth to have read the entire 26 volumes of the Warren Report. He fails to mention his willful, startlingly lax examination of the contradictions and omissions in the report.

After President Kennedy's head was exploded, Lee Harvey Oswald was discovered on the second floor of the Book Depository building drinking a Coke. His presence was verified by his boss, Roy Truly, and motorcycle patrolman Marion Baker. According to the Warren Commission, the three men's encounter was reenacted in two "tests" by the commission: In the first, Baker (walking!) reached the second floor landing in 1 minute, 30 seconds. In the second test; in his words: "at kind of a trot"; he finished the course in 1 minute, 15 seconds ... to "time" Oswald's movements, Special Agent John Howlett of the Secret Service (in another rigged "test") carried a rifle (there were three rifles found in the Depository on November 22: a German Mauser, a much joked about Italian Mannlicher-Carcano, and a British Enfield Rifle; but that's another story) from the "nest" and "placed" the Carcano on the floor near the site where it was actually found. The truth is the murderer hid the rifle, which would take longer than to "place it on the floor." The reality is (as Mr. Bugliosi knows full well if he "read" the Report as he claims) the Warren Commission reenactments of Baker's reaction times were done at a slower speed than his actual movements, according to Baker's own testimony he ran from his motorcycle and into the depository quickly but the reenactments had him purposely go slower to meet the needs of the Commission's desire to create the impression that there was time enough for the assassin to do his dirty deed. Let us now consider what Oswald was alleged to have accomplished, by some miracle, with his rickety ass misaligned bolt-action relic of a rifle: Fire three bullets, with deadly accuracy (of which one was "magic:" a theory concocted by Arlen Specter, at the behest of the Commission, that manages to suspend the laws of Newtonian physics!), squeeze out of the sniper's nest, wipe off the gun, go to the opposite end of the sixth floor, zigzagging and dodging stacks of books, wedge the weapon between two of the stacks, run down four flights of stairs (with landings, actually making it eight flights, I visited the Book Depository) then, according to page 679 of Volume XXVI of the Commission's Hearings and Exhibits ... exhibit No. 3076 quoting Officer Baker's deposition: "on the second floor where the lunchroom is located, I saw a man standing in the lunchroom drinking a Coke;" Oswald appeared completely calm and not the least out of breath or nervous at his chance encounter with patrolman Baker and Roy Truly (who remember ran up just one flight of stairs) in reality surely getting them there in more like SIXTY TO SIXTY FIVE SECONDS ladies and gentlemen: Therefore to repeat: IT WAS PHYSICALLY IMPOSSIBLE FOR OSWALD TO HAVE SHOT PRESIDENT KENNEDY!!! THANK YOU AND GOODNIGHT!

In conclusion I would have the distinguished prosecutor ponder two quotes:

"Let General de Pellieux allow me respectfully to point out that a piece of evidence, whatever it may be, cannot have any value and cannot constitute scientific proof before it has been subjected to cross-examination ... "

—Fernand Labori, defense attorney at the trial of Emile Zola.
Paris, February 17, 1898

And finally: *"There is a certain nobility about facing up to the truth ... "*

—Oxford scholar Richard Dawkins.

P.S. I highly recommend Josiah Thompson's masterpiece *Six Seconds In Dallas: A Micro-Study of the Kennedy Assassination*, Published by Bernard Geis Associates-Distributed by Random House, 1967; *The Oswald Affair-An Examination of the Contradictions and Ommissions of The Warren Report*, By Leo Sauvage, Published by The World Publishing Company 1966; and the most compelling, incredibly revelatory book ever written about the murder and all it's labyrinthian logistics and mysteries, *Ultimate Sacrifice*, by Lamar Waldron and Thom Hartmann, Published by Carrol & Graf 1966.

Conspiratorially Yours,

RICHARD BELZER

INTRODUCTION BY DAVID WAYNE

Governments tell lies, and most of us are learning to look at that as a reality. Forensic evidence stands in stark contrast, exhibiting the signposts of *truth* in a mute testimony that is almost timeless.

Those who commit crimes—be they governments, mobsters, or maniacs—inevitably make mistakes. And it's the evidence—in its silent but relentless integrity—which proves that which *actually* took place.

Even at its ugliest, evidence is somehow comforting, even beautiful: Purplish bruises (known technically as *lividity* marks) telling us that a body was moved post-mortem; dried vomit that ran up a cheek, informing us that the victim wasn't standing or sitting at the time of death *and* that any drugs involved were not fully ingested.

Evidentiary findings serve as a fixed beacon from which to navigate the shifting sands of time. They are of such significance that even what is *missing* helps us to solve the puzzle: an absence of sufficient blood determines what could *not* have happened at a crime scene; a stomach without refractive crystals screams to us that the victim could *not* have swallowed the drugs.

So, if you still believe that Marilyn Monroe overdosed on pills, or that Lee Harvey Oswald murdered JFK, or that Sirhan Bishara Sirhan killed Senator Robert Kennedy, then you better keep reading. In fact, you owe it to yourself as a witness to history. All the aforementioned allegations are quite literally *impossible*. If at first glance that seems arrogant, then just read those three chapters—it won't seem so after you have; for it is not a matter of opinions—those are the conclusions that the evidence necessitates. Examine the facts fairly and you will reach the same conclusions. Former FBI Special Agent Zack Shelton, whose excellent investigative summary, *The Shelton Report,* appears exclusively in our JFK chapter, summed up our work ethic best:

"I don't have any theories. All I have are the facts."

We include two types of entries: deaths that were alleged to be suicides or were originally ruled suicides, but have so many suspicious circumstances that they appear to have been murders and; deaths that were known to be murders but have so many irreconcilable issues that something is clearly amiss. In some cases, they were obvious: shooting one's self in the head five times with a bolt-action rifle is a bit of a stretch to term a suicide—even in Texas. In others, the flawed official reasoning was more subtle but, upon examination, every bit as clear.

In some chapters, we provide a brief summary of the major thinking that has developed regarding a specific death or assassination. Therefore, please note in sections following the subtitle *"possible scenarios"* that we at times may be leaving the field of facts and entering the arena of speculation—two very different places—and that we do not necessarily subscribe to a particular viewpoint.

Also note that forensic science isn't as simple as it sounds, or as we're too often led to believe on popular television shows. Cliff Spiegelman, distinguished professor of statistics and toxicology at Texas A & M University, is the author of many articles for peer-reviewed science journals, and is considered an expert in the field of forensic technology. Prof. Spiegelman observes:

> **"The application of forensic sciences is often lacking application of the scientific method. This is true in high-profile cases as well. Examples of misused forensic techniques include compositional bullet lead analysis (no longer used by the FBI Crime Lab) and firearm toolmarks (striations on bullets)."[4]**

Spiegelman and his colleagues have called for re-opening the investigation into the JFK assassination due to "fundamentally flawed" evidence procedures.

> **"The painful truth is that nearly all forensic procedures have been developed without much involvement from the statistical community or enough involvement from the independent, university-based scientific community or federal research labs. ... As a result, forensic results are typically stated with uncertainty statements that cannot be supported. For example, it is typical in firearm toolmark identifications to state that, to a practical certainty, the defendant's gun fired the bullets found in a decedent. Two recent National Research Council (NRC) reports (Strengthening Forensic Science in the United States: A Path Forward and Ballistic Imaging) conclude there is no statistical foundation for such an absolute statement. Also, some federal and state jurisdictions recently ruled that firearm toolmark examiners may only testify that it is more likely than not that the defendant's gun fired the bullets found in a decedent. (See State of Ohio v. Anderson (pdf) and U.S. v. GLYNN.) That is, the courts require only a better than 50-50 chance of a match.**
>
> **The broader scientific community has noted the blatant failures of forensic science, but the justice system has not paid careful enough attention."[5]**

---

[4] Clifford Spiegeleman, email to author, 31 May 2010.
[5] Clifford Spiegelman, "Weak Forensic Science Has High Cost," *AMSTAT News, Magazine of the American Statistical Association,* 1 Mar. 2010.

These observations are important; Spiegelman organized a "bulletproof" panel of scientific and forensic experts that included former FBI scientist William Tobin, an expert in evidentiary techniques as well as ballistic forensics. The blue-ribbon panel utilized the latest compositional analysis techniques that were not available in the 1960s. Conclusion? In the evidence techniques employed by the government after the JFK assassination:

> " ... evidence used to rule out a second assassin is fundamentally flawed."[6]

---

[6] Clifford Spiegelman, William A. Tobin, William D. James, Simon J. Sheather, Stuart Wexler and D. Max Roundhill, "Chemical and forensic analysis of JFK assassination bullet lots: Is a second shooter possible?," *The Annals of Applied Statistics*, Volume 1, Number 2 (2007), 285-634.

Dead Wrong

✳   ✳   ✳

CHAPTER 1

Frank Olson –
November 28, 1953
Head of Special Operations Division
(Top-Secret Research), CIA

Photo courtesy of *Frank Olson Legacy Project*,
FrankOlsonProject.org

VICTIM	FRANK OLSON
Cause of Death	Fell from the thirteenth-story window of his hotel in New York City.
Official Verdict	"SUICIDE": Coroner cited autopsy findings indicating that the victim jumped from his window. In 1975, the CIA admitted doping Olson with LSD that led to his suicide (what is known in intelligence parlance as a "limited hangout") and settled out of court with the Olson family for $750,000 <u>precluding further investigation</u>. Olson's family had the body exhumed and re-autopsied in the 1990s and forensic experts concluded that Olson was murdered; the New York District Attorney's office conducted a murder investigation but never filed criminal charges.

Actual Circumstances

Olson's death was a clear-cut case of "National Security homicide." As head of CIA bio-weapons research, he had extensive access to "state secrets." One of those secrets was that bombs with the anthrax virus had apparently been dropped on North Korea. He'd become increasingly outraged and vocal by what he saw as an immoral use of his research. He told colleagues he was disturbed about evidence of CIA torture-to-death interrogations in Germany and bacteriological warfare on North Korea. He was deemed a security risk and was interviewed by Military Intelligence. He was drugged with LSD without his knowledge (or permission) and further interrogated about his plans. On the Monday immediately preceding his death, he informed his boss that he was quitting his job (he died the following Saturday). That weekend, he was booked into the Hotel Statler in New York City accompanied by a CIA agent who was constantly guarding him. He was then visited by a military doctor, and once again drugged, and apparently clubbed and pushed out the window of the hotel (the window was <u>closed</u> at the time) and found dying on the sidewalk. A phone call was placed by the CIA agent immediately afterwards (and overheard by a hotel operator) in which the agent stated only: "Well, he's gone." Exhumation and autopsy revealed that he had suffered a severe hematoma to the skull (blow to the head) <u>prior</u> to the fall. It was a textbook murder taken directly from the CIA Assassination Manual.

Inconsistencies

1. A second autopsy demanded by relatives confirmed 'blunt force trauma' and that the victim was rendered unconscious *prior* to his fall. Forensic findings were also that there were no indications that the trauma could have come from the window and that the forensic evidence was "rankly and starkly suggestive of homicide."
2. The U.S. government conceded in an out-of-court settlement that LSD was administered to Olson without his knowledge or permission.
3. Forensic experts conducting a second autopsy concluded that the first autopsy report intentionally misrepresented the true facts in order to make it appear a suicide.
4. Contrary to the first autopsy report, no lacerations were found upon the victim, even though he had supposedly crashed through and out of a plate glass window at high

speed, plus a canvas shade and cloth curtain covering the shade. Even if the window shade had protected his body from cuts on the way through the window, the forensic literature reveals that individuals receive the most lacerations as parts of their body <u>withdraw</u> from the glass, not as they crash through it (i.e., on the way *out* of the window, not on the way through it), specifically causing multiple lacerations, especially upon the legs of the victim. Olson had none.[7]

5. The hotel room was so small that it would have been impossible for the victim to build up sufficient running speed, then catapult over the twin beds that intersected the room and crash through a plate glass window upon impact, especially one that was not very high.

6. Forensic examination determined that the body of the victim was medically consistent with the body having been dumped out the window in a semi-conscious state, rather than having intentionally crashed through it.

7. The CIA agent, Robert Lashbrook, who was "shadowing" the victim, kept changing his story about how the victim went out the window. The night manager at the hotel immediately realized that something was clearly amiss:

> "And here is Lashbrook sitting on a john in his skivvies and the police thought to question him and I heard him say, 'Well all I heard was a crash.' I walked around the room to look around. Nobody ever jumps through a window. They open the window and they go out, not dash through a shade and a sheer drape. You know, there's no sense to that."

8. Instead of calling the police or the hotel desk after "the accident" as might be expected, the CIA agent called his superior, CIA scientist Dr. Harold Abramson (who had sedated Olson earlier) and, in a conversation enabled and overheard by the hotel operator, stated only:

> "Well, he's gone."

9. Olson had been interviewed by Military Intelligence and deemed a security risk.

10. Nine days before his death, Olson was drugged (without his knowledge or permission) with LSD and a drug known to make a person more open and talkative and then, in a drugged state, was interrogated utilizing secret interrogation techniques garnered from *Artichoke*, the mind-control operation that Olson had been part of.

---

[7] James E. Starrs with Katherine Ramsfeld, *A Voice for the Dead: A Forensic Investigator's Pursuit of the Truth in the Grave* (New York: G. P. Putnam's Sons 2005).

11. Shortly before Olson's death, the CIA distributed its Assassination Manual to agents (it was declassified in 1997) which details the precise method of Olson's death as <u>the</u> most preferable method of assassination.

12. In training for the assassinations unit of the Israeli Mossad (Institute for Intelligence & Special Operations), the Olson murder has been used as an example of a perfect assassination.

"Frank Olson's murder is like a nuclear bomb in an 18th century naval battle. It stands out because of its context ... In the absence of oversight or accountability, sadism and stupidity compete for domination."[8]

Would it surprise you to learn that the CIA drugged an entire French village with LSD? Or that it "tested" LSD on unknowing U.S. citizens right in the middle of Manhattan; and on our own soldiers, prisoners, and mental patients locked-up in hospitals?[9] How about that the U.S. tested anthrax on American factory workers and used BW (Bacteriological Warfare) on civilians in North Korea? Or that the CIA secret prisons now known as black sites for "extraordinary rendition" (translation: kidnap-torture) bear their roots in the research of the 1950s? You won't be seeing those facts in high school history books any time soon, but they *did* happen; and Frank Olson was the man who attempted to intervene on behalf of humanity—an act which cost him his life.

Frank Olson, a gifted chemist, was a CIA officer and Acting Chief of Special Operations for the Central Intelligence Agency at the top-secret Special Operations Division at Camp Detrick in Detrick, Maryland. Biological warfare, LSD as a mind-control technique, terminal interrogations and assassination techniques were the realm of the Special Operations Division. Olson was an expert in the use of psychoactive drugs and biological warfare, including anthrax and other viral agents, and he had top security clearance.

A special CIA operation code-named Artichoke "involved the development of special, extreme methods of interrogation."

Robert Lashbrook was the identity of the CIA agent shadowing Olson, day and night.

Historical Perspective of Operation Artichoke

▶ **World War Two**

The "sweeping up" by the Allies following the fall of Nazi Germany includes Operation Dustbin, Operation Trashcan, and Operation Paperclip. The Allies perceived that both Russian and China were already enemies. Some generals recommend continuing on from

---

[8] David Swanson, "LSD, Murder and the CIA: Frank Olson, Enemy Combatant," *Counterpunch*, 26-28 Mar. 2010

[9] H. P. Albarelli Jr., *A Terrible Mistake: The Murder of Frank Olson and the CIA's Secret Cold War Experiments*, (Trine Day, 2011)

Berlin to Moscow in order to keep Eastern Europe from going Communist, while other generals counsel that land wars in Asia are unwinnable (wisdom that the U.S. later ignores in its wars against Vietnam-Laos-Cambodia, Iraq & Afghanistan).

Therefore, a contest ensues to capture the best of Nazi technology for use in the coming Cold War.

▸ Operation Paperclip

Operation Paperclip "saved" Nazi scientists. It was a mission to determine those scientists of value to the West in the Cold War. We interviewed Nazi scientists, including those who had conducted experimentation on human subjects in concentration camps such as Dachau, to determine what research was of value and potential use. One of these men was the infamous Kurt Blome. They were shielded from conviction at the Nuremberg war trials (although the evidence against them was substantial and they were clearly Nazi war criminals) and they were quite literally "rescued" from the gallows in exchange for their help with US research programs.

▸ Operation Artichoke

Artichoke continued where the research had left off in Nazi Germany, and Kurt Blome worked with the scientists on the program. Frank Olson, as Acting Director of CIA Special Operations Division, oversaw the work of this program. Artichoke largely dealt with mind-control techniques and brutal interrogation methods often ending in the death of what the CIA termed "expendables" (prisoners, suspected double agents, etc.). Olson witnessed these interrogations and apparently considered them immoral and very disturbing. "Tests" under Artichoke included combinations of hypnosis, torture, LSD and other hallucinogens, and "mind-opening" and "tongue-loosening" agents. These tests were in the direction of mind-control, maneuvering subjects into controllable states to manufacture "Manchurian candidates" (programmed killers) or, in the case of interrogations, will-less subjects who became totally compliant. Tests sometimes left victims in vegetative states and were other times fatal.

▸ Use of BW (Bacteriological Warfare) Against North Korea

Top secret order JCS 1837/26 dated September 21, 1951 from the US Joint Chiefs of Staff Command clearly authorized the "field testing" of anthrax weapons and there is evidence that testing was conducted on the civilian population of North Korea.[10] Eyewitnesses to the testing verify the reports.[11]

---

[10] Joint Chiefs of Staff 1837/26, "Biological Warfare: Memorandum by the Joint Advanced Study Committee for the Joint Chiefs of Staff," 21 September, 1951, Combined Chiefs of Staff 385.2, sec. 13, RG 330, NARA: JCS 1837/26, "Statements of Policy and Directives on Biological Warfare," 3 July 1952, Combined Chiefs of Staff 385.2, sec. 15, RG 273.

[11] Stephen Endicott & Edward Hagerman, *The United States and Biological Warfare: Secrets from the Early Cold War and Korea*, 1998

▶ **Murder of Frank Olson**

Olson became disturbed at the macabre events to which he was privy and became openly talkative and critical about the secret work the CIA was conducting. Among the things Olson apparently talked about, in addition to the lethal interrogation techniques, were the use of anthrax as a bacteriological weapon during the Korean War, and the fact that the "recanted confessions" of dozens of returning POWs who witnessed BW in North Korea were the apparent result of "debriefings" utilizing techniques garnered from Operation Artichoke.[12]

A close associate and colleague of Olson at Ft. Detrick, Norman Cournoyer, testified that Olson personally told him that in the course of Operation Artichoke, he had witnessed torture interrogations in Europe that had disturbed him deeply at a moral level, so much so that he was disgusted with the CIA and intended to leave. Cournoyer also stated Olson was convinced that, despite official denials, the U.S. had employed the use of biological weapons, including the use of anthrax, during the Korean War. A film, *Code Name ARTICHOKE,* documents the events surrounding the secret program and can be accessed on *YouTube.*

Close friends, family, and coworkers document that Frank Olson was a very decent man boxed into a corner by a very indecent position, who became increasingly outraged by what he saw.

Olson was deemed a security risk. The same advanced interrogation techniques under LSD and talk-inducing drugs that were perfected by his Special Operations Division were then used on Olson himself. He then informed the CIA that he was resigning his position, and a few days later he was apparently again drugged, subdued, and thrown out of a 13th floor window.

The methods of Operation Artichoke did not disappear. Quite to the contrary, some have apparently been applied at Guantánamo, Abu Ghraib, and most notably, in the CIA secret prisons for extraordinary rendition. Some have accused the government of using Artichoke-type techniques on José Padilla prior to his terrorism conviction in 2007 that made him into a "human vegetable."[13]

---

[12] Walker M. Mahurin, *Honest John: The Autobiography of Walker M. Mahurin,* (New York: G. P. Putnam's Sons, 1962)

[13] Amy Goodman, "An Inside Look at How U.S. Interrogators Destroyed the Mind of Jose Padilla," August 16, 2007, *DemocracyNow.org,* http://www.democracynow.org/2007/8/16/exclusive_an_inside_look_at_how (accessed 14 May, 2011)

Events Leading to Death of Frank Olson

▶ **Late 1940s**

In a secret facility at Fort Detrick, Maryland, a massive arms program was underway to develop bacteriological weapons, primarily anthrax spores, which were proven to be highly resistant and therefore suitable for biological warfare.

▶ **1949**

As Acting Director of CIA's highly secretive Special Operations Division, Olson was privy to many secrets. As a leader of Operation Artichoke (brainwashing & mind control interrogation techniques via drugs, hypnosis & torture), he witnessed unscrupulous experiments on human beings that resulted in their deaths. The experience leaves a noticeable mark on him, according to friends and family, and he begins to question the morality of their work.

▶ **October, 1949**

Olson's free-thinking and talkative lifestyle was considered dangerous in relation to his work in military secrets. He was suspected of disclosing government secrets (an accusation that was never proven) and interrogated by Military Intelligence. Olson was from then on considered a security risk. The Military Intelligence report stated that:

> "Olson is violently opposed to control of scientific research, either military or otherwise, and opposes supervision of his work. He does not follow orders, and has had numerous altercations with MP's ... "

Norman Cournoyer, a co-worker who was close to Olson, summarized:

> "He was very, very open and not scared to say what he thought. For that matter, to the contrary. He did not give a damn. Frank Olson pulled no punches at any time ... That's what they were scared of, I am sure."

▶ **April, 1950**

Olson was given a diplomatic passport, highly unusual for an Army scientist, and began making frequent trips to Europe, especially to Germany.

▶ **1950–1953**

In CIA safe-houses in Germany, Olson witnessed horrific brutal interrogations on a regular basis. Detainees who were deemed "expendable"; suspected spies or "moles", security leaks, etc., were literally interrogated to death in experimental methods combining drugs, hypnosis, and torture to attempt to master brainwashing techniques and memory erasing ... The "live" testing on human beings was designed to extract information from the detainee and then leave him in a blank mental state in which he was unaware what happened to him.

▶ **June, 1952**

Family and co-workers report that Olson's behavior had markedly changed. He became openly critical and talkative about the work being conducted at the CIA.

▶ **1952–1953**

CIA established that large doses of LSD are much better "tongue-looseners" than alcohol. They test the technique on unsuspecting victims right in New York City's Greenwich Village section, having prostitutes slip the drug into the drinks of customers who are then interrogated.

▶ **August, 1953**

After returning from another trip to Germany where he witnessed the CIA's torture-to-death interrogations, Olson became extremely moody. Friends and family comment that he began to behave like he was boxed into a corner and could not do anything about it. He informed close friend and co-worker, Norman Cournoyer, that he was planning on resigning his CIA position:

"He said 'Norm, you would be stunned by the techniques that they used. They made people talk! They brainwashed people! They used all kinds of drugs, they used all kinds of torture.'" "He said, that he was going to leave. He told me that. He said, 'I am getting out of that CIA. Period'"

Olson and Counoyer are both aware of two disturbing truths:

1. The use of anthrax as a biological weapon during the Korean War;
2. The fact that the "recanted confessions" of dozens of returning POWs who witnessed BW in North Korea were the apparent result of "debriefings" utilizing techniques garnered from Operation Artichoke.

▶ **Thursday, November 19, 1953**

The same LSD interrogation technique that was perfected by his Special Operations Division was then used on Olson himself. At a work retreat just prior to Thanksgiving, the CIA's "Dirty Tricks" Division met with ten of its scientists at a remote location. Olson was given a large dose of the drug, without his knowledge or permission, and was then interrogated under the influence of LSD using Artichoke techniques.

▶ **Friday evening, November 20, 1953**

Olson returned home to his family and was visibly and deeply disturbed. He told his wife that there were very serious problems with his work and that he had made "a terrible mistake."

▶ **Saturday & Sunday, November 21–22, 1953**

Olson stayed inside all weekend and was very quiet and thoughtful all weekend long. His children recall the weekend as being very somber and serious and vividly remember their father at that time as sitting for hours on the sofa and staring thoughtfully out the window.

▶ **Monday, November 23, 1953**

Olson informed his boss, Lieutenant Colonel Vincent Ruwet, that he "wanted out of the germ warfare business" to "devote his life to something else" and that he, therefore, was resigning from his position. LTC Ruwet refuses to accept Olson's resignation.

▶ **Tuesday, November 24, 1953**

Olson returned to the office of LTC Ruwet and again informed him that he was resigning from his position. Lt. Colonel Ruwet advised Olson not to resign and told him that they will take him to New York City to get treatment for his depression about his work.

▶ **Friday, November 27, 1953**

Olson was brought to New York City by Lt. Colonel Ruwet and was also in the constant accompaniment of a CIA agent who was assigned as his shadow. They check Olson and the CIA agent into room 1018a (which is actually the thirteenth floor when the first three unnumbered floors are counted) of the Hotel Statler (which is now the Hotel Pennsylvania). They are visited there by a CIA doctor who administers medication to Olson.

▶ **Saturday, November 28, 1953 at 2:30 AM**

In the early morning hours of Saturday night/Sunday morning, Frank Olson went through the closed thirteenth floor window of his hotel room, crashing through a canvas window shade, a cloth curtain covering the shade and a closed plate glass window, before landing on the 7th Avenue sidewalk.

▶ **Saturday, November 28, 1953, 2:30–2:35 AM**

Hotel manager Armand Pastore rushed outside, attempting to comfort the victim, who died in his arms.

▶ **Saturday, November 28, 1953, 2:30–2:35 AM**

CIA agent Robert Lashbrook phoned Dr. Harold Abramson (the doctor working with the CIA who had sedated Olson earlier) from the hotel room. Via the system in use in 1953, Lashbrook had to use the hotel operator to place the call to a number in Long Island. The hotel operator stayed on the line and heard the call in its entirety. After the call was connected and answered, the caller only stated the following:

> "Well, he's gone."

The other party then stated:

> "Well, that's too bad."

Both parties then hung up.

▶ **Saturday, November 28, 1953 at 2:40–3:00 AM**

Hotel manager Armand Pastore notified police and also determined that the victim must have fallen from Room 1018a on the thirteenth floor and that there was another occupant of that room. Pastore leads police to 1018a and opens the door for them. The police enter, guns drawn, and encounter the room's other occupant, Robert Lashbrook, seated on the toilet. The police say "What happened?" and Lashbrook responds: "I don't know, I just heard a crash of glass and then I see that Frank Olson is out of the window and he is down on the street."

▶ **Sunday, November 29 , 1953**

The case was classified as a suicide and immediately closed.

▶ **Post-Mortem—Summer, 1975**

The report of The Rockefeller Commission was released in which it was made public that the CIA had drugged U.S. citizens with LSD without their permission. The Olson family investigated the information contained in the report and confirmed that one of the subjects referred to was indeed Frank Olson. They held a press conference and demanded that the case of their father's death be investigated.

▶ **Post-Mortem—Summer, 1975**

Donald Rumsfeld and Richard Cheney, aides to President Ford, confidentially recommend to the President that he contain the "Olson matter" by settling out of court to preclude "the possibility that it might be necessary to disclose highly classified national security information," because it has become known that the CIA did indeed drug Frank Olson with LSD just prior to his death. Therefore, in what is known in Intelligence parlance as a "limited hangout," the CIA settled out of court with the Olson family for $750,000 retribution for past wrongdoing. Ten days after the memo from Rumsfeld and Cheney recommending retribution and an apology, President Ford hosted the Olson family at the White House for photos and handshakes with the family after the President apologizes on behalf of the U.S. Government.

▶ Post-Mortem

Former longtime CIA agent Ike Feldman investigated the circumstances of Olson's death:

"The source that I have was the New York City Police Department, the Bureau of Narcotics Agents and the CIA agents themselves. They all say the same thing: that he was pushed out of the window and that he did not jump.

People who wanted him out of the way said he talked too much and he was telling people about the things he had done which is American secret. If you work on a top government secret, a city secret, a state secret, and it spills out to people who should not know, there is only one way to do it: kill him."

▶ Post-Mortem—June 2, 1994

Olson's body was exhumed and autopsied at the insistence of relatives suspicious of foul play. Eminent forensic scientist James Starrs, Professor of Law and Forensic Science at the National Law Center at George Washington University, led the autopsy team, also selecting a diverse team of scientific experts in the appropriate fields. The team determined that the original medical report in 1953 was "manipulated" and "totally inaccurate in some very important respects." Forensic finding is that the victim suffered a severe hematoma, i.e., a blunt force trauma to the head, prior to his fall through the window:

"That is only reasonably explainable as having occurred by reason of his being shall we say silenced, being rendered unable to defend himself, so that he could be tossed out of the window."

Official finding of Professor James Starrs, George Washington University:

"HOMICIDE"

Regarding the assassination method detailed in the CIA Assassination Manual, Professor Starrs further states:

"What was spelled out in that 'Assassination Manual' was almost letter for letter what happened to Doctor Olson and it was a protocol, as we call it, for an assassination, which fit like the fingers in a glove."

Source material for the above chart was derived primarily from the following:

"The Frank Olson Legacy Project," http://www.frankolsonproject.org/Contents.html

Code Name: Artichoke; The CIA's Secret Experiments on Humans, film by Egmont R. Koch & Michael Wech, 2002, http://topdocumentaryfilms.com/code-name-artichoke/

A Terrible Mistake: The Murder of Frank Olson and the CIA's Secret Cold War Experiments; H.P. Albarelli Jr.; 2009, Trine Day.

"The Case of Frank Olson," Oliver Boothby, February 11, 1996: http://www.frankolsonproject.org/Student%20papers/Oliver.html

"Scientist was 'Killed to Stop Him Revealing Death Secrets'; So Did Cheney and Rumsfeld Cover Up a CIA Assassination?," Gordon Thomas, London Sunday Express, August 25, 2002.

"Frank Olson: Did a government scientist jump to his death from a New York hotel? Or was he pushed?," http://www.unsolved.com/ajax-files/une_frank_olson.htm

"LSD, Murder and the CIA: Frank Olson, Enemy Combatant," David Swanson, *Counterpunch*, March 26-28, 2010

The Biology of Doom: The History of America's Secret Germ Warfare Project, Ed Regis, 2000

Rumsfeld & Cheney's Dirty Little Spy Secret, Fintan Dunne, Editor, *GuluFuture.com,* March 6, 2006:
http://www.apfn.net/messageboard/03-06-06/discussion.cgi.31.html

The Men Who Stare At Goats, Jon Ronson, 2005

Robert Lashbrook was the identity of the CIA agent shadowing Olson, day and night.

Armond Pastore, who was the night manager at the hotel, had seen more than his share of accidents, and immediately took the police up to room 1018A so the police could investigate. They found the CIA agent sitting in the bathroom. Pastore recalled very clearly:

"And here is Lashbrook sitting on a john in his skivvies and the police thought to question him and I heard him say, 'Well all I heard was a crash.' I walked around the room to look around. Nobody ever jumps

through a window. They open the window and they go out, not dash through a shade and a sheer drape. You know, there's no sense to that." [14]

"The first call that Lashbrook made was not to the hotel management or the police, but to his superior, Dr. Sid Gottlieb, at his home in Virginia, to tell him what had happened. Then he reported to the hotel desk clerk and telephoned Dr. Abramson." [15]

"In those days all of the calls were manual. You call the operator and you tell her what number you want and she would dial it for you. And then she listened to see that you got connected. When the man in the room called this number he said, 'Well, he's gone.' And the man on the other end said, 'Well, that's too bad.' And they both hung up. I mean, what's more suspicious than that? You don't have to be a genius to figure out that there's something amiss. Or, Hamlet said, 'There's something rotten in Denmark.' I mean, I knew there was something rotten at the hotel that night." [16]

Kathryn Olmstead, Professor of History at the University of California, discovered documents indicating a White House-level cover-up of the Frank Olson case, related to the secret use of anthrax weapons. Dick Cheney and Donald Rumsfeld were directly involved in concealing information about Olson's death. Dr. Olmstead also said that part of Olson's work was the making of anthrax and other biological weapons.

Rumsfeld, at that time, was White House Chief of Staff to President Gerald Ford and Dick Cheney was a White House assistant.

One of the documents that Professor Olmstead obtained states:

"Dr. Olson's job was so sensitive that it is highly unlikely that we would submit relevant evidence." [17]

In another memo, Cheney acknowledges the following:

"The Olson lawyers will seek to explore all the circumstances of Dr. Olson's employment, as well as those concerning his death. In any trial, it may become apparent that we are concealing evidence

[14] Unsolved.com, "Frank Olson: Did a government scientist jump to his death from a New York Hotel? Or was he pushed?," http://www.unsolved.com/ajaxfiles/une_frank_olson.htm (accessed 2 Feb. 2011).

[15] Stephen Endicott, "Memo from Stephen Endicott, Professor of History, York University, analyzing the documents obtained by the Olson family from CIA Director William Colby in June 1975," *FrankOlsonProject.org*, February 4, 1999, http://www.frankolsonproject.org/Sources/Notes%20on%20items%20&%20events/Endicott-Analysis.html (accessed 16 Feb. 2011).

[16] Unsolved.com, "Frank Olson: Did a government scientist jump to his death from a New York Hotel? Or was he pushed?," http://www.unsolved.com/ajaxfiles/une_frank_olson.htm (accessed 2 Feb. 2011).

[17] Gordon Thomas, "Scientist was 'killed to stop him revealing death secrets'; So did Cheney and Rumsfeld cover up a CIA assassination?" *London Sunday Express*, August 25, 2002, http://www.frankolsonproject.org/Articles/LondonExpress.html (accessed 14 Jan. 2011)

for national security reasons and any settlement or judgment reached thereafter could be perceived as money paid to cover up the activities of the CIA."[18]

Many observers, therefore, have "connected the dots" and concluded that Cheney and Rumsfeld were given the task in the 1970s of covering up the details of Olson's death.

"The fact that Frank Olson had died shortly after being given LSD in a CIA experiment came out in 1975 as a consequence of President Ford's Rockefeller Commission investigation into the CIA's domestic activities. Further investigation was called for, but in a White House memo advisers to President Ford stated that this would risk revealing state secrets (probably meaning, in part, the use by the U.S. of germ warfare in Korea); further investigation was suppressed and the whole matter covered up. The names of those White House advisers were Dick Cheney, current U.S. Vice-President, and Donald Rumsfeld, current Secretary of Defense. They have never been questioned as to what they knew about Olson's death."[19]

Cheney-Rumsfeld: The "formative" years: Both handled the "limited hangout" under President Ford in 1975, settling with the Olson family for $750,000, a private audience and apology from President Ford and an apparent end to the uncomfortable issues surrounding Frank Olson's knowledge of bacteriological warfare by the US in North Korea and the "enhanced" interrogation techniques of *Project Artichoke*. The Olson family later learned that a "renewed coverup of the truth concerning this story was being carried out at the highest levels of government, including the White House."

---

[18] Gordon Thomas, "Scientist was 'killed to stop him revealing death secrets'; So did Cheney and Rumsfeld cover up a CIA assassination?" *London Sunday Express*, August 25, 2002, http://www.frankolsonproject.org/Articles/LondonExpress.html (accessed 14 Jan. 2011)

[19] Serendipity, "The Frank Olson Murder," http://www.serendipity.li/cia/olson2.htm (accessed 14 May 2011)

The following is a verbatim excerpt from the CIA Assassination Manual which was declassified in 1997; this document was written and put out to "agents in the field" only a short time prior to Olson's death:[20]

Professor Starrs, who led the autopsy team which concluded that the death was actually murder, concluded that the:

2. Accidents

For secret assassination, either simple or chase, the contrived accident is the most effective technique. When successfully executed, it causes little excitement and is only casually investigated.

The most efficient accident, in simple assassination, is a fall of 75 feet or more onto a hard surface. Elevator shafts, stair wells, unscreened windows and bridges will serve. Bridge falls into water are not reliable. In simple cases a private meeting with the subject may be arranged at a properly-cased location. The act may be executed by sudden, vigorous [next word excised] of the ankles, tipping the subject over the edge. If the assassin immediately sets up an outcry, playing the "horrified witness", no alibi or surreptitious withdrawal is necessary. In chase cases it will usually be necessary to stun or drug the subject before dropping him. Care is required to insure that no wound or condition not attributable to the fall is discernible after death.

Falls into the sea or swiftly flowing rivers may suffice if the subject cannot swim. It will be more reliable if the assassin can arrange to attempt rescue, as he can thus be sure of the subject's death and at the same time establish a workable alibi.

If the subject's personal habits make it feasible, alcohol may be used [2 words excised] to prepare him for a contrived accident of any kind.

Falls before trains or subway cars are usually effective, but require exact timing and can seldom be free from unexpected observation.

" ... evidence from 1953 demonstrates a concerted pattern of concealment and deception on the part of those persons and agencies most closely associated with—and most likely to be accountable for—a homicide most foul in the death of Dr. Olson ... The confluence of scientific fact and investigative fact points unerringly to the death of Frank Olson as being a homicide, deft, deliberate and diabolical."[21]

Olson's son, Eric Olson, who is Director of *The Frank Olson Legacy Project* and has literally spent decades researching the circumstances of his father's death, deserves the last word here and, frankly, no one could put it more eloquently:

"What this means for me is that a national security homicide is not only a possibility, but really it is a necessity, when you have a certain number of ingredients together. If you are doing top secret work that is immoral, arguably immoral, especially in the post-Nuremberg period, and arguably illegal, and at odds with the kind of high

---

[20] Central Intelligence Agency, *A Study of Assassination*, 1954 (National Security Archive Center, Washington University), Released via Freedom of Information Act, May 23, 1997.

[21] Starrs with Ramsfeld, *A Voice for the Dead*.

moral position you are trying to maintain in the world, then you have to have a mechanism of security which is going to include murder."[22]

BIBLIOGRAPHY

A Terrible Mistake: The Murder of Frank Olson and the CIA's Secret Cold War Experiments; H. P. Albarelli Jr.; 2009, Trine Day

The Biology of Doom: The History of America's Secret Germ Warfare Project, Ed Regis, 2000

The Men Who Stare At Goats, Jon Ronson, 2005

Code Name: Artichoke; The CIA's Secret Experiments on Humans, film by Egmont R. Koch & Michael Wech, 2002, http://topdocumentaryfilms.com/code-name-artichoke/

"The Frank Olson Legacy Project," http://www.frankolsonproject.org/Contents.html

"LSD, Murder and the CIA: Frank Olson, Enemy Combatant," David Swanson, Counterpunch, March 26-28, 2010

"Scientist was 'Killed to Stop Him Revealing Death Secrets': So Did Cheney and Rumsfeld Cover Up a CIA Assassination?," Gordon Thomas, London Sunday Express, August 25, 2002.

"The Case of Frank Olson," Oliver Boothby, February 11, 1996: http://www.frankolsonproject.org/Student%20papers/Oliver.html

"Frank Olson: Did a government scientist jump to his death from a New York hotel? Or was he pushed?," *Unsolved.com* http://www.unsolved.com/ajaxfiles/une_frank_olson.htm

"Rumsfeld & Cheney's Dirty Little Spy Secret," Fintan Dunne, Editor, GuluFuture.com, March 6, 2006, http://www.apfn.net/messageboard/03-06-06/discussion.cgi.31.html

---

[22] *Code Name: Artichoke; The CIA's Secret Experiments on Humans,* film by Egmont R. Koch & Michael Wech, 2002, http://topdocumentaryfilms.com/code-name-artichoke/

CHAPTER 2

Henry Marshall —
June 3, 1961
Inspector, U.S. Department of Agriculture

Spartacus Educational, www.spartacus.
schoolnet.co.uk/JFKmarshallH.htm

VICTIM	HENRY MARSHALL
Cause of Death	Five gunshots from a bolt action rifle.
Official Verdict	"SUICIDE" (ruling by County Sheriff Howard Stegall and Justice of the Peace Lee Farmer, who ordered the body to be buried without an autopsy)
Actual Circumstances	Investigator for U.S. Department of Agriculture, who uncovered vast financial scam being run by Billie Sol Estes and linked to Lyndon Johnson in Texas. Estes later testified that Johnson had ordered Marshall killed, using hit man Mac Wallace.

Inconsistencies

1. Initial death ruling never even addressed the impossibility of a person shooting himself five separate times with a bolt-action rifle.
2. The rifle was never checked for fingerprints; nor was Marshall's pickup truck, which his corpse was found laying beside.
3. No samples were taken of the blood stains on the truck and it was washed and waxed the following day.
4. No photographs were taken of the crime scene.
5. A Grand Jury later ruled that Marshall's body be exhumed and an autopsy revealed that he had suffered a severe blow to the head prior to his death and that his body contained a carbon monoxide concentration of fifteen percent. The doctor performing the autopsy estimated that the carbon monoxide concentration at the time of death was as high as thirty percent.

It may shock some to learn that Lyndon B. Johnson, the thirty-sixth President of the United States, was also apparently a mass murderer … but he was. Henry Marshall was one of several victims whom Johnson reportedly ordered his henchman, Mac Wallace, to murder.

Incredibly, the fact that Henry Marshall was shot five times with a bolt-action rifle did not preclude an official death verdict of "suicide." Think about *that* one for awhile. …

President Lyndon B. Johnson was, by many accounts, one of our most ruthless politicians, and his path to the presidency was littered with dead bodies and highly questionable circumstances. None was more obvious than Agricultural Inspector Henry Marshall, who had uncovered a huge financial scandal leading directly to LBJ's doorstep.

Marshall, in his capacity as a U.S. Department of Agriculture Investigator, saw through a false paper trail and uncovered the fact that Billie Sol Estes was receiving millions of dollars in federal agricultural subsidies for crops of cotton that were non-existent. The profits raked in from the scheme represented a major source of Lyndon Johnson's political funding.

One thing that can, however, be said of Lyndon Johnson, is that he attempted simpler solutions prior to employing the use of murder. When Marshall got too close to the big financial scam that Johnson's associate Billie Sol Estes was running, Johnson apparently arranged for a fat promotion for Marshall to the Washington, D.C. office of the Department of Agriculture. Perceiving it as a bribe, Marshall refused the promotion and continued his efforts to prosecute the corruption he had discovered. That refusal was apparently tantamount to signing his death warrant.

Billie Sol Estes has testified that he had a meeting with Lyndon Johnson and his closest associates, Cliff Carter and Ed Clark, on January 17, 1961, and the purpose was to discuss what to do about Marshall, since he refused the promotion to Washington. Lyndon Johnson reportedly made the decision: "It looks like we'll just have to get rid of him."[23] It was also decided at that meeting that the assignment was to be given to Mac Wallace, who was a hit man used by Johnson.

On June 3, 1961, Marshall was found dead next to his pickup truck on a remote portion of his farm.

Early in 1962, several months after Henry Marshall's death, Billie Sol Estes was arrested by the FBI and officially charged with fraud and conspiracy. That arrest inspired the Robertson County Grand Jury to order that the body of Marshall be exhumed and autopsied. The autopsy revealed that Marshall had suffered a severe blow to the head prior to his death and had an extremely high level of carbon monoxide in his body prior to the gunshots. The suicide ruling was overturned.

It should be noted that even morally-challenged FBI Director J. Edgar Hoover took pause on the impossibility of the initial death ruling, writing that:

"I just can't understand how one can fire five shots at himself."[24]

Senator John McClellan also later concluded:

"It doesn't take many deductions to come to the irrevocable conclusion that no man committed suicide by placing the rifle in that awkward position and then cocking it four times more."[25]

BIBLIOGRAPHY

The Texas Connection: The Assassination of John F. Kennedy, Craig I. Zirbel, 1991

Captain People, Texas Ranger: Fifty Years a Lawman, James M. Day, 1980

A Texan Looks at Lyndon, J. Evetts Haley, 1964

Captain People, Texas Ranger: Fifty Years a Lawman, James M. Day, 1980

JFK and Sam, Antoinette Giancana, John R. Hughes, DM OXON, MD, PHD & Thomas H. Jobe, MD, 2005

"Henry Marshall," John Simkin, *Spartacus Educatonal.* http://www.spartacus. schoolnet.co.uk/JFKmarshallH.htm

"Did LBJ Order the Killing of Henry Marshall?," John Simkin, *Education Forum,* January 30, 2006, http://educationforum.ipbhost.com/index. php?showtopic=5988

---

[23] John Simkin, "Clifton C. Carter: Biography," *Spartacus Educational,* http://www.spartacus.schoolnet.co.uk/ JFKcarter.htm (accessed 14 Mar. 2011)

[24] John Simkin, "Billie Sol Estes: Biography," *Spartacus Educational,* http://www.spartacus.schoolnet.co.uk/JFKestes. htm (accessed 2 May 2011)

[25] John Simkin, "Henry Marshall: Biography," *Spartacus Educational,* http://www.spartacus.schoolnet.co.uk/ JFKmarshallH.htm (accessed 4 May 2011)

"Letter to Stephen S. Trott, U.S. Department of Justice", Douglas Caddy, August 9, 1984

"Interview with Douglas Caddy," John Simkin, January 20, 2006

"The Killing of Henry Marshall", Bill Adler, November 7, 1986, *The Texas Observer*

"Convicted Swindler Billie Sol Estes," David Hanners & George Kuempel, March 24, 1984, Dallas Morning News, http://www.spartacus.schoolnet. co.uk/JFKmarshallH.htm

CHAPTER 3

George Krutilek –
April 4, 1962
Accountant

VICTIM	GEORGE KRUTILEK
Cause of Death	Carbon Monoxide poisoning
Official Verdict	SUICIDE
Actual Circumstances	Krutilek was the accountant for the financial scam being run by Billie Sol Estes and linked to Lyndon Johnson in Texas. Estes later testified that Johnson had personally ordered that Krutilek be killed, using hit man Mac Wallace.
Inconsistencies	A large bruise on Krutilek's head indicated that he had been bludgeoned unconscious prior to inhaling the carbon monoxide. Carbon monoxide poisoning was the modus operandi of hit man, Mac Wallace.

Like Henry Marshall, the death of George Krutilek was directly linked to the financial scandal involving Billie Sol Estes and Lyndon Johnson.

Krutilek was the accountant for Billy Sol Estes and had close knowledge of the gigantic scam of subsidies for nonexistent crops that was fleecing taxpayers, claiming government credits for cotton that was never actually grown, but listed as grown and in storage. The "invisible cotton" was then also used as collateral to secure large fraudulent loans that weren't repaid.

A day after being questioned by the FBI, April 3, 1962, Krutilek was found dead from carbon monoxide poisoning. The following day, Billy Sol Estes was indicted by a Federal Grand Jury on fifty-seven counts of fraud and conspiracy. Three men were arrested with Estes and two of them died under suspicious circumstances.

LBJ did whatever it took to win. His political history was laced with blatant corruption. Johnson had failed in his bid for U.S. senator in a Texas election, losing by a margin of very few votes. Six days *after* the election, 203 "extra" votes turned up from a tiny town in Alice, Texas and, in an amazing anomaly in the laws of probability, 202 of those 203 votes were for Lyndon Johnson. He was declared the winner by 87 votes and that was why LBJ was mockingly referred to as "Landslide Lyndon"

> **" ... the election judge in Alice (Texas) admitted that he had helped rig the election." [26]**

But that didn't stop LBJ from blazing a path of corruption across the state of Texas and into the halls of the United States Senate. As veteran CIA operative (and Texas native) John Stockwell put it, everyone in Texas knew that:

> **" ... Lyndon Johnson was corrupt to the core, with mob ties, with murders sometimes associated with his political campaigns." [27]**

To convey an idea of the extent of pervasive corruption wreaked by Lyndon Johnson's political organization in Texas, one need look no further than the trial of his henchman, Mac Wallace. Described as Johnson's hit man, Wallace was found guilty of First Degree Murder with eleven jurors recommending the death penalty and the twelfth juror recommending life imprisonment. But in an incredibly obvious example of a corrupt system known at the time as "Texas Justice," the judge over-ruled the jury, technically sentencing Wallace to five years imprisonment, which was "suspended" by the judge, and Wallace was immediately freed.

It is duly noted that, as an American citizen, even Lyndon Johnson deserved his day in court. Here, however, is a glimpse of what that day would have looked like. Douglas Caddy, Esq., the attorney formally representing Billie Sol Estes, contacted the United States Attorney's Office on August 9, 1984 informing them that his client had personal and direct knowledge of, and was willing to testify that, Lyndon Johnson was responsible for ordering the murders of:"

- Henry Marshall
- George Krutelik
- Harold Orr
- Coleman Wade
- Josefa Johnson
- John Kinser
- President John F. Kennedy

---

[26] Thomas E. Woods, Jr., *The Politically Incorrect Guide to American History*, (Regnery, 2004)
[27] John Stockwell, *The Praetorian Guard: The U.S. Role in the New World Order*, (South End Press, 1999)

The statement to the U.S. Department of Justice included the following: "Mr. Estes is willing to testify that LBJ ordered these killings, and that he transmitted his orders through Cliff Carter to Mac Wallace, who executed the murders." [28]

Adding further fuel to that same fire is another amazing fact. The fingerprints of Lee Harvey Oswald, the accused assassin of President Kennedy, were nowhere to be found at the so-called sniper's nest in Dallas. But the fingerprint of another man was positively identified there, by a certified expert in that field, who determined a clear 14-point identification, exceeding the legal requirement of proof for a match. If you guessed that the name of the man whom that fingerprint belonged to was Mac Wallace, you are correct. [29]

BIBLIOGRAPHY

The Texas Connection: The Assassination of John F. Kennedy, Craig I. Zirbel, 1991

A Texan Looks at Lyndon, J. Evetts Haley, 1964

Politically Incorrect Guide to American History, Thomas E. Woods, Jr., 2004

The Praetorian Guard: The U.S. Role in the New World Order, John Stockwell, 1991

"George Krutilek", John Simkin, *Spartacus Educational.* http://www.spartacus. schoolnet.co.uk/JFKkrutilek.htm

"LBJ and the Deaths of George Krutilek, Harold Orr & Coleman Wade", John Simkin, February 4, 2006, *Education Forum.* http://educationforum. ipbhost. com/index.php?showtopic=6044

"Letter to Stephen S. Trott, U.S. Department of Justice", Douglas Caddy, August 9, 1984

"Interview with Douglas Caddy," John Simkin, January 20, 2006

Convicted Swindler Billie Sol Estes ..., David Hanners & George Kuempel, March 24, 1984, Dallas Morning News

---

[28] John Simkin, "Douglas Caddy: Biography," *Spartacus Educational,* http://www.spartacus.schoolnet.co.uk/ JFKcaddyD.htm (accessed 12 May, 2012)

[29] Alan Kent, et al., "Mac Wallace fingerprint?" *The Education Forum,* http://educationforum.ipbhost.com/index. php?showtopic=4966 (accessed 14 May 2012).

CHAPTER 4

Marilyn Monroe –
August 4, 1962
Actress

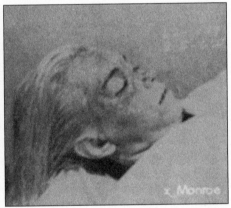

VICTIM	**MARILYN MONROE**
Cause of Death	Acute barbiturate poisoning
Official Verdict	SUICIDE — "a self-administered overdose of sedative drugs" (Deputy Medical Examiner penciled in the word "probable" on his report)
	Marilyn Monroe had an affair with President Kennedy and also a brief relationship with his brother, Attorney General Robert Kennedy. On one occasion, while still in bed with the President, Marilyn Monroe placed a post-coital call to

her masseur and he gave her and JFK advice on how to help his ailing back. In another confirmation, the head of the Medical-Legal Division at the District Attorney's office was granted permission to listen to recordings of Marilyn's private psychiatric sessions and concluded from the tapes that Marilyn had relationships with the President, and then the Attorney General: "It could be inferred almost conclusively from what she had to say about President Kennedy. It was specific as to Robert Kennedy."[30] The relationships were also common knowledge in show business circles and even as a confidential matter among police departments. L.A. Police Chief Tom Reddin stated: "The Kennedy connection was a matter of common knowledge at the Police Department level I was at. The Kennedy—I should say Kennedys'—relationship with Marilyn Monroe was pretty generally accepted."[31] Marilyn considered both relationships serious, not at all frivolous. Previously, she reportedly had an affair with Mob-linked Frank Sinatra and was good friends with Chicago Mafia boss Sam Giancana, Johnny Roselli (also Chicago Mob), and others, amid what one writer has called "an astonishing array of indiscretions."[32] But what set off alarm bells in U.S. intelligence was her friendship with Frederick Field and other known Soviet intelligence agents. Her phones were tapped and her home had listening devices, with eavesdropping conducted by the government and (independently) by the Mob. Her home was "sanitized," i.e., swept of bugs and sensitive materials in the hours after her death, accounting for the "missing six hours" before anyone finally called the police.

Actual Circumstances

Inconsistencies

1. No trace of tablets were found in her stomach or intestines, even though she had enough Nembutal and Chloral Hydrate in her bloodstream to kill an elephant. Computer analysis that compiled all the pharmaceutical data concluded that, to reach those levels, Marilyn would have had to swallow a total of 77 to 88 pills (60 to -70 Nembutal and 17 -to 18 Chloral Hydrate).[33] Digestion stops at death, therefore, victims who swallowed pills always have undigested tablets and refractive crystals (the active ingredient of any drug) in their stomach. So there should have been

[30] *Say Goodbye to the President*, dir. by Christopher Olgiati (1988; British Broadcasting Company, 1998 dvd).

[31] David Marshall, *The DD Group: An Online Investigation Into the Death of Marilyn Monroe*, (iUniverse, 2005), 134.

[32] Donald H. Wolfe, *The Last Days of Marilyn Monroe*, (New York: William Morrow and Company, 1998).

[33] Tony Plant, "How Did Marilyn Monroe Die?," July, 2004. http://southernwingsaircraft.com/howmarilyndied.html

substantial residue, and there are always refractive crystals in an oral overdose. But none were found, even using a polarized microscope.

Medical Examiner Thomas Noguchi:

"I found absolutely no visual evidence of pills in the stomach or the small intestine. No residue. No refractile crystals."[34]

2. No refractile crystals means she *could not* have swallowed the pills—period. The Coroner's Report states:

"A smear made from the gastric contents and examined under the polarized microscope shows no refractile crystals."[35]

Dr. Sidney S. Weinberg, Chief Medical Examiner, Suffolk County, NY:

"It would have been impossible for her to have taken the barbiturates orally and not have some residue turn up in the stomach. The evidence points to all the classic features of a homicide, much more so than suicide—and certainly not an accidental death."[36]

Inconsistencies

3. In addition to the huge amounts of Chloral Hydrate (known colloquially as "knockout drops" or "Mickey Finns") and Nembutal (a strong barbiturate) in her bloodstream, Marilyn also had 2.88 times that much Nembutal in her liver, per the two toxicologists attached to the autopsy (we don't know how much Chloral Hydrate was in her liver because her organs literally *disappeared* before that could be tested. Dr. Noguchi re-requested the additional toxicology tests on her organs to establish with certainty *how* the drugs had been introduced, and he was told that the organs could not be located!). That's enough drugs to kill an elephant—literally. Yet *none* of the drugs were in her stomach.

4. Dr. Noguchi also stated that her stomach was almost completely empty. She had not eaten on her last day, nor had she consumed any alcohol. The fact that the stomach was virtually empty leads to the logically necessary conclusion that Marilyn was given a drug-laced

[34] Jay Margolis, *Marilyn Monroe: A Case for Murder* (iUniverse, 2011), 25.

[35] T. Noguchi, M.D., Deputy Medical Examiner, *County Coroner's Report on the autopsy of Marilyn Monroe*, August 13, 1962. http://news.google.com/newspapers?nid=1299&dat=19730809&id=YslHAAAAIBAJ&sjid=8IsDAAAAIBAJ&pg=4892,2503573

[36] Margolis, *A Case for Murder*, 10–11.

enema. Her body was fully examined for needle marks or puncture wounds; injection of the drugs was eliminated as a possibility. John Miner, who was head of the Los Angeles District Attorney's Medical-Legal Section and attended Monroe's autopsy, concluded that the vehicle of entry was an enema:

> "Noguchi and I were convinced this was absolutely the route of admitting the fatal dose."[37]

The original Medical Examiner, the highly respected Thomas Noguchi, later called for a new official investigation, citing the strong possibility of murder:

Dr. Noguchi: "She had a bruise, on her back or near the hip that has never been fully explained, There is no explanation for it, and it is a sign of violence."

Interviewer: "Murder?"

Dr. Noguchi: "Could be."[38]

Inconsistencies

5. Her body was found lying face down, however, secondary lividity marks on her back and posterior aspects of the arms and legs indicate that at some point during the first four hours after death (when lividity occurs) her body was moved onto its back for a considerable period of time (evidenced by strong secondary lividity marks) and then placed back in the face down position before police arrived. Lividity doesn't lie— it is "fixed" four hours after death and does not change afterward—and that's what the markings clearly indicate.

6. Cyanosis (turning blue) was present, a medical indication that her death may have occurred very quickly. This correlates with the timeline in which people spoke to her on the phone near the time of her death and stated that she seemed normal; indicating that death may have been very sudden, which is inconsistent with typical sedative ingestion.

7. The first officer at the death scene (LAPD Watch Commander Jack Clemmons) concluded that the death scene had been cleaned up and staged and that Monroe had actually been murdered. He said there was a major cover-up at LAPD and publicly disputed the official findings:

> "It was the most obviously staged death scene I have ever seen."[39]

Forensic expert, Dr. Sidney S. Weinberg, explains:

[37] Christopher Claire, "Why the Mafia had to Murder Marilyn Monroe," July 28, 2002, *News.Scotsman.com*
[38] Margolis, *A Case for Murder*, 144 (citing ABC's Eyewitness News, October, 1985).
[39] Anthony Summers, *Goddess: The Secret Life of Marilyn Monroe* (Macmillan, 1985).

"People who have died as a result of excessive ingestion by mouth of barbiturates, in their agonal stages, as they're dying, they throw up. They have regurgitation and this regurgitated material comes out onto the pillow cases or whatever they're resting on."[40]

8. There is a gap of over six hours between the time that she died and the time at which authorities were finally called. Combined with official observations, this gap is highly indicative of a "clean-up"; when Sgt. Clemmons arrived, he noticed that everything was too clean and that the maid was already doing her third load of laundry at 4:45 AM

9. Although Marilyn was a dramatic person in a dramatic profession, there was no suicide note.

10. Victim was reported by witnesses to have been "in good spirits" on both the day and the evening of her death. Witnesses who spoke to her on the phone shortly before her death testified that she sounded "normal." Marilyn had very specific plans for her future and was demonstrably excited about those prospects. The tape-recordings of her sessions with her psychiatrist prompted a member of the L.A. District Attorney's office to conclude that "there was no possible way this woman could have killed herself. She had very specific plans for her future. She knew exactly what she wanted to do."[41]

Inconsistencies

11. The locked filing cabinet in which Marilyn kept her most important personal papers was forcibly broken into on the night she died.[42]

12. A White House phone number was reportedly found scribbled on a small piece of paper in her bed. The note later "disappeared."[43]

13. The laboratory tests that Dr. Noguchi originally requested on Marilyn's organs were never done. When he *re-requested* they be done, he was told that the laboratory specimens (her *organs*) had "disappeared"; a Deputy District Attorney stated:

"In the entire history of the L.A. County Coroner's Office there had never been a previous instance of organ samples vanishing."[44]

[40] Margolis, *A Case for Murder*, 10.
[41] Associated Press, "Ex-prosecutor claims Monroe wasn't suicidal," *MSNBC.com*, August 5, 2005. http://today. msnbc.msn.com/id/8841843/ns/today-entertainment/t/ex-prosecutor-claims-monroe-wasnt-suicidal/
[42] Wolfe, *Last Days of Marilyn Monroe*
[43] Wolfe, *Last Days of Marilyn Monroe*
[44] Wolfe, *Last Days of Marilyn Monroe*

An attendant stated:

> "Knowing Coroner Curphey (who was Noguchi's supe-
> rior at the time), and that he supervised the autopsy,
> it's difficult to imagine that those specimens just disap-
> peared. It wouldn't have happened."[45]

14. Original autopsy report is reportedly missing.
15. Original police report is also missing. Donald Wolfe
    writes: "So what ever happened to the obviously very
    important police file on Marilyn Monroe, one might
    ask?

Lieutenant Marion Philips told us:

> "In 1962 Chief Parker took the file to show someone in
> Washington. That was the last we heard of it." [46]

16. Her official medical reports have reportedly also
    disappeared.
17. Telephone records of Marilyn's calls in the days
    preceding her death were apparently seized by the
    FBI and then "disappeared."
18. Wiretaps and tapes of professional eavesdropping—
    conducted by the U.S. Justice Department and,
    independently, also by Organized Crime—at Marilyn's
    home and also at Peter Lawford's Santa Monica beach
    house (where she sometimes met with the Kennedys),
    are known to have been recorded but, *alas,* they too
    have "disappeared."

Sergeant Jack Clemmons was on duty as Watch Commander at the West Los Angeles Division Headquarters of the Los Angeles Police Department when he received a phone call from Marilyn Monroe's doctor stating that she was dead. He noted the time in his logbook: 4:25 AM on Saturday night, technically Sunday morning. He told the doctor that he'd be right over.

En route to the home, he radioed for back-up, and then pulled into the driveway of Marilyn Monroe's fashionable Brentwood home. He noted several other cars parked in the driveway as he parked his police unit. He was the first officer on the scene.

He knocked on the door and waited, hearing footsteps and whispering inside the house, which lasted for a full minute, before finally seeing the porch light turn on. The housekeeper finally opened the door and he entered the home. She led him to Marilyn's bedroom where she lay dead upon the bed. A sheet was pulled up over her body, leaving only her head exposed. Marilyn's

[45] Wolfe, *Last Days of Marilyn Monroe*
[46] Wolfe, *Last Days of Marilyn Monroe*

physician, Dr. Engleberg, was seated in a chair near the bed. Dr. Ralph Greenson, Marilyn's psychiatrist, was also in the room, standing near the bed.

The doctors blurted out that Marilyn had committed suicide and, gesturing to an empty bottle of Nembutal on the nightstand, said that she had taken "all of those." Sgt. Clemmons pulled down the sheet as the two doctors watched. The first thing that struck him as odd was the fact that the body was obviously bruised. He also noted that a telephone cord ran over one side of the bed and was underneath her. He then noticed that the body was perfectly straight in what is known as the "soldier's position" (face down, arms at the sides, legs straight), and he knew from experience that it's not a position that overdose victims die in—they end up in a contorted position due to the involuntary spasms caused by the overdose. It's also usually very messy because OD victims typically vomit in the throes of death, as their body attempts to reject the semi-digested drugs.

Sgt. Clemmons immediately asked the doctors if the body had been moved. They answered that it had not. He then asked them if they had tried to revive her. Dr. Greenson stated flatly that they had not, that it was too late. But Sgt. Clemons considered their attitudes out of context with the situation; they were defensive and, uncharacteristically for doctors, wouldn't volunteer any further information. Clemmons found their attitudes totally "off," especially of Dr. Greenson:

> **"He was cocky—almost challenging me to accuse him of something. I kept thinking to myself, 'What the hell's wrong with this fellow?' Because it just didn't fit the situation."[47]**

Sgt. Clemmons said he wanted to speak to the housekeeper and, walking over to the laundry room, he found Eunice Murray there, folding clothes, with the dryer running. He immediately thought it quite odd that she would be doing laundry at that hour of the night, actually almost 5:00 AM, especially while her employer lay dead in the other room. He also noted that the housekeeper had a very agitated and nervous demeanor, just as she had when she had finally answered the front door for him.

As the housekeeper nervously folded clothes, Sgt. Clemmons asked her at what point had she known that something was wrong. Mrs. Murray answered that it was about midnight that she had woken up to go to the bathroom and noticed that the light was still on in Marilyn's room, as she could see light under the door. She said that she knocked on Marilyn's door, but Marilyn didn't answer. She tried to open the door, but it was locked from the inside; so she called Dr. Greenson, who arrived about 12:30 AM. She stated that when Dr. Greenson arrived, again trying Marilyn's door and getting no response, the Dr. went outside and looked through the bedroom window and could see Marilyn lying motionless on the bed, so he broke the window and then came through the window, unlocked the door and told her "We've lost her."

---

[47] Wolfe, *Last Days of Marilyn Monroe*

Sgt. Clemmons found it very troubling that the body had been discovered at 12:30 AM, but no one had called the police until 4:25. Four hours is a long time to wait. Furthermore, the precise manner in which the housekeeper stated the events to Sgt. Clemmons made him even more suspicious, because it sounded too rehearsed.

He asked the housekeeper what she'd been doing all night. She answered that she realized that there'd be a lot to do and that a lot of people would coming over, so she called someone to repair the broken window.

What else?

She answered that then she collected all of her personal belongings from Marilyn's home and gathered them in a basket.

It sounded extremely insufficient to Sgt. Clemmons. He then returned to the doctors and asked them the same question.

They responded that they hadn't called the police immediately because they had to call Marilyn's studio and get permission.

Sgt. Clemmons was astounded.

"Permission?"

They explained that, basically, that's how it is in the movie business—they had to clear everything with her publicist.

"What did you do during those hours?"

They answered that "We were just talking."[48]

"What were you talking about for four hours?"

The doctors didn't have an answer for that one and responded inaudibly, simply shrugging their shoulders.[49]

Sgt. Clemmons knew that the doctors were protected by professional confidentiality and didn't legally have to answer his questions. He also knew that their attitudes were absolutely bizarre for the situation and that things simply were not adding up.

He then pointed out to the two doctors that, although there was an empty bottle of pills, there was no glass or drink of any kind that she could have used to help her swallow all the pills. Stumped by that very cogent observation, the doctors then "helped" Sgt. Clemmons look around for a drinking glass … none was found.

However, they *did* find that the water in Marilyn's bathroom was completely shut off, making it an even more troublesome point.

Sgt. Clemmons then asked the doctors if Marilyn was in the habit of injecting drugs with a syringe. They answered that she always took her drugs orally.

Clemmons then backed them up and asked them again.

"How was the body discovered?"

Dr. Greenson related the same story about being called by the housekeeper and then breaking the bedroom window to find Marilyn dead in bed. He added that her hand was firmly gripping the telephone when he reached her and that he took the phone out of her hand. He said that Marilyn must have been trying to call for help.[50]

---

[48] Wolfe, *Last Days of Marilyn Monroe*
[49] Wolfe, *Last Days of Marilyn Monroe*
[50] Wolfe, *Last Days of Marilyn Monroe*

That conclusion immediately struck Sgt. Clemmons as yet another oddity. *Why would the victim be calling for help on the telephone when she had her own housekeeper right down the hall, just a few feet away from her?*

Sgt. Clemmons completed taking statements from the witnesses and concluded that he had not been told the truth. Why wasn't there even a glass of water next to the neatly lined up pill bottles when the LAPD first arrived, and how come one was placed near them later on? The officers confirmed that it was definitely *not* there when they first arrived. That seems just a tad suspicious.

We know now that she actually died *prior* to the time police were told; at least *six* hours before the phone call was made to the police. When Marilyn's corpse was picked up, the level of rigor mortis in the body was observed by experts and they then estimated the time of death at 9:30 to 11:30 PM … so they waited over *six hours* to call the police? What was taking place during those six hours, and why?

We also know that the washing machine was running when the police arrived at shortly after 4:30 AM. Isn't that a rather odd time to being doing laundry? *Too* many irregularities, *too* much out of place. The story given to police was that she'd locked herself in her bedroom, but it was obvious that the story being told wasn't true.

Along with the questionable responses by both the two doctors and Mrs. Murray, there were many other signs that showed the death of Marilyn Monroe to have been a "staged suicide."

SIGNS OF FORCED ENTRY: An often overlooked fact is that the window of Marilyn's bedroom (the one that did not have "anti-burglar" bars on it) was forcibly broken. A basic fact of crime scene investigation is that a broken window is *always* classified as inconsistent with suicide. That's because a broken window—especially in the room where the decedent is found—is a clear and precise indication of a possible forced entry. That may very well be why the broken window became part of the cover story during the many long hours prior

Classic Crime Scene Red Flags

As the Chief of the Investigative Support Unit at The FBI Academy writes: "Red Flags:

Offenders who stage crime scenes usually make mistakes because they arrange the scene to resemble what they believe it should look like. In so doing, offenders experience a great deal of stress and do not have the time to fit all the pieces together logically. As a result, inconsistencies in forensic findings and in the overall 'big picture' of the crime scene will begin to appear. These inconsistencies can serve as the 'red flags' of staging, which serve to prevent investigations from becoming misguided."

(*Violent Crime Scene Analysis: Modus Operandi, Signature, and Staging*, John E. Douglas, Ed.D., Special Agent & Chief, Investigative Support Unit FBI Academy & Corinne Munn, Honors Intern, FBI Academy, February 1992, FBI Law Enforcement Bulletin)

* * *

Sgt. Jack Clemmons, Watch Commander at LAPD, was the first officer on the scene at Marilyn's home. Experienced in homicides and overdoses, he knew what to look for, he knew what to ask. From the moment he entered the crime scene, Sgt. Clemmons immediately noted some dramatic inconsistencies. The whole scenario made no sense and Sgt. Clemmons knew it.

1. When he arrived and announced his presence, there was a delay in answering the door as he heard whispering voices behind the door. Normally, when police are called in such a case, they are eagerly awaited and immediately ushered inside. Sgt. Clemmons said that, after knocking, the door wasn't answered until a "good minute or so later."

2. There were too many cars parked in the driveway for the small number of people inside the home.

3. Sgt. Clemmons asked the two doctors if they had attempted to revive the deceased and they answered that no, they had not. They simply stated that "It was too late."

4. The body had obviously been moved after death. A sheet had been pulled up over her head and the body was lying almost perfectly straight, face down in the pillow, head turned to one side, arms out, in what is known as the "soldier's position."

5. The body of the deceased had several fresh bruises.

6. Sgt. Clemmons immediately asked the two doctors present if the body had been moved and they responded that it had not—and appeared quite defensive about the questioning.

7. The corpse was far too neat and tidy for a drug overdose. Involuntary spasms and vomiting in the moments before death inevitably leave a very messy victim in a contorted position. Marilyn was lying perfectly straight in her bed as though she had been positioned there. Sgt. Clemmons later concluded:

"It was the most obviously staged death scene I had ever seen. The pill bottles on her bedside table

to the time when police were finally called—the fact that there was a broken window had to be accounted for. So, Dr. Greenson made up a story (or was told to), which we now know to be false.

He told police that the door to Marilyn's bedroom was locked. We now know that is not true because the housekeeper finally admitted that Marilyn almost never locked her bedroom door and that, indeed, she had not locked it on her final night. Even so, by saying that it was locked made it feasible for Dr. Greenson to have broken the window in order to get in and try to help Marilyn. We know that the window was not broken during the day or evening hours because Mrs. Murray, the housekeeper and support worker caring for Marilyn, made no effort to address a broken window. She certainly would not have let the world's most famous movie star go to bed with an unprotected window—she was charged with Marilyn's care by her psychiatrist and was very attentive and industrious in that regard (and did, in fact, immediately address the issue of the broken window at the moment that she knew of it, even in the very difficult early morning hours, by calling her son-in-law to come over and repair it). Therefore, <u>the window was apparently broken close to the time of Marilyn's death</u>.

The locked filing cabinet in which Marilyn kept her most important personal papers, which was located in her guest cottage, was also forcibly <u>broken into</u> on the night that she died.

had been arranged in neat order and the body was deliberately positioned. It all looked too tidy."

8. The bed was made with fresh linen, and it appeared that the sheets had just been changed. Clemmons observed that the whole death scene had obviously been sanitized.

9. Marilyn's psychiatrist, Dr. Greenson, stated that she was found clutching the telephone, apparently trying to call for help during her last moments. Sgt. Clemmons found that very odd because, if she'd wanted help, she could have just yelled for the housekeeper who was right down the hall, just a few feet away. The fact that her hand was dramatically clutching for the telephone as though she'd wanted to call for help (as stated by her doctors) seemed staged, just like the rest of it.

10. Marilyn's doctors told Sgt. Clemmons that she had committed suicide by swallowing all the pills, gesturing to the empty pill container on her nightstand. But, as Clemmons quickly noted, how would she have swallowed all the pills they said she had when there was nothing in the room to swallow them with? There was no water glass or anything sufficient. So, how did she swallow them? When Clemmons pointed this out to her doctors, they were feeble, lost for answers, and helped Clemmons search the room for a drinking glass. None was found. To further confound anyone who had actually been trying to swallow something, their search revealed that the bathroom water had even been turned off for some remodeling work (there was nothing to drink from in the bathroom either).

Sgt. Clemmons, first officer on the scene, was certain that there was no glass or bottle with which Marilyn would have been able to swallow the pills. Later, and just in time for the police photos, an empty glass is present in Marilyn's bedroom. Sgt. Clemmons was

SIGNS OF A STRUGGLE: Many fresh bruises were noted on the victim's body, especially a very large bruise on the lower left side of her back. The medical examiner later stated that the large bruise was clearly a "sign of violence" that should have been investigated as such. Also noted were bruises on her arms and on the backs of both legs. Autopsy report reads "The colon shows marked congestion and purplish discoloration;" which the head of the medical/legal section at the District Attorney's office considered the "smoking gun," indicating homicide.

VICTIM DID NOT HAVE ACCESS TO DRUGS THAT KILLED HER: Marilyn was being successfully "weaned" off of Nembutal by her two doctors—who were working together, gradually reducing both her reliance upon and her access to the drug; so she was taking much less of a dosage. The prescriptions filled during the last five weeks of Marilyn's life are almost completely accounted for. The only Nembutal that Marilyn had even possible access to was a prescription on August 3, 1962 for twenty-five capsules. Yet, the autopsy revealed a <u>massive overdose,</u> many times more than the amount to which she had access.

Her clear lack of access is further evidenced by the fact that, on her final day, her psychiatrist—after a two hour Saturday afternoon session at Marilyn's home—telephoned Marilyn's doctor to ask if he could come over and give her something to help her sleep because she had had a tough day

adamant, however, that it was not there initially; as he had searched.

11. When Sgt. Clemmons asked how they first knew that something was wrong, Eunice, the housekeeper answered that it was around midnight when she had gotten up to go the bathroom and she then noticed under Marilyn's bedroom door that the light was still on and the door was locked.

In their initial story to police, the witnesses (including two doctors) placed Marilyn's time of death at slightly before 12:30 AM (the time they said that they found her). But professionals are able to easily determine a clear time window of death by observing the specific stage of rigor mortis. Rigor (stiffening of the muscles) begins about three to four hours after death and is in full effect at about twelve hours. Mortician Guy Hockett arrived at Marilyn's home at 5:40 AM. He inspected the body, and, based on the level of rigor mortis, determined a time window for her death of 9:30 to 11:30 PM. That concurs with what we now know about exactly when her "handlers" were informed. We know that Marilyn actually was dead prior to 10:00 PM. because shortly after 10:00, her lead publicist, Arthur Jacobs, was urgently interrupted, at a concert, with the message "Come with us right now please, Mr. Jacobs—Marilyn Monroe is dead."

12. In their initial story (which all three witnesses later changed at the exact same time), the housekeeper and the two doctors stated that Marilyn had locked herself in her bedroom. So, to gain access, Dr. Greenson had gone outside and smashed the window open with a fireplace poker. Sgt. Clemmons noted, however, that If her doctor had only smashed through the window from the outside to get in, the shards of

(her doctor was unable to comply). Upon leaving Marilyn's home that evening, Marilyn's psychiatrist was professionally confident that Marilyn had calmed down and would be fine and, as a failsafe, even asked the housekeeper (who watched over Marilyn and reported directly to her psychiatrist) to spend the night at Marilyn's home, just to keep an eye on her.

The lack of access is further evidenced by the fact that Marilyn called Dr. Greenson later in the evening to relay some good news, and she used that occasion to ask him if he had taken her Nembutal prescription. Dr. Greenson answered that no, he had not—but he was therefore cognizant of the fact, and relieved, that Marilyn had no access to any Nembutal. It is further confirmed via the testimony from a friend who stated that Marilyn telephoned her between 9:00 and 9:30 PM, told her she was having trouble getting to sleep and asked her if she had any sleeping pills that she might be able to bring over to Marilyn (the friend was unable to comply). Minutes later, Marilyn was dead.

METHOD OF DEATH: The only way that the massive amount of drugs could have entered Marilyn's body was anally. (Forensic experts ruled out all other possibilities.) Combined with her bruises and, especially her bruised colon, this is a clear indicator of possible murder. The chief of the Medical/ Legal Division for the D.A. later stated: "That autopsy, Dr. Noguchi and I saw a considerable area of the sigmoid colon, which is the lower portion of the large intestine,

glass would have only fallen inside the room, not outside where he also saw some of the glass shards.

13. The housekeeper was doing the laundry at 4:30 AM while her employer lay dead in the bedroom. Both the washer and dryer were running and the housekeeper was folding clean laundry and nervously fidgeting with it as she did so. Several loads were being done, so he knew she'd been at it for hours:

> "She had already washed one complete load and was doing a second. A third load of linens had been folded and put on a counter."

14. The housekeeper related her story in a very even and precise manner as though her statements had been very rehearsed and prepared.

15. It was very disturbing that witnesses stated the body was found at 12:30 AM, but the police were not called until 4:25 AM. Moreover, the explanations of what transpired during that four-hour gap were feeble and vague. Finally, Sgt. Clemmons asked the doctors directly: "What were you doing for four hours?" "Talking," they responded. "For four hours? What were you talking about for four hours?" They shook their heads, no verbal response.

> As established above, the actual time of death was prior to 10:00 PM, making it actually a gap of at least six and a half hours that she was dead, before the police were finally called.

16. Why were the witnesses behaving so strangely, either nervously avoiding Sgt. Clemmons questions, or, in the case of one of her doctors, almost challenging him to doubt their story? Contrary to typical experience with physicians, who were readily informative and didn't need to be probed, these two seemed to be holding back, reluctant to provide information; one doctor seemed despondent and uncommunicative; the other seemed very strange, defensive, and almost cocky, "almost challenging me to accuse him of something. I kept thinking to myself, 'What the hell's

which was congested and dark purplish in color. This is totally anomalous. I've seen many other autopsies of barbiturate deaths and I have never seen that phenomenon.'"

INDICATIONS OF RAPID DEATH: Rapid death is a sign of possible murder because it is inconsistent with a typical overdose. In a typical drug suicide, the victim succumbs slowly and usually vomits and experiences muscle contortions as their body attempts to expel the toxic substance. There were <u>no signs of these typical reflex actions</u> at Marilyn's death scene. Instead, the body lay perfectly straight with no mess from vomiting or gagging.

It was a known fact among her friends that Marilyn had difficulty swallowing pills and often gagged when taking only one. To posit that she swallowed scores of capsules <u>without gagging</u> or vomiting is simply <u>not believable</u>.

The victim also displayed cyanosis (bluish discoloration of the extremities) and still had stool in her colon.

Cyanosis is the deep bluepurplish discoloration to the skin, gums, fingers, or mucous membranes that occurs from a sudden and overall lack of oxygen in the blood. An overall lack of oxygen is usually the result of a trauma, such as strangulation, choking, suffocation, or drowning. A heart attack or blood clot can cause cyanosis because they also quickly cut off the oxygen supply.

When present in a drug overdose, cyanosis can be an indication of a <u>massive amount of drugs introduced rapidly</u> into the victim's

wrong with this fellow?' Because it just didn't fit the situation."

17. An official police investigative unit arrived at the house at about 5:30 AM and re-interviewed the witnesses; it was led by Sgt. Robert Byron and overseen by Lieutenant Grover Armstrong, Chief of Detectives, West Los Angeles, LAPD. The unit leader agreed with Sgt. Clemmons' suspicions.

Regarding the housekeeper, Sgt. Byron concluded:

> "My feeling was that she had been told what to say. It had all been rehearsed beforehand. She had her story and that was it."

Regarding the doctors, Sgt. Byron's conclusion was:

> "I didn't feel they were telling the correct time or situation."

18. Sgt. Clemmons kept investigating the case on his own for the rest of his life. He concluded:

> "I knew at the time that the doctors and Mrs. Murray were lying to me. Now I know that they must have moved the body and invented the locked room story. The District Attorney wouldn't listen to me. I kept telling them that the death scene was arranged, and they said I was hallucinating."

Sgt. Clemmons always maintained the belief that Marilyn's death was a Homicide and that a cover-up hid the true facts of her murder.

body. For example, a heroin addict who ODs by injecting an inordinately strong dose of heroin would be likely to have cyanosis.

In Marilyn's case, we know that she did not suffer from the most common medical causes of cyanosis, i.e., she did not suffer a heart attack, severe blood clot, cyanide poisoning, severe lung disease, pulmonary embolism, or cyanotic heart disease; nor did she suffer a trauma that cut off her breathing—the autopsy would have revealed that. So, her cyanosis was quite possibly <u>caused by a massive amount of drugs entering her system in a rapid manner</u>.

The fact that she still had stool in her colon is <u>another indication of rapid death:</u> Had she been conscious when a deadly amount of drugs entered her anally, the logical reaction is to intentionally evacuate the bowel in order to expel the lethal enema content.

The <u>significance of the rapidity of death</u> did not go unnoticed by the Medical Examiner. As Dr. Noguchi later noted:

No one has been able to explain why Marilyn "was laughing happily" on the telephone "and dying only thirty minutes later."

ABSENCE OF SUICIDE NOTE: Marilyn was a dramatic person. If she had actually planned to commit suicide, it is <u>very surprising</u> that she would not leave a note.

VICTIM WAS NOT DEPRESSED: Marilyn's last phone calls and other conversations on her final day provide a verifiable record of her *not* being in a suicidal frame of mind. Moments prior to closing her bedroom door for the final time, she was bubbling with so much laughter that it literally made her housekeeper smile at the fact of so much happiness in the home.

SIGNS THAT BODY WAS MOVED POST-MORTEM: One thing is definitely for sure: Lividity never lies. Lividity (the bluish markings that result from the settling of blood after death) is "fixed" within four hours post-mortem. That means that during the period of the first four hours following death—and *only* during that period—any movement of the body creates marks that will not go away. The lividity marks tell a very precise story of exactly how the body was moved during those four hours, and since Marilyn's body was not officially moved prior to 6:00 AM (over eight hours post-mortem, which is too late for lividity), we, therefore, can be sure that no lividity markings were the result of transporting her body or any other officially known capacity. Marilyn had "primary" lividity (very pronounced markings) on the front of her head, neck, and upper chest. She also had "secondary" lividity on her back. Tertiary lividity (mild and general) also appears on the front side of her body. Therefore, there is <u>clear evidence that she was actually moved twice</u>. We know from that evidence that Marilyn died with her head down—in fact, the lividity is so pronounced that it indicates that she died with her head down and even hanging off the edge of the bed. The body was then moved twice. The lividity markings define precisely how and when the body was moved: At a point between approximately 10:00 PM to 2:00 AM, Marilyn's body was turned from its original face-down death position and was placed flat on her back. Her body remained in that position, *not* for just a couple of minutes, or time for a "quick clean-up," but for a substantial period of time. Her body was then turned back to its original death position of face-down upon her bed, as it was positioned at the time that the police arrived. And that's nobody's "theory" either—it's hard forensic science from clear forensic facts.

SIGNS THAT DEATH SCENE WAS STAGED: The first officer on the scene—and an experienced Division Watch Commander, at that—flatly stated:

> **"It was the most obviously staged death scene I have ever seen."**

That is a pretty big red flag. All the witnesses were extremely evasive, their cover story had holes, the body had obviously been moved, and the room had most certainly been sanitized. It wasn't that just a few things were a little bit off—everything was very noticeably false, and the officers' interpretations clearly reflected that.

POLICE WERE NOT CALLED IMMEDIATELY: Police were not called for <u>over six hours</u> after the time that Marilyn's entourage (her doctors, career managers, etc.) knew that she was dead. The six-hour gap is almost completely unaccounted for; plus the witnesses on the scene gave very feeble excuses. During that time period, it is known that a professional wire tapper came to Marilyn's home and "swept it" of electronic bugs. All sensitive materials (such as things linking her to President Kennedy or Attorney General Robert Kennedy) were also removed from the home and the crime scene was clearly "sanitized," and the housekeeper was already on her third load of laundry when police arrived at about 5:00 AM.

SIGNS OF AN OBVIOUS COVERUP:

- Federal agents immediately seized Marilyn's telephone records in a move directed from very high in Washington;
- Marilyn's housekeeper finally admitted that Attorney General Robert Kennedy had been at Marilyn's home that day and that, after her death, "Robert Kennedy's protectors" had to step in to shield him from political ruin. That protection apparently included everything from the seizure of records to "sweeping" her home clean of eavesdropping equipment in the pre-dawn hours;
- Police Department files, to this day, have still not been released. And a proper investigation of Marilyn's death was never ordered or conducted;
- Key witnesses were never required to testify. One (the housekeeper) was allowed to immediately leave for an extended stay in Europe even though it was known that her story simply did not add up. Another, Peter Lawford, was "unavailable" to make a statement to police, until he finally availed himself and made a statement in 1973, *eleven years later*;
- A Grand Jury Foreman in 1985 stated his goal of re-opening the case of Marilyn's death and requested the appointment of a special prosecutor, and, as he was holding the press conference to detail that, it was announced by a Superior Court Judge that he was replacing him with a new Grand Jury Foreman;
- The records of the suicide prevention team (which took statements from Marilyn's friends and family regarding her state of mind) have, to this day, never been released;
- Even though "doctor-patient confidentiality" legally ends at death, Marilyn's psychiatric records and the tapes of her sessions, which are known to exist, have never been released;
- Even though it was known that tapes were made of the results of electronic eavesdropping at Marilyn's home (by both the FBI and, independently by the Mafia), those tapes have never surfaced;
- Although TV programs like *Unsolved History* purport to be open-minded, it is apparent that they begin with the pre-formed conclusion that Marilyn's death was intentional suicide. They distort the truth by asserting, for example, that the disorderliness of Marilyn's bedroom and absence of photographs or other personal mementos were indicative of a severely depressed person who had decided days earlier to commit suicide. The actual truth of the matter, however, was that Marilyn was in the midst of redecorating her entire home and had saved her own room for last and that is why it looked the way it did. They also misrepresent the strong probability that the drugs were introduced via enema, by focusing only on the old-fashioned bag-and-hose type enema and how problematic it would have been, and not the simple bulb-type syringe enema, which would have been the type actually used. They also dramatically reduced the estimate of drugs in Marilyn's body by ignoring the drug content in the liver, rejecting the results of the two toxicologists

attached to the autopsy, not figuring in the factor of absorption and assuming that Marilyn had the tolerance of a person who had never taken Nembutal before (when, in fact, her body was extremely tolerant to the drug).

The cover-up was effective because it succeeded in skewing perceptions to the point where crime scene inconsistencies were no longer obvious red flags:

A broken bedroom window was not viewed as it should have been: a sign of possible forced entry;

Severe fresh bruising was not viewed as it should have been: a sign of possible struggle;

Forced entry into Marilyn's personal filing cabinet was inconsistent with a suicide scenario, but was obscured by the coverup.

VICTIM WAS CLOSE TO CRIMINAL ELEMENTS: The Chicago Mafia clearly played a major role in Marilyn's career, and, to her final days, she maintained a close friendship with Sam Giancana, Don of the Chicago Mob (and the most powerful mobster in the country in 1962), as well as Johnny Roselli, Chicago's top man in Hollywood.

VICTIM'S CRIMINAL FRIENDS HAD OBVIOUS MOTIVE: It has become apparent that the Mob had motive to kill Marilyn as a means of attempting to ruin the political career of Attorney General Robert Kennedy, the Mob's arch-enemy. It is known that Robert Kennedy visited Marilyn at her home on the day of her death, and it is also known that the two had a romantic affair. Especially in the context of 1962 America, that behavior was not publicly acceptable.

Source material for the above chart was derived primarily from the following:

Files of The Los Angeles Police Department; *Coroner*, Thomas T. Noguchi, M.D. & Joseph Dimona, 1983; *The DD Group: Marilyn Monroe: An Online Investigation Into the Death of Marilyn Monroe*, David Marshall, 2005; *The Last Days of Marilyn Monroe*, Donald H. Wolfe, 1998.; *Goddess: The Secret Life of Marilyn Monroe*, Anthony Summers, 1985; *Marilyn: The Last Take*, Peter Harry Brown & Patte B. Barham, 1992; *Say Goodbye to the President* (Documentary), Produced by George Carey & Christoper Olgiati, Directed by Christopher Olgiati, 1985; *Unsolved History: Death of Marilyn Monroe* (Documentary), 2003, Discovery Communications, Inc.

First and foremost, let's examine the physical evidence, because it's very revealing in this case. The autopsy was performed early on Sunday morning at about 10:30 AM (time of death was about twelve to thirteen hours earlier on Saturday night) by Dr. Thomas Noguchi of the Los Angeles County Morgue. Thomas Noguchi was then a Deputy Medical Examiner and was charged with the study of Marilyn's corpse. Deputy District Attorney John Miner was also present during the autopsy. Miner was head of the Los Angeles County District Attorney's Medical-Legal Division and was a man at the very top of his field in medically-related law. In addition to being a prosecutor in L.A. for many years as Deputy District Attorney for Los Angeles County, Miner also co-founded the University of Southern California's *Institute of Psychiatry, Law and Behavioral Science* in 1963.

The autopsy was supervised by Coroner Theodore Curphy, and others noted that it was the very first time that anyone could remember Coroner Curphy being present for an autopsy, let alone supervising one, as he ordinarily concerned himself with the running of the Coroner's office.

Noguchi and Miner were aware of the reported circumstances: that Marilyn had died in a locked room, that her doctors believed she'd died from an ingestion of pills, and they had also studied the pill bottles themselves. It should also be noted that the autopsy confirmed that no stomach pump had been used to remove the contents of Marilyn's stomach.

NO NEEDLE MARKS—FRESH BRUISING—MASSIVE OVERDOSE

Marilyn's body was first thoroughly examined for needle marks because they had been informed that it was a drug overdose, so that was considered a highly possible vehicle of entry into her body for the drugs. They did a full-body search, closely examining her entire body with a magnifying glass. They stated very clearly in the autopsy that their thorough examination concluded that Marilyn had <u>no needle marks</u> of any type, anywhere on her body. It has been posited by some writers that needle marks can quickly disappear, which is a good point. However, in the case of the massive and lethal amount of drugs in Marilyn's body, the medical reality is that *any* injection, *anywhere* on her body, would have left very clear markings, simply as a result of the huge quantity of drugs involved. Dr. Noguchi specifically noted that the injection of any large quantity of barbiturates would have produced large swellings in the area of the injections, and both the puncture wounds and the swelling would have remained visible, because the healing process stops at death and death would have been rapid.

There were many small bruises on Marilyn's arms and on the backs of both legs. That was noted when the body was first viewed, and it was even filled out on an initial intake form at the Coroner's Office; however, those bruises were not part of the official report of Coroner Curphey ... but one of her bruises was too big *not* to note: a large, deep bruise on her left hip that ran all the way from her lower left back, down her left buttock, and which Dr. Noguchi later termed a "sign of violence." Noguchi eventually questioned the official findings of that autopsy, noting "That bruise has never been fully explained"; that it was a "sign of violence" and it clearly should have been investigated as such.

While Marilyn drank no alcohol on her final day, as none was found in her system, they found enough drugs in her bloodstream to kill an elephant ... literally. Over fifteen times a fatal dose. Yet, the internal examination of Marilyn's body revealed an amazing discovery: her stomach was almost completely empty and there was absolutely no trace of the drugs in her stomach. Nembutal is coated with a thick yellow die, therefore, the doctors immediately knew that if he she had actually swallowed a large number of the Nembutal tablets (and a large number of Chloral Hydrate capsules), as her personal physicians reported that she had, some of the yellow dye should have been present in her stomach, especially in an almost empty stomach … but it wasn't yellow because there were no drugs in her stomach.

Dr. Noguchi stated that they "found absolutely no visual evidence of pills in the stomach or the small intestine."[51] Yet, the toxicology examination that was conducted by Dr. R.J. Abernathy proved conclusively that Marilyn died from a massive overdose of the drugs pentobarbital (the active ingredient in Nembutal) and Chloral Hydrate, both of which were found in *huge* amounts in her bloodstream.

Chloral Hydrate has the street-names "Mickey Finn" or simply "Mickeys" or "knockout drops," because it's a powerful drug that quickly renders a victim unconscious. It's also known as the "date-rape drug." Its use is often implied in TV shows and motion pictures when we witness someone slipping something into a drink and then see the person passed out a short time later. Its use was apparently common by the Mafia, especially circa early 1960s:

> " … the hypnotic drug had been used the previous year in a number of brutal underworld killings and was the mafia's pharmaceutical murder weapon of choice."[52]

The forensic contradictions led Noguchi back to the toxicology report, which was limited in nature and did not contain results of testing of the kidney, stomach, urine, and intestines, for which Noguchi had sent specific samples, because they would reveal how the barbiturates had entered Marilyn's body.

Noguchi's request for the test results of these samples was met with a response that was hard for even a Medical Examiner to digest: There *were* no results and, furthermore, the samples had all "disappeared."

Deputy District Attorney John Miner was as shocked at the disappearance as Noguchi was:

> "In the entire history of the L.A. County Coroner's office there had never been a previous instance of organ samples vanishing."[53]

At that point, it was apparently too late to obtain further samples.

But the forensics clearly establish that if she *had* swallowed the pills, then the autopsy findings would have been, by necessity, much different than they actually were.

> "The forensic medicine establishes that there is no case on record of a fatal dose by oral ingestion involving such HIGH concentration in the blood of both "Pentobarbital" and "Chloral Hydrate"; the victim inevitably dies before the fatal concentration can approach such a high blood level. Monroe would have been dead before even reaching 35% of the total barbiturates had been

---

[51] Margolis, *A Case for Murder*, 25

[52] Christopher Claire, "Why the Mafia had to Murder Marilyn Monroe," July 28, 2002, *News.Scotsman.com*

[53] Wolfe, *Last Days of Marilyn Monroe*

absorbed from the digestive track into her bloodstream. It is not possible that the remaining 65% to be absorbed by the digestive track, vanished without a trace, because when the heart stops beating, the blood stops circulating, and the bodily functions shut down."[54]

Deputy D.A. Miner confirmed that if she had taken the pills orally, there necessarily would have been undissolved capsules in her system:

"With that massive amount of intake, there would have been undissolved capsules. She would have died before all of those capsules had been absorbed."[55]

That rules out oral ingestion. Miner confirmed that:

"So the notion of oral intake of the barbiturates simply does not scientifically stand up. It just didn't happen that way."[56]

Also note that it takes less Nembutal to kill a person when others drugs are taken with it — and Chloral Hydrate was present in high quantity (a minimum of 17 tablets).

It's also not very feasible that such a lethal dosage could have been taken accidentally by the victim *or* "over-administered" accidentally by her physicians. It's just *too much dope* to be accidental.

- It should be noted that "in the thousands of fatal cases involving acute barbiturate poisoning due to the ingestion of an overdose, not one case involves the ingestion of over twelve capsules in which no residue has been found in the digestive tract";[57]
- As high as the percentile of drugs was in her blood, her liver was even more lethal, containing a level of concentration 2.88 times higher than the level in her bloodstream;
- "No case has ever been reported in which the victim has as high as 4.5 mg. percent pentobarbital and eight percent chloral hydrate in the blood and no refractile crystals or concentrations found in the stomach or intestinal tract";[58]
- There is <u>no</u> case on record in the entire history of forensic medicine of the oral ingestion of a fatal dose with such extremely high concentrations of pentobarbital and Chloral Hydrate in the bloodstream. The reason is simple: The patient inevitably dies before the concentrations can get that high;

---

[54] Wolfe, *Last Days of Marilyn Monroe*
[55] "History's Mysteries: Marilyn Monroe" October 12, 2009, http://www.youtube.com/watch?v=dddee3vSmaI
[56] "History's Mysteries: Marilyn Monroe"
[57] Wolfe, *Last Days of Marilyn Monroe*
[58] Wolfe, *Last Days of Marilyn Monroe*

- If the drugs had been orally ingested, Marilyn would have been dead before the absorption into her blood of even a third of the total amount of barbiturates;
- Digestion stops at death. Therefore, the remaining two thirds of the drugs should have been present in her stomach and digestive tract, but none of the drugs were, which is impossible;
- Pentobarbital actually slows the digestive process. Therefore, the more Nembutal in her system, the slower her stomach would have digested it, further increasing the amount of undigested drug that should have been present;
- Therefore, as biographer Donald Wolfe correctly concluded from the analytical evidence:

"Technology of the modern world of forensic medicine gives the final verdict — Case #81128 was a homicide victim."[59]

One extensive investigation concluded that:

"When Dr. Noguchi mentioned in his *Omni* magazine interview that the drug levels in Marilyn's liver were three to four times that which was found in her blood, alarm bells should have gone off. If the levels in the liver were that outrageously high then the case could not possibly have been suicide, probable or otherwise."[60]

Medical research, however, suggests that we can't just *add* the liver content to the equation to reach a higher total, as some researchers have done. The reason is because her liver was in the process of breaking down the same Nembutal that had been in her bloodstream. Tony Plant, a superb medical researcher who has spent many years researching the case of Marilyn's death, cautions us concerning the liver content:

"The liver concentration is important but not anything we can use to determine how much Nembutal was in her system. It just means that the Nembutal was not injected or administered intravenously or she would have died long before the liver started removing the Nembutal from her blood. And the liver does store Nembutal until it breaks it down into waste and with Nembutal being a drug that clings to fat tissues well, the liver would take awhile to break it down to where it would not test as Nembutal. So we can't use the liver concentration to figure any Nembutal in her system. What is important is that she had a high tolerance to Nembutal so her body learned how to get rid of the Nembutal faster. It's her body weight and blood concentration of Nembutal that matters."[61]

---

[59] Wolfe, *Last Days of Marilyn Monroe*
[60] Marshall, *The DD Group*
[61] Tony Plant, email to author, September 3, 2011

The above statement is demonstrative of the fact that Mr. Plant conducts medical research in a manner that is quite precise, conscientious and cautious—bear that in mind when we view his conclusions very shortly.

Lividity

As earlier established, lividity doesn't lie and in this case it clearly reveals that Marilyn's body was moved twice before the telephone call was made to the police.

Abnormal Colon—Signs of Violence

As noted, the autopsy revealed an abnormally discolored colon and a large fresh bruise on Marilyn's left hip that the Deputy Medical Examiner classified as a "sign of violence."[62]

INVESTIGATIVE CONTEXT

Unlike the literary landscape of most celebrities, the literature on Marilyn's death is incredibly diverse. At one extreme, biographer Donald Wolfe concludes that her death was basically a national security assassination by the Kennedy Administration; while at the other, respected biographer Donald Spoto paints a pristine picture in which neither Robert nor President Kennedy had anything to do with the woman. The truth, as usual, is somewhere in between.

There is also an unfortunate tendency among researchers to divide into pro-Kennedy and anti-Kennedy "camps," and to separate the literature on Marilyn's death accordingly. That may be a good practice for conducting a debate, but it's a very poor method for discerning the truth.

The DD Group: An Online Investigation Into the Death of Marilyn Monroe is an excellent examination of the major works regarding Marilyn and the circumstances of her death. Its author, David Marshall, makes a good point: It is worth reading everything about Marilyn because, even those works which one disagrees with, may contain very important information. In the same vein, we cannot completely discount specific information just because it is contained in a book in which the conclusions appear to be incorrect. And sometimes, the best information even tends to be obscure.

We've read most of the literature, and the best evidence we've found is some of the least publicized. For the most comprehensive scientific analysis of the chemistry of Marilyn's death, we strongly recommend *How Did Marilyn Monroe Die?* by Tony Plant. It's the definitive document available. Plant conducted a multi-year medical research study involving long days and weeks spent with pharmacologists, doctors, medical examiners, charts, and medical details and history. He immersed himself in the medical evidence, and his findings were not at all general, they were highly specific.

Key findings of the drug study conducted by Tony Plant were the following:

- Computer chemical analysis determined that to reach the drug levels present, she must have ingested the contents of not less than seventy-seven and not more than eighty-eight pills: sixty to seventy Nembutal and seventeen to eighteen Chloral Hydrate;

---

[62] Margolis, *A Case for Murder*, 144 (citing ABC's *Eyewitness News*, October, 1985).

- Pharmacy record research determined that Marilyn did not have access to more than twenty-five Nembutal capsules;
- She did not swallow the pills because it is impossible that she would not have *any* refractive crystals present, since her stomach contained only twenty cc's of fluid. The Chloral Hydrate would have even *slowed down* the passing of the Nembutal out of her stomach—it slows down the absorption rate and also the rate at which the liver removes the Nembutal. So that would have actually made it an even *better* probability of finding Nembutal in her stomach, had she actually swallowed it;
- The high level of drugs in her body could not have been the result of previous drug use that her body had "stored";
- She could not have "accidentally" swallowed too many pills because to get the amount of drugs found in her system, she would have had to swallow twice as many capsules as a person who was non-tolerant to the drug (Marilyn had a high tolerance);
- If she had swallowed that many capsules, she would have died long before the entire amount had been digested. Therefore, there would have been drug crystals undigested. No crystals mean that she did not swallow the drugs that killed her.

The pills could not have been swallowed because (*aside* from the fact that there was nothing nearby to swallow them with!) the victim dies before they can digest that many pills. When the victim dies, the heart stops and so does the digestive system, inevitably leaving *un*digested traces of the drugs in the stomach and intestines- which she didn't have!

> **Therefore, "with this amount she would have died long before the entire amount had completely digested past her stomach and completely past her small intestine. So in simple terms it would have taken so many capsules to kill Marilyn that there should have been undissolved capsules and been a lot of drug crystals found in her digestive system. No crystals mean that she did not swallow the drugs that killed her."[63]**

If she had swallowed the pills, then:

- The fact that there was no yellow die in her stomach from the pills *may* be explainable, but is certainly not likely;
- The fact that there was no capsule residue at all found in her stomach or intestines is *almost impossible* to explain;
- The fact that there were no refractive crystals found anywhere in her stomach or intestines is *literally impossible* to explain (if the drugs were ingested orally);
- Proving to a scientific certainty that she did not swallow the pills. The drugs—by scientific necessity—were ingested by a means <u>other than oral,</u> i.e., either anal or injection.

---

[63] Tony Plant, "How Did Marilyn Monroe Die?"

Marilyn had far in excess of a fatal dose. And when her established high tolerance for the drug is factored into the equation, it was a *massive* overdose—one of 77-to-88 pills, and one that could not have been ingested orally (impossible), *or* via injection or IV (both would have bruised her substantially making the marks easily identifiable at autopsy). Therefore the vehicle of ingestion was anal:

> **"Marilyn did not swallow the drugs that killed her. She didn't have any oral Nembutal in her possession. Still it was a very large amount of Nembutal that killed her and since it wasn't swallowed or injected that only leaves enema bulb or IV (which would have taken a long time and left a mark)."[64]**

Nor could it have been the result of some horrible medical miscalculation. That possibility has been suggested, because liquid Nembutal can also be administered via enema. The largest bags it was medically distributed in, circa 1962, were fifty cc bags of the drug. So, it has been posited that possibly someone meant to give her five cc's but accidentally gave her all fifty cc's instead.

However, that would *not* account for the huge amount of drugs that were found in Marilyn's body. A full bag was 50cc's of liquid Nembutal, equal to 37.5 grains, the equivalent of 25 1.5-grain tablets of Nembutal. Marilyn had <u>over double</u> that much Nembutal in her bloodstream (leaving liver content totally out of the equation), almost triple that much (the most accurate medical method comes out to the equivalent of between sixty to seventy Nembutal capsules). And she had no access to Nembutal. Even if we pushed it and factored in the missing twenty-five capsules prescribed to her, it's still not nearly enough Nembutal (and since there were no refractive crystals in her digestive tract, they could not have been swallowed anyway). Now note the very clear conclusion of medical researcher Tony Plant:

> **"My calculations actually come up with more than fifty cc's in her blood and if so then she was murdered on purpose."[65]**

Non-Suicidal Frame of Mind

An examination of Marilyn's actions on the last day of her life provides a profile of a person who is clearly *not* contemplating suicide. The Timeline which follows tells us a great deal about Marilyn's frame of mind.

When reconstructing a crime scene, it's often helpful to "work-the-evidence backwards"; to start at the end and come forward. Doing so in the case of Marilyn's death, we can begin with the fact that there was an obvious cover-up. There is substantial evidence that—for whatever reason—facts were covered up, stories were changed, and evidence linking Marilyn to an affair with President Kennedy and/or Attorney General Robert Kennedy was "taken care of" to protect the White House. That fact is indisputable.

---

[64] Tony Plant, email to author, August 19, 2010
[65] Tony Plant, email to author, September 3, 2011

COMPREHENSIVE TIMELINE

Reconstruction of Last Day of Marilyn Monroe's Life Saturday, August 4, 1962

Shortly after FBI Director Hoover warned President Kennedy and Attorney General Robert Kennedy about the Administration's vulnerability to blackmail from the President's "liaisons" (February, 1962), JFK broke off his relationship with Marilyn. It has been established that, somehow, during that process, Marilyn became romantically involved with Robert Kennedy, and then that relationship got "cut off" at some point (quite possibly on August 4).[66]

It is also well-established that Marilyn's home was "wired;" her phones were tapped, and there were also covert listening devices in it. The Justice Department had her phones tapped and the mob, via Jimmy Hoffa (arch-enemy of Robert Kennedy), had her under electronic surveillance. The mob also had Peter Lawford's Santa Monica beach home wired, the presumed purpose being to "get dirt" on the Kennedys (who often visited there), just as Hoover had warned. Lawford (who is the brother-in-law of the Kennedy brothers and their protector in Hollywood) actually knew that his phones were bugged and went to pay phones when he needed to talk to the President (and was patched right through by standing orders to the White House operator). FBI surveillance of Marilyn on her vacation to Mexico City revealed that a friend of hers was also a high-ranking Communist, which also worried the FBI.[67]

---

[66] *Say Goodbye to the President,* dir. by Christopher Olgiati (1988; British Broadcasting Company, 1998 dvd).

[67] John William Tuohy, "Bugging of a Goddess: The Marilyn Monroe Tapes," http://www.scribd.com/MansonCaseFile/d/53839213-Bugging-of-a-Goddess-The-Marilyn-Monroe-Tapes (accessed 14 Jan. 2012).

However, bear in mind that, as we noted in our introduction, those who cover up a crime are not necessarily the ones who commit it. Cover-ups occur for any number of reasons, often under the guise (and protection) of "National Security." And if the White House is compromised, that *is* National Security.

Furthermore, the Kennedy brothers were clearly *not* in the habit of murdering girlfriends to keep them quiet. There is no precedent in their highly detailed histories to suggest anything close to resorting to murder as a means of "damage control." As Attorney General and President of the United States, they had much more effective means at their disposal and there is every indication that they utilized those means thoroughly and successfully. Every bit of evidence linking Marilyn to a romantic affair or sexual liaison with President Kennedy suddenly vanished off the face of the earth in the immediate aftermath of Marilyn's death. And, in the context of 1962 America, there were very prescient reasons to make sure that it did.

Press coverage documents the fact that Bobby Kennedy arrived in San Francisco with his wife and four of their children on Friday afternoon, August 3, 1962. They were visiting friends for the weekend at the ranch of the Bates family in Gilroy, about 50 miles south of San Francisco International Airport.

"But in the process of his Monroe investigation, LAPD Captain

8:00 AM Saturday, August 4, 1962

Housekeeper Eunice Murray arrives at Marilyn's home at 12305 5ᵗʰ Helena Drive in Brentwood, a classy suburb close to Hollywood. Mrs. Murray is a regular at Marilyn's home (she also uses her son-in-law, Norman Jeffries, for small repairs at the property). At this moment, Marilyn is still in her bedroom and house guest Pat Newcomb, who spent the night, is still asleep in the guest room.

9:00 AM

Marilyn comes into the kitchen, Mrs. Murray gives her a glass of grapefruit juice, and the two start to chat. Marilyn explains that her publicist (and friend), Pat Newcomb, has spent the night because she is suffering from bronchitis (Pat had planned on checking into a hospital, but Marilyn convinced her to spend the night at her home instead, hoping that some good rest and lots of sunshine would nurse her back to health without hospitalization). So Marilyn says to let her sleep for her bad cold and then maybe in the afternoon she can "bake it out" at poolside.

9:30–10:00 AM

Marilyn meets at the house with Larry Schiller of *Playboy Magazine* regarding a proposal for a photo shoot and cover story on Marilyn. Schiller says Marilyn "looks fresh, unworried and without a care."[68] Even though it is Saturday, among her plans today, in addition to meeting with *Playboy*, include a designer fitting with the renowned Jean Louis, a meeting with famed actor/dancer Gene Kelly regarding the *I Love Louisa* project (the name was later changed to *What A Way To Go!* when actually made), and making plans for her upcoming trip to New York City,

Thad Brown discovered something quite startling: the Attorney General had been in Los Angeles on Saturday, August 4ᵗʰ"[147]

But you can cover a lot of ground when you're Attorney General of the United States and have the entire Department of Justice, including the FBI, following your direction.

"Further evidence uncovered by Summers suggests that as soon as Monroe died, RFK persuaded J. Edgar Hoover to save him from scandal by obliterating all evidence—such as telephone company records linking him to Monroe. Summers mentions that LAPD Chief of Detectives Thad Brown knew of the affair and notes that speculation in the newspapers that LAPD Chief William H. Parker had kept RFK's name out of the investigation into Monroe's death "to curry favor with the Kennedys." Summers also suspects that LAPD officers helped private detectives hired by RFK to obscure the senator's links to Monroe. In 1975, the LAPD conducted a reinquiry into Monroe's death under the supervision of Daryl Gates, who refused to make the investigative files public."[148]

In that context, the cover-up forced the hand of other investigative agencies. Evidence seemed to be disappearing much quicker

---

[68] Eunice Murray, *Marilyn: The Last Months* (Pyramid, 1975)

[147] Wolfe, *Last Days of Marilyn Monroe*

[148] Andy Boehm, "The Killing of RFK: Will we ever know the truth?," http://www.skeptictank.org/files/socialis/rfkplot.htm (accessed 12 Oct. 2012).

during which she has planned a meeting with composer Jule Styne to work on Marilyn's proposed musical version of *A Tree Grows In Brooklyn*, an interview and photo essay with *Esquire Magazine*, meeting with executives from *20th Century Fox* about resuming filming of *Something's Got To Give*, and scheduling a meeting with Italian film producers on some possible future film projects.[69]

10:00–11:50 AM

A small piece of furniture, a nightstand that Marilyn had ordered, is delivered to her home and Marilyn writes a check for and receives it.[70]

Marilyn makes a phone call to friend Ralph Roberts, and they discuss a singer whom Marilyn is trying to help along in his career. Marilyn asks Ralph if he can try to locate an unreleased record of him. They also discuss a possible barbecue dinner at Marilyn's home tomorrow (Sunday) and agree to talk again a little bit later.[71]

Marilyn receives a phone call from Sidney Skolsky. He asks her what her plans are for the evening and she says that she is expecting to see one of the Kennedys at a dinner at Peter Lawford's home.[72]

11:00 AM

A helicopter arrives at the landing pad at *20th Century Fox* movie studios. This has previously been the method that Robert Kennedy takes to visit Marilyn; landing at the helicopter pad at *Fox*, being driven to Peter Lawford's beach home in Santa Monica, then visiting Marilyn either at her home or at Lawford's. There are eighteen credible witnesses to Robert Kennedy's presence in Los Angeles on August 4, 1962, from police officers, to neighbors who were familiar with his

than those investigating the crime could unearth it. Therefore, under the probable guise of "National Security," the agencies with less clout were apparently placed in a position in which they were forced to play ball, succumbing to the efficiently wielded bureaucratic power coming from higher up.

> **"Summers notes the DA's office no longer possesses the reports on Monroe and RFK filed years ago by one of its own investigators, Frank Hronek, now deceased. On the November 5, 1988 edition of Fox TV's The Reporters, former Deputy DA John Miner said his own report on Monroe is also missing from the DA's office."[149]**

In any cover-up, there are obviously facts that an individual or individuals believe *need* covering up; and in the case of Marilyn's death, that fact would certainly appear to be the affairs with President Kennedy and then Attorney General Robert Kennedy. A cover-up could also be the result of obscuring the fact that others were trying to make that fact public knowledge. There were reportedly wiretaps of Marilyn's phone lines that were *not* authorized by the Justice Department; the suggestion being that someone, such as organized crime, was attempting to obtain proof of an affair between Marilyn and one of the Kennedys and then use that

---

[69] Peter Harry Brown & Patte B. Barham, *Marilyn: The Last Take*, (Dutton, 1992)

[70] Murray, *The Last Months*

[71] Summers, *Goddess*

[72] Summers, *Goddess*

---

[149] Boehm, "The Killing of RFK"

comings and goings. He was positively identified arriving at the *20th Century Fox* helicopter pad, and also entering the homes of both Marilyn Monroe and Peter Lawford later that day.[73]

11:50 am–12:30 PM

Pat Newcomb wakes up and joins Marilyn and Eunice in the kitchen. Eunice prepares one of her fresh herb omelets for Pat, but Marilyn does not eat (this is confirmed by the fact that the autopsy also showed that she had not eaten anything on Saturday). Marilyn and Pat end up in an argument. Some of Marilyn's biographers have theorized that the argument was because Pat had slept so well and Marilyn, who has difficulty sleeping, was jealous of that fact. That simply doesn't hold up to scrutiny—the reason Pat spent the night to begin with was because Marilyn knew Pat had a terrible cold and wanted her to rest. Other reports from witnesses make much more sense—that Marilyn saw Pat as always defending the Kennedys (which was very true; she even went to work with Robert Kennedy after Marilyn's death). Marilyn was becoming more and more convinced that those closest to her were not taking her side in matters related to the Kennedy brothers (which was also true).[74]

12:30–2:00 PM

The tension between Marilyn and Pat cools off and the two spend some time around the house. Pat rests and gets some sun for her cold. Marilyn occupies herself with a bunch of trees that have been delivered for her yard's new landscaping. Furniture had recently been delivered (in addition to the nightstand that was delivered this morning) and Marilyn concerns herself with these matters around the house. She is in the process of redecorating her home, the first that she has ever owned.

evidence to blackmail or smear the White House.

> **"If Summers is correct, local police and prosecutors were investigating Monroe's death at the same time the FBI was eradicating local evidence of her affair with RFK. Local officials therefore had to know of Hoover's illegal effort to save Kennedy from scandal. Certainly, it is hard to imagine that LAPD Chief Parker didn't know the FBI was seizing or destroying evidence on his turf. That the affair remained secret for years suggest that the LAPD and the DA acquiesced or assisted in, Hoover's cleaning up after RFK."[150]**

In short, the simple fact of the matter was that Marilyn apparently (and admittedly) had an extramarital sexual liaison with the President of the United States and then had a sexual relationship with the Attorney General- and that *could not* be made public. Combine that with the fact that the Attorney General was drawn into the crime scene near the actual time of death and you've got a whopper of a cover-up to come up with. But the Kennedys knew how to play hardball, even with the tough guys from the rough side of town, and in 1962, they had their horses all lined up to play it to perfection ... and they did.

---

[73] Marshall, *The DD Group,* 97-150.
[74] Marshall, *The DD Group,* 33-41.

[150] Boehm, "The Killing of RFK"

2:00 PM

Joe DiMaggio, Jr. telephones for Marilyn; Joe Jr. is the son of Marilyn's former husband, baseball hero, Joe DiMaggio, and she remains close with both of them. The call is "Collect, for Marilyn" and is operator-assisted. Joe Jr. states that Mrs. Murray (Eunice) answered the phone and told the operator that Miss Monroe was not in to take the call.[75]

Shortly after 2:00 PM

Mrs. Murray's car is delivered. It had been in the shop for repairs, and a man from the repair shop had dropped her off at Marilyn's earlier today. She then drives to the market to stock up on some supplies that are needed for the house.[76]

(Here, it should be noted that one of Marilyn's chief biographers, Donald Spoto, injects that Dr. Greenson, Marilyn's psychiatrist, arrives at her house shortly after 1:00 pm. Spoto is the only biographer who makes this assertion and it seems highly unlikely-to-impossible. The purpose appears to be the "cleansing effect" pertaining to the presence of Robert Kennedy at Marilyn's home. Spoto states that Robert Kennedy was never there and changing this point in the timeline facilitates it. However, Robert Kennedy quite definitely was there, as we shall soon see.)

Approximately 3:00 PM

Elizabeth Pollard, Marilyn's neighbor across the street in the cul-de-sac, later reports that while she and her friends are playing cards as they often do on Saturday afternoons, they clearly see Robert Kennedy get out of a parked car. She vividly recalls one of her guests remarking excitedly "Oh look, there's Robert Kennedy!" and that they all

---

Evidentiary Indications of Violence

- An abrupt change quite obviously took place at Marilyn's home on the night of her death because she quickly went from "laughing and joking" on the telephone with "her laughter ringing through the house" during the calls just prior to her death—to a corpse at a crime scene. As Chief Medical Examiner Thomas Noguchi later noted in his book *Coroner*:

  > No one has been able to explain why Marilyn "was laughing happily with Joe DiMaggio, Jr." and then "dying only thirty minutes later." (*Coroner*, Thomas T. Noguchi, M.D. & Joseph Dimona, 1983)

- Several friends who spoke to her shortly prior to her death reported that she sounded fine, i.e., there was nothing suicidal in her behavior during the final moments. She was planning things, making a hair appointment, and expressing her desire to continue conversations. As Dr. Noguchi noted: "Monroe's friends and associates said that her career, which had been in a decline, was now on an upswing. So, they insisted, there was no

---

[75] Margolis, *A Case for Murder*, 252.
[76] Murray, *The Last Months*

watched as he and two other men then walked up the drive to Marilyn's home.[77]

(We examined this account and it is highly credible. Some authors have tried "pushing" it to later in the evening, putting it closer to the time of death, but Pollard's original statement was that it actually occurred at about 3:00 PM—that would also coincide with the timing of Ward Wood's testimony and with other credible sightings of Robert Kennedy in Los Angeles that day.)

(Caretaker Norman Jeffries tells a different story many years later, however, being Eunice's son-in-law and on very bad terms with her in later years, he clearly has an axe to grind and his account has been determined not credible.)

Approximately 3:00 PM

Years later (not at the time of questioning), housekeeper Eunice Murray admits (on more than one occasion) that Robert Kennedy was indeed at Marilyn's home that afternoon. She says it was a surprise visit, that he wasn't expected, which was evidenced by the fact that Marilyn wasn't "ready" for him; she hadn't had her hair, makeup, and nails done, and wasn't dressed up as she normally would be. The autopsy photos confirm that her dark roots were showing, and she hadn't shaved her legs or done her nails, so there was no way she was expecting a visit from Robert. The exact words of Eunice regarding his presence that day and its ramifications, are: "Oh sure, yes—I was in the living room when he arrived. She was not dressed. It became so sticky that the protectors of Robert Kennedy had to step in."[78]

4:30 PM

After Robert Kennedy's visit, Eunice finds Marilyn very upset and she calls

---

[77] Marshall, *The DD Group*, 97-150.
[78] *Say Goodbye to the President*, BBC.

reason for her to have suddenly committed suicide." Therefore, we have a very non-suicidal victim, closing her bedroom door for the last time, in a very non-suicidal frame of mind, and entering a bedroom which does not at that time have a <u>broken window allowing access from the outside</u> (as it did a short time later).

- That broken bedroom window on the window without burglar bars is very consistent with <u>forced entry</u>.
- Her final phone call reportedly contained a highly suspicious event in which the caller stated that she put down the telephone to go and check on a noise that she had heard and never came back to the call.
- Victim was quickly incapacitated. She is checking on a noise one moment, and is dead a few minutes later. Something apparently rendered her incapable of further action.
- The high presence of Chloral Hydrate (known as "knockout drops" for their quick debilitating effect) at a level of seventeen to eighteen tablets minimum, suggests it may have been used to silence the decedent (it is clearly far in excess of anything close to a normal dose and, at the level present, would

Dr. Greenson, Marilyn's psychiatrist, who is basically on-call to handle her "issues."[79]

4:30 PM

Joe DiMaggio Jr. again calls collect for Marilyn and the operator is again told that Miss Monroe is unavailable to take the call.[80]

"Late afternoon"

Marilyn telephones her good friend Sidney Guilaroff, the world-renowned hairdresser. She is in tears and tells Sidney that "Robert Kennedy was here, threatening me and yelling at me." He asks her why he was there, and Marilyn answers because "I'm having an affair with him." She told Sidney that he then left with Peter Lawford. Sidney consoles her a bit, and she is less depressed, but the visit quite obviously upset her.[81]

"Late afternoon"

Ward Wood, next-door neighbor of Peter Lawford's Santa Monica beach home (which the Kennedys are known to frequent), later tells police that Robert Kennedy arrives at Lawford's late in the day, and that he clearly remembers seeing him as he steps out of a Mercedes. He makes the identification with informed certainty.[82]

5:00–5:10 PM

Peter Lawford states that at this time he phones Marilyn and invites her to a dinner party he is having this evening at his home in Santa Monica. Marilyn answers that she's not sure, but she'll think about it. Lawford tells Marilyn he hopes to see her there.[83]

render a person defenseless and unconscious).

- Large, fresh bruise reaching from lower-left back down left hip. Dr. Noguchi later stated that this bruise was an obvious "sign of violence" that should have been thoroughly investigated and was not.

> "On Monroe's lower left back was an area of slight ecchymosis, a dark reddish-blue bruise that results from bleeding into the tissues through injury. And the color of the bruise indicated that it was fresh rather than old. A bruise means wreckage. Human tissue and blood vessels have broken under the impact of an external blow … "

> "There is no explanation for that bruise. It is a sign of violence."

- In addition to the large hip bruise, the Coroner's initial examination report also noted bruises on victim's arms and on the backs of both legs. That's an indication that force had possibly been used to hold the victim down.
- Bruised colon. The autopsy report reads: "The colon shows marked congestion and purplish discoloration." According to John Miner, head of the Medical-Legal Division of the D.A.'s Office,

[79] Marshall, *The DD Group*, 240.
[80] Margolis, *A Case for Murder*, 252
[81] Wolfe, *Last Days of Marilyn Monroe*
[82] Marshall, *The DD Group*, 99.
[83] Donald Spoto, *Marilyn Monroe: The Biography* (Harper Collins, 1993).

5:00– 5:10 PM

While Marilyn is on the phone with Lawford, on the other line, Marilyn gets a call from Isadore Miller (father of playwright and Marilyn's former husband, Arthur Miller. Marilyn has remained close to Isadore. He was even her escort to the JFK birthday gala at Madison Square Garden earlier in the year). Eunice tells Isadore Miller that Marilyn is busy, and she'll have to call him back. Marilyn does not return Miller's phone call.[84]

Note: Marilyn's home has two separate phone lines (two different phone numbers) and her closer friends are aware of both. Both of the phones are kept in the guest room. The home has two guest bedrooms. The one that Pat Newcomb slept in last night (and that Eunice Murray is in tonight) is at the end of the hall, which is up from Marilyn's bedroom. The other guest room, the one where the telephones are kept, is near the first, and the two guest rooms are connected via a joint bathroom.

5:15 PM

Dr. Greenson arrives and confers with Marilyn in her bedroom. He spends a long time in her room, only exiting occasionally, coming out into the hallway and appearing deep in thought, then returning to her room.[85] He later states to a close colleague who had also once treated Marilyn that she was distraught at the time that he arrived, but had clearly settled down during their long session and was okay by the time that he left. However, Greenson later tells the "Suicide Prevention Team" that Marilyn was "depressed and drugged," "furious" and "in a rage" this afternoon due to her having been involved sexually with "important men in government" and that she was "feeling rejected by some of the people she had been close to."[86]

[84] Spoto, *Marilyn Monroe*
[85] Marshall, *The DD Group*, 240.
[86] James Spada, *Peter Lawford: The Man Who Kept the Secrets* (Bantam, 1991)

this was the "smoking gun" that pointed to homicide.

- Both Medical Examiner Noguchi & District Attorney's Office Miner later concluded that the vehicle of ingestion was anal:

  "Noguchi and I were convinced this was absolutely the route of admitting the fatal dose."

- Massive and obviously fatal overdose delivered anally is further indicative of homicide (oral ingestion, injection and I.V. were medically ruled out). Her body had enough toxicity to kill fifteen people and that's way over-kill, by any stretch of the imagination. That's the type of math used by killers, not by suicides.

- Victim had restricted access to Nembutal. It has been clearly established that Marilyn did not have access to anywhere near that much Nembutal. She *may* have had a prescription for twenty-five capsules (although that was missing, per her psychiatrist), but she clearly did not have access to more. The drug levels in her blood were far in excess of twenty-five Nembutal capsules.

- The conflicting statements in witness testimony are separable into two distinct groups: all her friends, who had no reason to lie, stated

6:00 PM

Dr. Greenson is nearing the end of a therapy session in Marilyn's home and telephones Marilyn's personal physician, Hyman Engleberg, asking him to come over and give Marilyn an injection of a sedative so that she can get some rest. They are in the process of "weaning" Marilyn off her reliance upon the sedative Nembutal, so there are apparently none in the house. Marilyn only had a prescription for twenty-five Nembutal, and she can't find them, apparently accusing Pat of flushing them down the toilet. Dr. Engleberg had only given Marilyn this prescription to stave off any withdrawal symptoms because he knew that he was going to be unavailable in the short term to give her any injections. In any case, since she was disturbed by the visit from Robert Kennedy, Greenson thinks she needs something to calm her. However, Engleberg declines because he has his own dramas to deal with (his wife was in the process of leaving him).[87]

6:30 PM

Ralph Roberts, Marilyn's friend and masseur, telephones. Roberts is on his way to the grocery store to pick up some things that he and Marilyn need for a barbecue they have scheduled the following day. Dr. Greenson answers the phone, telling Roberts that Marilyn isn't there and then hanging up on him (Roberts recalls the event specifically and remembers wondering why Dr. Greenson would be at Marilyn's house at all if Marilyn wasn't there).[88]

6:30 PM

Pat Newcomb, Marilyn's press agent, who had spent the night at Marilyn's house, now leaves Marilyn's home. There is an undercurrent of suspicion between Marilyn and Pat—even though she is supposed to be looking out for Marilyn

that she sounded fine; and all of her "handlers" (doctors, lawyer, housekeeper, and Peter Lawford), who were quite obviously covering something up and got caught changing their stories, stated that she was very, very upset.

- Even though her two doctors (who certainly knew better) were present at scene, the police were not called for <u>over six hours</u>. When the police asked them what they were doing all that time, they answered "talking." When asked what they were talking about, they simply gestured blankly. Something was obviously wrong, and a cover story was obviously being prepared. The body had definitely been moved and the witness statements were transparently false.

- Drawers and cabinet in Marilyn's guest cottage were reportedly broken into on the day of her death and things were obviously taken. It was known by friends that the cabinet in the cottage was where she usually kept her personal journal, in which some said they had witnessed her taking notes about Attorney General Robert Kennedy's comments, at times even in his presence. The existence of her journal, or diary, has been disputed. However,

---

[87] Marshall, *The DD Group,* 240.
[88] Summers, *Goddess,* 309.

as her publicist, Marilyn accuses her of being a watchdog for the Kennedys and reporting everything back to them (which was true). Earlier in the day, Marilyn had ordered Pat out of the house, but Pat had stayed there anyway. Dr. Greenson eventually comes out of their closed-door session in Marilyn's bedroom after calming her down, and he pointedly addresses Pat with a rejoinder to the effect of: "Are you leaving now, Pat?" (This is apparently letting Pat know that Marilyn has confided in him that she had ordered Pat out of her house, and that Pat didn't leave). Pat then apparently leaves the house in a huff without saying a word to anyone (according to the housekeeper, she is quite indignant in her exit).[89]

Dr. Greenson is still at Marilyn's home when Pat Newcomb leaves, along with Marilyn and housekeeper Eunice Murray. Newcomb later states: "When I last saw her, nothing about her mood or manner had changed ... she even said I'd see her tomorrow."[90]

6:45– 7:00 PM

After spending almost two hours at the house, most of it alone with Marilyn, Dr. Greenson then leaves. Before going, he tells Eunice that Marilyn is much calmer now, but to keep an eye on her, suggesting she spend the night there (which she did not ordinarily do on Saturday nights). Eunice agrees to do precisely that. Dr. Greenson later characterizes Marilyn's mood that day by saying that she was a bit depressed, but that he had "seen her many, many times in much worse condition." Eunice later confirms that there was no serious concern about Marilyn at this particular point. Dr. Greenson tells Marilyn to give him a call in the morning, but also adds that he will be available again in a few hours and that she can call him later at home should she need him.[91]

her filing cabinet had definitely been broken into on the night of her death and her home had obviously been "sanitized."

Therefore, we have an intelligent, successful woman, retiring to bed at 7:50 p.m. on a Saturday night, in an excellent and notably non-suicidal frame of mind, bringing her phone into her bedroom for the last time, not locking her bedroom door (as Mrs. Murray eventually concedes), near a window that is obviously not broken at that time as far as the knowledge of she and Mrs. Murray (because had they thought it broken, they surely would have addressed a broken, unbarred window allowing access to the world's most famous star's bedroom—and, further to that point, Mrs. Murray indeed said she did immediately address the issue of the broken window as soon as she learned of it, by calling her son-in-law to come over and board it up— and that was even in the middle of the night). Therefore, that broken window, allowing access from the outside, was not, to their knowledge, at that time, broken—and it was broken later that night. That spells foul play. Her last caller referred to her hearing a noise and then never coming back to the phone. No tape marks on mouth doesn't rule out foul play.

[89] Marshall, *The DD Group*
[90] Wolfe, *Last Days of Marilyn Monroe*
[91] Marshall, *The DD Group*, 261.

7:15 PM

The son of Marilyn's former husband Joe DiMaggio, Joe DiMaggio Jr., again telephones Marilyn and the two converse amiably for quite some time (his father, the baseball hero, had become very disturbed at the fact that medical types, whom he considered detrimental, had attached themselves to Marilyn. He reportedly quit his job with a military supplier a few days earlier on August 1, planning to ask Marilyn to remarry him, a rumor that had been spreading nationally after the two had again become close). Joe, Jr. tells Marilyn the "big news"—that he has broken off his engagement to be married—and Marilyn is thrilled to hear it because she had been against it all along. DiMaggio, Jr. later states that, during their phone call, Marilyn sounded fine.[92] Housekeeper Eunice Murray also states that Marilyn was in very good spirits both during and after the call, her bubbly laughter ringing through the whole house, which Eunice greeted with relief after the day's earlier events. Eunice describes her right now as: "Happy and in good spirits; gay, alert. Anything but depressed."[93]

7:40 PM

Marilyn phones Dr. Greenson, who has already arrived at his home and is now shaving because he is getting ready to go out to dinner with his wife. Marilyn informs him of the good news that Joe Jr. has broken off his wedding engagement and Greenson welcomes her enthusiasm. Later during the call, Marilyn asks Dr. Greenson if he took her Nembutal and he answers that no, he hasn't. Dr. Greenson is a bit taken aback by the question, but recalls being relieved by the fact that Marilyn obviously didn't have any Nembutal at the house. Greenson says Marilyn sounded "quite pleasant and more cheerful."[94]

---

[92] Summers, *Goddess*
[93] Marshall, *The DD Group*, 261.
[94] Barbara Leaming, *Marilyn Monroe* (Crown, 1998).

If she wasn't subdued, she could have simply yelled for Mrs. Murray, who was certainly within earshot. But note that if Chloroform had been used to control her, it would likely not show up at the autopsy. As Dr. Michelle Dupre, Medical Examiner and forensic pathologist states: "But if the person, say, was given Chloroform to knock them out, it is not likely that that would show up."[151] But severe bruising did show up at autopsy, and some of the bruising was consistent with having been held down.

- John Miner, head of the Medical-Legal Department at the D.A.'s Office, was the only person granted the opportunity to listen to Marilyn's taped private psychiatric sessions, and even then only under the legally binding condition that he not discuss their contents:

  "But what he heard on the tapes, and his debriefing interview with Dr. Greenson, had convinced him that Marilyn Monroe had NOT committed suicide." (Marshall, *The DD Group*, p. 399, emphasis in original)

- Medical Examiner Noguchi concluded:

  "Thus, if Miner's evaluation in 1962 was correct,

---

[151] Dr. Michelle Dupre, "HLN: Dr. Baden Statement about Chloroform in Hair," CNN.com, http://youtu.be/ hAyHAiWqXyo (accessed 29 Aug. 2011).

Note that Marilyn does have access to at least two bottles of Librium, a potent tranquilizer that she has been prescribed—she does not take any (there was no Librium in her body at autopsy). The following morning, the two bottles of Librium are found on the table near her body: one contained twenty-seven capsules, the other contained seventeen.

7:45 PM

Marilyn says goodnight to Mrs. Murray and tells her that she is retiring early. She is still in an excellent mood (two hours later, she is dead). As was her regular custom, she takes the telephone from its table in the guest room and brings it with her into her bedroom, closing her door with the phone cord beneath the door. Typically, she later replaces the telephone in the guest room as part of her nightly ritual, at the point when she is ready to go to sleep—as Eunice later puts it, "Putting the phones to bed was one of Marilyn's nightly habits."[95] Before going to sleep, she would return the telephone to the guest room and cover both telephones with pillows to muffle the ring and not disturb her sleep. On this night, Marilyn does not return the phone to the guest room which, later, reportedly alerts the housekeeper that something is amiss—because "she hadn't put the telephone to bed." From this point forward, Eunice Murray does not hear anything further from Marilyn. Eunice soon retires to the guest room and is in bed, reading. The next time that she hears the telephone ring will be a bit after 8:30 when Marilyn's attorney, Mickey Rudin, calls (Rudin is also Dr. Greenson's brother-in-law). Bear in mind that Eunice will hear the phone ring on the second line, not on the telephone which Marilyn has taken into her bedroom. Also note that Eunice does not pass by Marilyn's bedroom to answer the phone in the guest room— she simply walks through the bathroom which adjoins the two guest rooms.

[95] George Carpozi, Jr., "I was there the night Marilyn Monroe died," *Ladies' Home Journal,* v90, Nov. 1973, 54+.

the only conceivable cause of Monroe's death was murder."

• Dr. Sidney B. Weinberg, Chief Medical Examiner, Suffolk County, New York, investigated the case and concluded:

"The evidence points to all of the classic features of a homicide, much more so than a suicide."

• Sgt. Jack Clemmons, Night Watch Commander, LAPD, who was the first officer on the scene, maintained to his dying day that it was murder. Decades later, he stated:

"In my opinion, Marilyn Monroe was murdered that night. In fact, it was the most obvious case of murder I ever saw."

Based on the work and statements of Dr. Thomas T. Noguchi, M.D., Chief Medical Examiner, Los Angeles County, California; John Miner, Deputy District Attorney, County of Los Angeles, California; Dr. Sidney B. Weinberg, Chief Medical Examiner, Suffolk County, New York; Sgt. Jack Clemmons, Los Angeles Police Department. See: Coroner, Thomas T. Noguchi with Joseph DiMona, 1983; "Did Marilyn Monroe Commit Suicide? Or was she murdered because of her political involvement?", Sherman A. Meeds, Jr., May 19, 2009.

8:00 PM

Peter Lawford originally states that during a phone call with Marilyn "nothing seemed unusual, only that Marilyn said she was tired and would not be coming over, wishing instead to go to bed early that night. She said she was feeling sleepy and was going to bed. She did sound sleepy, but I've talked to her a hundred times before, and she sounded no different."[96]

Lawford then changed his story, stating that he received a phone call from Marilyn around 8:00 PM and that she had slurred speech and was at times inaudible. According to Lawford, Marilyn's voice "drifted off" and he says he tried calling back several times, but the line was busy. He said that he considered going over to Marilyn's home, only ten minutes away, but that instead he called his manager, Ebbins, and Ebbins instructed him that it would look bad: "For God's sakes, Peter, you're the President's brother-in-law. You can't go over there. Your wife is out of town, the press will have a field day." Ebbins then phones Marilyn's attorney, Mickey Rudin, to call Marilyn to see if she's okay.[97]

Lawford's original version appears much more credible due to the fact that his sense of panic regarding Marilyn actually occurs much later in the evening, at around 11:00 PM (and he never attempted to call Marilyn on her other phone line).

8:00 – 8:30 PM

Henry Rosenfield, a close friend of Marilyn's, telephones Marilyn and later states that they discussed the upcoming trip to New York and taking in some theater while there, i.e., enjoying some Broadway plays together while in New York City. He states that Marilyn seemed normal; she sounded a bit groggy, but was not at all unusual and he was not concerned.[98]

---

96 *Los Angeles Herald Examiner*, August 8, 1962
97 Marshall, *The DD Group*, 294-308.
98 Chris Ellis & June Ellis, *The Mammoth Book of Celebrity Murders* (Carroll & Graf, 2005) 123.

MEDICAL & LEGAL IMPLICATIONS

It's not really the *cause* of Marilyn's death that's observably noteworthy from an evidentiary standpoint; it's the *vehicle of delivery*. We know that her bloodstream contained a huge amount of the two powerful tranquilizers, Nembutal and Chloral Hydrate; enough to kill fifteen people. However, <u>as a clear result of the autopsy</u>, we know that they were not ingested into her body in typical fashion. Her stomach and digestive tract were thoroughly examined and revealed an extremely curious finding: there were <u>no traces of the drugs in the stomach</u>.

Nembutal contains a strong yellow dye that usually leaves yellowish traces in the digestive tract. Yet there was <u>none</u> of the dye in her stomach. Furthermore, there were no needle punctures on her body, therefore, the drugs were not injected either. To a forensic scientist, these facts imply a clear indication: the drugs entered her bloodstream by a method other than swallowing all of those pills.

As the character Sherlock Holmes famously put it: "Once you eliminate the impossible, whatever remains, no matter how improbable, must be the truth." Therefore, the drugs had to get into her body via a different method of delivery. That delivery was apparently anal, via a drug-laced enema. That method is also supported by additional autopsy findings. It's also supported by other medical evidence.

It has never been officially acknowledged that an enema was

8:25 PM

Mickey Rudin's exchange (circa 1962, before the age of voicemail, many people, especially in Hollywood, had an answering service to take their messages on phone calls that they missed and they often referred to that service as their "exchange") receives a call from Milt Ebbins (Lawford's manager).[99]

8:30 PM

Rudin's exchange relays the message to Mickey Rudin that he should call Milt Ebbins.[100]

8:30 PM

Ralph Roberts' (Marilyn's good friend) answering service receives a call for him. The caller is a "fuzzy-voiced woman" who asks for Ralph but leaves no message. Roberts had only given this phone number to four people, one of whom was Marilyn. He checked with the other three and they confirmed the fact that they had not called him, so he is sure that it was Marilyn.[101]

8:40 PM

Marilyn telephones famous hairdresser and good friend, Sidney Guilaroff, to talk and to arrange an appointment to have her hair done the following day. Guilaroff says she was upset when they had talked earlier during the afternoon but had calmed down and now is much "more composed" during this second conversation. They chat a bit and agree that they'll talk more about things in the morning at her hair appointment. Sidney says "I never imagined we would never speak again."[102]

---

[99] Marshall, *The DD Group*, 287.
[100] Marshall, *The DD Group*, 287.
[101] Fred Lawrence Guiles, *Legend: The Life and Death of Marilyn Monroe* (Stein and Day, 1984)
[102] Wolfe, *Last Days of Marilyn Monroe*

the delivery vehicle of the sedatives. Yet, via the elimination of all other possibilities, it quite literally *had* to be an enema. A drug-filled suppository can also be ruled out because that would apparently have caused much more obvious inflammation on the lining of the colon than was present or visible.

We can even deduce what type of enema was used. A traditional bag-and-hose enema would have been very problematic (this is the old-fashioned type enema with a long, extended hose that was and still is commonly used to combat constipation). It's unlikely that an enema of this type was used for several reasons. If this type had been used, it most likely would have emptied her bowel—and we know from the autopsy that her bowel was <u>not</u> empty as there was the presence of "formed stool" clearly noted on the autopsy. Yet none of the police officers noted a scent of stool at the house. The bag-and-hose type enema also would have created inflammation on the lining of the colon, just as a suppository would, which would have been visible at autopsy.

A much simpler type of enema is the small syringe-type, with no bag, that is basically just a small bulb that is gently squeezed, forcing its contents up into the colon. This is the type of enema that appears to have been used. The purplish discoloration noted in Marilyn's colon is *precisely consistent* with the use of the bulb-type enema, because it squirts the enema solution upward inside the rectum until it hits the wall of the lining of the colon:

8:30– 9:00 PM

Marilyn's attorney, Mickey Rudin stated that he called Marilyn's house and asked housekeeper Eunice to check on Marilyn and see if she's okay. (Eunice later tells police that Rudin called her at about 9:00 pm). Eunice came back to the phone in a minute and told Rudin that she checked and Marilyn is fine. Rudin calls back Ebbins (Lawford's handler) and tells him Marilyn is fine. Ebbins then tells Lawford that things are fine, but Lawford later states that he was still worried about her condition. Rudin's official statement to investigators is: "Believing Miss Monroe was suffering from one of her despondent moments, Mr. Rudin dismissed the possibility of anything further being wrong."[103]

9:00 – 9:15 PM

Marilyn calls an old friend, Jeanne Carmen—who states that she didn't look at the clock but knew that it was somewhere between 9 and 9:30 (on another occasion she states that it was 9:00, so apparently it was closer to 9:00 than to 9:30). Marilyn asks her if she has a couple of sleeping pills she could bring over to her house because she doesn't have any and can't get to sleep. Carmen basically responds that she's sorry, Marilyn, but she's "hammered" (drunk), already going to bed herself and not in any condition to go over to anybody's house. Other than that, Carmen reports that Marilyn sounded fine—she was used to hearing Marilyn when she was drunk or sedated (the two, according to Carmen, had been pin-up girls, models, together and then next-door neighbors at a previous residence of Marilyn's), and she didn't sound anything like that during the call—she simply sounded like an old friend who couldn't get to sleep.

Carmen adds that her telephone rang again a bit later and, figuring it was Marilyn again, she didn't answer.[104]

[103] Sgt. R.E. Byron, West Los Angeles Detectives, "RE- Interview of Persons Known to Marilyn Monroe," August 6, 1962
[104] Wolfe, *Last Days of Marilyn Monroe*

that's *exactly* the location that the heavy purplish discoloration was present. Therefore, it was via a disingenuous method—false appearances that were factually misleading—that the *Discovery Channel* documentary, *Unsolved History: Death of Marilyn Monroe* in 2003 was able to arrive at the conclusion that an enema could not have been how the lethal drugs were introduced: because they focused *solely* on the old-fashioned and messy bag-and-hose type enema, and they <u>completely ignored</u> that the simple syringe-type enema could have easily been used. Furthermore, both the crime scene evidence and the forensic evidence, especially the colon discoloration, *fit* perfectly with the use of the syringe-type enema.

Another possibility that investigators have looked at, is a theory that Marilyn was *accidentally* given an enema containing too much of the drug—i.e., a tragically fatal medical miscalculation. After all, enemas were popular in 1962, actresses used them for weight control, and it's known that Marilyn sometimes used them and that they had been administered to her in the past by her housekeeper, Mrs. Murray. However, we thoroughly investigated that possibility and we can say this with complete confidence that it was not the case.

Medical research specialist Tony Plant examined the possibility that Marilyn had somehow died as the result of a horrible medical miscalculation. A seemingly plausible scenario goes like this: Since Dr. Greenson did not give injections to Marilyn him-

9:30 PM

Former boyfriend Jose Bolanos telephones Monroe and later states that Marilyn sounded normal during their conversation. However, in mid-conversation, Marilyn hears some kind of disturbance and goes to check on it, laying down the phone without hanging it up. She never returns to the phone, and Bolanos never hears back from her.[105]

9:30–10:00 PM

We now know that, during this time period, Eunice had to have discovered that Marilyn was near death and placed an urgent call to Dr. Greenson who rushes right over (Dr. Greenson soon places a call from Marilyn's home, so he's obviously there). Eunice admits, later in her life when the heat from these tragic events has subsided, that Marilyn was still alive when Dr. Greenson came to the house, and that an ambulance was called and arrived before she died. One thing she later states very clearly is that "the doctor" was with Marilyn when she died, while Eunice waited in the living room.[106]

10:00 PM

Marilyn's housekeeper, Eunice, later states that, at 10:00, she got up and walked past Marilyn's bedroom door and saw a light on under the door, but decided not to disturb her. Note that this is almost definitely in reference to the same call from attorney Mickey Rudin that came earlier. Eunice keeps changing the times of these events over the ensuing years, but the call certainly seems to have come much earlier because there is a clear record of Ebbins' call to Rudin's answering service at 8:25, prompting Rudin's call to Eunice. Eunice later stated that the call came at about 8:30 which would fit with the forwarded message to Rudin and with the manner in which events transpired. Eunice's exact words regarding the call from Mickey Rudin are "He asked if Marilyn was alright. I said as

[105] Summers, *Goddess*
[106] *Say Goodbye to the President*, BBC

self and always relied on Marilyn's internist, Dr. Engleberg, for that, and since Engleberg was unavailable on Marilyn's last evening, it's possible that Dr. Greenson could have arranged to pick up a solution of *liquid* Nembutal, to be administered via enema, to be given to Marilyn later that night so that she could get some sleep. *Then*, it's possible that Mrs. Murray, an in-home support worker for Dr. Greenson's clients, could have mistakenly administered an entire bag of liquid Nembutal in the enema solution (fifty cc's), rather than the *intended* dosage of five cc's, resulting in the massive overdose. It's *possible— or is it?*

We determined that we can medically rule out the possibility that fifty cc's of Nembutal were accidentally given to Marilyn instead of a prescribed dosage of five cc's of Nembutal liquid solution. *Had that been the case*, the enema would have been prepared by her housekeeper. Marilyn's psychiatrist (who saw her almost daily), Ralph Greenson, also knew Marilyn's housekeeper very well. Greenson knew he could trust her: It was Dr. Greenson who had placed Mrs. Murray in the job at Marilyn's home, so Greenson knew that he could count on her, and Eunice faithfully reported back to him on Marilyn's habits and health.

On the day of Marilyn's death, Dr. Greenson had made a very rare visit to Marilyn's home in Brentwood in the late afternoon. It was rare due to the fact that he normally never treated her at her home. But

far as I know she is. The light was on in her room and the telephone (cord) was under the door and these were indications that she was still awake." Therefore, we can ascertain that there was no concern noted as of 8:30, but that a sense of emergency then surfaces about 10:00; that is also in accordance with the estimated time of death via the rate of rigor mortis.[107]

Around 10:00 PM

Norman Jeffries, the caretaker, states that he was working at Marilyn's home all day on August 4. Jeffries states that he saw Attorney General Robert F. Kennedy and two other men arrive and park their car around 10:00 pm. They enter Marilyn's home and tell Jeffries and Eunice to leave them alone there. Jeffries and Eunice wait at a neighbor's until the three men leave at approximately 10:30 PM.[108]

(Uncorroborated by neighbors)

10:00– 10:30 PM

From Marilyn's home, Dr. Greenson telephones attorney Mickey Rudin and tells him that Marilyn is dead. Rudin says he'll drive right over and he proceeds to do so. Mickey Rudin then calls Arthur Jacobs (Marilyn's lead publicist), and Milt Ebbins (Lawford's manager), and Ebbins then calls Peter Lawford.[109]

10:30 PM

This is the moment we can say it is a certainty that Marilyn is dead. Marilyn's agent Arthur Jacobs (Pat Newcomb's boss), receives an urgent message at a concert he is attending at the Hollywood Bowl. He returns to his guests, informs his future wife that something horrible has happened—Marilyn is dead—and they leave hurriedly. The call is from Marilyn's lawyer, Mickey Rudin.

---

[107] *The Legend of Marilyn Monroe* (Documentary), Produced by David Wolper, Directed by Terry Sanders, Narrated by John Huston, 1964 (cited in Marshall, *The DD Group, 287*)
[108] Wolfe, *Last Days of Marilyn Monroe*
[109] Spoto, *Marilyn Monroe*

it was reported to him that Marilyn was very upset (probably as a result of the now-established visit to her home that afternoon by Robert Kennedy), so Greenson made an exception and paid her a house call. Not only did he treat her at her home on a weekend, he conducted a lengthy psychiatric session of over two hours, not leaving until he was sure that Marilyn had settled down and was back in control of herself. Greenson was concerned enough for her well-being that he also made sure that Mrs. Murray planned on spending the night and keeping an eye on her. Greenson was relieved when Marilyn called him later that evening to tell him about her phone call with Joe, Jr., conveying the news that he was not getting married, which Marilyn was very happy about. Marilyn also asked Dr. Greenson during that same phone call, if he had taken her Nembutal prescription because she couldn't locate it. Greenson responded that he had not, but he was actually relieved to hear it confirmed that Marilyn did not have access to *any* Nembutal at that time. After being "weaned down" on her use, she was usually given an injection of Nembutal by Dr. Engleberg, when deemed necessary. Since Dr. Engleberg knew he was going to be unavailable for injections for a short period of time in the upcoming days, he had given Marilyn a prescription for twenty-five Nembutal, in the event she needed it to stave off any remaining withdrawal symptoms from the drug. Normally though, she was taking Chloral Hydrate if needed, to calm her nerves, and

Jacobs quickly drops off his fiancée and then goes straight to Marilyn's house.[110]

Approximately 10:30 PM

Joe Naar and his wife Dolores leave Peter Lawford's house. They state that everything seems fine at the time they left. Peter Lawford was pretty drunk by the end of the night but, in any event, he certainly never let on that anything unusual was going on, and everything seemed perfectly normal. Dolores said "There wasn't a word about Marilyn." Her impression and later conclusion was "Peter probably called Jack or Bobby and was told to take care of things—do whatever he had to do. And do it yourself—don't involve anybody else under any circumstances. [111]

10:30–11:00 PM

Peter Lawford calls the White House immediately after getting the news from Rudin. Some writers have pointed out that President Kennedy was in Hyannis Port, not in Washington; however, the White House operator was capable of patching calls through to the President almost anywhere in the world and did so for Lawford's calls, which were given high priority. This call was confirmed by Dr. Robert Litman, a member of LAPD's "Marilyn Monroe suicide investigation team."[112]

10:30–11:00 PM

Peter Levathes, Chief Production Executive at 20th Century Fox receives a "panicked call" from Fox publicist Frank Nell that Fox security guards be rushed over to Marilyn's home—and they quickly are.[113]

10:45–11:15 PM

Los Angeles Chief of Police Bill Parker is awakened by an urgent phone call that has been routed through the main LAPD

Dr. Greenson knew that she had that if needed; so, he was happy to hear that there was <u>no Nembutal in the house.</u> Anyone else observe here that this very noteworthy confirmation even comes to us via the very person who was forced by circumstances into helping create the cover story that Marilyn had committed suicide?

It's only remotely conceivable that Mrs. Murray recklessly and mistakenly placed an entire bag of liquid Nembutal, containing fifty cc's of the drug, in an enema solution. However, also recall that no drugs were swallowed or injected into Marilyn's body that night.

We can also rule out the possibility that Marilyn administered the enema herself as a method of committing suicide. Recall that Marilyn's doctor made sure that Marilyn's housekeeper was spending the night, because they wanted to keep an eye on her after her having been upset that afternoon. Following the two-hour in-home psychiatric session, Dr. Greenson felt she was well enough to stay at home, rest, and maybe even have Mrs. Murray take her for a drive later along the beach if she was feeling better. So, even if her doctors actually had sent over a bag of liquid Nembutal for an enema, and even if it *had* been fifty cc's of Nembutal in the bag, they most certainly would not have left Marilyn alone with it after she had been in a disturbed state earlier that day. Furthermore, when Marilyn went to her bedroom for the last time at 7:45, she casually said goodnight to Mrs. Murray and added "I guess we won't be taking

switchboard. Chief Parker then notifies members of the LAPD Intelligence Squad of a special meeting at 7 a.m. the next morning.[114]

Very close to 11:00 PM

Joe Naar arrives at their home with his wife and after going in and putting on his pajamas, gets a phone call from Peter Lawford. Lawford asks Naar, who lives very close to Marilyn's house, if he can run over and check on her. Naar agrees to go over and check on her, but just as he is leaving, receives a phone call from attorney Rudin informing him that now he needn't bother because Dr. Greenson has simply given her a sedative and everything is okay.[115]

11:00 PM

Arthur Jacobs arrives at Marilyn's house. Confirmation that Marilyn was now dead comes via Jacobs' later statements that he had seen her when "I went out there at eleven o'clock." By the time that Jacobs arrives, there are already many "others present."[116]

10:30 PM & After

According to Norman Jeffries, he and the housekeeper return to the house and find Marilyn, apparently dead, in the guest house, face down in the bed there. Eunice calls an ambulance and then calls Dr. Greenson. Greenson tells Eunice to call Dr. Engleberg also. Jeffries states that he was waiting at the front gate for the ambulance and then saw Peter Lawford and Pat Newcomb (Marilyn's press agent) arrive at the house. Newcomb became hysterical, screaming at Eunice who was very distraught. Jeffries takes Eunice into the house as he hears the ambulance, and then Dr. Greenson arrives at the house. Jeffries states that "After that, all hell broke loose—it was horrible"; that Dr. Engelberg arrived

114 Brown & Barham, *The Last Take*
115 Marshall, *The DD Group*
116 Summers, *Goddess*, 514.

that drive after all." Mrs. Murray had no idea what she meant at the time, but later learned that Dr. Greenson had suggested the drive as a possibility. That was a very natural exchange between two people. The point though, is that *had* Mrs. Murray been instructed to prepare an enema containing Nembutal, she would have already done so prior to the time that Marilyn retired to her bedroom for the evening. Therefore, the facts simply don't support any possibility that a liquid Nembutal solution had been sent to Marilyn's home by her doctors and fifty cc's of Nembutal had been prepared in the enema solution, by accident *or* by design (i.e., suicide).

With all this information, there shows that some strong reasons exist which virtually eliminate the possibility of medical miscalculation:

a.) There is absolutely no evidentiary indication whatsoever that a bag of liquid Nembutal was obtained from Dr. Engleberg (or from anyone else, for that matter);

b.) Given the fact that Dr. Greenson and Dr. Engleberg were both deeply involved in the current and successful treatment of Marilyn's addiction to Nembutal and were gradually weaning her off its use, it is almost impossible to imagine them not being careful with the dosage and not mentioning the specific dosage for the support worker (bear in mind that Marilyn's housekeeper is a

around midnight and they moved Marilyn's body from the guest cottage into her bedroom in the main house; that the "locked room suicide scenario was formulated by some plainclothes officials"; that police cars were arriving, fire trucks, a police helicopter landing at the golf course, and another ambulance. He stated that the place was swarming with about a dozen plainclothes officers (he had no idea who they were) and then they disappeared as suddenly as they had arrived.[117] *(As noted, Jeffries testimony is suspect)*

Jeffries' testimony is corroborated, however, by ambulance driver James Hall, who states that he and his partner arrived at Marilyn's home a few minutes after receiving a "Code-3" call. Hall confirmed the presence of Peter Lawford, Dr. Greenson, and identified the hysterical woman as Pat Newcomb. Hall states they found Marilyn in a comatose state on the bed in the guest cottage, placed her upon the floor and attempted to resuscitate her. Dr. Greenson then directed them to remove the resuscitator and attempt manual CPR, which they did, as Greenson attached a heart needle to a syringe and attempted to inject adrenaline directly into her heart. But the needle hit a rib, Dr. Greenson leaned into the injection anyway, according to Hall, and Marilyn "succumbed" to death a few moments later.[118]

(Note that no evidence of needle marks was found at autopsy even though they specifically examined for same.)

Investigator Anthony Summers located two employees of an ambulance company who echoed the same story; one stating that he was one of two attendants who were summoned to Marilyn's home but that "She was dead and they wouldn't let us take her." (Apparently California law technically prohibited transport of a corpse in an ambulance.) An executive at the ambulance company also told a District Attorney investigator that Marilyn was in a coma from an overdose when their ambulance arrived

companion placed in her home by Dr. Greenson) to give her at bedtime. Marilyn was Greenson's prized patient, and it is well-established that he cared for her. It was in both his professional and personal interest to look out for her safety;

c.) Even if her housekeeper had mistook fifty cc's for five cc's and mistakenly given her a fatal dose, there is *no way* she would have added a huge dosage of Chloral Hydrate to the Nembutal (bear in mind that Marilyn's bloodstream also had the equivalent of at least seventeen tablets of Chloral Hydrate— she had been taking a few every day while being weaned off of the Nembutal—but a few a day is a far cry from seventeen all at once);

d.) If it *had* been some horribly unfortunate form of medical miscalculation, at no time in the several decades following did anyone ever imply it—and you'd think it would have been a relief to mention it—in addition to the aspect of cleansing their conscience, medical accident is a much more comforting scenario to most than is murder or suicide.

e.) When we also consider the amount of Nembutal in the liver (2.88 times the amount in her bloodstream), the total amount of Nembutal in Marilyn's body at autopsy is dramatically in excess of the amount in a fifty cc's bag of liquid Nembutal (and that was the largest size bag of liquid Nembutal that was distributed to doctors

---

[118] Wolfe, *Last Days of Marilyn Monroe*
[117] Wolfe, *Last Days of Marilyn Monroe*

at her home, and that she died at Santa Monica Hospital; Summers concluded that the body was then returned to the home as part of the cover-up. There are, however, credible sightings of an ambulance by neighbors, as additional evidence that one was summoned. Yet Marilyn was on the bed in the bedroom of the house when police arrived, not in the cottage.[119]

Mr. & Mrs. Abe Landau, who lived next door, reported that when they returned home late on Saturday night (at about 1:00 a.m.), they saw an ambulance and a police car parked in the cul-de-sac in front of Marilyn's home. Other neighbors reported hearing a helicopter immediately overhead around midnight. Mr. Landau stated that "the place was like Grand Central Station. The cars were all the way up the alley … Some limousine was here … And, of course, police cars and the ambulance."[120]

Housekeeper Eunice finally admitted the truth much later. In an interview for the 1985 documentary *Say Goodbye* to the President, she at first stuck to the original cover story. When the cameras stopped rolling (but the microphone was still on), she said, "Why, at my age, do I still have to cover up this thing?" They asked her what she meant, and she revealed that she had seen Bobby Kennedy at Marilyn's house that afternoon and that had obviously been the reason that Marilyn was so upset. She confirmed the two were definitely having a romantic affair. She also stated that when she called for help, Marilyn was still alive when "the doctor and an ambulance arrived" and also confirmed the coverup, explaining: "It became so sticky that the protectors of Robert Kennedy, you know, had to step in and protect him."[121]

It was also confirmed by investigator Billy Woodfield and several former LAPD officers that the leader of the plainclothes officers at Marilyn's home late that night was Captain James Hamilton, head of the LAPD Intelligence Division

in 1962). A fifty cc bag contains thirty-seven and one half grains of Nembutal, the equivalent of twenty-five of the capsules she'd been prescribed. But Marilyn's Nembutal levels were more than *double* that number, in fact, almost triple—and that's just counting the amount in her bloodstream, not in her liver.

f.) Furthermore, if it had been an accident, then she wouldn't even have been conscious to be on the phone calls that she was apparently on later that evening. And she certainly wouldn't have needed to phone old friend Jeanne Carmen about 9:00 on the night of her death and ask her to bring over a couple of sleeping pills!

The facts also preclude the possibility of oral ingestion or hypodermic injection. The drugs entered her body anally via a drug-laced enema. That's not a theory, it's a fact. That's how the woman died. We can, therefore, deduce from those known facts that only one of three possibilities occurred:

1. The drug-laced enema was self-administered suicide;
2. Medical miscalculation gave her a lethal dose;
3. Her killers subdued her and then administered the enema.

One of the above is true. Since Marilyn did not have access to the liquid Nembutal that would be used in an enema, and since her doctors were weaning her off the drug, they clearly would not have *given* her access (especially on a day that had

---

[119] Summers, *Goddess*
[120] Margolis, *A Case for Murder*, 164.
[121] *Say Goodbye to the President*, BBC.

and an ardent Kennedy ally. LAPD Chief Bill Parker was another staunch Kennedy ally and was rumored to be the Kennedy's choice to soon replace Hoover as Director of the FBI.[122]

Two former LAPD Chiefs of Police, Daryl Gates and Tom Reddin, stated that informant sightings placing Robert Kennedy at the Beverly Wilshire Hotel on August 4, 1962 had been reported to them. It was also confirmed that the two individuals at times accompanying Robert Kennedy during his visit were two detectives who had been assigned to him.[123]

The important thing to take away from all this information is that an <u>ambulance was definitely called</u>, and Marilyn was apparently still alive when help first arrived. There were plainclothes police officers at Marilyn's home. They can deny it for a million years (and probably will), obfuscating the facts with disappearing documents and an obvious stonewall cover-up—but that's what actually happened.

12:10 AM

Beverly Hills police officer Lynn Franklin testified that he pulled over a dark sedan traveling east on Olympic Boulevard at a speed of approximately 75 miles per hour. Officer Franklin cautiously approached the vehicle and, shining his flashlight into the car, immediately recognized the driver as being Peter Lawford and one of the two other occupants as being Attorney General Robert Kennedy; a third man he later confirmed as Dr. Ralph Greenson. Lawford informed Officer Franklin that he was driving the Attorney General to the Beverly Hilton Hotel on an urgent matter. Officer Franklin reminded Lawford that he was in a 35 m.p.h. zone and waved him on.[124]

Lynn Franklin is the most highly decorated officer in Beverly Hills Police history.[125] He recalled the above event with certainty.

[122] Summers, *Goddess*
[123] *Say Goodbye to the President*, BBC
[124] Lynn Franklin, *The Beverly Hills Murder File*, (Epic, 1999); Wolfe, *Last Days of Marilyn Monroe*; Margolis, *A Case for Murder*, 181-82.
[125] Franklin, *Beverly Hills Murder File*

been stressful to begin with), we can rule out self-administered suicide. Since the largest bags that liquid Nembutal was medically distributed in, circa 1962, contained fifty cc's, and her actual Nembutal levels in her bloodstream were almost *triple* that level, we can also rule out medical miscalculation. That leaves Murder. The fact that there was obvious bruising of the hips and marked discoloration of the colon are indications that, just as Medical Examiner Noguchi later stated, there were "signs of violence."

The facts, therefore, necessitate the conclusion that the case was actually a murder. Examine the evidentiary implications in their entirety: Marilyn had fifteen times a fatal dose in her body–enough to kill an elephant. No doctor in the world would make an error of such a huge magnitude. It would have been an accident of gigantic proportion, difficult to imagine even with bad doctors and a typical patient—and Marilyn actually had *good* doctors, and she was their most famous patient! So we can effectively rule out accident, we can definitely rule out oral ingestion, and we can also rule out self-administered injection. We can actually rule out injection by *anyone* because the autopsy was specifically *looking* for that and found nothing.

Therefore, our conclusion stands up to intense scrutiny. Marilyn Monroe, to the logical exclusion of all other possibilities, was murdered via a drug-filled syringe-type enema. The evidence itself confirms that the victim was murdered. And please note that we intentionally use the word

Around midnight

A helicopter lands at Peter Lawford's Santa Monica beach house. Investigator Billy Woodfield gained access to the flight logs of the helicopter company that Peter Lawford usually used, and the logs revealed a notation that a flight had been dispatched to Lawford's Santa Monica home for a trip to the LA airport at "around midnight." The flight records at Culver Field in Santa Monica showed a pickup of one passenger at the Lawford house and a trip taking that passenger to LA airport.[126]

12:00 AM or just after midnight

Housekeeper Murray states to police (initially), that at this time she noticed the light under the door again and knocks but gets no reply. She tells police she immediately telephoned Dr Ralph Greenson, Monroe's psychiatrist.[127]

12:30 AM

Dr. Greenson states to police (initially), that at this time he arrives and tries to break open the locked bedroom door but fails. He states to police later that, he looks through the French windows outside and sees Monroe lying on the bed holding the telephone, apparently dead, so he breaks the glass to open the locked door and checks her. He calls Dr. Hyman Engelberg.[128]

Note that Eunice Murray later admits that Marilyn's bedroom door was not locked that night.[129]

12:00– 12:30 AM

Peter Lawford contacts private investigator Fred Otash, a surveillance expert, and the two arrange to meet shortly at Otash's office.[130]

---

[126] Summers, *Goddess*
[127] *Los Angeles Herald Examiner*, August 8, 1962
[128] Marshall, *The DD Group*
[129] Marshall, *The DD Group*
[130] Marshall, *The DD Group*, 346-351.

"murder" rather than "homicide." The legal definition of homicide is that the death was simply facilitated by the actions of another person. That means that homicide includes the possibility that a doctor accidentally over-drugged a patient, as was the case with Michael Jackson's death. Murder implies intent. So it's 100% certain that it was a homicide; and furthermore, appears to be First-Degree Murder.

That's more than simply a conclusion—it's an *inevitability* determined by the evidence: <u>Marilyn died from a lethal enema</u> that was *not* administered accidentally via a medical miscalculation, and was *not* administered herself as a method of suicide. Therefore, we can conclude from a standpoint of science and logic that Marilyn Monroe was murdered and, furthermore, she was murdered not on August 5, which is officially the date of her death, but <u>on August 4,</u> between 8:00-10:00 PM.

As the Deputy D.A. concluded:

**"I don't know who killed her.
But I do know that she didn't kill herself.
So someone must have killed her."**[152]

Let's also take a quick recap of some of the circumstantial evidence. No suicide note? An *actress*? Committing *suicide*? Because of a huge *drama*? And *no note*? You *gotta* be kidding ...

Would she really make an appointment to get her hair done (as has been confirmed that she did at 9:00 p.m. on the night of her

---

[152] John Miner, "The Death of Marilyn Monroe," episode of *History's Mysteries* (The History Channel), http://www.youtube.com/watch?v=KfcBarDpOeI (accessed 4 Jan 2012).

1:00 AM

Peter Lawford is supposedly informed by attorney Mickey Rudin that Marilyn is dead.

This, again, smacks of cover-up. As we can see in the previous post, Lawford was already well aware that Marilyn was dead and was already busy covering tracks.

1:00 AM

A neighbor of Marilyn's, Abe Landau, arrives home and notices a lot of cars and activity at Marilyn's house. Landau states that he asked what was happening, and he was told that Marilyn had died.[131]

1:30 AM

Attorney Milt Ebbins speaks on the phone to Peter Lawford.[132]

2:00 AM

Peter Lawford meets private investigator Fred Otash at Otash's office as the two had arranged in the earlier call. Lawford explains that Marilyn is dead, and that Robert Kennedy had been at the house, so there is an urgent need to get over to her home and "sweep" it of all listening devices, as well as making sure that there is nothing in the home linking her to the Kennedys. Otash had apparently wiretapped Marilyn's house and knew she was under surveillance. Lawford's wife (Patty Seaton Lawford) also verified that Lawford had gone to see Otash right after Marilyn's death. Otash verified that the tapes revealed that Robert Kennedy had been at the house that day. Two other witnesses also heard the tape and confirm that.[133]

3:00 AM

Ebbins calls Peter Lawford to talk to him again but this time there is no answer at Lawford's home.[134]

---

[131] Margolis, *A Case for Murder*
[132] Margolis, *A Case for Murder*, 184.
[133] Marshall, *The DD Group*
[134] Margolis, *A Case for Murder*, 184.

death) if she was about to commit suicide? Would you? Would anybody?

And if she had and was about to take enough sleeping pills to kill an elephant (many times a fatal dose) then why would she ask her doctor if he had taken her Nembutal? Why would she reportedly call an old friend shortly before her death and ask her if she had any sleeping pills? Jeanne Carmen was Marilyn's friend and she certainly believed that she was murdered. Why else, she reasons, would Marilyn have called her up late on the evening of her death to ask if she could bring over a sleeping pill? According to Carmen, Marilyn said:

"Carmen, do you have any sleeping pills? If you do, can you bring them over?" And I said "I can't."[153]

Jeanne Carmen had been a neighbor of Marilyn's at the home she'd had prior to Brentwood. The actual level of their friendship has been disputed by researchers, many of whom feel that there are "hangers-on" who attach themselves to the Marilyn story for their own personal aspirations to fame. Many researchers classify Robert Slatzer in that category, and some also include Jeanne Carmen. However, it seems clear that she and Marilyn were, at the very least, one-time neighbors and casual friends.

If you're wondering what Jeanne Carmen's conclusion about it all was, here it is:

---

[153] "The Marilyn Tapes," 2006 episode of 48 Hours Mystery (CBS, April 22, 2006).

Early AM hours

Surveillance expert Fred Otash, acting on instructions received via Peter Lawford, arrives at Marilyn's home and checks and removes the listening devices from it.[135]

Early AM hours

Men described as "Federal Agents" arrive at the Santa Monica headquarters of the General Telephone Company and, even though it is after hours, demand, receive and seize the telephone records of Marilyn Monroe.[136]

3:50 AM

Dr. Engleberg, Marilyn's real doctor (remember that Greenson is simply her psychiatrist) states that he gets a phone call at 3:50 a.m., informing him that Marilyn is dead, so he heads over to the house right before the police are called.[137]

4:00 AM

Ebbins states that he gets a call from attorney Mickey Rudin who tells him "I'm at Marilyn's house now and she's dead."[138]

4:00 AM

Pat Newcomb gets a wake-up call from Mickey Rudin, who tells her he is at Marilyn's house and that Marilyn is dead. Pat throws a jacket over her pajamas and heads over to Marilyn's house. A bit later, around dawn, she is caught screaming viciously at the reporters who hover just outside Marilyn's driveway: "Vultures! Are you happy now? ... Vultures"[139]

4:25 AM

Police are finally called. Dr. Greenson places the call from Marilyn's home

---

[135] Summers, *Goddess*
[136] Summers, *Goddess*
[137] Marshall, *The DD Group*
[138] Summers, *Goddess*
[139] Summers, *Goddess*

"I would bet my life on the fact that she did not take an overdose. She was murdered, period."[154]

The fact that Robert Kennedy had an affair with Marilyn Monroe was still a career-killer as late as 1985 when ABC News' *20/20* produced an extremely well-researched segment for the show that was cancelled at the last minute by an ABC executive closely linked to Ethel Kennedy. Research from the segment, however, still exists. Sylvia Chase asked former housekeeper Eunice Murray if Marilyn was romantically involved with Robert Kennedy. Murray responded by detailing a visit of Robert Kennedy's to Marilyn's home in June, 1962 and said *"I would call it a romantic involvement—yes."*

Former U.S. Senator George Smathers, a personal friend of JFK's, also disclosed that President Kennedy had confided in him that Bobby and Marilyn were having an affair after his own affair with Marilyn basically ended.

An even more explosive aspect of the ABC *20/20* segment was the fact that they established a highly credible link concerning the Mafia blackmailing of the Attorney General and President of the United States. In their interview with surveillance expert Fred Otash, he documented that he had been contracted by the Kennedy brothers' arch enemy—Mob-affiliated Teamster boss Jimmy Hoffa—to wiretap and record Marilyn's liaisons with Robert and President Kennedy. The tapes clearly demonstrated the

---

and it is received by Sgt. Clemmons, Night Watch Commander at the West Los Angeles Police Station. (By some accounts, the phone call is placed by Dr. Engleberg. In any event, one of her doctors calls the police, and both doctors are present when Sgt. Clemmons arrives). Sgt Clemmons verifies the death and then heads over to Marilyn's house personally.[140]

Shortly after 4:30 AM

Police arrive. Housekeeper Eunice and the two doctors are questioned, and they initially indicate a time of death of around 12:30 a.m. Police note the room is extremely tidy, and that the bed appears to have fresh linen on it. The police note that Murray was washing sheets when they arrived. Police also note that the bedside table has several pill bottles but the room contains no means to wash pills down as there is no glass and, furthermore, that the water is turned off due to remodeling. Later, a glass or other type of drinking vessel is found lying on the floor by the bed, but a police officer who was present states that it was not there previously when the room was thoroughly searched and that a glass was one of the items they were specifically looking for.[141]

5:40 AM

The undertaker, Guy Hockett, arrives and notes that Marilyn is in an advanced state of rigor mortis, and that the state of rigor mortis indicates a time of death between 9:30 and 11:30 p.m. However, the time is <u>later altered to match the witness statements.</u>[142]

6:00 AM

Eunice changes her story to police and now says she went back to bed

[140] Wolfe, *Last Days of Marilyn Monroe*
[141] Wolfe, *Last Days of Marilyn Monroe*
[142] Wolfe, *Last Days of Marilyn Monroe*

sexual nature of their relationships with Marilyn. The potential for blackmail was blatantly obvious. *20/20* segment producer Stanhope Gould spelled it out crystal clear:

"It was the documentation, coupled with the Mob angle that made it a story—the fact that the President and the Attorney General of the United States had put themselves in a position to have the nation's most powerful criminals eavesdrop on their affairs with the nation's most famous actress, and were exposed to blackmail. That was one hell of a story."[155]

You can judge the gravity of an event by its fallout: Hugh Downs, Sylvia Chase, and Geraldo Rivera all protested what they viewed as censorship and then resigned from ABC.[156]

HISTORICAL CONTEXT

By 1962, in addition to most "industry people" in Hollywood,

[155] John Simkin, "The Death of Marilyn Monroe," http://educationforum.ipbhost.com/index.php?s=eda8d6a61ec90 723172b46491db1c72c&showtopic=3716&st=0 (accessed 12 May 2011).
[156] Hugh Downs, "Marilyn Monroe story proves to be greatest '20-20' conflict," *Houston Chronicle*, 15 Jan. 1987, 2. http://www.chron.com/CDA/archives/archive.mpl/1987_435393/on-camera-marilyn-monroe-story-proves-to-be-greate.html (accessed 12 Jan 2012).

at midnight and only called Dr. Green-son when she awoke at 3:00 a.m. and noticed that the light was still on.

Both doctors also change their stories and now claim Monroe died around 3:50 AM (for the obvious purpose of closing up all the missing hours before police were called). Police note that Eunice Murray appears quite evasive and extremely vague—she would eventually change her story several more times. Despite being a key witness, Murray travels to Europe and is not questioned again. Since there is not a Coroner's Inquest or any official crimi-nal investigation, the witnesses are <u>not required to testify</u> under oath.[143]

6:04 AM

Peter Lawford calls President Kennedy (verified by White House phone log). The White House operator patches the call through to Hyannis Port, Massaa-chusetts, where the President is spend-ing the weekend, and the call lasts for a little bit over 20 minutes.[144]

August 6, 1962

One day after Marilyn's death is made public, Attorney General Robert Ken-nedy announces that J. Edgar Hoover has been doing a great job as FBI Director and will be kept on in that position even though he is past the age of mandatory requirement. This is nothing less than a <u>complete reversal</u> of an established goal of the Kennedy Administration, which was to force Hoover out and replace his important position with a true Kennedy ally. Hoover was bitter enemies with the Kennedy brothers (with Robert Kennedy in particular—it was a known fact that the two men despised each other, both personally and professionally). Bobby and his Justice Department were literally at war with the Mob, while Hoover was still officially denying that the Mafia even existed. So Bobby had been pushing JFK

most politicians in Washington also knew of JFK's affair with Mar-ilyn, and the pressure was increas-ing to break it off before it threat-ened the upcoming elections. For example, when it became known that Marilyn planned to sing *Happy Birthday* to the President at his gala event at Madison Square Garden in New York, the Kenne-dys advised her not to attend, and Marilyn's studio sent her attorney a two-page legal threat of dismissal for contract violation if she went to the party. When Marilyn asked the Kennedys to use their influ-ence with the board members of her studio, whom they knew, the Kennedys declined. Reports of the outrage of Democratic Party lead-ers were reaching JFK and prior to the event, three Democratic Sena-tors and six Democratic Congress-men went so far as sending tele-grams to the President urging him to cut Marilyn from the program at the huge birthday ceremony.

The heat was *on*. Marilyn went anyway.

In an event that mirrored the dissolving distance between the pri-vate and public lives of President Kennedy, the gala event held in honor of his 45th birthday was a cel-ebration of 15,000 friends, colleagues and contributors—including report-ers from around the world—that was held on May 19, 1962 at Madi-son Square Garden in New York City and was nationally televised. The entertainment included a song for the President from Marilyn, whom many knew was engaged in a roman-tic affair with President Kennedy.

Marilyn almost seemed to be making a "go-for-it-all" attempt

---

143 Wolfe, *Last Days of Marilyn Monroe*
144 Anthony Summers, *Official and Confidential: The Secret Life of J. Edgar Hoover* (G.P. Putnam's Sons, 1993), 301.

to fire him, and it was considered evident that Hoover's days were numbered (and a low number, at that). Even Bobby's statement is seething with ridicule, if one examines it closely: "the FBI Director has done an outstanding job of controlling the Communist Party in the United States, and I hope he will serve the country for many, many years to come."[145] (Bobby openly considered the "threat" of Communists in the U.S. to be little more than a joke at this point, designed in part for the purpose of shielding the truer threats to security). The fact that Robert Kennedy makes such a dramatic reversal one day after the death announcement is indicative of dramatic goings-on behind the scenes. Marilyn's home was bugged, her phones were tapped and she was being followed under extensive surveillance by the FBI. Therefore, Hoover obviously had access to that info (he had ordered it) and would have known that Robert Kennedy was at her home on the day of her death. The obvious inference is that a secret accord was reached to accede to Hoover's wish to continue as Director, in exchange for his cooperation in the cover-up, especially in relation to Robert Kennedy's presence in Los Angeles that day. Politics isn't pretty. There are actually 18 credible citings of Robert Kennedy being in L.A. that day—he may have had witnesses who swore that he never left Northern California on August 4—but he was in L.A. However, it bears noting, that Robert Kennedy's presence there in no way implies his involvement in Marilyn's death—if anything, quite the contrary. If Robert Kennedy would have had any indication there would be violence at Marilyn's home, he would not have even set foot in the state of California, let alone be at her house. Therefore, it appears she was killed for the very reason of implicating him by his presence there (just as Hoover had warned), in an effort to smear the Kennedy brothers with a public

to capture President Kennedy by strongly implying what many already knew. To sweeten the pot, she appeared on stage dressed in a form-fitting see-through gown. The revealing dress was actually a sheer slip, so tight against her naked body that she—quite literally—had to be sewed into the dress. The sequin-studded slip was composed of 2,500 luminous rhinestones and prompted UN Ambassador Adlai Stevenson to remark:

> "I don't think I had ever seen anyone so beautiful as Marilyn Monroe that night. She was wearing skin and beads—I didn't see the beads."[157]

The event was so dramatic that when Marilyn finally walked out on stage, there were audible gasps:

> "The figure was famous and, for one breathless moment, the 15,000 people in Madison Square Garden thought they were going to see all of

---

[145] *Seattle Intelligencer, August 7,* 1962 (cited in Marshall, *The DD Group,* 146).

---

[157] Lisa Waller Rogers, "Marilyn Monroe: Gentlemen Prefer … Skin and Beads," 16 September, 2009, http://www.lisawallerrogers.wordpress.com/2009/09/16/marilyn-monroe-gentlemen-prefer-skin-and-beads/ (accessed 14 Jan. 2012).

the Kennedy brothers with a public scandal that would ruin them politically (which, in the context of 1962 America, was a very realistic expectation). The "cover-up" which followed, appears to be a very clear effort to foil that attempt by the swift and almost surgical removal of any and all links to the Kennedy brothers at Marilyn's home by LAPD, with full coverage (especially on phone records) by the FBI and Justice Department, and the accompanying emergency exit—getting the Attorney General out of L.A. in the tumultuous hours after her murder.[146]

146 Summers, *Goddess*

it. Onto the stage sashayed Marilyn Monroe, attired in a great bundle of white mink. Arriving at the lectern, she turned and swept the furs from her shoulders. A slight gasp rose from the audience before it was realized that she was really wearing a skintight flesh-toned gown."[158]

As Hugh Sidey of *Time Magazine* put it: "When she came down in that flesh-colored dress, without any underwear on, you could just smell the lust."[159]

Marilyn then stunned the crowd by singing a long, slow, and sultry song to President Kennedy—actually a slowed-down and very sexed-up version of "Happy Birthday (Mister President)." Reporter Dorothy Kilgallen noted that it was like "making love to the President in the direct view of forty million Americans."[160] First Lady Jackie Kennedy wasn't steaming in the shadows because she was smart enough to have seen the whole thing coming. The moment that she heard that Marilyn would be singing at the event, she canceled her plans to attend the party and left town. All indications are that she was all-too-aware of the affair between her husband and Marilyn.

The combination of the sultry song, the mesmerizing performance, and the dress that left little to the imagination, certainly captured the complete attention of

Emblematic of the event's significance, the dress she wore that night was sold at auction at Christie's in New York in 1999 for $1,260,000.

everyone in the arena. It was a very difficult situation to handle, yet, true-to-form, President Kennedy handled it well. After the song, he went to the podium, smiled with a commandeering charm and then stated, very *under*whelmingly:

158 Waller Rogers, *Skin and Beads*
159 Waller Rogers, *Skin and Beads*
160 Waller Rogers, *Skin and Beads*

> **"I can now retire from politics after having had** *Happy Birthday* **sung to me in such a sweet, wholesome way."**[161]

White House control over the press was exercised forcefully. Following the party after the event at Madison Square Garden, U.S. Secret Service agents reportedly seized photos of the Attorney General dancing with Marilyn. At 2:30 AM, Secret Service agents knocked on the hotel door of White House reporter Merriman Smith:

> **"They wanted to make sure I didn't write about Marilyn and Bobby."**[162]

Early the next morning, U.S. Secret Service agents went to the photo lab of *Time Magazine* and demanded they hand over the photographs of the Kennedys and Marilyn at the party.

After the party, President Kennedy broke off the affair, and Marilyn never saw JFK again. Since it was more for political purposes than personal reasons, it's not too hard to see how things got quite dicey. Taking the counsel of Washington insiders, JFK cut off all contact with Marilyn—her calls were no longer accepted at the White House switchboard, and the private number that the President had given her to contact him at was disconnected.

[161] Waller Rogers, *Skin and Beads*

[162] "The Kennedys and Marilyn Monroe," *The Copa Room*, http://www.angelfire.com/jazz/thecoparoom/kennedysmarilyn.html (accessed 14 Jan 2012)

Although it was a well-established fact that JFK had numerous extramarital affairs, in the context of 1963 America, the press would not publicize that fact—in the perspective of the era, that simply wasn't done. Furthermore, JFK's charm and wit helped him establish an excellent rapport with the White House and Washington press corps. Additionally, JFK benefited from a vast network of media assets and contacts that stemmed from the business empire of his father Joseph Kennedy. In short, the press was very deferential to the charismatic President Kennedy.

Therefore, JFK's sexual exploits—Marilyn Monroe, Judy Campbell, Ellen Rometsch and Mary Pinchot Meyer were some of the more prominent names— were well-known but were kept out of the press. The danger—as FBI Director J. Edgar Hoover pointedly warned—was the potential for blackmail as a result. In that regard, Ellen Rometsch was deported when she was suspected of being an East German Spy; and JFK abruptly halted his affair with Judy Campbell after being warned by Hoover that he was aware of her close ties to Sam Giancana, the Chicago Mafia chieftain.

No Love Lost Here, Folks: FBI Director J. Edgar Hoover warned President Kennedy that he was very vulnerable to blackmail because FBI surveillance had confirmed his sexual escapades with women linked to the Mafia and the Communist Party. Robert Kennedy also implored his brother to curtail his sexual indiscretions, especially those that made him vulnerable to the Mafia—Marilyn Monroe and Judy Campbell. President Kennedy eventually succumbed to this pressure, and his relationship with Marilyn ended a short time later, a few months before her death.

Although President Kennedy had an excellent relationship with the press, his multiple sexual relationships were becoming a bit too public. The numerous extramarital activities were pushing the limits of acceptability—especially in 1963 America. JFK then ended his relationship with Marilyn Monroe.

Marilyn had reportedly benefited professionally from her friendship with Johnny Roselli, the high-ranking Mafia associate of Sam Giancana. The Chicago Mafia was reportedly responsible for Marilyn Monroe's success. Her career was said to have been launched and pushed hard by Tony Accardo, predecessor to Sam Giancana as chief of the Chicago Mob.

> **"The extensive influence the Chicago mafia had over Hollywood is best illustrated in 1948 when Chicago Mafia boss Tony Accardo had told John Rosselli to force powerful Columbia Pictures' president Harry Cohn into signing then-unknown actor Marilyn Monroe to a lucrative multi-year contract. The usually highly combative Cohn quickly complied without opposition, mainly because Cohn had obtained control of Columbia through mob funds and influence provided by both Accardo and Rosselli."[163]**

So through Johnny Roselli, the Chicago Mafia bought its way into the film industry in Hollywood through their backing of Harry Cohn, head of Columbia Studios. This gave the Chicago mob a strong trajectory into show business, which they reportedly leveraged to their advantage in promoting the careers of Marilyn Monroe and Frank Sinatra, among others. Harry Cohn is rumored to be the producer depicted in the "horse's head" incident in the film, *The Godfather*. In the "real-life" version, Roselli was sent by "Chicago" to tell Cohn that Sinatra would star in the film. Cohn resisted:

> **"In a tense meeting in Cohn's office, Roselli reportedly ordered Cohn to give Sinatra the part of Angelo Maggio in the film. Cohn not only refused, he told Roselli, 'John, if we have a problem here, I'm going to have to make some phone calls,' referring to Cohn's own considerable contact in the underworld.**
>
> **But Roselli had the backing of the entire national syndicate behind him and knew that Cohn was defenseless. 'Harry,' he said, 'If we have a problem here, you're a fucking dead man.'**
>
> **In the end Sinatra got the part and the Academy Award to boot."[164]**

The exact same links to Organized Crime apparently played roles in the deaths of both Marilyn Monroe in 1962 and President Kennedy in 1963.

---

[163] "Hollywood and the Mafia," www.chicagosyndicate.com (accessed 2 Feb 2006)

[164] John William Tuohy, "King Cohn and the Horse's Head," June 2002, http://www.americanmafia.com/Feature_Articles_214.html (accessed 8 Aug. 2012)

POSSIBLE SCENARIOS

The Kennedys

Some books have pointed to the possibility that the Kennedys had Marilyn killed because she was getting too public about her affair with the President. This theory is usually dismissed due to the fact that JFK and his brother Robert may have had their affairs and they may, at times, have gotten messy—but one thing that *has been* established is that neither one of them went around killing their girlfriends. Their interest in Marilyn was quite obviously of a more carnal nature, and it was simply on a different playing field than murder. Robert Kennedy in particular seemed genuinely concerned about the poor woman's well-being and, well, let's just say that murder is a bit of a stretch in that particular case. However, there is substantial evidence that Robert Kennedy was in town, and that he got out of town very quickly following her death.

CIA

The next group that can probably be eliminated from most serious discussions is the CIA. Some have posited that the CIA killed her to avenge the Kennedys for what some Agency people perceived as their betrayal of the intelligence community at the Bay of Pigs fiasco in Cuba.

But the biggest problem with "the CIA did it" theory is very well-evidenced by one simple question:

> **"If the CIA wanted to implicate the Kennedys in murder, why make it look like suicide?"[165]**

Mob

But if the Mob did it ... then it would have been a stroke of brilliance to make it appear a suicide. That's another theory out there and, frankly, one that makes a lot more sense.

That was the scenario that was reported in the revealing Mob book, *Double Cross* (written by Giancana family members) and it's also the scenario suspected by many Mob investigators. The Chicago outfit reportedly sent Tony "The Ant" Spilotro and Frank "The German" Schweihs to kill Marilyn (chloroforming her and then giving a lethal Nembutal enema) and to make it look like an overdose.[166] Other accounts from Mob insiders posit that it was a different team of hit men—but they are consistent that they were sent by "Chicago."[167]

---

[165] *Publisher's Weekly*, "Review of *Marilyn's Last Words: Her Secret Tapes and Mysterious Death*," Reed Business Information, division of Reed Elsevier, Inc. http://www.amazon.com/Marilyns-Last-Words-Secret-Mysterious/dp/0786713801

[166] "The Deepest Family Secret," Chuck Goudie, Investigative Report, WLS-TV, 8 May 2008. http://abclocal.go.com/wls/story?section=news/local&id=6129222 (accessed 2 Jan. 2012)

[167] Sam Giancana & Chuck Giancana, *Double Cross: The Explosive Inside Story of the Mobster Who Controlled America* (New York: Skyhorse, 2010). Adela Gregory & Milo Speriglio, *Crypt 33: The Saga of Marilyn Monroe-The Final Word* (New York: Citadel, 1993).

It's also very interesting to note that Chloral Hydrate (which was found in Marilyn's body at a level of over seventeen capsules worth), is related to chloroform; hence the nickname of "knockout drops."

It's no secret about the war that was going on between Robert Kennedy's Justice Department and Mafiosos like Sam Giancana and Carlos Marcello who felt that they had been completely double-crossed by the Kennedys.

What better way to cause the total career-collapse of Robert Kennedy than to have it go public that his heart-broken extramarital lover had felt so rejected by him that she decided to end it all? The evidence was right there at the death scene for discovery, in letters, notes and her diary. That's why—so the theory goes—there was a long gap between her death and its being reported—it had to take time to clean up the crime scene and protect the Attorney General and President of the United States from being blackmailed by a bunch of hoodlums.

We looked into that scenario and, actually, quite a bit of it makes sense. We do not know exactly what happened at the time of Marilyn's death, but we *do* know, bear in mind, what happened after it. And it gets pretty messy.

So somebody (or, more accurately, a *lot* of somebodys) went to a lot of trouble to cover the tracks that led to the White House. That much we know.

> **"If mobsters had hoped to use the Monroe connection to destroy Robert Kennedy, they were thwarted by the successful cover-up, however, worked largely thanks to Edgar. By grabbing the telephone records on their behalf, he made the Kennedys more beholden to him than ever."**[168]

According to a true crime author Christopher Claire, the hypnotic drug Chloral Hydrate had been used in murders by the Mob, to the extent that it was the Mafia's pharmaceutical murder weapon of choice. In the year previous to Marilyn's murder it was reportedly used in a number of Mafia murders.[169]

Looking at the big picture, a very complicated dance was taking place and it wasn't just on Marilyn's shag carpet either. It has been documented that Joe Kennedy, father of the president, went to Chicago prior to the 1960 election and enlisted the support of Organized Crime there. Some say they delivered the state of Illinois to JFK. Others say the Mob actually delivered Illinois *and* West Virginia. In any event, they certainly helped.

That fact certainly would have led the Mob, collectively, to believe that they had some "help" in Washington. Contrary to their expectations, the Kennedys in general and Robert in particular centered their careers around public attacks on the Mafia. Yet, contrary to this public posture, the CIA continued to enlist the support of the Mafia—and it has been documented that the CIA was working with the Mafia—especially in attempts to assassinate Fidel Castro, of which Robert Kennedy, who oversaw the intelligence community's *Operation Mongoose*, was to some extent, probably aware. And, in this strange but real dance, that cooperation with the Mob continued even after publication of Robert Kennedy's

---

[168] Summers, *Goddess*, 300-301.
[169] Claire, "Why the Mafia had to Murder Marilyn Monroe"

book, *The Enemy Within*, which warned of the venomous dangers of Organized Crime. Yet, at the same time that Robert Kennedy's Department of Justice was waging war in vigorous prosecutorial efforts against the Mafia on a nationwide basis, others connected to the Kennedy Administration continued to work *with* them against Cuba.

So another possible scenario is that, rather than being villain and threatening to go public with info about the Kennedys, Marilyn was probably the victim.

The Mob was trying to get at the Kennedys *any* way that they could and they'd tried a lot of ways; through Sinatra's friendship with them that the Kennedys finally halted due to Sinatra's many Mob connections; through trying sexual blackmail by wiretapped conversations catching JFK with another woman; and who knows what else. Setting up Marilyn via blackmail, and/or killing her to implicate a Kennedy, were *exactly* the type of things they were looking for. Marilyn's house was bugged for exactly that reason.[170]

So the notion that Marilyn was going to "spill the beans" on her affairs with the Kennedy brothers or on the plans to kill Castro, doesn't really hold up to scrutiny, nor does the claim that she was afraid of what the Kennedys might "do" to her.

Quite contrary to her "dumb blonde" screen image, Marilyn was nobody's fool. She worked hard to construct a career that had taken her all the way to the top of the ladder. Why would she jeopardize that? She had an important career to protect; a career that she'd planned and strategically maneuvered to achieve. She wouldn't risk that over a jilted love affair; she even cited that fact as the reason that her marriage to Joe DiMaggio could never have worked. Revealing a security secret or an affair with the President, especially in the context of 1960s America, would have sent her entire career crashing down faster than you can say Hollywood scandal. So the rumor that she was "going public" about her affairs, simply doesn't hold up.

In conclusion, there's a very good reason that the police always ask if the victim was linked to anyone with a criminal history, and if there's anyone you can think of who might have wanted to see her harmed for any reason. On those last two notes, you can almost hear Marilyn's friend, Frank Sinatra, singing:

"Chicago, Chicago ... "

BIBLIOGRAPHY

"How Did Marilyn Monroe Die?," Tony Plant, July, 2004; http://southernwingsaircraft.com/howmarilyndied.html

The DD Group: An Online Investigation Into the Death of Marilyn Monroe; David Marshall, 2005

Coroner, Thomas T. Noguchi, MD & Joseph Dimona, 1984

---

[170] Claire, "Why the Mafia had to Murder Marilyn Monroe"

Toxicology and Pathological Studies on Psychoactive Drug-Involved Deaths, Louis A. Gottschalk, MD, 1980

Goddess: The Secret Lives of Marilyn Monroe, Anthony Summers, 1985

Marilyn: The Last Take, Peter Harry Brown & Patte B. Barham, 1992

The Strange Death of Marilyn Monroe, Frank Capell, 1964

Marilyn Monroe: The FBI Files, Tim Coates, 2003

Chief: My Life in the LAPD, Darryl Gates, 1992

Double Cross, Sam Giancana & Chuck Giancana, 1992

Crypt 33: The Saga of Marilyn Monroe—The Final Word, Adela Gregory & Milo Speriglio, 1993

Norma Jean, Fred Lawrence Guiles, 1969

Legend: The Life and Death of Marilyn Monroe, Fred Lawrence Guiles, 1984

His Way: The Unauthorized Biography of Frank Sinatra, Kitty Kelly, 1987

Marilyn Monroe, Barbara Learning, 1998

Marilyn, Norman Mailer, 1973

Marilyn: The Last Months, Eunice Murray, 1975

Roemer: Man Against the Mob, William F. Roemer, Jr., 1989

Peter Lawford: The Man Who Kept the Secrets, James Spada, 1991

The Peter Lawford Story, Patricia Seaton, 1988

Marilyn Monroe, Donald Spoto, 1993

Marilyn and Me, Susan Strasberg, 1992

Conversations with Marilyn, W. J. Weatherby, 1976

The Last Days of Marilyn Monroe, Donald H. Wolfe, 1998

The Assassination of Marilyn Monroe, Donald H. Wolfe, 1999

Joe DiMaggio: The Hero's Life, Richard Ben Cramer

The Show Business Nobody Knows, Earl Wilson, 1973

Show Business Laid Bare, Earl Wilson, 1975

Nemesis: The True Story of Aristotle Onassis, Jackie O, and the Love Triangle That Brought Down the Kennedys, Peter Evans, 2004

A Question of Character: A Life of John F. Kennedy, Thomas C. Reeves, 1997

The Dark Side of Camelot, Seymour Hersh, 1997

50 Greatest Conspiracies of All Time: History's Biggest Mysteries, Coverups, and Cabals, Vankin & Whalen, 1994

The Mammoth Book of Celebrity Murder: Murder Played Out in the spotlight of maximum publicity, Chris Ellis & Julie Ellis, 2005

"The Killing of RFK: Will we ever know the truth?," Andy Boehm; http://www.skeptictank.org/files/socialis/rfkplot.htm

"Skinny D'Amato," Atlantic City Newsletter, Archie Black, March, 2000; http://www.ratpack.biz/rat-pack-archive.php?id=34&SkinnyDAmatoAtlanticCity

"Why the Mafia had to Murder Marilyn Monroe," Christopher Claire, July 28, 2002, News.Scotsman.com; http://www.scotsman.com/news/international/why-the-mafia-had-to-murder-marilyn-monroe-1-1375559

"Marilyn Monroe: the unseen files," Tim Auld, February 27, 2011, The Telegraph; http://www.telegraph.co.uk/culture/8340357/Marilyn-Monroe-the-unseen-files.html

"Did Marilyn Monroe Commit Suicide? Or was she murdered because of her political involvement?," Sherman A. Meeds, Jr., May 19, 2009; http://www.mysterioustimes.net/doc/PageView.php?pg=5

"The JFK Assassination Chronology," Ira David Wood III; http://www.jfkresearch.com/JFK%20Chronology%201.pdf

"Marilyn and Her Monsters," Sam Kashner, Vanity Fair, November, 2010

Files of the Los Angeles Police Department

" Marilyn Monroe," Rachael Bell, TruTV Crime Library

"Interview with Ken Hunter, an ambulance attendant," CBS News, Monroe Investigation Interviews, April 22, 2006, transcript of audio recorded in 1982

"Inquiry requested in Marilyn's death," Spokane Chronicle, Associated Press, October 8, 1985

"The Assassination of Marilyn Monroe," Mel Ayton, 2005, Crime Magazine;

"Joe DiMaggio Would Appreciate It Very Much If You'd Leave Him the Hell Alone," Robert Huber, 1999, Esquire 131, no. 6: 82. Academic Search Premier, Seattle Intelligencer, August 7, 1962)

"Hollywood and the Mafia," TheChicagoSyndicate.com; http://www.thechicagosyndicate.com/2005/11/hollywood-and-mafia.html

"The Kennedys: Power, Seduction and Hollywood" (Jeanne Carmen), 1998, E! True Hollywood Story

"Say Goodbye to the President" (Documentary), Produced by George Carey & Christoper Olgiati, Directed by Christopher Olgiati, 1985

"Unsolved History: Death of Marilyn Monroe" (Documentary), Discovery Communications, 2003

"History's Mysteries: Marilyn Monroe," October 12, 2009; http://www.youtube.com/watch?v=dddee3vSmaI

HLN, "Coverage of Casey Anthony Murder Trial and use of Chloroform (Dr. Michelle Dupre, Medical Examiner, Forensic Pathologist)," CNN.com; http://youtu.be/hAyHAiWqXyo

"The Deepest Family Secret," Chuck Goudie, Investigative Report, May 8, 2008, WLS-TV, Chicago, IL; http://abclocal.go.com/wls/story?section=news/local&id=6129222

"Celebrity Obituaries: John Miner," The Telegraph, March 4, 2011; http://www.telegraph.co.uk/news/obituaries/celebrity-obituaries/8362737/John-Miner.html

CHAPTER 5

John F. Kennedy –
November 22, 1963

U.S. President

VICTIM	**PRESIDENT JOHN F. KENNEDY**
Cause of Death	MULTIPLE GUNSHOTS
Official Verdict	President Kennedy was assassinated by a lone gunman, Lee Harvey Oswald, who fired three rifle shots from behind the motorcade, from a window of the sixth floor of a building.
	Purpose of trip to Texas was political "fence-mending" within the Democratic Party. But JFK had some very serious enemies in Texas—conservatives, mafia, "Big Oil," and even his own Vice-President, Lyndon Johnson.

Actual Circumstances	The "lone assassin" nonsense has been thoroughly disproved by the JFK research community—the circumstances of the ambush (too many bullets from too many angles) literally necessitate multiple shooters. Oswald had clear links to the intelligence community, was set up to "take the fall" and a massive government cover-up followed.
Inconsistencies	1. The kill-shot came from the front and the evidence proves it (Oswald was at the rear of the motorcade during the shooting). Footage of the assassination clearly documents the President's head being driven sharply backward from the impact of a frontal shot. The blood spatter evidence and eyewitness and ear witness testimony also confirm shots from front. An exhaustive review of the medical evidence concludes that: " … multiple witnesses saw the intact entry hole high in the right forehead at the hairline."[170] Sworn testimony of the emergency room doctors in Dallas confirms an additional frontal entry wound in the President's throat. [172] The evidence of gunshots from the front is simply overwhelming and, by any reasonable standard, meets all requirements of proof. 2. Oswald could not possibly have done the shooting that is officially attributed to him. The best sniper in military history tried and couldn't match it, so how could Oswald?[173] "Oswald was a patsy. There's no question about it."[174] —COLONEL L. FLETCHER PROUTY, MILITARY LIAISON TO CIA FOR CLANDESTINE OPERATIONS (Focal Point Officer between the CIA and the Air Force for Clandestine Operations per National Security Council Directive 5412 and Briefing Officer for the Secretary of Defense) 3. More than three shots were fired at the motorcade which necessitates a conspiracy involving several shooters. The utterly preposterous "single-bullet theory" was literally invented to address the existence of too many bullets.

[171] David W. Mantik, M.D., Ph.D., *"Inside the Assassination Records Review Board (AARB)* by Douglas Horne: A Nearly-Entirely-Positive Review," 26 Feb. 2010. http://assassinationscience.com/HorneReview.pdf (accessed 3 Jan. 2012).

[172] Douglas P. Horne, *Inside the Assassination Records Review Board: The U.S. Government's Final Attempt to Reconcile the Conflicting Medical Evidence in the Assassination of JFK* (Douglas P. Horne, 2009).

[173] Craig Roberts, *Kill Zone: A Sniper Looks at Dealey Plaza* (Consolidated Press, 1994), 89-90.

[174] Colonel L. Fletcher Prouty, "The Col. L. Fletcher Prouty Reference Site," http://www.prouty.org/ (accessed 12 May 2011).

4. Oswald was operational with U.S. intelligence, and over a dozen Intelligence veterans have verified that fact. Indications are that he was "working penetration" on plots against the President and was set up as the "patsy" by renegade operatives. Oswald's recorded voice holds up to the scrutiny of Voice Stress Analysis which indicated that he was actually speaking truthfully when he said "I didn't kill anybody. I'm a patsy."[175]

"That's not an allegation—that's a fact. Oswald was Military Intelligence."[176]

—William Robert Plumlee, former Military Intelligence operative and CIA "Special Ops" pilot

5. A blatantly obvious cover-up was instituted by the government to blame the assassination on Oswald, to ignore, reject, or obfuscate all evidence to the contrary, to mask Oswald's associations with U.S. intelligence agencies, and to preclude a genuine investigation.

Alarm bells went off all over Washington the second that Oswald's name was mentioned, because U.S. intelligence had been dramatically compromised.

"You may never get the truth in your lifetime, and I mean that seriously."

—Supreme Court Chief Justice Earl Warren, head of the *Warren Commission*, entrusted with investigating the JFK Assassination on behalf of the American people

THE EVIDENCE PROVES CONCLUSIVELY THAT SHOTS WERE FIRED FROM THE FRONT OF THE MOTORCADE, AS WELL AS FROM THE REAR

Frames 312-to-320 of the film, below, of the JFK assassination (taken by Abraham Zapruder), reveal in shocking detail the frontal head shot that killed President Kennedy. The President had already been shot through the throat and Governor Connally, seated in front of JFK in the presidential limousine, has also reacted to at least one bullet that has passed through his own body. So at Frame 312, First Lady Jackie Kennedy, aware that something is dreadfully wrong, is leaning over toward the President, who is lurching forward in reaction to his throat wound. A frontal shot of extremely high velocity then strikes

---

[175] George O'Toole, *The Assassination Tapes: An electronic probe into the Murder of John F. Kennedy and the Dallas coverup* (Penthouse Press, 1975).

[176] William Robert Plumlee, interview with author, 12 June 2006.

The assassination of President Kennedy was filmed at a rate of about 18 frames per second. At frame 312, the President is clutching his throat, precisely where emergency room physicals indicated an entry would. Governor Connally, to the President's right, is also reacting to a wound from a different gunshot, which came from the rear. Frames are courtesy of the Combined Costella Edit, produced by John P. Costella, Ph.D., at the web site of www.assassinationresearch.com/zfilm/, an electronic journal for advanced study of the death of JFK, edited by James H. Fetzer, Ph.D.

President Kennedy in his upper right forehead and drives his head and entire body sharply backward and to his left. The impact of the shot was such that it literally drove blood, bone, and brain matter of President Kennedy into the air and splattered onto the windshields of the two motorcycle officers flanking the limousine at the left rear of the car.

The backward impact is even more dramatic when viewed in the film footage. When the Zapruder film finally made it to the light of day for an American television audience, viewers were stunned at how obviously it revealed a shot from the front. An enhanced print of the Zapruder film is available online— every American who can, *should* view this important historical footage. The frontal impact of the bullet is vivid and unmistakably clear: http://youtube/ iU83R7rpXQY

A large piece broken off from the skull of President Kennedy is also visible in the film footage. It flies off his head immediately after impact, traveling backwards onto the trunk of the limo. First Lady Jackie Kennedy instinctively

At frame 313, a high-velocity round impacts at the right front of the President's head, near the hairline.

reaches backwards to grab the piece of her husband's head which had "flown off" (her exact words). The common myth was that Jackie was attempting to help Secret Service Agent Clint Hill climb onto the trunk of the limo, which is erroneous. She was reaching for the large skull fragment of President Kennedy which had been driven backward out of her husband's head as she stared at him; she reaches backward, grabs the skull fragment in her hand, and returns to the limo, her hand never touching Clint Hill, who then climbs aboard without her assistance.[177] The above is clearly discernable in the film footage at: http://jfkhistory.com/jackie.html

Jackie Kennedy also confirmed that, repeatedly stating:

"I have his brains in my hand."[178]

---

[177] Robert Harris, "Jackie on the Trunk?," http://jfkhistory.com/jackie.html (accessed 2 Mar. 2012).

[178] Harris, "Jackie on the Trunk?"

By frame 317, the President is already driven violently backward and to his left from the impact of a high-velocity frangible round (exploding ammunition).

The evidence regarding the final shot is dissected and diagrammed frame-by-frame in the excellent video study, *The JFK Assassination—the Last Shot* by Bob Harris.[179] It can be accessed at: www.youtube.com/watch?v=IVfIh-8nXyQ

Note that some of the forensic evidence in the Harris study indicates that President Kennedy was actually struck by *two head shots*, striking him almost simultaneously: one from the front, one from the rear. However, note that for the verification of multiple assassins, all that requires being established is *one frontal gunshot*. There were undeniably at least two frontal shots: The shot that entered the right-front forehead, verified by the exhaustive analysis of evidence and testimony conducted in Douglas P. Horne's epic "*Inside the Assassination Records Review Board: The U.S. Government's Final Attempt to Reconcile the Conflicting Medical Evidence in the Assassination of JFK*, 2010; and the shot that entered the President's throat, verified by the sworn testimony of the doctors who treated him at the emergency room in Dallas.[180]

It is very clear that Jackie Kennedy was holding a piece of the President's head in her hand. Moreover, large skull fragment would not be driven backward

179 Robert Harris, "The JFK Assassination—the Last Shot," http://www.youtube.com/watch?v=IVfIh-8nXyQ (accessed 1 Mar. 2012).
180 Horne, *Inside the ARRB*

At frame 320, less than half of one second after impact, the President's body is farther back and to his left, indicative of a high-velocity shot from the front and right of the limousine. He is soon slumped over completely to his left, low in the backseat.

in the split-second immediately following impact unless there was a shot from the front; skull fragmentation would only be driven backward from a frontal impact.

Minutes later, when emergency room physicians were scrambling to do what little could be done for President Kennedy at Parkland Hospital, Jackie Kennedy nudged one of the doctors and showed him what she had been closely guarding in her hands: a large piece of the President's brain. Dr. Marion Jenkins confirmed that:

> **"As she passed by, she nudged me with an elbow and handed me what she had been nursing in her hands—a large chunk of her husband's brain tissue."[181]**

The blood spatter evidence (his blood, bone, and brain matter immediately splattered the windshield of the two motorcycle officers who were flanking the presidential limo at the left-rear) is consistent with the frontal-right entry wound seen in the Zapruder film.

---

[181] Richard B. Trask, *Pictures of the Pain: Photography and the Assassination of President Kennedy* (Yeoman Press, 1994).

Sherry Gutierrez Fiester is a retired Certified Senior Crime Scene Investigator and Court-Recognized Expert in Crime Scene Reconstruction and Blood Spatter Analysis. Based on her detailed reconstruction of the crime scene and decades of scientific analysis, she has reached the following professional conclusions:

- "The head injury to President Kennedy was the result of a single gunshot fired from the right front of the President."[182]
- "I believe the shooter's location for the fatal headshot was from a location near the south end of the triple underpass. That position mathematically supports trajectory with angle and elevation; provides concealment, even from those standing on the overpass; and with unhindered access to an adjacent parking lot, offered ready vehicular egress from the scene. Moreover, as Kennedy was looking generally toward that location, it was almost a straight on shot—only slightly right of center—a trajectory that corresponds with the medical evidence indicating the injury to Kennedy's head was confined to his right side."[183]

Contrary to a study sponsored by the *Discovery Channel*, which was calculated upon parameters and assumptions not proven to have existed at the actual time, the blood spatter evidence actually at the crime scene is clearly indicative of a frontal shot. (The *Discovery Channel* Study in 2008 was flawed in many respects.[184] For example, the car in which they studied the blood spatter was not the car in which President Kennedy was shot; it was a test vehicle that supposedly "matched" as far as having the same wounds upon the "victim" after a simulated shooting. However, the wounds that "matched" were only those professed by the official government version of the event and not the actual wounds that were apparently inflicted. Put simply, they "proved" the official version by assuming that it was already true. They did so via a legal faux pais known as assuming facts not proven in evidence. Put simply, they took points that are hotly contested and assumed that the official answers to those points are correct. That's much like saying the following: If we assume that women have prostate glands, they then have the same prostate problems that men have. In the field of logic, that's known as the fallacy of falsely assumed premises—it matters not what the conclusion is, because the premises are totally corrupt.)

It has also been clearly established from many reports that the presidential limousine slowed dramatically after the first two shots, almost to a complete stop. Therefore, the directional momentum of the vehicle itself is virtually a moot point as regards the blood spatter evidence.

[182] Sherry Gutierrez Fiester, *JFK HOMICIDE: Forensic Reconstruction, Bloodspatter Analysis in the Kennedy Murder: Proving a Frontal Headshot* (2010, JFK Lancer, dvd). http://www.jfklancer.com/catalog/gutierrez/index.html

[183] Sherry Fiester, email to author, 5 Aug. 2011.

[184] Robert Harris, *The Discovery Channel Scam, JFKHistory.com*, http://www.jfkhistory.com/Youtube.html (accessed 2Jan. 2012)

More Blood-Spatter Evidence of Frontal Gunshot:
In the above photo, note how far back and to the left of the limo the two motorcycle officers Bobby Hargis and B. J. Martin are riding behind the President's limousine (they are actually nearer to the Secret Service Follow-Up car). The fact that both of their windshields were splattered with large amounts of blood and brain spatter immediately after the head shot is highly indicative of a shot from the right-front of the limousine.

Officer Bobby Hargis, Dallas Police Motorcycle Officer (riding flank left-rear side, immediately behind President Kennedy's limousine):

> "When President Kennedy straightened back up in the car the bullet hit him in the head, the one that killed him and it seemed like his head exploded, and I was splattered with blood and brain, and kind of a bloody water ... well, at the time it sounded like the shots were right next to me."[185]
>
> Officer Hargis then dropped his motorcycle and ran up the knoll embankment, as did scores of others, who all thought the shot came from up above that grassy area.

Motorcycle Officer B. J. Martin was also riding flank left-rear behind President Kennedy. His position was even *farther* out (he was to the left of Officer Hargis) from the vehicle, and his windshield was also splattered with blood, bone, and brain matter from the head shot to the President.[186]

U.S. Secret Service Special Agent Paul Landis
Special Agent Landis was riding in the Secret Service Follow-Up car, the car immediately behind the President. He was standing on the right-side running board of

---

[185] Robert Hargis, "Deposition of Robert Hargis," 18 April, 1964

[186] Fiester, *Forensic Reconstruction*

the car and was therefore directly behind and only a few feet away from where the President was seated. At the time of the last shot, SA Landis can be seen in the photographic evidence, focusing all his attention exactly where he testified it was:

> "My reaction at this time was that the shot came from somewhere towards the front, right-hand side of the road."[187]

THE MEDICAL EVIDENCE

Overwhelming medical evidence proves conclusively that at least two shots in the President's body were frontal entry wounds: An entry wound in the front of the throat and another wound of entry high in the right forehead at the hairline. Furthermore:

> "multiple eyewitnesses saw the intact entry hole high in the right forehead at the hairline."[188]

In his 2010 exhaustive examination of every document available relating to the medical evidence in the JFK assassination (a five-volume study totaling 1,807 pages), Douglas Horne documents that:

> "Multiple witnesses, who were medically and otherwise credible, confirmed that they clearly saw an entry wound in the FRONT of President Kennedy's head, in his upper right forehead at the hairline."[189]

As Researcher Bob Harris points out in his video study of the assassination, the issue of a frontal shot is a medical certainty:

> "The 3 top independent experts to study the JFK X-rays at the National Archives were Dr. Joseph Riley, Dr. Randy Robertson and Dr. David Mantik. They each did their research at different times and formed their conclusions independently. But all 3 of them expressed absolute certainty that the President was hit in the head twice."[190]

Dr. Joseph Riley, Ph.D. in Neuroscience and Neuroanatomy, independently concluded:

> "John Kennedy was struck in the head by two bullets, one from the right front and one from the rear."[191]

Dr. Randy Robertson, M.D. and Board Certified Radiologist, independently concluded:

[187] Paul Landis, "Secret Service Report of Paul E. Landis," 22 November, 1963.
[188] Mantik, M.D., Ph.D., *Review of Inside the ARRB*
[189] Horne, *Inside the ARRB*
[190] Robert Harris, *JFK Assassination, part 7* (video study), *JFKHistory.com*
[191] Harris, video study.

"In sum, it is a medical and scientific fact that the damage to the President's skull did not result from a single shot but was instead caused by two separate bullets."

Dr. David Mantik, M.D., Ph.D. in Physics, Board Certified Radiologist, independently concluded:

" ... there were two shots which struck the head."[192]

The medical consensus of the Dallas doctors on the frontal entry wound clearly identifiable in the President's throat was also certain; it was also certain on the fact that the entry wound at the front of the head caused a massive exit wound at the rear. One hundred percent of the medical personnel who viewed President Kennedy at Parkland Memorial Hospital described a large exit wound at the back of the President's head and have testified as such for the historical record:

- Dr. Charles J. Carrico was a treating physician on the emergency medical team that treated President Kennedy in Dallas. He described a large exit wound at the right rear area of the President's head. The circumstances were vividly memorable and the recollection is with certainty.[193]
- Dr. Charles Crenshaw was a treating physician on the emergency medical team that treated President Kennedy in Dallas. He described a large exit wound at the right rear area of the President's head. The circumstances were vividly memorable and the recollection is with certainty.[194]
- Dr. Richard Dulaney was a treating physician on the emergency medical team that treated President Kennedy in Dallas. He described a large exit wound at the right rear area of the President's head. The circumstances were vividly memorable and the recollection is with certainty.[195]
- Dr. Ronald Jones was a treating physician on the emergency medical team that treated President Kennedy in Dallas. He described a large exit wound at the right rear area of the President's head. The circumstances were vividly memorable and the recollection is with certainty.[196]
- Dr. Robert McClelland was a treating physician on the emergency medical team that treated President Kennedy in Dallas. He described a large exit wound at the right rear area of the President's head. The circumstances were vividly memorable and the recollection is with certainty.[197]

---

[192] Harris, video study.

[193] Gary L. Aguilar, M.D., "John F. Kennedy's Fatal Wounds: The Witnesses and the Interpretations From 1963 to the Present," August 1994, *Electronic Assassinations Newsletter*, http://www.assassinationweb.com/ag6.htm

[194] Aguilar, M.D., "Fatal Wounds"

[195] Aguilar, M.D., "Fatal Wounds"

[196] Aguilar, M.D., "Fatal Wounds"

[197] Aguilar, M.D., "Fatal Wounds"

- Dr. Paul Peters was a treating physician on the emergency medical team that treated President Kennedy in Dallas. He described a large exit wound at the right rear area of the President's head. The circumstances were vividly memorable and the recollection is with certainty.[198]
- Dr. Kenneth E. Salyer was a treating physician on the emergency medical team that treated President Kennedy in Dallas. He described a large exit wound at the right rear area of the President's head. The circumstances were vividly memorable and the recollection is with certainty.[199]
- ER Nurse Audrey Bell was a member of the emergency medical team that treated President Kennedy in Dallas. She described a large exit wound at the right rear area of the President's head. The circumstances were vividly memorable and the recollection is with certainty.[200]
- FBI agent Frank O'Neal was present at Bethesda and observed the President's body. He confirmed the existence of a massive wound at the right and rear of the President's head.[201]
- Radiographer Jerrol Custer X-rayed the President's body at Bethesda. With absolute certainty, he vividly recalls a gaping hole at the back and right portion of the President's head: "It was *gone*."[202]
- Floyd Riebe, an autopsy technician at Bethesda, stated in a filmed interview that he personally observed a huge exit wound at the right and rear of the President's head.[203]
- Paul O'Connor, an autopsy technician at Bethesda, stated in a filmed interview that he personally observed a huge exit wound at the right and rear of the President's head.[204]

Six of the Dallas physicians reported that they even observed a large portion of the cerebellum oozing out of the back of the President's head and onto the ER table he was laying upon. When these physicians were asked if they remembered that with certainty, they basically responded that you quite simply just don't forget a thing like that, especially when it's the President of the United States.

Eighty percent of the eyewitnesses to the murder of President Kennedy reported that a shot came from the west (the site of the "official sniper's nest" was east in the Texas School Book Depository building). The closest eyewitnesses reported that the upper knoll was the direction from which the fatal headshot occurred (west). Their reports were with certainty and were not instinctual—they heard the shot and it was different from the other shots. They reported statements such as the fact that the last shot was so close to them that it seemed as if it went right over their heads and

---

[198] Aguilar, M.D., "Fatal Wounds"

[199] Aguilar, M.D., "Fatal Wounds"

[200] *History Matters Archive*, "ARRB Bell Interview," http://history-matters.com/archive/jfk/arrb/medical_interviews/audio/ARRB_Bell. htm (accessed 11 Feb. 2012)

[201] Aguilar, M.D., "Fatal Wounds"

[202] Aguilar, M.D., "Fatal Wounds"

[203] Aguilar, M.D., "Fatal Wounds"

[204] Aguilar, M.D., "Fatal Wounds"

they even dove to the ground seeking cover from the imminent danger registered in them by the last gunshot.[205]

SECRET SERVICE TESTIMONY:

Forrest Sorrels, SAIC (Special Agent in Charge), Dallas District, U.S. Secret Service (in Lead car; the car ahead of President Kennedy):

At the moment of the assassination, Special Agent Sorrels was a passenger in the lead car of the presidential motorcade. He was seated in the right rear of the lead car and was peering out the right rear window at the time of the shots. He testified that:

> **"I looked towards the top of the terrace to my right as the sound of the shots seemed to come from that direction."[206]**

Special Agent Paul E. Landis, White House Detail, U.S. Secret Service (in Follow-Up car, the car immediately behind President Kennedy):

> **"My reaction at this time was that the shot came from somewhere towards the front."[207]**

Thomas L. "Lem" Johns, Assistant to the Special Agent-in-Charge, Vice-Presidential Detail, U.S. Secret Service (riding with the Vice-President, two cars behind President Kennedy):

> **"The first two (shots) sounded like they were on the side of me towards the grassy knoll."[208]**

The collective testimony of U.S. Secret Service special agents has been well-documented in Vince Palamara's book, *Survivor's Guilt*. The immediate focus of many special agents was on the area that had been *in front* of the limousine because that was from where it had seemed that shots had been fired.[209] It has been established that in the moments immediately following the gunshots, virtually all attention of law enforcement personnel was focused on the area that had been in front of the motorcade at the shooting (the overpass area, the railroad yard near it, and the grassy knoll area where scores of witnesses were rushing up the hill which they had determined as the location source of the gunfire).

Witness the very first police radio reports:

---

[205] *JFK: The Case for Conspiracy*, dir. by Robert J. Groden, (2003, Delta, dvd).

[206] Forrest Sorrells, "Secret Service Report of Special Agent-In-Charge Forrest V. Sorrells," 28 November, 1963.

[207] Paul Landis, "Statement of United States Secret Service Special Agent Paul E. Landis," 27 November, 1963.

[208] *House Select Committee on Assassinations*, "Interview of Special Agent Thomas L. Johns," 8 August, 1978.

[209] Vincent Michael Palamara, *Survivor's Guilt: The Secret Service and the Failure to Protect the President* (Assassination Research.com, 2006). http://www.assassinationresearch.com/v4n1.html (accessed 1May 2011).

Jesse Curry, Chief of Police, Dallas, Texas (in Lead car; the car ahead of President Kennedy):

DALLAS POLICE RADIO TRANSMISSION: November 22, 1963, 12:30PM

> Chief Curry: "Get a man on top of that Triple Underpass and see what happened up there."[210]

Chief Curry later acknowledged that:

> "We don't have any proof that Oswald fired the rifle, and never did. Nobody's yet been able to put him in the building with a gun in his hand."[211]

Bill Decker, Sheriff of Dallas County (in Lead car; the car ahead of President Kennedy):

DALLAS POLICE RADIO TRANSMISSION: November 22, 1963, 12:30PM

> Sheriff Decker: "Have my office move all available men out of my office into the railroad yard to try to determine what happened in there and hold everything secure until Homicide and other investigators should get there."[212]

Officer Clyde Haygood, Dallas Police motorcycle officer (riding flank right-side behind President Kennedy):

TESTIMONY OF OFFICER CLYDE A. HAYGOOD

> QUESTION: "What did you do after you heard the sounds?"
>
> OFFICER HAYGOOD: "I made the shift down to lower gear and went on to the scene of the shooting."
>
> QUESTION: "What do you mean by 'the scene of the shooting?'"
>
> OFFICER HAYGOOD: " ... I could see all these people laying on the ground there on Elm. Some of them were pointing back up to the railroad yard, and a couple of people were headed back up that way, and I immediately tried to jump the north curb there in the

[210] Stewart Galanor, "The Art and Science of Misrepresenting Evidence," http://www.history-mattewrs.com/analysis/Witness/artScience.htm (accessed 2 Mar. 2012).

[211] Jim Marrs, *Crossfire* (New York: Carroll & Graf, 1989).

[212] Galanor, "Misrepresenting Evidence"

	400 block, which was too high for me to get over."
QUESTION:	"You mean with your motorcycle?"
OFFICER HAYGOOD:	" ... And I left my motor on the street and ran to the railroad yard."
QUESTION:	" ... Did you see any people running away from there?"
OFFICER HAYGOOD:	"No. They was all going to it."[213]

Officer Haygood, along with over one hundred other eyewitnesses and law enforcement officials, ran up the knoll embankment to the railroad yard in the minutes immediately following the shots.

JAMES TAGUE was an eyewitness in Dealey Plaza who noted for the historical record that the Texas School Book Depository was not at all the focus of early attention:

"If you go back to Dealey Plaza at 12:30 and get the photographs and police tapes, there was really no action taken on the School Book Depository for seven minutes. True, there were a couple of policemen who said they rushed in, which looks good on a sergeant's report, but it didn't happen that way. In those seven minutes, I think Oswald may have assisted in letting people into the building by saying they worked there or whatever. During that time, they could have moved an army in and out of the Texas School Book Depository.

In viewing the Zapruder film, there's overwhelming evidence that there was a frontal shot. They keep saying that there was possibly a neurological reaction, but if you view the film in slow motion, the Groden enhancement, the power of that shot even throws the body backward. The car was barely moving, so it wasn't from the acceleration, and I've never found anybody yet that has seen a kill of an animal where they fall toward the shot. As a result, there very definitely had to have been a shot from the grassy knoll."[214]

Therefore, six primary evidence chains indicate a frontal shot:

1. The dramatic backward movement of head and body;
2. A large fragment of skull or brain material visibly driven backward at moment of impact;
3. Immediate blood and brain spatter on the windshields of the left-rear flanking motorcycles;

---

[213] Clyde Haygood, "Testimony of Clyde A. Haygood to the President's Commission (a.k.a. Warren Commission)," 9 April, 1964. http://jfkassassination.net/russ/testimony/haygood.htm

[214] James Tague, "Eyewitness Statement of James Tague," http://karws.gso.uri.edu/jfk/History/The_deed/Sneed/Tague.html (accessed 2 Feb. 2012).

4. At least twenty-five credible eyewitness reports of smelling street-level gunpowder and/or seeing gun smoke down at street level (Oswald was supposedly on 6th floor);[215]

5. Over 100 witnesses reported seeing and/or hearing at least one shot from the grassy area at street-level in front of the motorcade. That area is precisely where law enforcement personnel rushed in the moments after the assassination amid live on-scene reports of gunfire there;[216]

6. The medical evidence, especially at Parkland Hospital where the President was taken immediately after the shooting, *overwhelmingly* indicates that at least two shots in the President's body were frontal entry wounds: an entry wound in the front of the throat and another intact entry wound high in the right forehead at the hairline.[217]

OSWALD COULD NOT POSSIBLY HAVE ACCOMPLISHED THE SHOOTING THAT IS OFFICIALLY ATTRIBUTED TO HIM

"Now if I can't do it, how in the world could a guy who was a non-qual on the rifle range and later only qualified 'marksman' do it?"[218]

—Gunnery Sergeant Carlos Hathcock, Senior Instructor, Quantico, U.S. Marine Corps Sniper Instructor School

The most accomplished combat sniper in the entire history of the U.S. military is Marine Corps Gunnery Sergeant Carlos Hathcock. Hathcock's skills are legendary; as a sniper, he was officially credited with ninety-three confirmed kills. He was also senior instructor for the U.S. Marine Corps Sniper Instructor School at its headquarters at Quantico, Virginia. Hathcock and his crew meticulously reconstructed the entire shooting scenario in the JFK assassination and concluded that the shooting was not possible from one gunman on the 6th floor of the building.

"'Let me tell you what we did at Quantico,' Hathcock recalls. 'We reconstructed the whole thing: the angle, the range, the moving target, the time limit, the obstacles, everything. I don't know how many times we tried it, but we couldn't duplicate what the Warren Commission said Oswald did.'"[219]

[215] Walt Brown Ph.D., *The Guns of Texas Are Upon You* (Last Hurrah Press, 2005). William Robert Plumlee, "Affidavit of William R. Plumlee," notarized 27 July 2010. Mark Lane, *Rush to Judgement* (Thunder's Mouth, 1992). Palamara, 2006. John Simkin, "George Hickey: Biography," *Spartacus Educational*, http://www.spartacus.schoolnet.co.uk/JFKhickey.htm (accessed 12 Jan. 2012)

[216] *JFK: The Case for* Conspiracy, Groden

[217] Horne, *Inside the ARRB*

[218] Roberts, *Kill Zone*

[219] Roberts, *Kill Zone*

SNIPER SNAPSHOT
of Dealey Plaza

LOGISTIC	PROFESSIONAL ASSESSMENT	DEGREE OF DIFFICULTY:
Weapon:	A C2766 bolt-action 6.5 mm Mannlicher-Carcano is an extremely unprofessional choice. After the first shot, potential for succeeding fire is severely limited.	Implausible
Location:	The 6th floor window of Book Deposit Building is a terrible choice for a professional shooter to set up. The angles are very poor. Sniper's choice would be the Dal-Tex Building (which was also precisely the location of professional assassin Chuck Nicoletti, per testimony of Chicago Mafioso James Files).	Highly Implausible
Angle of Engagement:	Kill zone is obscured by tree branches. Wall and vertical pipes prevent shooter from positioning properly for shot. Only a professional sniper could correctly gauge/scope the exact high-to-low angle formula necessary for a kill shot.	Virtually Impossible
Shot Choice:	Especially if 6.5 Carcano is weapon, shot choice is when target is approaching or beneath window, not when target has trailed off and moving away.	Extremely Implausible
Sequence Of Shots:	In any realistic shooting scenario, the first shot is the most accurate. In the assassination, it was the least accurate, missing the entire limousine, as well as the target—leading to very logical speculation that first fire was actually a warning shot in an attempt to thwart the assassination.	Extremely Implausible

Timing Of Shots:	"Re-enactment" could not duplicate shots/hits assigned to Oswald because it never happened that way in reality. If the best combat sniper in U.S history could not accomplish the shooting, it literally could not have been done by Oswald.	Literally Impossible

Based primarily on the work of Lt. Colonel Craig Roberts and Gunnery Sergeant Carlos Hathcock, both of whom were professional snipers.

Lt. Colonel Craig Roberts was a Marine sniper in Vietnam and a police sharp-shooter with an urban SWAT team. Roberts examined the technical details of the shooting, and of Dealey Plaza itself, and wrote the book *Kill Zone: A Sniper Looks at Dealey Plaza*. Roberts puts it very simply:

> **"The reason I *knew* that Oswald could not have done it, was because *I* could not have done it."[220] (emphasis in original)**

As a professional sniper, Lt. Colonel Roberts knew the moment that he looked at the target angles from the 6th floor window that the shooting wasn't all done from there.

> **"I walked away from the window in disgust. I had seen all I needed to know that Oswald could not have been the lone shooter."[221]**

> **"Roberts places at least one shooter on the infamous grassy knoll overlooking Elm, ahead of Kennedy and to his right. He places another in the building across Houston Street from the Book Depository: the Dal-Tex Building, as it was in 1963."[222]**

Roberts has also studied the entrance/exit transit of the head shot and has concluded with absolute certainty that the final shot came from the front.

> **"Some of the supporters of the Warren Commission ... stated that the bullet came from the rear because the eruption of brain matter and blood came out of the front of the president's skull. I saw something else. In a head shot, the exit wound, due to the buildup of hydrostatic pressure, explodes in a conical formation in the down-range direction of the bullet. Yet in the Zapruder film, I**

---

[220] Roberts, *Kill Zone*

[221] Roberts, *Kill Zone*

[222] Steve Badrich, "Postcards from the Labyrinth: Thirty Years After, J.F.K. Researchers Gather in Dallas," (NameBase Newsline, No. 4, Jan.-Mar. 1994), http://the-puzzle-palace.com/files/NEWSLINE.194

could plainly see that the eruption was not a conical shape to the front of the limo, but instead was an explosion that cast fragments both up and down in a vertical plane, and side to side in a horizontal plane. There was only one explanation for this: an exploding or 'frangible' bullet. Such a round explodes on impact—in exactly the manner depicted in the film."[223]

"With his extensive combat experience, Roberts is scathing about the mysterious 'jet force' that supposedly blows Kennedy's head backwards, towards Oswald, in the famous Zapruder home movie of the assassination. 'In that film,' says Roberts, 'we see Kennedy take a shot from the front.'"[224]

The alleged rifle was such a piece of junk that it was also very difficult to fire succeeding shots. As former Governor Jesse Ventura, an Expert Marksman and Navy UDT (Underwater Demolition Teams, now known as Navy SEALs), established beyond doubt in a 2010 shooting re-enactment, it is impossible to get off three shots with that rifle in six seconds, as is officially alleged.[225]

An exhaustive scientific study that was recently published confirmed Ventura's opinion; it concluded categorically that the rifle cannot be re-fired in 1.6 seconds, as the government officially claimed. The same study also confirmed that the head snap of the President was evidence of a frontal shot, with autopsy evidence of that as well. It also concluded that the government clearly acted in a pattern that established their need to arrive at a non-conspiracy conclusion, and that Oswald cannot be placed as one of the shooters.[226]

So, bear in mind, that's if Oswald was even *there*—as the Chief of Police said:

"We don't have any proof that Oswald fired the rifle and never have."[227]

—Jesse Curry, Dallas Chief of Police

The task of the shooting, therefore, for one lone shooter would have been impossible, even for an expert marksman. And Oswald was nothing close to an expert marksman. His fellow soldiers, in fact, recalled that he was "a relatively poor shot."[228]

Furthermore, Oswald's rifle wasn't even *sighted in* (lined up correctly), which means that a person shooting it wouldn't even hit what was lined up in the sight! As historian Walt Brown puts it:

---

[223] Roberts, *Kill Zone*

[224] Badrich, "Postcards from the Labyrinth"

[225] *Conspiracy Theory with Jesse Ventura*, 2010, truTV

[226] *Hear No Evil: Social Constructivism & the Forensic Evidence in the Kennedy Assassination*, Donald Byron Thomas, 2010

[227] Marrs, *Crossfire*

[228] Mark Lane, *Rush To Judgment*, (Thunder's Mouth Press, 1992), 125.

"It would also have made a difference if the expert rifleman was using an expert rifleman's weapon of choice, not a piece of war surplus Italian junk whose inadequacies were massively compounded by the conclusion that the weapon was assembled and fired without ever having been sighted in. Ask your friend, the hunter. He'll tell you *it can't be done.*"[229]

TOO MANY BULLETS NECESSITATE MULTIPLE SHOOTERS

"There had to be more than three shots, gentlemen."[230]

—Official testimony of Roy Kellerman, U.S. Secret Service Special Agent-in-Charge White House Secret Service Detail, Dallas trip

TOO MANY BULLETS

(Official FBI & Warren Commission findings were three shots only)

Shot #1	The first rifle shot missed, hitting the street behind President Kennedy's limousine and creating sparks. Even the Warren Commission categorizes this as a miss. It is an astonishing feat that the first shot misses and later shots hit the target. Any professional assassin would expect their first shot to be their best. This fact has caused rampant speculation that if Oswald actually fired at all, it was this, as a warning or diversionary shot, in an attempt to throw off the timing of the assassination plot he had penetrated and to save the life of President Kennedy, not take it.
Shot #2	Hit President Kennedy in his throat from the front, just as the emergency room doctors in Dallas described it. The doctors observed the wound and described it as a "wound of entry" which they then utilized in order to make their tracheostomy incision.
Shot #3	Hits at street level, then ricochets, wounding bystander James Tague in his cheek.
Shot #4	Hits Governor Connally in the back, traveling through his chest, cracking a rib and exiting through his right nipple.
Shot #5	Hits President Kennedy in his back, four inches below the nape of his neck and to the right of his spine (fired from the rear of the limousine).

---

229 Brown, *Guns of Texas* (emphasis in original).
230 Palamara, *Survivor's Guilt*

Shot #6	Shot enters and shatters Governor Connally's right wrist, traveling through-and-through and then enters his thigh. (When Governor Connally died, investigators attempted to obtain permission to autopsy his wrist, to examine the fragments of metal still lodged within it. Those efforts were denied.)
Shot #7	Strikes the windshield of the President's limousine, traversing through-and-through. The bullet hole was observed by at least two Dallas Police Officers: Sergeant Stavis Ellis and Officer H. R. Freeman, as well as journalist Richard Dudman, while the limo sat parked near the emergency room at Parkland Memorial. The bullet hole was "just left of center" in the front windshield. Sergeant Ellis testified that he observed what he determined was a bullet hole in the windshield; that it was not chipped glass: "You could put a pencil through it."[231]
Shot #8	Hits President Kennedy in the back of his head from the rear. This shot was only milliseconds prior to the final head shot, causing the slight forward motion in the President's head which is clearly visible before the final shot (see the full examination by Dankbaar at www.jfkmurdersolved.com).
Shot #9	Hits President Kennedy from the front, entering at his right temple, causing a massive blowback exit from the right rear of his skull and forcefully driving his head and entire body backward and to his left.

(Based on the work of Walt Brown, Ph.D., Robert Groden, Douglas Herman, Craig Roberts, and Wim Dankbaar: Groden, 1993, Harvard Science Center; Herman; 2005; Dankbaar, 2006; Roberts, 1994. Also see "The Shots in Dealey Plaza," William Orchard, 2010. http://theshotsindealeyplaza.com/?page_id=12)

Ballistics expert Orlando Martin reached much the same conclusions in his 2010 study that has been termed the "Preeminent Ballistics Analysis of the JFK Assassination":[232]

- At least five shots were fired;
- From three shooters in three different locations;
- With bullets that were different loads and weights.[233]

It has been scientifically established that *different* bullets were used, meaning that they had to be the product of multiple weapons. While most of the bullets were normal rounds, the bullet from the fatal frontal shot was clearly a "frangible" bullet, known as a "hot load" or exploding ammo. Physics, *not* the Warren Commission, *proves* conclusively that it was a bullet of this type

---

[231] Douglas Horne, "Photographic Evidence of Bullet Hole in JFK Limousine Windshield 'Hiding in Plain Sight'", 1 June, 2012. http://insidethearrb.livejournal.com/

[232] *Amazon.com*, "Reviews of 'JFK: The Analysis of a Shooting'," http://www.amazon.com/JFK-Analysis-Shooting-Ultimate-Ballistics/product-reviews/1608443159 (accessed 1 Mar 2012)

[233] Orlando Martin, JFK, *The Analysis of a Shooting: The Ultimate Ballistics Truth Exposed* (Dog Ear, 2010).

that struck President Kennedy's forehead. The lack of copper in the bullet that missed the motorcade and hit the curbstone, also indicates that a weapon other than Oswald's alleged rifle *had* to have been used that day.[234]

Professor James Fetzer is also a former Marine Corps officer who supervised recruit training and marksmanship instruction at the same rifle range and depot where Oswald took his training. His 2000 study of the science of the assassination brought together an amazing collection of highly qualified research:

"The contributors whose work has been brought together in this volume include the leading authority on the Secret Service (Vincent Palamara); the most knowledgeable student of the Presidential limousine (Douglas Weldon, J.D.); a leading expert on the medical evidence at Parkland and at Bethesda (Gary Aguilar, M.D.); the single most highly qualified person to ever study this case (David W. Mantik, M.D., Ph.D.); the Senior Analyst for Military Records for the ARRB (Douglas Horne); a legendary photoanalyst who advised the House Select Committee during its reinvestigation (Jack White); a world-famous philosopher who received the Nobel Prize for Literature in 1950 (Bertrand Russell); a prize-winning director and playwright, who has produced a brilliant chronology (Ira David Wood III); and a philosopher of science who has published more than twenty books and 100 articles in his fields of expertise (James H. Fetzer, Ph.D.)."[235]

That study concluded that:

> **"An absolute minimum of six shots had to have been fired during the assassination, where the total was more likely eight, nine, or even ten."[236]**

There are other very credible reports of additional shots; one striking the chrome trim strip of the limousine's windshield and one striking the freeway sign on Elm Street (see Roberts; 1994). There were, in fact, *so many* gunshots, that their precise reconstruction proves very difficult. That is why the Secret Service agent in charge on the scene described the event as:

> **" ... a flurry of shots"[237]**

> **—Roy Kellerman, U.S. Secret Service Special Agent in Charge,
> White House Secret Service Detail, Dallas trip**

A rarely publicized fact is that substantial bullet fragments were retrieved from *inside* the limousine:

> **"Gerald Posner, writing in Case Closed, wrote that over sixty *grams* of fragments were recovered from inside the limo. That is a hell of a lot of fragments."[238]**

---

[234] G. Paul Chambers, *Head Shot: The Science Behind the JFK Assassination* (Prometheus, 2012). Martin, *Analysis of a Shooting.*

[235] James H. Fetzer Ph.D., *Murder in Dealey Plaza: What We Know Now that We Didn't Know Then* (Open Court, 2000).

[236] Fetzer, *Murder in Dealey Plaza*

[237] Palamara, *Survivor's Guilt*

[238] Douglas Herman, "Count the Bullets: Blow away all arguments," 27 June 2005, (emphasis in original), http://strike-the-root.com/51/herman/herman16.html (accessed 2 Jan. 2012)

The man in charge of the White House Secret Service Detail at ground-level in Dealey Plaza that day was Roy Kellerman. He was riding in the front passenger seat of the Presidential limousine, in front of President Kennedy. In his testimony for the Warren Commission, Special Agent Kellerman was very challenging toward the quickly-conceived conclusions of the Commission. His summary of the event is that they suddenly thought they had driven right into an ambush because they were taking fire from all directions as "a flurry of shells came into the car." He didn't *think* there were more than three shots, he *knew* there were:

> **"President Kennedy had four wounds, two in the head and shoulder and the neck. Governor Connally, from our reports, had three. There have got to be more than three shots, gentlemen."[239]**

CIA veteran John Stockwell analyzed the assassination from a professional tactical standpoint and concluded:

> **"Kennedy was shot at very close range from firing stations, probably four of them, where the assassins fired eight to ten shots. He was hit in the back, throat, and twice in the head, two bullets each from the front and from the back. Texas Governor John Connally was hit twice. Two bullets were fired into the concrete, one on each side of the convoy."[240]**

The Fetzer study also proved that:
- The weapon that Oswald is alleged to have used could not have fired the bullets that killed JFK: the carbine was not a high-velocity weapon.[241]
- "Everyone, including Posner, agrees that the muzzle velocity of the Mannlicher-Carcano was 2,000 fps (feet per second). The death certificates, autopsy report, and Warren Commission declared he was killed by the impact of high-velocity bullets. High velocity would be 2,600 fps and up."[242]
- The shot striking the right forehead was from a frangible or "exploding" bullet, as evidenced by the extensive shockwaves of damage through the brain; Oswald's bullets were standard copper-jacketed military ammunition which could not have inflicted frangible damage.[243]

[239] Palamara, *Survivor's Guilt*

[240] John Stockwell, *The Praetorian Guard: The U.S. Role in the New World Order* (South End Press, 1999).

[241] Fetzer, *Murder in Dealey Plaza*

[242] James H. Fetzer Ph.D., email to author, 30 June, 2010.

[243] James H. Fetzer Ph.D., "JFK and RFK: The Plots that Killed Them, The Patsies that Didn't," 13 June 2010. http://jamesfetzer.blogspot.com/2010/06/jfk-and-rfk-plots-that-killed-them.html (accessed 1 Mar. 2012)

U.S. Military Intelligence operative William Robert "Tosh" Plumlee, witnessed the assassination from a close vantage point on the south knoll of Dealey Plaza (to the left-front of the motorcade) and also witnessed more than 3 gunshots, also referring to it as "a flurry of shots":

> "Sergio and I at that time were standing on the south knoll, about 150 yards east of the Triple Overpass and about 5 feet up on the side of that hill, in line with the lamp posts down on the street.
>
> Then all of a sudden, all hell broke loose—a flurry of shots—at least four, and we both thought more probably five; two of which were very close together."[244]

The two shots that Intelligence veteran Tosh Plumlee refers to as "very close together" pose an additional gunfire inconsistency that also eliminates the possibility of a lone gunman:

TWO CLOSELY-SPACED SHOTS:

Many extremely credible witnesses heard two simultaneous shots; two separate shots that were so close together they could not have been fired from the weapon reportedly used. Among these witnesses were law enforcement officials very familiar with gunfire, from the U.S. Secret Service, Military Intelligence, Dallas Police Department, and Dallas County Deputy Sheriffs.[245]

If even one of the many accounts of two closely-spaced shots is correct, then the position of the Warren Commission falls apart like a house of cards:

> "Any two closely spaced (authentic) shots are incompatible with a single gunman firing a Mannlicher-Carcano. If *only one* of these ear witnesses is correct, the Warren Report is wrong."[246]

SHOT FROM WEST (FRONT) OF MOTORCADE: Numerous eyewitness reports, including officials of the U.S. Secret Service, Military Intelligence, Dallas County Deputy Sheriffs, and officers of the Dallas Police Department reported a shot coming from the west, or front, of the motorcade.[247]

In conclusion, there were too many shots, too close together, from too many directions, with different types of bullets, to be the work of a single shooter. It is now ludicrous to look at all the evidence and not conclude there was more than one gunman.

PROOF THAT OSWALD WAS U.S. INTELLIGENCE

At least eighteen U.S. intelligence veterans with direct and pertinent knowledge concluded that Lee Harvey Oswald was operational with U.S. Intelligence.[248]

[244] William Robert Plumlee, interview with author, 12 June 2006

[245] *JFK: The Case for* Conspiracy, Groden. Palamara, *Survivor'sGuilt.* Plumlee, "Affidavit of Plumlee."

[246] James H. Fetzer Ph.D., *Assassination Science: Experts Speak Out on the Death of JFK* (Open Court, 1998) (emphasis in original)

[247] Palamara, *Survivor'sGuilt.. JFK: The Case for* Conspiracy, Groden. Plumlee, "Affidavit of Plumlee".

[248] Eighteen Intelligence veterans indicating Oswald was U.S. Intelligence are listed and their affiliations follow: William R. Plumlee, U.S. Military Intelligence, Richard Case Nagell, U.S. Military Intelligence, James Southwood, U.S. Military Intelligence, Victor Marchetti, CIA, David Atlee Phillips, CIA, Colonel L. Fletcher Prouty, Liaison to CIA for Clandestine Operations, Colonel William

Marina Oswald, widow of the accused, has also gone on record that she believes her husband was working for U.S. Intelligence.[249]

Former Military Intelligence "Special Ops" Operative William Robert "Tosh" Plumlee was one of the first (if not *the* first) to go public about Iran-Contra and ongoing intelligence matters with "secret crews" in Costa Rica. He was originally recruited at Ft. Bliss, Texas for secret military "off-the-books" operations in 1954 and then went on to participate in the CIA's secret anti-Cuban operations. His *bona fides* can be verified at: http://toshplumlee.info/

> **"Oswald was Military Intelligence. He was operational in military ops. I know that from both direct experience and from liaison with my superior Intelligence officers. That's not an allegation—that's a fact. Oswald was Military Intelligence."[250]**

Affidavit of William R. Plumlee

My name is William Robert "Tosh" Plumlee. I was an associate member of an Army Military Intelligence unit which was secretly assigned to the Pentagon. I was attached "TDY" (Temporary Duty) status as a "coded field operative" to the CIA (Central Intelligence Agency). My assigned operational duties were classified; however I was primarily an aircraft pilot, flying secret covert missions for the CIA's JM/WAVE operations during the infamous Cuban Project of the early sixties.

In the spring of 1961, I was attached to a little-known unit within the project, known as "Task Force W". In the early days of the Cuban conflict, this unit, and its many splintered support groups, acted as a special top secret strike force for emergency military actions in support of Presidential policies of the time. This secret unit with all its fail-safe "cut-outs" was on some occasions used by the Secret Service for Presidential protection and security. Some TFW operational units were attached directly to the Pentagon and our dispatches and orders came at the direction of a high-level covert action group, embedded deep within the Pentagon, CIA and the NSC (National Security Council) White House staff; as well as directly from the President of the United States.

In the early to mid-1960s, a "special group" was formed and was soon referred to as the 5412 and later as the 5412/2. This planning and operational group at times met within the Oval Office and the White House Situation Room. Orders for my TFW unit usually came via chain of command from the President or from this special group

C. Bishop, Senior Military Officer *Executive Action,* Dr. John M. Newman, National Security Agency, John Stockwell, CIA, Frank Camper, *Special Operations Group,* E. Howard Hunt, CIA, Zack Shelton, FBI, William Turner, FBI, James Wilcott, CIA, Ronald Augustinovich, CIA, Chauncey Holt, CIA, George De Mohrenschildt, CIA, William Morrow, CIA.

[249] Jesse Ventura, *Conspiracy Theory with Jesse Ventura,* 2010, *tru*TV
[250] William Robert Plumlee, interview with author, 12 June 2006

and its counterpart—known within the CIA as "Operation 40"—an administrative branch of the military OMC (Operations Military Covert) and the CIA's Covert Action Group (CAG). OMC dispatched orders for military-type action and assault groups, such as the CIA's own WH/Task Force Division W (Western Hemisphere, Task Force Division W) These operational approvals were handed down from administrative functions such as OPS-40 or the 5412, Pentagon, Joint Chiefs of Staff, or at the President's discretion.

Therefore, the Military Industrial Complex had, embedded within it, these secret military teams that acted as a "Praetorian Guard" for Presidential protection or special use, at the whim of the President of the United States. The CIA acted as logistical support for these teams. However, there would never be any paperwork to that effect, especially not to an FOIA (Freedom of Information Act) request. Our units were military, not CIA, and paper trails were carefully avoided.

My assigned operative name, used on covert operations, was William H. "Buck" Pearson. My codename, before and after the Bay of Pigs, was "Zapata". I have a secret classified file, as defined within the National Security Statutes, under the above names, assigned by the Miami CIA Cuban Desk (1960-63 MI/CIA OMC-TFW-7; Section C; locator Tabs B & D- classified information); portions of this file were declassified in August, 1998. I held a classified QC-2 type clearance, sometimes erroneously referred to as a "crypto type 2 clearance".

I have provided secret closed-door testimony to the U.S. government on four occasions, including to the FBI's Special Agent in Charge of the Denver Colorado, OO (Office of Origin) in February of 1964; to the Department of Justice, FBI Director J. Edgar Hoover, also in 1964. I have also provided testimony to investigators for Senator Church's Committee in 1975-76; as well as to the House Select Committee on Assassinations, (HSCA). In 1989 and 1991, I testified to Senator John Kerry's Committee concerning drug smuggling and the Iran/Contra affair. These investigations of me, and testimonies by me, remain sealed and classified as "Top Secret; Committee Sensitive" to this day.

I have previously made the following statements voluntarily to various law enforcement and investigative bodies, only for the historical record, and too, without remuneration. I do not make any implication further than the factual statements previously made and which follow below.

- Lee Harvey Oswald was a Military Intelligence operative. I had associations with Lee Harvey Oswald in the course of his Intelligence training and also in the course of my Intelligence service. I first met Oswald at Illusionary Warfare training (propaganda, language instruction, false identities, maintenance of cover stories, etc.) at Nag's Head, North Carolina in 1957. Oswald was taking language courses at the same complex where I was taking Illusionary Warfare training classes. These courses, at the time, were referred to as "Spook School" and were preparatory to "going covert in international operations." Everybody who was there was CIA or Military Intelligence, or at least they were in some form of government training for their particular covert mission.

At the time, I had no reason to focus on Oswald or his training. He was just one more of many—as I also was one of many—at that training facility. I ran across Lee Harvey Oswald again, in Hawaii, after I completed a course in jungle warfare training, which was held on the big Island of Hawaii. Oswald was shipping out for Japan at that time. I did not know him, nor did I talk to him. Several years later, in 1962, I accidentally ran into Oswald again in Dallas at a Cuban "safe house"—an apartment house behind the house where he had rented a room on North Beckley Street in Oak Cliff. I thought it strange that he was present in the course of a government-sanctioned gunrunning operation in which I was a participant. Oswald also had access to another safe house for a very short time on Elsbeth Street, a few blocks from the Beckley street address where a Cuban, whom I knew by the name of Fernandez, had a room. These individuals were known by me to be functioning operationally at that time with the Alpha 66 anti-Castro group out of Miami, Florida. My operational understanding and assumption was that Oswald was working some form of military operations associated with the Dallas gunrunning operations of the time. When I asked about this strange encounter or coincidence, I was told that Oswald was somehow associated with ONI Intelligence. It was also confirmed to me by my associates that Oswald was connected in some format as an operative of sorts. At that early date, that was as far as it went. This limited information was passed to me through my liaison with Captain Edward G. Seiwell of the Fourth Army Reserve, Dallas, Love Field, and Captain Gilbert C. Cook of a special unit from the 49th Armored Division, 156th Tank Battalion, connected to the 112th MIG (Military Intelligence Group), Dallas, Texas and San Marcos, Texas. I was informed by them that Oswald was somehow attached to ONI (Office of Naval Intelligence) and was or had been, active at two known ONI facilities in the Dallas area; Hensley Field in Grand Prairie, Texas and a facility at Bachman's Lake, near Dallas' Love Field. They were confident in their statements, regarding Oswald's affiliation with ONI.

- I piloted many covert missions for the United States government in the years just prior to the assassination of President Kennedy. John Roselli, also known to me by his Intelligence codename "Colonel—Ralston" a.k.a. "Rawlston"—was a passenger on many of my flights in Florida, Cuba, and Texas. I knew Roselli was part of covert Intelligence operations and I have personally had irrefutable confirmation on many occasions to that fact. Roselli was so well-known in covert Intell circles that he was usually referred to simply as "The Colonel". I was aware of the ongoing assassination attempts toward Fidel Castro at the time. I also transported Charles Nicoletti on two separate occasions; to Santa Barbara, California and Las Vegas, Nevada. I knew Nicoletti as "Raven"; a codename given to me by my case officer as the person I was to transport. I do not think this was a covert assigned name for Nicoletti and I am not sure if he, like Roselli, was connected directly with military operations or CIA activities.

- I co-piloted a flight that infiltrated a Military Intelligence team into Dallas on the morning of November 22, 1963, in an attempt to abort the assassination of President John F. Kennedy. This mission was at the direction of the Pentagon with CIA logistical support. John Roselli was a passenger on that flight. Intelligence for our mission, after some confusion, had identified Dealey Plaza as the sight for the operation of an assassination attempt. The detailed "inside" information as to how this operation came about, I would not know. I could only speculate as to how this information, which led to the formation of the abort team, was obtained or deciphered.

Upon reaching Dealey Plaza, the Intell Team split in three directions, looking for three or more shooters or teams that could form a triangulated crossfire. I was asked to act as a spotter, reconnoitering the south knoll in this operation with my friend and operational partner, "Sergio". We were also looking for a diversionary act, something that would give shooters an opportunity to secretly set up. Therefore, while people were congregating around Elm Street and the Book Depository and we heard sirens coming closer, instead of looking toward the commotion, we looked away from it, scanning the perimeter and looking for a shooter or shooters attempting to set up triangulation shooting in a kill zone that we had identified.

We arrived at the plaza too late to abort the assassination; there was not enough time, our people were not in position and our communications between scattered team members were very poor. Shortly after the limo turned from Houston Street and came into our view, Sergio and I both heard at least four shots, very distinctly from our vantage point on the south knoll. Two of those shots were very close together, basically on top of each other—and my partner and I were both aware that it was not the result of an echo-effect, but two clear and distinct rifle reports that were very close together. One of the shots was also from a different direction than the others; one came from the southwest, meaning from the front of the limousine, not the rear. We both knew that with certainty. When my partner and I debriefed each other later that day, we were both sure on that one different-sounding shot. That fact was hard for us to miss because the other shots came from the north and east of us and that one shot from the southwest of us had a totally different sound and came whizzing right over our heads. We were both experienced veterans of gunfire, and very familiar with its sound, and we were both certain that one gunshot came from a westerly direction.

We knew we had to ex filtrate the scene immediately because we both had extensive secret Intelligence associations and liaison, which would provide no legitimate reason to logically explain our being there as the President was fired upon. As we cleared the area, Sergio and I both caught the distinct smell and "taste" of gunpowder at a location high on the south knoll of Dealey Plaza, near the south structure of the overpass.

We flew out of Dallas a couple hours after the assassination, from Redbird Airport. We flew VFR (Visual Flight Rules) coming into and out of Redbird, because we did not have to file a flight plan which would establish a record and flight log. John Roselli was not a passenger on the flight that left Dallas after the assassination. Everyone on board the flight out of Dallas was very quiet and dejected. It was a very somber experience; heads were low, with nothing said.

I do not know the names of most of the men who were on that mission because those type of operations are intentionally structured in a manner that minimizes individual knowledge. In "Black Operations" one does not ask questions of others—that is an unwritten rule. The official post-mission debriefing took place at West Palm Beach, Florida on November 25th, my birthday. That debriefing was conducted by Rex Beardsley, Bob Bennette and Tracy Barnes.

I hereby declare that the above statements stem from my personal knowledge and direct experience and are true and correct to the best of my knowledge.

Signed and dated this 27th day of July, 2010
William Robert "Tosh" Plumlee *(NOTARIZED)*

It should be noted that Tosh Plumlee's long career in covert operations has spanned many decades. At this writing, he is involved in intelligence operations against the deadly drug cartels in Mexico, working with a joint American/Mexican Military Task Force as a "contract advisor"; he is currently at work on his memoir entitled *Deep Cover, Shallow Graves*.

The testimony of former high-ranking CIA officer Victor Marchetti completely corroborates Plumlee's testimony regarding Oswald's intelligence training at Nag's Head, North Carolina and the ONI False Defector Program in which Oswald participated:

STATEMENTS OF FORMER CIA OFFICER VICTOR L. MARCHETTI

(Marchetti was Executive Assistant to Deputy Director, CIA; resigned, 1969)

> "One of these activities was an ONI (Office of Naval Intelligence) program which involved three dozen, maybe forty, young men who were made to appear disenchanted, poor, American youths who had become turned off and wanted to see what communism was all about. Some of these people lasted only a few weeks. They were sent into the Soviet Union, or into eastern Europe, with the specific intention the Soviets would pick them up and 'double' them if they suspected them of being US agents, or recruit them as KGB agents. They were trained at various naval installations both here and abroad, but the operation was being run out of Nag's Head, North Carolina."[251]

> "Interviewed from his Northern Virginia home, Marchetti confirmed the existence of the ONI base to me privately, saying the plan was to send young men to the Soviet Union as defectors, but who in actuality were hoping to be picked up as agents by the KGB. This process is known as "doubling," as the young men would then in effect be double agents for both American and Soviet Intelligence. Once placing an agent in the KGB, American Intelligence could then begin funneling in disinformation. According to Marchetti, this was the plan for Oswald."[252]

Oswald's operational activities certainly coincided precisely with the operational activities of the ONI False Defector Program described by Marchetti.

(The following is from Marchetti's testimony regarding Oswald's mysterious phone call from the Dallas jail to an otherwise unknown person:)

QUESTION: "But there is a call mechanism set up?"

Mr. MARCHETTI: "Yes."

QUESTION: "So it is conceivable that Lee Harvey Oswald was—"

Mr. MARCHETTI: "That's what he was doing. He was trying to call in and say, 'Tell them I'm all right.'"

QUESTION: "Was that his death warrant?"

---

[251] Anthony Summers, "Interview of Victor Marchetti," in John Simkin, "Lee Harvey Oswald: Biography," *Spartacus Educational*, http://www.spartacus.schoolnet.co.uk/JFKoswald.htm (accessed 4 Nov. 2011) (emphasis added).

[252] Proctor, "The Raleigh Call," http://www.groverproctor.us/jfk/jfk80.html (accessed 1 Jan 2011).

Mr. MARCHETTI: "You betcha. Because this time he went over the dam, whether he knew it or not, or whether they set him up or not. He was over the dam. At this point it was executive action [assassination]."

QUESTION: "Is the contact person's name ever the name of someone who is not necessarily an active agent but is just a contact person?"

Mr. MARCHETTI: "That's right."

QUESTION: "Then that person would go up to the next level?"

Mr. MARCHETTI: "That's right, and it would be a 'funny name'—a pseudonym. Like for example, you would have a number to call. If you were my agent, and you got yourself into a peck of trouble, you might try to contact me, but maybe you can't get through."

QUESTION: "I would contact you by telephone, right?"

Mr. MARCHETTI: "Yes. But I might have covered my tracks real good so you can't contact me by telephone. In other words, I contact you, you don't contact me. But I give you a [unintelligible] number. So you call him, but I've already talked to him and said, 'Don't touch him.' You're screwed up."

QUESTION: "But you would use, for that middle man, people who were not necessarily active agents or agency people, right?"

Mr. MARCHETTI: "That's right. Most likely they would be cut-outs. You would have to call indirectly."

QUESTION: "Could Oswald have had a name? ... "

Mr. MARCHETTI: "He was probably calling his cut-out. He was calling somebody who could put him in touch with his case officer. He couldn't go beyond that person. There's no way he could. He just had to depend on this person to say, 'Okay, I'll deliver the message.' Now, if the cut-out has already been alerted to cut him off and ignore him, then ... "[253]

"The FBI, while publicly embracing the Warren Commission's 'one man acting alone' conclusion, has always privately known that there were three gunmen."[254]

[253] Proctor, "The Raleigh Call"

[254] John Simkin, "Victor Marchetti: Biography," *Spartacus Educational*, http://www.spartacus.schoolnet.co.uk/JFKmarchetti.htm (accessed 8 Nov. 2011).

Multiple use of Oswald cover names

A great deal of evidence also suggests that there were actually *two* Intelligence operatives using the name Oswald as a component of their operation in the False Defector Program. The evidence is extensive, from several authors: John Armstrong has researched that particular point for decades, and his book *Harvey & Lee* examines that issue in precise detail. It is also well summarized in the 2010 book *American Conspiracies* by Jesse Ventura and Dick Russell:

> "My hunch is that they were both part of a false defector program that James Angleton and his friends in counterintelligence were running out of the CIA. While Harvey was over in Russia, Lee was working with anti-Castro Cubans in Florida planning to bump off Castro (he was seen by a number of people down there at the same time). Harvey, the wimpy-chinned one in the photographs, was married to Marina. Lee, the thick-necked one, was used to set up Harvey. I believe it's Harvey laying in the grave, and whatever happened to Lee, I have no idea."[260]

BOMBSHELL DROPPED FROM HIGH LOCATION

David Atlee Phillips, Director, WHO (Western Hemisphere Operations), CIA

Dave Phillips was a twenty-five-year CIA officer and one of very few in history to be awarded the Career Intelligence Medal. He rose from full-time operative, to CIA Chief of Station, and then all the way to Chief of All Operations, Western Hemisphere. During that time he handled "the night watch" at CIA and was privy to a great degree of inside knowledge.

Phillips made this astounding admission late in his life:

"My final take on the assassination is there was a conspiracy, likely including American intelligence officers."[255]

Phillips also used a literary vehicle with which to give us an amazing clue to the actual context of the assassination. In addition to being a brilliant strategist, Phillips was also a gifted writer. In an unpublished manuscript that he'd made sure would be discovered, he apparently utilized that to tell us what really happened in the JFK assassination. Intelligence veterans have often used manuscripts, that are technically not works of non-fiction, as vehicles for making statements in a manner that skirts the security obligations of their lifetime secrecy agreements.

[255] Larry Hancock, *Someone Would Have Talked: The Assassination of President John F. Kennedy and The Conspiracy to Mislead History* (JFK Lancer, 2006).

[260] Jesse Ventura & Dick Russell, *American Conspiracies* (New York: Skyhorse, 2010).

The unpublished manuscript was entitled The AMLASH Legacy. AMLASH was the CIA program to assassinate Fidel Castro, with which Phillips was closely familiar. He details characters who closely mirror himself, Oswald and others at CIA.

Then, in a climactic explanation of what actually happened, the character explicitly based on Phillips himself reveals:

"I was one of the two case officers who handled Lee Harvey Oswald ... we gave him the mission of killing Fidel Castro in Cuba ... I don't know why he killed Kennedy. But I do know he used precisely the plan we had devised against Castro. Thus the CIA did not anticipate the president's assassination, but it was responsible for it. I share that guilt."[256]

To a brilliant tactician like Phillips, every word was important. Therefore, the key phrase is:

"I do know he used precisely the plan we had devised against Castro."[257]

That's highly indicative that an intelligence operation that had been planned against Castro was "hijacked" and redirected at President Kennedy. That would explain why alarm bells went off all over Washington the second that Oswald's name was mentioned. That would explain the coverup and rush for closure and why Attorney General Robert Kennedy participated in it and at times even directed it. That would explain that there were actually two conspiracies:

1. The JFK murder with Oswald set-up as the patsy;
2. The massive government cover-up that was rushed into place when it seemed apparent that U.S. Intelligence had been completely compromised.

RFK registered immediate recognition of Oswald's name. He immediately called the anti-Castro camp in Florida, dramatically shouting into the telephone: "One of your guys did it!"[258]

That may very well have been the "dark beauty" of the hijacked "black op":

It forced the victims into covering up the crime.

And then abracadabra—the enigma becomes clear.

Regarding much of the above information, see Our Man in Mexico, page 238:

"The notion that David Phillips or Angleton and his Counterintelligence team ran a closely held operation involving Oswald in the weeks before Kennedy was killed has become less implausible as more records have come into public view. Phillips himself entertained such a scenario later in life. In addition to two nonfiction memoirs, Phillips

---

[256] David Atlee Phillips, The AMLASH Legacy (unpublished manuscript).
[257] Phillips, The AMLASH Legacy
[258] Lamar Waldron & Thom Hartmann, Ultimate Sacrifice (New York: Carroll & Graf, 2005).

also wrote novels of espionage. When he died in 1987, he left behind an outline for a novel about the Mexico City station in 1963, entitled "The AMLASH Legacy." The leading characters were explicitly based on Win Scott, James Angleton, and David Phillips himself. The role of the Phillips character in the events of 1963 was described as follows:

"I was one of the two case officers who handled Lee Harvey Oswald. After working to establish his Marxist bona fides, we gave him the mission of killing Fidel Castro in Cuba. I helped him when he came to Mexico City to obtain a visa, and when he returned to Dallas to wait for it I saw him twice there. We rehearsed the plan many times: In Havana Oswald was to assassinate Castro with a sniper's rifle from the upper floor window of a building on the route where Castro often drove in an open jeep. Whether Oswald was a double-agent or a psycho I'm not sure, and I don't know why he killed Kennedy. But I do know he used precisely the plan we had devised against Castro. Thus the CIA did not anticipate the President's assassination but it was responsible for it. I share that guilt."[259]

[259] Jefferson Morley & Michael Scott, *Our Man in Mexico* (University Press of Kansas, 2008)

Oswald's role-playing may have also been related to the "Gary Powers incident."

"On May 1, 1960, a U-2 spy plane piloted by Francis Gary Powers was shot down by the Soviets while photographing Soviet military installations. The United States first denied that it was on a spy mission but later conceded that it was. The major incident is curiously absent from Lee's 'historic diary,' even though he had certainly been aware of and perhaps even involved in the missions in Atsugi. Powers, who survived the crash, believed that it was information from Lee that gave the Soviets the ability to find the U-2 and shoot it down."[261]

INTELLIGENCE HISTORY OF LEE HARVEY OSWALD:

- **United States Marine Corps**: 1956-1959;
- **Illusionary Warfare Training**: Propaganda, language instruction, false identities, maintenance of cover stories, etc.; CounterIntelligence training for ONI's (Office of Naval Intelligence) False Defector Program at Nag's Head, North Carolina. 1957 *1;
- **Military Intelligence operative**: Top Secret security clearance, Marine Air Control, Atsugi, Japan (main CIA base in Far East); activities related to U-2 spy plane missions; Assignments

[261] Robert Groden, *The Search for Lee Harvey Oswald: A Comprehensive Photographic Record* (Penguin, 1995).

related to "hostesses" at Queen Bee Night Club, Tokyo *2, and the defection-targeting of Soviet Colonel Nikolai Eroshkin; 1957-1959 *3;

- **Calculated Duality**: Though extremely patriotic, Oswald carefully builds a reputation of spouting Communist beliefs and Marxist leanings: "So at this point in his life, Oswald has talked like a Communist, but what he really does is join ultra-patriotic American military organizations (such as David Ferrie's Civil Air Patrol) and work on behalf of U.S Intelligence against communism. The next major step in his life, long before leaving the Marine Corps, is to make plans to go to Russia." (Bob Harris, February 23, 2008); 1958-1959;

- **Advanced Russian**: 1959; at U.S. Army Monterey School of Languages, or (more likely) Oswald's Intelligence "double" was a native Russian speaker *4;

- **Constructs Intelligence 'Legend'**: 1959; Formally applies for early military discharge; methodically plans mission into Soviet Union; applies to Albert Schweitzer College in Switzerland—"Consider that coming fresh out of the Marine Corps, he needed a way to establish a cover as a legitimate seeker of knowledge rather than an agent of the United States. The materials that the Schweitzer College mailed back to him gave him something he could present, to at least give that appearance." (Bob Harris, February 23, 2008);

- **Granted U.S. Marines Dependency Discharge**: Immediately prior to his Soviet "defection" because his "mother injured foot" (a minor injury which actually occurred six months prior to the discharge); applies for passport the very next day; then travels to Europe, determining Helsinki, Finland as easiest point of entry to Russia; gains entry to Moscow, via U.S.-friendly Helsinki entry point; 1959;

- **CounterIntelligence Operative**: In an obvious infiltration effort, Oswald applies to Patrice Lumumba University in Moscow, a notorious terrorist incubation center and a high value target to U.S. Intelligence (Carlos 'The Jackal' and other revolutionaries and guerrillas were trained there); KGB (Soviet equivalent of CIA) is highly dubious of Oswald's bonafides; his application to Patrice Lumumba University is formally denied and Oswald is faced with deportation; on the day that he has been ordered to exit the country, he dramatically slits his wrist at precisely the time he is to meet Rimma Shirakova, his "guide"—who has been instructed by KGB to have Oswald on the 3:00 pm train back to Helsinki; when Oswald fails to appear in the lobby at the arranged time, Shirakova has his hotel door broken down; after the perceived suicide attempt, Oswald is granted permission to remain in Soviet Union; 1959;

- **CounterIntelligence Operative**: 1959-1962; Participant in the False Defector Program of U.S. Intelligence; "defected" to the Soviet Union, as an orchestrated Intelligence maneuver; Oswald is one of several false defectors—Americans with constructed legends who are feigning Russian sympathy and Marxist ideology; Oswald "offered to give up radar secrets along with 'something of special interest'" *5; Top-secret U-2 flight of Gary Powers is shot down while Oswald is in the Soviet Union; the incident literally changes history, torpedoing scheduled plan for a Big Four Summit Meeting (U.S., the Soviet Union, Britain & France), the effect of which is a very expensive continuation of the Cold War (Powers later expressed his belief that Oswald gave Soviets info for the shoot-down); "There is a very strong likelihood that Lee's defection was designed to provide the fertilizer to allow the Soviets an excuse to end the talks. This is exactly what did happen. On May 17, 1960, the peace talks fell apart. Khrushchev cited the U-2 incident and referred to America's 'aggressive actions.' If this was Lee Oswald's mission, it succeeded." (Robert Groden, 1995);
- **Admitted, U.S. Customs**: Re-entry to the United States was granted to Oswald and his young Russian bride without being detained or questioned, despite his defection to the Soviet Union at the height of the Cold War and his formal attempt to renounce his U.S. citizenship; his return trip to the United States was financed by the U.S. government (as the U.S. State Department confirmed in its June 7, 1962 letter to Oswald's mother), just as the trip to Moscow had been financed; 1962;
- **Intelligence Debriefing**: Oswald is then debriefed by U.S. Intelligence, even though the CIA later lied about it, saying that the debriefing never took place (a former CIA officer confirmed his viewing of the CIA debriefing report of Oswald); 1962 (*Who Was Lee Harvey Oswald*? November 20, 2003, Frontline, PBS)
- **CounterIntelligence Operative**: Simultaneously pro-Castro/anti-Castro; Infiltration of Fair Play for Cuba Committee and possible penetration of anti-Castro group planning assassination of President Kennedy; Operational with ONI (Office of Naval Intelligence) at Hensley Field in Grand Prairie, Texas and ONI facility at Bachman's Lake, near Love Field, Dallas, Texas; Involved with Alpha 66 anti-Castro Cubans at CIA "safe houses" in Dallas and government-sanctioned gunrunning operations; 1962-1963 *6;
- **Covert Operations**: It has been proved that two different individuals—"Lee Oswald" and "Harvey Oswald"—were melded into the single Intelligence profile of "Lee Harvey Oswald" as a specific intelligence function of covert operations. *7;
- **CIA assumed Marina Prusakova (Marina Oswald) was KGB**: Several facts caused the CIA to conclude that Oswald's

bride was KGB (Soviet Intelligence). Chief among them: At the height of the Cold War, how was it possible that a teenage Soviet girl managed to meet the 2nd and 3rd U.S. defectors to the Soviet Union, in cities hundreds of miles apart, speak to them in English, and marry one of them (Oswald) within days of their first meeting, and then leave the Soviet Union with him a year later, without any exit difficulties, at the height of the Cold War?—that wasn't simply rare, it was virtually unheard of at that time—it wasn't known as the Iron Curtain without reason and people didn't come and go as they do today: If you were in, you stayed in—that's why it was called the Iron Curtain. *8 Additionally, Marina's uncle was Ilya Prusakova, a Colonel in the MVD (Ministry of Internal Affairs, a.k.a. Soviet Secret Police), who reportedly approved the very sudden marriage between his niece and the American defector. Thus, in the cat-and-mouse culture of Counterintelligence, it then became a question of "Who's playing whom?" U.S. Intelligence then utilized George de Mohrenschildt, a Russian émigré and CIA asset who befriended Oswald in Dallas, to attempt to keep track of the Oswald-Marina Prusakova situation;

1. The False Defector Program at Nag's Head and Oswald's presence there have been confirmed independently by former CIA officer Victor Marchetti and former Military Intelligence operative William "Tosh" Plumlee, respectively.
2. "A curious entry in Oswald's Marine medical records for Sept. 16, 1958 states that he was being treated for gonorrhea and that the ailment originated '[i]n the line of duty, not due to his own misconduct'" (*The Search for Lee Harvey Oswald*, Robert Groden, 1995). Note that the prostitutes with whom Oswald was associating were suspected by U.S. Intelligence of passing the secrets they acquired from American soldiers on to the Communists. Oswald's assignment was obviously linked to that, and that mission's expenses were also the only way he could have afforded the very expensive prostitutes at the club.
3. Refer to *The Man Who Knew Too Much* by Dick Russell for a detailed history of the Eroshkin incident (Russell; 2003)
4. Oswald failed a Russian proficiency test on February 25, 1959. Only 6 months later he was totally fluent in the difficult language, as witnessed by 2 native Russian speakers; his wife, Marina and George de Mohrenschildt. "In 1974, a document classified by the Warren Commission ... revealed that Oswald had attended the U.S. Army's School of Languages at Monterey. Monterey is not open to just anyone who happens to have a language hobby. One is sent by the

government, for training in a specific language pertaining to a specific assignment. Oswald learned Russian at Monterey." (Parenti; *Dirty Truths;* 1996) (Parenti's claim has been disputed.) There is also substantial and reliable evidence that Oswald's Intelligence "double" was a native of the Soviet Union (see *Harvey and Lee,* John Armstrong, 2003)

5. Oswald's Military Intelligence file was secretly destroyed by the Department of Defense (House Assassinations Committee Final Report; 1978; pp. 223-24); Quotation above is from Dr. John M. Newman, former Executive Assistant to Director, National Security Agency

6. Former Military Intelligence operative Tosh Plumlee has testified that in addition to training with Oswald at the Nag's Head facility, he received confirmations on two separate occasions from his Military Intelligence superior officers "that Oswald was ONI." (Interview with author; 2006)

7. For a very thorough dissection of the profiles of the two separate Oswalds, see "Harvey and Lee: Military Records-Soviet Union," John Armstrong, in *JFK Deep Politics Quarterly*, July, 2011

8. See "Harvey and Lee: Military Records-Soviet Union," John Armstrong, in *JFK Deep Politics Quarterly,* July, 2011

Also see: *Who Was Lee Harvey Oswald?* November 20, 2003, Frontline, PBS; http://www.pbs.org/wgbh/pages/frontline/shows/oswald/etc/script.html

Lee Harvey Oswald, Parts 1 and 2, Robert Harris, February 23, 2008, July 17, 2008; http://www.jfkhistory.com/Youtube.html

On the surface, the incident was a huge public relations disaster and of major embarrassment to the United States. Historically, however, its effect was much more dramatic. The eventual result of the incident was not just the shoot-down of the plane, but the torpedoing of the Big Four Summit Meeting (United States, Soviet Union, Great Britain and France) of great importance between the superpowers, and hence, an extremely expensive continuation of the Cold War.

President Eisenhower refused to apologize for the incident to the satisfaction of the Soviets, and the would-be peace talks came to an abrupt halt as a result.

> **"There is a very strong likelihood that Lee's defection was designed to provide the fertilizer to allow the Soviets an excuse to end the talks. This is exactly what did happen. On May 17, 1960, the peace talks fell apart. Khrushchev cited the U-2 incident and referred to America's 'aggressive actions.' If this was Lee Oswald's mission, it succeeded."[262]**

---

[262] Groden, *The Search for Lee Harvey Oswald*

Powers reportedly blamed radar secrets leaked to the Russians by Lee Harvey Oswald as the reason for the shoot-down of the U-2 spy plane Powers had piloted. Oswald had a Top Secret security clearance and may have had access to radar secrets and classified information on the U-2 surveillance flights, which he helped monitor from the Atsugi, Japan base where he had been recently stationed. More importantly from an intelligence standpoint, especially if the mission was to torpedo the peace talks—it would have been *perceived* that he could have had access to those secrets.

The conclusions of Gary Powers, an experienced CIA operative, merit serious attention—he was one cool customer. When asked how high he was flying in his spy plane when he was shot down in Soviet air space, Powers calmly responded:

"Not high enough."[263]

COLONEL L. FLETCHER PROUTY

Colonel L. Fletcher Prouty was a twenty-three-year military veteran who became the model for "Mr. X" in the film *JFK* by Oliver Stone. He rose to the level of Focal Point Officer, the key liaison between the CIA and the Air Force for covert operations, after having also been the Briefing Officer for the Secretary of Defense. In short—at the highest levels of government—he was privy to many secrets, in general, and in matters of espionage, in particular. His website is a wealth of information for researchers, historians, and students: http://www.prouty.org/

Colonel Prouty's conclusions about Lee Harvey Oswald are stark and direct:

"Oswald was a patsy. There's no question about it."[264]

Evidence Exonerating Lee Harvey Oswald:

1. Oswald paraffin-tested negative for gunfire residue on his cheek, which is highly indicative that he had not fired a rifle recently. Although the presence of gunfire residue, detected by paraffin-testing, is not necessarily indicative of having recently fired a weapon, its absence is highly indicative of not having recently fired a weapon. See "Bugliosi Fails the Paraffin Test," Pat Speer, 24 July, 2007; http://jfkaccountability.type-pad.com/reclaiming_history/2007/07/bugliosi-fails-.html

2. Oswald's fingerprints were not found anywhere on the rifle by the FBI. It is quite reasonable to assume that the FBI very thoroughly examined the weapon supposedly responsible for the murder of the President of the United States. They initially

---

263 *RoadrnnersInternationale*, http://roadrunnersinternationale.com/powers_gary.html (accessed 2 Mar 2012).

264 Colonel L. Fletcher Prouty, "The Col. L. Fletcher Prouty Reference Site," http://www.prouty.org/ (accessed 12 May 2011).

found no prints of Oswald's anywhere on the weapon. After a highly questionable chain-of-evidence and a very mysterious FBI visit to the funeral home where Oswald's body was in the process of being embalmed for burial, a partial palm print of Oswald's was supposedly later identified on the same weapon that had been previously examined in great detail. The funeral director testified that he knew that the FBI came to the funeral home and took both fingerprints and palm prints of Oswald because, after they left, he had to clean off the ink to prepare the body. See testimony of mortician Paul Groody of Miller Funeral Home: "'Agents' fingerprinted Oswald corpse"; http://youtu.be/P2W_-ID8RMI

3. Ballistics testing did not incriminate Oswald in any way. The FBI performed both neutron activation analysis and emission spectography for the Warren Commission and reported that the tests were inconclusive (Fuhrman, 2006). Furthermore, the FBI Lab's chief metallurgy expert for more than two decades, William A. Tobin, concluded that the lead analysis used for the initial one-gunman conclusion was fundamentally flawed and that bullets from another gun also struck President Kennedy. See "Study Led By Former FBI Scientist Says Multiple Shooters In JFK Assassination," John Solomon, May 17, 2007, *Washington Post*; accessible at: http://www.informationliberation.com/?id=22026

4. Officer J. D. Tippit was shot with an automatic and Oswald had a revolver, and there are obvious and marked ballistics differentiations between the two. Two very experienced witnesses (a police Sergeant and a former combat Marine) testified they were certain that the crime scene gun at the shooting of Officer Tippit was an automatic, not a revolver (Oswald had a revolver). See: "Did Oswald Shoot Tippit?", Michael T. Grifith, 2002; http://www.kenrahn.com/jfk/the_critics/griffith/With_Malice.html

5. No witness could ever place Oswald at the actual crime scene. As Dallas Chief of Police Jesse Curry noted:

"We don't have any proof that Oswald fired the rifle, and never did. Nobody's yet been able to put him in that building with a gun in his hand."

—Jesse Curry
Chief of Police
Dallas Police Department
(*Dallas Morning News*, Nov. 6, 1969, in Jim Marrs, *Crossfire*, 1990)

6. The rifle discovered in the Book Depository building was initially identified as a 7.65mm Mauser (an excellent rifle), not as a 6.5 mm Mannlicher-Carcano (an extremely poor rifle) by the

members of the search team which found it. They made that identification with certainty, even having read that word on the rifle itself, and were veteran police officers experienced with weapons (one had even owned a gun shop). Officer Weitzman, who had operated a sporting goods store, was extremely familiar with rifles and described the weapon found on the sixth floor in no uncertain terms: "This rifle was a 7.65 Mauser bolt action equipped with a 4/18 scope, a thick leather brownish-black sling on it." Roger Craig, who was also part of the search team, even recalled seeing the word "Mauser" inscribed on the metal of the rifle. Weitzman and Craig refused to alter their testimony and were harassed for the remainder of their short lives. See: *The Guns of Dealey Plaza*, John S. Craig: www.acorn.net/jfkplace/09/ fp.back_issues/11th_issue/guns_dp.html

7. The sight on the supposed murder weapon was not even aligned properly, meaning that a shooter would not actually have hit what had been lined up in the sight. A 6.5 mm Mannlicher-Carcano was a notoriously poor weapon and would no doubt have been one of the last choices an assassin would have made. It was nicknamed "The Peacekeeper" by Italian soldiers because if you fired at what was lined up in your sight, it was joked that you would never actually hit anyone. Much has been written about the absurdity of an assassin even considering as ludicrous a weapon choice as the 6.5 Mannlicher for an assassination attempt.

8. Colonel William C. Bishop was the Senior Military Intelligence member of the CIA's Executive Action assassinations project. Colonel Bishop was not only an expert on assassins, he actually collected them for Executive Action and was also personally responsible for making the hit on President Trujillo of the Dominican Republic in 1961. Colonel Bishop stated flatly:

"Oswald was a decoy. There's no way in hell he could have fired three shots in that space of time, with that accuracy, with that weapon … I'll tell you one damn thing. Whoever set up that poor little son of a bitch did a first-class job."

See: *The Man Who Knew Too Much*, Dick Russell, 1993

9. ONI (Office of Naval Intelligence) conducted its own secret investigation of the JFK assassination that reached the following conclusions:
   ▸ Oswald was not the shooter
   ▸ Oswald was incapable of masterminding the assassination See *Ultimate Sacrifice*, Waldron & Hartmann, 2006

10. Scientific voice analysis and evaluation of Oswald's recorded voice overwhelmingly indicated that Oswald was being

truthful about his innocence. Psychological Stress Evaluation (PSE) is a scientific method of measuring voice stress. George O'Toole explains the function: "Stress is a necessary, but not sufficient, condition of lying; it must be interpreted, and therein lies the margin of error. But the absence of stress is a sufficient condition of truthfulness. If someone is talking about a matter of real importance to himself and shows absolutely no stress, then he must be telling the truth." As historian Michael Griffith notes: "The PSE has been shown to be reliable in several tests. It is used by hundreds of U.S. law enforcement agencies, and it is accepted as evidence in more than a dozen states."

- "Oswald denied shooting anybody—the president, the policeman, anybody. The psychological stress evaluator said he was telling the truth."
- "There is no other plausible interpretation of the Oswald PSE charts than the explanation that Oswald was simply telling the truth."
- "My PSE analysis of these recordings indicates very clearly that Oswald believed he was telling the truth when he denied killing the president."

—Lloyd H. Hitchcock, who conducted the tests
(O'Toole, in Scott, Hoch & Stetler; 1976)

See: *The Assassinations: Dallas and Beyond: A Guide to Cover-Ups and Investigations*, Professor Peter Dale Scott, Paul Hoch & Russell Stetler (Eds.), 1976

"Where Was Oswald From 11:50 to 12:35 P.M. on the Day of the Assassination?," Michael T. Griffith, 1998; http://www.mtgriffith.com/web_documents/wherewasoswald.htm

"Hasty Judgment: A Reply to Gerald Posner—Why The JFK Case Is Not Closed," Michael T. Griffith, 1998; http://karws.gso.uri.edu/jfk/the_critics/griffith/Hasty_Judgment.html

A GOVERNMENTAL COVER-UP INTENTIONALLY BURIED THE FACTS

Almost as much has been written about how the government covered up the truth about the circumstances of the assassination as has been written about the assassination itself. Suffice to summarize that it's absolutely accurate to say that The Warren Commission wasn't formed to find the true facts—it was formed to send the true facts to their official burial ground.

The U.S. Department of Justice even made the mistake of documenting the cover-up for the historical record. In a memo from Acting Attorney General Nicholas Katzenbach (in Bobby Kennedy's absence), the Government clearly mandates closing the book on any speculation about a conspiracy, ensuring Oswald was convicted in the court of public opinion and that it was perceived that he had acted as the lone assassin.

THE SMOKING GUN OF THE COVER-UP:

The following is a verbatim copy of the Justice Department memo from the Acting Attorney General of the United States to President Johnson aide Bill Moyers (written shortly after Oswald was murdered), documenting the cover-up in the historical record:

November 25, 1963
MEMORANDUM FOR MR. MOYERS

It is important that all of the facts surrounding President Kennedy's Assassination be made public in a way which will satisfy people in the United States and abroad that all the facts have been told and that a statement to this effect be made now.

1. The public must be satisfied that Oswald was the assassin; that he did not have confederates who are still at large; and that the evidence was such that he would have been convicted at trial.

2. Speculation about Oswald's motivation ought to be cut off, and we should have some basis for rebutting thought that this was a Communist conspiracy or (as the Iron Curtain press is saying) a right-wing conspiracy to blame it on the Communists. Unfortunately the facts on Oswald seem about too pat—too obvious (Marxist, Cuba, Russian wife, etc.). The Dallas police have put out statements on the Communist conspiracy theory, and it was they who were in charge when he was shot and thus silenced.

3. The matter has been handled thus far with neither dignity nor conviction. Facts have been mixed with rumour and speculation. We can scarcely let the world see us totally in the image of the Dallas police when our President is murdered.

I think this objective may be satisfied by making public as soon as possible a complete and thorough FBI report on Oswald and the assassination. This may run into the difficulty of pointing to inconsistencies between this report and statements by Dallas police officials. But the reputation of the Bureau is such that it may do the whole job.

The only other step would be the appointment of a Presidential Commission of unimpeachable personnel to review and examine the evidence and announce its conclusions. This has both advantages and disadvantages. I think it can await publication of the FBI report and public reaction to it here and abroad.

I think, however, that a statement that all the facts will be made public property in an orderly and responsible way should be made now. We need something to head off public speculation or Congressional hearings of the wrong sort.

Nicholas deB. Katzenbach
Deputy Attorney General

(R) – ITEM IS RESTRICTED

The cover-up was apparently necessitated by the exposure and implication of covert U.S. intelligence anti-Castro operations which were utilizing the Mafia to attempt to assassinate Fidel Castro. It is an often overlooked fact that in the immediate aftermath of the assassination, Robert F. Kennedy was the most powerful person in the United States—more so than even new President Lyndon B. Johnson. In the hours after the murder, it was Robert Kennedy and Kennedy loyalists who controlled the autopsy, the doctors, the body of President Kennedy, and the actions of much of the Secret Service, law enforcement, and emergency personnel. It was also Attorney General Robert Kennedy's Justice Department which ultimately controlled the evidence and instituted the cover-up process via the memo from Deputy Attorney General Nick Katzenbach stating that the imperative and overriding directive was that the public must believe that Oswald acted alone. Obviously, Robert Kennedy was not involved in the death plot against his brother. But just as obviously, his hand was forced into covering up the true circumstances surrounding the murder. It was through his office, from those loyal to both he and President Kennedy, and at times at his own direction, that the actual facts concerning the assassination were intentionally (and *necessarily*, from their standpoint) obscured.

> "The Federal Bureau of Investigation and the Central Intelligence Agency engaged in a cover-up of highly relevant information when the Warren Commission was investigating President John Kennedy's assassination ... President Johnson and Attorney General Robert F. Kennedy became party to the effort which consisted of withholding key facts from the Warren Commission."[265]

Investigation and analysis by the CIA's John Stockwell noted that:

> "After the shooting stopped, the convoy raced away. The FBI and other branches of the government immediately launched the coverup. The new President, Lyndon Johnson, ordered the limousine in which Kennedy was killed be flown to Chicago and destroyed. The announced goal of President Johnson was to 'reassure' the nation by proving that the killing was the work of lone assassin Lee Harvey Oswald."

[265] Waldron & Hartmann, *Ultimate Sacrifice*

" … CIA operatives far from Dallas were waiting with biographic information about Oswald to feed to the media."[266]

CONCLUSIONS

We do not know with exact certainty how President Kennedy was murdered, but we most certainly *do* know with exact certainty how he was *not* murdered. We know what did *not happen*. We know (and with certainty) that Lee Harvey Oswald acting alone did not do it because the evidence proves conclusively he could not have:

1. Frontal shots preclude the possibility of a single shooter.
2. Oswald was incapable of doing the shooting. The best combat snipers in history tried to match the shots/hits attributed to Oswald and *could not do it*. And Oswald wasn't even in the same league with them as a shooter. Oswald's fellow Marines judged him a "rather poor shot."
3. There were far too many shots fired (more than the shots that the Warren Commission focused upon by completely ignoring the others) to have come from one shooter alone.
4. Oswald was operational in U.S. Military Intelligence.[267] The "Hidell" operational cover name was not being used only by Oswald—it was what is termed a "floating alias" in covert intelligence, and was also being used by other operatives in Military Intelligence.[268]
5. A blatant Government cover-up followed, intentionally obfuscating the facts, particularly concerning Oswald's involvement in the anti-Castro operations of the U.S. intelligence community.

Zack Shelton was a twenty-eight year FBI veteran, twenty-five of those years as a Special Agent. Special Agent Shelton was part of the Organized Crime squad in Kansas City for four and a half years and the Organized Crime squad in Chicago for eight years. He was part of many high-profile investigations, including the FBI team that ran the Mob "skimming" operation out of Las Vegas in the infamous "Strawman Operation" (upon which the film *Casino* was based); the team that solved the truck-dragging death of James Byrd in Jasper, Texas; the capture of the armed robbers who held up the Stardust Hotel in Las Vegas; and the arrest of a corrupt Texas sheriff for drug smuggling. He's an expert on criminal investigation who knows where to look and what to look at when he gets there. Put simply, he's very familiar with the territory.[269]

Shelton was hired by Wim Dankbaar, a wealthy Dutch industrialist, to investigate the circumstances surrounding the JFK assassination and attempt to reach fact-based conclusions based upon his investigation. The lengthy investigation

---

266 Stockwell, *The Praetorian Guard*
267 Plumlee, "Affidavit of William R. Plumlee"
268 Russell, *The Man Who Knew Too Much*"
269 Zechariah Shelton, Interview with author, 11 August, 2006

by Shelton revealed a long collection of Organized Crime confessions—culled from FBI wiretaps, reliable informants, and cooperating witnesses—which reveal direct Mafia involvement in the assassination of the 35th President of the United States. Therefore, it is not a matter of it being his personal opinion, it is based on the results of a professional who went where the evidence led him. As former Special Agent Shelton puts it:

"I don't have any theories. All I have are the facts."[270]

The following is former Special Agent Shelton's summary of the evidence obtained from his lengthy investigation into the assassination of John F. Kennedy:

Z. Shelton & Associates, Inc.

THE SHELTON REPORT:

▸ **Summary of Facts in the JFK Assassination**

Prepared by:
Z. Shelton & Associates, Inc.
Zechariah Shelton
Investigator; twenty-five year FBI Special Agent, retired.

The following are the results of my extensive investigation into the evidence in the JFK assassination.
In summarizing the JFK Assassination, one must look at the facts, not at theories. The following are the irrefutable facts that have surfaced in my investigation. This is a summary of my investigation, spotlighting significant events that led to the assassination, the events of the day and the cover-up, which indicate that there was a conspiracy to kill the president.

April–November 21, 1963

Chauncey Holt (CIA Operative)	Approximately April of 1963—Holt begins to produce IDs for Lee Harvey Oswald, including all of his aliases. June—Travels to New Orleans, Louisiana to deliver the IDs to Guy Bannister. Holt is photographed by news reporters in the same photo with Oswald. September–October—Holt is instructed by his handler to prepare Secret Service Identification Pins for the President's trip to Dallas. November 16—Holt receives a letter from Peter Licavoli stating that Chuck Nicoletti is at the

	Grace Ranch in Arizona and for Holt to come and drive Nicoletti to Dallas.
	November 21 - Holt drives Nicoletti to Dallas.
Jack Ruby	Had extensive and numerous connections to Organized Crime throughout his adult life. He worked directly for Sam Giancana of Chicago Mafia (see Brandt, 2004), was connected to New Orleans Mafia, led at the time by Carlos Marcello; also closely associated with Organized Crime in Dallas.
	September through November 1963 - Numerous out-of-state telephone calls are placed by Ruby to well-known Mafia figures. These calls are twenty-five times the amount of calls placed during other periods of 1963. The last week before the assassination, Ruby is visited by numerous well-known Mafia figures in Dallas. (see Scheim, 1991; Waldron & Hartmann, 2005)
Carlos Marcello **Jimmy Hoffa** **Santo Traficante**	Within months before the assassination, these three individuals were making death threats against the President. These comments came from reliable Federal Sources.
	(see Scheim, 1991; Waldron & Hartmann, 2005)
James Files	Approximately six months before the assassination, Files receives word from Chuck Nicoletti that they have a contract to kill President Kennedy. There was a meeting at Tony Accardo's house and present were Accardo, Giacanna and Nicoletti. Nicoletti left the meeting and informed Files.
Jim Wagner	Jim Wagner is a retired FBI Organized Crime Supervisor from Chicago. In September of 1963, a reliable informant stated that Tony Accardo sent $100,000.00 to Mexico City to finance an operation. This fact comes directly from the files of the FBI.

November 22, 1963

Chauncey Holt	Drove Chuck Nicoletti into Dallas. According to Files, Nicoletti was one of the four on the hit team. Holt delivers the Secret Service Pins. He drives into the railroad yard in a white 1959 Oldsmobile Station Wagon. This is corroborated by the testimony of Bowers. Holt was instructed to go into Dealey Plaza and participate in an anti-Castro demonstration and

if there was a problem, he was to report to a designated boxcar. He stated that Dealey Plaza looked like "Old Home Week". This meant that there were a lot of CIA Operatives in Dealey Plaza. Files also reported some of the names that Holt mentioned. When the shots rang out, he reported to the boxcar as instructed and met with Charles Harrelson and Charles Rogers (known to Holt as Richard Montoya). All three of these individuals were detained by the Dallas Police Department and later released. Several photographs were taken of these three men and they are known as the three tramps. Lois Gibson, respected forensic artist, verifies the three as Holt and Charles Harrelson and Charles Rogers, two violent criminals.

Tosh Plumlee He states that he was a CIA pilot and flew John Roselli into Dallas on the morning of the assassination. This flight was a military flight. Files corroborates this when he says that Roselli arrived in Dallas on a military aircraft.

James Files He states that he drove into Dealey Plaza in Nicoletti's vehicle, a 1963 Chevy Impala Super Sport, white over maroon. He drove Roselli and Nicoletti and parked face in, on the side of the Dal-Tex Building. The Beztner film shows the vehicle parked where Files says it was. Files stated he took the head shot from the grassy knoll behind the picket fence. Where he says he stood, the House Select Committee puts a shooter by means of an acoustic test. Files smoked Pall Mall Cigarettes and there were the same brand found where he says he was standing. Bowers saw an individual by the picket fence. Files says Dealey Plaza looked like "Old Home Week" and mentions three or four names, as did Chauncey Holt. Files states he shot with an XP 100 Fireball with a .222 cartridge. He bit into a .222 casing and left it at the scene. Gary Radermaker found a .222 casing in 1987 that had a tooth mark in it. Files stated that it was he, Roselli, Nicoletti and one other individual who were the hit team that day.

Zapruder Film This film clearly shows Kennedy's head violently pushed to the left rear when the head-

	shot occurred. This provides evidence that the headshot came from the right front.
The Irrefutable Testi mony Of Holt, Plumlee And Files	Three separate testimonies, from Chauncey Holt, Tosh Plumlee and James Files, all cross-corroborate each other. There is no way each individual could have known what the other person had said or was going to say, yet they all said the same thing.
Witnesses in Dealey Plaza	The majority of the witnesses in the Plaza said there were shots from the grassy knoll.
The Mary Moorman Photograph	At the exact same spot where Files said he shot and the House Select Committee said the shooter was, is a figure in the photograph behind the picket fence.

AFTER NOVEMBER 22, 1963

House Select Committee	The Acoustic Test proved that there was a shot from the grassy knoll and it came from the exact spot where Files says he was standing. (*House Select Committee on Assassinations*, 1978)
Bill Bonanno	He states in *Bound By Honor* (Bonanno, 1999) that Roselli confessed to him about killing Kennedy and there were four people on the hit team.
Sam Giancana John Roselli	They state in *Double Cross* (Giancana & Giancana, 1993) that Roselli was in on the hit of Kennedy.
Chuck Nicoletti	Roselli expressed direct knowledge about his and other Mafia involvement in the JFK assassination, on several occasions. (*Washington Post*, 1976; *House Select Committee on Assassinations*, 1978).
Sam Giancana John Roselli Chuck Nicoletti	All three were scheduled to testify before Congress. All three were murdered just prior to their dates to testify. All three had established involvement in the CIA-Mafia plot to kill Fidel Castro and in the assassination of President Kennedy.

Carlos Marcello
Santo Trafficante   FBI documents reveal that Marcello confessed his involvement in the JFK assassination on several occasions (see FBI Document 124-10182-10430; Waldron & Hartmann, 2005; O'Leary & Seymour, 2003). FBI wiretaps reveal Trafficante expressed knowledge of his involvement, even making a deathbed statement to his attorney. (see Ragano & Raab, 1994; Waldron & Hartmann, 2005)

Joe Granata   Joseph Granata was a member of the Chicago crime family and close associate of Chuck Nicoletti. Granata became an FBI informant and a reliable witness against Organized Crime, who went into the Federal Witness Protection Program. Granata has verified the involvement of Roselli, Nicoletti, Marshall Caifano and Jimmy Sutton (a.k.a. James Files) in the assassination of President Kennedy. Granata verified that Chuck Nicoletti, top hit man for the Chicago Mafia, confided in him, on several occasions, the involvement of Nicoletti, Roselli, Sutton and Caifano, whom Nicoletti stated were all in Dealey Plaza with him at the time of the murder when "We blew his brains out." (Dankbaar; 2006)

Frank Sheeran   Frank Sheeran was a notorious Mafia hit man and Jimmy Hoffa associate. Sheeran made deathbed confessions in *I Heard You Paint Houses* (2004) and many experienced law enforcement officials give veracity to his accounts. Sheeran stated that he and Hoffa provided "high-powered rifles for the Kennedy hit in Dallas". Sheeran also stated that Hoffa confessed high-level Mafia involvement in the JFK assassination, stating: "They had fake cops and real cops involved in it. Jack Ruby's cops were supposed to take care of Oswald but Ruby bungled it. That's why he had to go in and finish the job on Oswald. If he didn't take care of Oswald, what do you think they would have done to him—put Ruby on a meat hook. Don't kid yourself. Santo and Carlos and Giancana and some of their element, they were all in on Kennedy. Every single one of the same cast of characters that were in on the Bay of Pigs. They even had a plot to kill Castro with Momo (Giancana) and Roselli." (see Brandt, 2004)

Possible Scenarios

An electrifying realization occurs when we challenge our assumptions about the JFK assassination. We always assume that the operation was successful because it ended in the death of President Kennedy. But what if it was *unsuccessful*? What if that wasn't the complete end goal? What if it was also trying to accomplish something else? Then, suddenly, all the crazy pieces of the puzzle magically fit right together. What had seemed to be going in two different directions at the same time has then only been going in one all along. Allow us to explain.

It has become apparent that there were actually two aims of the assassination. One was to kill JFK and the other was—by making it look like Cuba was to blame for it—necessitating an invasion of the island of Cuba. Under that matrix, suddenly everything adds up clearly. Under that matrix, the actions of RFK covering up the real circumstances of his own brother's murder make complete and concrete sense. *Then*, covering up Oswald's links to U.S. Intelligence suddenly becomes comprehensible. The obvious "national security" cover-up that followed is then logical. If we look at the events through that refreshed perspective, we begin to finally understand what it really is that we've been looking at all this time. There's more on that point below.

Now let's look at some of the scenarios out there. Many theories exist for the real cause of the JFK assassination—and many can be easily dismissed as implausible. For example, the Russians being involved makes absolutely no sense whatsoever—if anything, they were actively involved in attempting to *thwart* the assassination (see *The Man Who Knew Too Much* by Dick Russell). The Soviets knew beyond a shadow of a doubt that they had much better political prospects with JFK remaining President. They were in the throws of enduring severe economic hardships as a result of the costs of the Cold War and were eager for continuing the softening of those pressures that the Kennedy Administration was offering in the post Cuban Missile Crisis environment.

Here are some others:

Oswald Acted Alone

The theory that Oswald killed JFK is exactly that—a theory, and a preposterous one at that. It has been touted in books by The Warren Commission, Gerald Posner, Vincent Bugliosi. They are what we call "conspiracy-closers"; they're like closing pitchers in baseball games who come in to try to slam the door shut on the opposition. They have an *agenda*. They typically "begin" by concluding that Oswald acted alone, rather than objectively weighing *all* of the evidence. The evidence, objectively evaluated in its totality, indicates that it wasn't even *possible* that Oswald acted alone. If that isn't clear by now then, *Homework Assignment*: read the JFK chapter of this book.

Mafia "Hit"

> "The minute that bullet hit Jack Kennedy's head, it was all over. Right then. The Organized Crime Program just stopped, and Hoover took control back."[271]

> —Bill Hundley, Organized Crime Section, U.S. Dept. of Justice

The word on the streets of Chicago in 1963 was that if Chuck Nicoletti got a contract with your name on it, *you were already dead*—you just didn't know it yet. Charles (Chuck) Nicoletti was the premier hit man in the 1950s and 60s for "Chicago"—the Organized Crime empire stretching across the nation and dominating most organized criminal enterprises in Chicago, Las Vegas and Miami Beach.

It has been established that Nicoletti was in Dallas with a high-powered rifle on the morning of the assassination.[272] In his "work book," a professional calendar of sorts, Nicoletti reportedly made the following entry for November 22, 1963, chilling in its stark simplicity:

> "Dallas—JFK"[273]

Few Americans are fully aware of the dramatic findings of the 1979 *Report of the House Select Committee on Assassinations*, which concluded:

> "There is solid evidence that ... Hoffa, Marcello, and Trafficante— three of the most important targets for criminal prosecution by the Kennedy Administration—had discussions with their subordinates about murdering President Kennedy. Associates of Hoffa, Trafficante, and Marcello were in direct contact with Jack Ruby, the Dallas nightclub owner who killed the 'lone assassin' of the President. Although members of the Warren Commission, which investigated President Kennedy's assassination, had knowledge of much of this information at the time of their inquiry, they chose not to follow it up."[274]

The preceding conclusion is practically an open indictment of the main investigative body of the assassination of the 35th President of the United States. That bears noting.

271 Richard Mahoney, *Sons and Brothers: The Days of Jack and Bobby Kennedy* (Arcade Publishing, 1999) 304.

272 Wim Dankbaar, *Files on JFK* (BookSurge, 2005). *Spooks, Hoods and the Hidden Elite*, dir. by Wim Dankbaar (Trine Day, 2008, dvd). Chauncey Holt, "Case Closed: Stampede of the Apologists," 2005, *Assassination Research: Journal for the Advanced Study of the Death of JFK*: Vol. 3, No. 2; 2005, http://www.assassinationresearch.com/v3n2/v3n2holt.pdf

273 Dankbaar, *Files on JFK*. Shelton, Interview with author, 2006.

274 *Report of the House Select Committee on Assassinations*, United States House of Representatives, 1979.

CONFESSIONS REGARDING THE MURDER OF JOHN F. KENNEDY

"Their own confessions now show that three Mafia bosses—Carlos Marcello, Santo Trafficante, and Johnny Rosselli—were behind JFK's assassination. They used parts of the secret coup plan to kill JFK in a way that forced Attorney General Robert Kennedy, President Lyndon B. Johnson, FBI Director J. Edgar Hoover, and high CIA official Richard Helms to withhold crucial information not only from the public and the press, but also from each other and sometimes their own investigators."[275]

The following conversation took place between Florida godfather Santo Trafficante and his friend and Miami businessman, Jose Aleman, shortly before the assassination of President Kennedy:

TRAFFICANTE: " … have you seen how his brother is hitting Hoffa … mark my word, this man Kennedy is in trouble and will get what is coming to him."

JOSE ALEMAN: "Kennedy will be re-elected."

TRAFFICANTE: "You don't understand me. Kennedy's not going to make it to the election. He is going to be hit."[276]

Government wiretaps and Mafia informants have provided detailed confessions of direct involvement in the assassination of President Kennedy.

• "Recently declassified FBI documents confirm that just a few years before his own death, **Carlos Marcello** confessed on three occasions to informants that he had had JFK killed."[277]
• "**Santo Trafficante** had been recruited in the CIA's plots to kill Castro months before JFK became president. Like Marcello, Trafficante later confessed his involvement in JFK's assassination."[278]
• "**Johnny Roselli**, according to his biographers, also claimed to know what really happened in Dallas … Internal CIA reports admit that they recruited Roselli and Trafficante for their own plots to assassinate Castro prior to JFK's election in 1960."[279]

Confessions of involvement in the JFK assassination came in later years from Carlos Marcello, Santo Trafficante, Johnny Roselli, John Martino and David Morales. Deliberate misinformation that was planted to link the assassination to Cuba was also traced to the above-named.

[275] Lamar Waldron & Thom Hartmann, *Legacy of Secrecy: The Long Shadow of the JFK Assassination* (Counterpoint, 2008).
[276] Waldron & Hartmann, *Ultimate Sacrifice*
[277] Waldron & Hartmann, *Ultimate Sacrifice*
[278] Waldron & Hartmann, *Ultimate Sacrifice*
[279] Waldron & Hartmann, *Ultimate Sacrifice*

Carlos Marcello: Marcello stated: "I had the little son-of-a-bitch killed, and I'd do it again … I wish I could have done it myself."[280] (spoken to FBI informant; FBI Document 124-10182-10430)

Santo Trafficante: Trafficante stated: "Carlos fucked up. We should not have killed John. We should have killed Bobby."[281] (deathbed statement to his attorney; spoken in Sicilian)

Santo Trafficante: Mafia figures who were scheduled to talk to investigating committees add up to another bit of circumstantial evidence that is not easy to ignore. When Sam Giancana was found shot to death with five bullet holes around his mouth, Santos Trafficante said, "Now there are only two people who know who shot Kennedy. And they aren't talking."[282] (spoken telephonically on FBI wiretap in 1975, after the murder of Sam Giancana)

David Morales: "Well, we took care of *that* son of a bitch, didn't we?"[283] (spoken to associates, during a drunken rant on JFK)

John Martino: Confessed to his role in the organizational involvement of the JFK assassination (on several occasions to family members and also to two friends, shortly before his death).[284]

Johnny Roselli: "Before he died, Roselli hinted to associates that he knew who had arranged President Kennedy's murder. It was the same conspirators, he suggested, whom he had recruited earlier to kill Cuban Premier Fidel Castro."[285] (Jack Anderson; *Washington Post*; September 9, 1976; cited by: Louis Stokes, House Select Committee on Assassinations; September 28, 1978)

Joe Granata: Granata was a credible FBI informant and close associate of notorious Chicago Mafia hit man Chuck Nicoletti. Granata testified that Nicoletti confessed to him, on several occasions, the direct involvement of Nicoletti, Johnny Roselli, Jimmy Sutton (a.k.a. James Files) and Marshal Caifano in the assassination of John F. Kennedy.[286] It should be added that Roselli's role would almost certainly not have been as an actual shooter—he was known as "Handsome Johnny" and renowned for being a charmer, not a killer—however the story apparently evolved into that over the years, as Mafia folklore has the habit of doing.

Frank Sheeran: Sheeran was a well-known Mafia hit man. He made deathbed confessions in 2004 that he and **Jimmy Hoffa** provided high-powered rifles for the Kennedy assassination and that Hoffa confessed to him that he had direct knowledge of high-level Mafia involvement in the murder.[287]

[280] Bradley S. O'Leary & L.E. Seymour, *Triangle of Death: The Shocking Truth About the Role of South Vietnam and the French Mafia in the Assassination of JFK* (WND Books, 2003).

[281] Frank Ragano & Selwyn Raab, *Mob Lawyer* (Random House Value, 1996).

[282] Jerome A. Kroth, *Conspiracy in Camelot: A Complete History of the John Fitzgerald Kennedy Assassination* (Algora Publishing, 2003), 190.

[283] John Simkin, "David Morales: Biography," *Spartacus Educational*, http://www.spartacus.schoolnet.co.uk/JFKmorales.htm (accessed 3 Mar. 2012).

[284] Hancock, *Someone Would Have Talked*

[285] Jack Anderson, "Behind John F. Kennedy's Murder," 7 September, 1976, *The Washington Post.*

[286] Dankbaar, *Files on JFK*

[287] Charles Brandt, *I Heard You Paint Houses: Frank 'The Irishman' Sheeran and the Inside Story of the Mafia, the Teamsters, and the Final Ride of Jimmy Hoffa* (Steerforth, 2004).

Frank Fiorini a.k.a. Frank Sturgis: "We did Watergate because Nixon wanted to stop the leakage of information on our role in the assassination of Kennedy."[288]

CIA Coup

The most common theory—"The CIA Did It"—is problematic because it contains several flaws in reasoning—and the most common reason contains the most fallacious reasoning. As it's often stated: The CIA (therefore, the Government) had to have done it because *only* the Government could have covered it up. That almost sounds logical, until we fully examine the premises and conclusion of the equation.

For openers, one person who was instrumental in the cover-up was none other than Robert F. Kennedy. The acts of Robert Kennedy in the immediate aftermath of the assassination clearly reveal a pattern in which he was actually a *primary* player in the construction of the cover-up.

It's an often overlooked fact that the most powerful person in the United States on the afternoon of November 22, 1963 was actually *not* the newly sworn-in President Lyndon Johnson. He had not yet fully taken the reins of power. It was Robert F. Kennedy. Johnson, on the afternoon of November 22, 1963, was basically a figurehead. Allegiance, as well as real authority, was rested in the Attorney General. While President Kennedy was alive, it was often commented that the Administration was really like a "dual-Presidency"—one in which RFK shared as much of the real power and responsibility as JFK. At the moment that President Kennedy was assassinated, true rank-and-file allegiance immediately shifted, by default, from President Kennedy to Attorney General Kennedy.

So what was Robert Kennedy actually doing on the afternoon of November 22 and afterward? Drastic actions were afoot:

- We know that he contacted a "security agent" whom he knew he could trust: CIA operative Hugh Huggins, who immediately boarded a jet, personally attended the autopsy, and reported directly to Bobby Kennedy.[289]
- We know that he immediately registered recognition of the name "Oswald" and called a contact in the anti-Castro camp in Florida, yelling into the telephone: "One of your guys did it!"[290]
- We know that he quickly called the Director of the CIA, screaming into the telephone: "Did the CIA kill my brother?!"[291]
- *And* we know that it was Bobby Kennedy's very own Attorney General's Office which actually *originated* the coverup, via the memo from staunch Kennedy ally Nick Katzenbach.

[288] Claudia Furiati, *ZR Rifle, The Plot to Kill Kennedy and Castro: Cuba Opens Secret Files* (Ocean Press, 1994).
[289] Bill Sloan & Jean Hill, *JFK: The Last Dissenting Witness*, (Pelican Publishing, 1992).
[290] Waldron & Hartmann, *Ultimate Sacrifice*
[291] Waldron & Hartmann, *Ultimate Sacrifice*

Bobby Kennedy called the CIA Director:

"Bobby said that 'at the time' of JFK's death, he 'asked (CIA Director John) McCone ... if they had killed my brother, and I asked him in a way that he couldn't lie to me, and they hadn't.' This statement is important, because Bobby said he asked McCone 'at the time' JFK died, meaning something about JFK's murder made him quickly suspect that the CIA might have been involved.

Second, how could Bobby ask McCone 'in a way that he couldn't lie to me' unless there was some particular operation both men knew about? Clearly, Bobby was asking McCone if a plan meant for Castro had been used on his brother instead ... Bobby Kennedy also said that 'McCone thought there were two people involved in the shooting.'"[292]

RFK registered immediate recognition of Oswald's name:

Robert Kennedy registered immediate recognition of Oswald's name because he knew that Oswald was a component of the anti-Castro operations which RFK headed.

According to recent research:

> **"Oswald was one of ten dossiers given to RFK to assassinate Castro."[293]**

> **"'Alba's sources for this information' included 'John Rice of the Secret Service (who parked his car in Alba's garage)'. Alba's 'sources also told him that after the assassination, RFK was seen in the Justice Department wailing, 'I've killed my own brother!'"[294]**

Historian John Simkin makes a very astute observation:

"One thing that has always puzzled me is the behavior of Robert Kennedy after the assassination. It must have been clear within hours of it happening that his brother had been killed by the Mafia with the support of rogue elements in the CIA and FBI. Yet, rather than calling for a full investigation into this possibility, he even took measures that attempted to cover up the conspiracy (taking control of the brain and autopsy X-rays that showed he had been hit in the front as well as in the back) ... John F. Kennedy did not in fact order an end to Executive Action. What he tried to do was to bring it under his own control. The plan to assassinate Fidel Castro now became known as Operation Freedom and was to be run by his brother Robert Kennedy ... Now consider the reaction of Robert Kennedy to the news that the man he had arranged to kill Castro had killed his brother. Any full investigation of Oswald and the Kennedy assassination would reveal details of Operation Freedom. What (the conspirators) had cleverly done was to implicate Robert Kennedy into the killing of his brother. He could now be guaranteed to join in the cover-up."[295]

---

[292] Waldron & Hartmann, *Ultimate Sacrifice*

[293] Gus Russo, *Live by the Sword: The Secret War Against Castro and the Death of JFK* (Bancroft, 1998).

[294] Waldron & Hartmann, *Ultimate Sacrifice* (citing Gus Russo).

[295] John Simkin, "Robert Kennedy and the Death of JFK," 13 March 2004, The Education Forum, http://educationforum.ipbhost.com/index.php?showtopic=512 (accessed 12 May 2010).

The fact that Oswald was manipulated into the tangled web of the JFK plot, assured that no official investigation ever could be made into his identity. Alarm bells went off all over Washington the moment that Oswald's name was mentioned because, those in a position to know, knew that U.S. intelligence had been seriously compromised. As some researchers conclude:

> **"The rifle fire in Dallas that killed John F. Kennedy didn't just start a frantic effort to find his assassins. JFK's murder also launched a flurry of covert actions by officials like Robert F. Kennedy, Lyndon Johnson, and Richard Helms to hide the fact that the United States was on the brink of invading Cuba as part of a JFK-authorized coup only ten days away. The plan's exposure could have cost the life of JFK's coup leader, Cuban Army Commander Juan Almeida, and led to a nuclear confrontation with the Soviets, just a year after the Cuban Missile Crisis."[296]**

Therefore, in the eyes of many in the JFK research community, the assassination was clearly a double-edged sword that was also a provocation for war:

> **"The assassination of President Kennedy was, to put it simply, an anti-Castro 'provocation', an act designed to be blamed on Castro to justify a punitive American invasion of the island. Such action would most clearly benefit the Mafia chieftains who had lost their gambling holdings in Havana because of Castro, and CIA agents who had lost their credibility with the Cuban exile freedom fighters from the ill-fated Bay of Pigs invasion."[297]**

The dark "beauty" of the "black op" that killed President Kennedy was that—by its very nature—it **forced the victims to cover up the crime**. Why else would Robert Kennedy have been handcuffed? He was still the Attorney General of the United States with a vast army of investigators at his disposal. Yet he refused to investigate the murder of his own brother. President Johnson did not handcuff Robert Kennedy—the Attorney General was free to pursue his tasks as he saw fit. His actions were handcuffed by the *very nature* of the operation which took JFK's life.

It should also be noted that RFK personally blamed Carlos Marcello for his brother's death, and that was something that Bobby confided to several associates.[298]

As we mentioned in the Marilyn Monroe chapter, there is an unfortunate tendency among researchers to divide into what they consider "pro-Kennedy" and "anti-Kennedy camps." The resulting polarization creates a type of "block" among some in the research community, who seem to be in denial that the Kennedy brothers (John and Robert) had extramarital affairs (both clearly did), and that Robert Kennedy was present at the home of Marilyn Monroe on the day of her death (which he clearly was). In much the same manner, many

---

[296] Waldron & Hartmann, *Legacy of Secrecy*

[297] Robert D. Morrow, *First Hand Knowledge: How I Participated in the CIA-Mafia Murder of President Kennedy* (S.P.I. Books, 1992).

[298] Waldron & Hartmann, *Ultimate Sacrifice*

researchers divide into camps on the JFK assassination, the most popular of which is that "the CIA did it." The problem is that, as a result, at least to some in the JFK research community, anything that suggests less than a total belief in the theory that the CIA "did it" tends to be perceived as somehow less than respectful to the Kennedy legacy.

The above notion is both mistaken and misinformed. Genuine research does not *color* itself according to political alliances; it simply follows wherever the evidence truly leads. The fact of the matter is that *collectively*, the CIA couldn't order a pizza—they are a huge organization composed of thousands of individuals of myriad factions and persuasions.

Instead, when we analyze both pre- and post-assassination actions, what we see is a clear pattern of CIA action (as an *agency*) that is in *opposition* to the plots to kill JFK.

The CIA Almost Went Public:

CIA veteran Victor Marchetti, former Executive Assistant to Deputy Director, CIA, in the book he co-authored, *The CIA and the Cult of Intelligence*, exposed an astonishing revelation of which he had direct knowledge:

> " ... at one time the CIA Director considered a public admission that some CIA field agents had been involved in the Kennedy assassination."[299]

Logic demands, however, that we realize that the converse of that is then also true; the CIA, as an agency, did not actively plan the assassination. That's *why* they actually considered "going public" about the actions of several agents (here, those who mistakenly consider themselves Kennedy "loyalists" would point out the intelligence technique known as a "limited hangout"—but that's an inappropriate attachment to the aforementioned point because there was clearly no *need* to go public). We also know that because, rather than smashing the conspiracy that killed his brother, Robert Kennedy used his office as Attorney General of the United States in 1963 to *cover up* that conspiracy.

CIA officer Victor Marchetti and others in a position to know such as David Atlee Phillips, also gave their personal opinions that although rogue agents were involved, the CIA itself ("as an agency") was not to blame for the assassination.

Former CIA officer Victor Marchetti made it clear in his work and his writing that he cared deeply about divulging the truth to the American people on intelligence matters. Yet he astutely adds:

> Mr. MARCHETTI: "But I had no evidence of the CIA's involvement in the assassination of President Kennedy. I will go a step further. I will volunteer that in my opinion, the CIA, as an institution, was not involved in that assassination. That does not mean that certain other individuals act-

---

[299] Victor Marchetti & John D. Marks, *The Cia and the Cult of Intelligence* (Knopf, 1974). Stockwell, *The Praetorian Guard*, 169.

ing on their own may not have been involved somehow, some way."

QUESTION: " ... Well, why would the CIA need to resort to a limited hangout if it had no role in that assassination?"

Mr. MARCHETTI: "To protect its role in the cover-up that began shortly after the assassination in the withholding of information and the deceiving of the Warren Commission and the subsequent hemming and hawing on the part of the Agency and its refusal to come clean for its own reasons, which I do not know. I can only speculate ... I think there was some sort of a connection in the assassination with CIA personnel, either officers, agents, or former officers or agents, that the Agency wanted to cover up, for one thing."[300]

Dr. John Newman—who was privy to high levels of intelligence while serving as Executive Assistant to Director, National Security Agency—agrees with Victor Marchetti's opinion that the documentary evidence does not suggest that the CIA, as an agency, was behind the assassination. However, he also notes that: "we can finally say with some authority that the CIA was spawning a web of deception about Oswald weeks before the president's murder, a fact that may have directly contributed to the outcome in Dallas."[301]

David Phillips, former Director of Western Hemisphere Operations at CIA, concluded basically the same—rogue intelligence agents *were* involved, but not the CIA as an *agency*:

"My final take on the assassination is there was a conspiracy, likely including American intelligence officers."[302]

It has also been documented that a Military Intelligence "Abort Team" (operating with CIA logistical support) succeeded in bringing Johnny Roselli to Dealey Plaza in an attempt to *thwart* the assassination of President Kennedy.[303] Presumably, the intended role of bringing Roselli (who was very active in U.S. Military Intelligence) was to, in effect, cancel the assassination, by making it known that the "game was up."

---

[300] Victor Marchetti, "Deposition of Victor L. Marchetti in *Hunt, Jr. vs. Liberty Lobby*," 9 July, 1984

[301] John Newman, *Oswald and the CIA: The Documented Truth About the Unkown Relationship Between the U.S. Government and the Alleged Killer of JFK* (New York: Skyhorse Publishing, 2008).

[302] Hancock, *Someone Would Have Talked*

[303] Plumlee, "Affidavit of William R. Plumlee"

> "A few key officials … —like Bobby Kennedy, Richard Helms, and others—would also believe that Oswald had done it (at least initially), but not for the reasons most others did. They would think that a US asset like Oswald had 'turned,' for some reason. Yet that reason couldn't be publicly revealed—or even fully investigated … "[304]

> "In a memo kept classified for ten years, the Warren Commission lawyers wrote that 'the motive of' the 'anti-Castroites' using Oswald 'would, of course, be expectation that after the President was killed," that 'Oswald would be caught or at least his identity ascertained. Law-enforcement authorities and the public would then blame the assassination on the Castro government, and the call for its forcible overthrow would be irresistible.'"[305]

The apparent reason for all the misrepresentation and the massive cover-up that ensued was that it was necessary for purposes of national security to avert war with Cuba and the Soviets, which had been the apparent intention of the assassination. Those "several CIA agents" mentioned above apparently hijacked a "black op" planned for Castro and redirected it against President Kennedy. David Atlee Phillips, CIA Director, WHO (Western Hemisphere Operations), alluded to that when he wrote:

> "I was one of the two case officers who handled Lee Harvey Oswald … we gave him the mission of killing Fidel Castro in Cuba … I don't know why he killed Kennedy. But I do know he used precisely the plan we had devised against Castro."[306]

That is further supported by the fact that, in a scenario surpassing the *Seven Days in May* thriller, moments after the President was shot, a false statement blaming Cuba was sent from U.S. Army Intelligence in Texas to the U.S. Strike Command in Florida and armed fighter planes were actually launched to attack Cuba.[307]

FBI agent James Hosty (who was Oswald's "handler" for the FBI), wrote that he learned of the near attack from two independent sources, and that shortly after Oswald's arrest:

> " … fully armed warplanes were sent screaming towards Cuba. Just before they entered Cuban airspace, they were hastily called back. With the launching of airplanes, the entire U.S. military went on alert."[308]

---

[304] Waldron & Hartmann, *Ultimate Sacrifice*

[305] Waldron & Hartmann, *Ultimate Sacrifice*

[306] Phillips, *AMLASH Legacy*

[307] Peter Dale Scott, *Deep Politics and the Death of JFK* (University of California Press, 1993). James P. Hosty Jr. & Thomas Hosty, *Assignment Oswald: From the FBI agent assigned to investigate Lee Harvey Oswald prior to the JFK assassination* (Arcade Publishing, 1997).

[308] Hosty Jr. & Hosty, *Assignment: Oswald*

The United States military went to the alert level "DEFCON 3" (Defense Condition 3) immediately after the assassination of President Kennedy. DefCon 3 is an extremely elevated formal defense posture; it is "the equivalent of loading and locking your weapon, and then placing your finger on the trigger. The power cells within Washington were in a panic."[309] War planes were "sent screaming towards Cuba" from the U.S. Strike Command at MacDill Air Force Base in Florida. They were then suddenly called back at the last moment before breaching Cuban air space—"the Air Force and CIA sent a 'Flash' worldwide alert" for U.S. flights to immediately "return to their bases lest the Soviet Union be provoked."[310]

USSTRICOM (United States Strike Command) apparently launched the Cuba-bound aircraft after it received an extraordinary cable on November 22, 1963:

> "The cable, from the Fourth Army Command in Texas to the U.S. Strike Command at MacDill Air Force Base in Florida, linked Oswald to Cuba via Cuba's alleged Communist 'propaganda vehicle,' the Fair Play for Cuba Committee. It also transmitted two statements about Oswald, both false, which had come via army Intelligence from the Dallas police."

> * "Assistant Chief Don Stringfellow, Intelligence Section, Dallas Police Department, notified 112th Intelligence Group, this Headquarters, that information obtained from Oswald revealed he had defected to Cuba in 1959 and is a card-carrying member of the Communist Party."[311]

Fortunately, cooler heads prevailed. For obvious reasons, the event has never been publicized. As Professor Peter Dale Scott observes,

Therefore, " … one can see the abundance of reasons behind the consensus, apparently generated by Hoover, for establishing that Oswald was just a nut who acted alone."[312]

Luckily, the recall code was issued before that strike was initiated and—there you have it, folks—a full-scale national security cover-up, resulting in *The War That Never Was*. And if that scenario is correct, then:

It was not the assassination of the 35th President of the United States that the government cover-up subverted; what the cover-up precluded was the military confrontation that was intended as a result of the assassination—hence the term, "national security" cover-up, which was even acknowledged by Robert F. Kennedy.

Rogue elements of the CIA, however, most probably were actively involved in the JFK assassination; and that actually *is* where the evidence truly leads.

---

[309] Hosty Jr. & Hosty, *Assignment: Oswald*

[310] Hosty Jr. & Hosty, *Assignment: Oswald*. Waldron & Hartmann, *Ultimate Sacrifice*

[311] Peter Dale Scott, *Deep Politics*

[312] Peter Dale Scott, *Deep Politics*

Elements of Mafia, US. Intelligence in the anti-Castro effort & Texas Millionaires

In a brief but astute article entitled *Toward a JFK Assassination Theory,* longtime JFK researcher Martin Shackelford makes a very coherent case for the melding of various factions whose "blended" interests are all present in the events of November 22, 1963:

1. CIA agents
2. Anti-Castro Cubans
3. Mafia figures
4. Lyndon Baines Johnson
5. "Texas Oil"[313]

Shackelford's right. All those factions appear to have played a role in the assassination. All of the above seem to contain elements of truth. Therefore, what clearly appears to be the most likely actual scenario, and what many researchers have come to believe, is that a "mix" of these various elements was responsible for the assassination: Mobsters like Charles Nicoletti and Johnny Roselli with strong links to Military Intelligence (from the crime families of Sam Giancana, Carlos Marcello, and Santos Trafficante), working in concert with several "renegade" U.S. Intelligence agents, and financed by the same group of Texas millionaires who had the very corrupt Texas politician Lyndon Johnson "in their pockets" and wouldn't at all mind seeing him become the next president who oversaw a Cold War, hijack a plan from within the anti-Castro operations.

> "the assassination was probably the work of a conspiracy involving elements of the CIA, Mafia and anti-Kennedy Cuban exiles—a cabal that was working to terminate Castro's reign (by any means necessary) and turned its guns instead against Kennedy. This is precisely what Robert Kennedy himself immediately suspected on the afternoon of Nov. 22, 1963 ... "[314]

To CIA veteran John Stockwell, it all seemed obvious:

> "A team of CIA, Cuban exile, and Mafia-related renegades organized a simple military ambush in Dallas and successfully gunned him down. The ambush and its coverup were brazen and astonishingly open. In fact several plots, in Chicago, Miami, and Houston, to kill Kennedy had misfired or been thwarted."

---

[313] Martin Shackelford, "Toward a JFK Assassination Theory," 5 November, 1996. http://www.acorn.net/jfkplace/03/MS/4gen.html (accessed 2 Mar. 2011)

[314] David Talbot, "Case Closed? A new book about the JFK assassination claims to finally solve the mystery," 1 December 2005, *Salon. com,* (review of *Ultimate Sacrifice*). http://www.salon.com/2005/12/01/review_161/

> "I personally believe, from my knowledge of the CIA that elements of the CIA's ZR/RIFLE program (an assassination group that was a component of OPERATION MONGOOSE) were probably involved in the conspiracy, along with Cuban exiles, and Sam Giancana, John Roselli, and Charles Nicoletti of organized crime. ZRRIFLE was exposed by the Senate Church Committee. The CIA's Chief of Operations, Richard Bissell, admitted to its existence as did its founder, a rough impetuous man named William Harvey, who boasted of his criminal connections."[315]

OPERATION MONGOOSE was the conglomeration of CIA, military, and Mafia resources that were directed at Cuba's leader Fidel Castro. Based in south Florida, it was this program that included many of the "renegades" suspected of turning their sights against President Kennedy.

Other evidentiary indications are that, much like a Shakespearean drama, Lyndon Johnson, the 36th President of the United States, was directly involved in the "removal" of the 35th President. Johnson had a long and sordid political career that was littered with murdered adversaries and corruption involving mobsters. And once you're President of the United States States, you're very well-positioned to control a cover-up.

"Robert Kennedy 'regarded the Warren Commission as a public relations exercise to reassure the public.' According to a variety of reports, Kennedy suspected a plot as soon as he heard his brother had been shot in Dallas. And as he made calls and inquiries in the hours and days after the assassination, he came to an ominous conclusion: JFK was the victim of a domestic political conspiracy."[316]

In fact, Robert Kennedy sent a special envoy to the Soviet Union shortly after the assassination with a message that read, in part:

> "We know that it was a domestic high level political conspiracy ... "[317]

Veteran CIA officer E. Howard Hunt testified in a deathbed statement that President Lyndon Johnson coordinated the assassination operation- codenamed "The Big Event"- through CIA agents Cord Meyer (JFK was having a serious affair with Cord Meyer's wife), David Morales and William Harvey, who also contracted a French assassin who fired from a location ahead of the limousine. Hunt even diagrammed the "Chain of Command" in his own handwriting (the bottom entry reads "French Gunman Grassy Knoll")[318]:

---

[315] Stockwell, *The Praetorian Guard*

[316] David Talbot, "The mother of all cover-ups," 15 September, 2004, *Salon.com*, (citing Evan Thomas, *Robert Kennedy: His Life* (New York: Simon & Schuster, 2002).

[317] David Talbot, *Brothers: The Hidden History of the Kennedy Years* (Free Press, 2007).

[318] *The Last Testament of E. Howard Hunt*, dir. by Saint John Hunt (Dreamland Productions, 2007, dvd). http://www.saintjohnhunt.com/testament.html

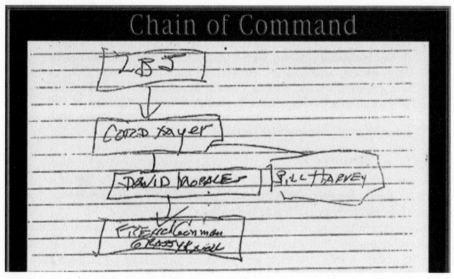

Courtesy of Saint John Hunt, www.SaintJohnHunt.com

Johnson's deep resentment of President Kennedy is well-documented. Sometimes a picture really *is* worth a thousand words—check out the two which follow:

Employing French mafia for the assassination would be consistent with the documentation from Bill Harvey, leader of the U.S. assassinations unit and a man who, for obvious reasons in that profession, left very little in writing. But the following notation from Harvey did survive:

> **"William Harvey's notes recommend using Corsicans, since 'Sicilians could lead to the Mafia.'"**[319]

Michel Mertz, a ruthless professional assassin for the Corsican Mafia who often used the alias of his arch-enemy and former freedom-fighter Jean Souetre, is often mentioned as the Corsican assassin that "Wild Bill" Harvey hired.

> **"Mertz was part of the French Corsican Mafia, though not Corsican himself (the same way the Jewish Jack Ruby worked for the Mafia)."**[320]

There is evidence that Mertz was in Dallas on November 22, 1963, again using Souetre as his alias.[321]

> **"Twenty-four parallels (lettered A-X) between the CIA's acknowledged European assassin recruiter (1960 to 1964) code-named QJWIN and Michel Victor Mertz, whom a CIA memo said was**

[319] Waldron & Hartmann, *Legacy of Secrecy*

[320] Waldron & Hartmann, *Legacy of Secrecy*

[321] Henry Hurt, *Reasonable Doubt: An Investigation into the Assassination of John F. Kennedy* (Holt, Rinehart & Winston, 1986). Michael T. Griffith, "Suspects in the JFK Assassination," 19 December 2002, http://www.mtgriffith.com/web_documents/suspects. htm. Waldron & Hartmann, *Ultimate Sacrifice*. Marrs, *Crossfire*.

deported from Dallas shortly after JFK's murder. Michel Mertz was an experienced assassin and a kingpin for the French Connection heroin network that involved both Carlos Marcello and Santo Trafficante."[322]

This mix of professional assassins and renegade Intelligence agents from the anti-Castro project in Florida appears to be responsible for the ambush in Dealey Plaza that was orchestrated with military precision. It should be noted that the U.S. Military Intelligence team that attempted to stop the assassination was looking for exactly that: A military-style ambush with 3 shooter teams in triangulated fire from the north knoll, south knoll, and the area of the Dal-Tex Building. They arrived too late and had bad communication between team members that day—and we know what happened then.[323]

The fact that the Military Intelligence abort team flew Johnny Roselli into Dallas on the morning of the assassination is a highly probable indication that Roselli (who in addition to being hooked up with the Chicago Mob, was also very hooked up with U.S. Intelligence and its anti-Castro ops) was crucial in the penetration of the plot to kill JFK. The intent of bringing him to Dallas with the abort team is indicative that he was to inform his co-conspirators that the game was up and to abort the assassination. Johnny Roselli apparently did what U.S. intelligence had told him to do, bringing in that message—right into Dealey Plaza itself—that "the CIA had called the hit stopped."[324] As a result, Roselli also reportedly balked at being specifically involved in the shooting. As Chuck Nicoletti, the premier hit man in the entire country at the time, put it:

> "Well, he doesn't want to go against the orders of the CIA. What he wants, he wants to call it off. He flew in here as an abort team. They flew a plane in here especially with him on it, to tell us to call it off."[325]

U.S. intelligence knew about the assassination attempt, even to the point of being aware of the specific location for the planned hit—having penetrated the plot through Roselli—so they frantically rushed in an elite Military Intelligence unit to abort the assassination, and *even* got the message to "stand down" to the shooting team.[326] However, according to the scenario from the Chicago Mafia's James Files—subscribed to by former FBI Special Agent and Organized Crime expert Zack Shelton—Nicoletti countered with an argument of his own: that it was "The Man" (Sam "The Man" Giancana, head of Chicago Mafia) who had written this "contract" and only The Man himself could call it off:

> " ... you know we can't call this off. Only one man can stop it ... I'm not going on somebody else's word ... As far as it is right now, I have a go from the boss."[327]

[322] Waldron & Hartmann, *Legacy of Secrecy*

[323] Plumlee, "Affidavit of William R. Plumlee"

[324] Dankbaar, *Files on JFK* (in "Interview of James Files by Robert G. Vernon, March 22, 1994").

[325] Dankbaar, *Files on JFK* (in "Interview of James Files by Jim Marrs and Wim Dankbaar").

[326] Plumlee, "Affidavit of William R. Plumlee"

[327] Dankbaar, *Files on JFK* (in "Interview of James Files by Jim Marrs and Wim Dankbaar").

So the hit was a "go" anyway. According to the hearsay evidence (Nicoletti told his bodyguard, who then told it to us)—in what was arguably one of the most important conversations of the entire twentieth century—Nicoletti trumped Roselli's argument with history—changing logic that could be traced straight back to the streets of Chicago:

> **"Fuck 'em. We** *go.***"**[328]

And then, reportedly, they "went"—it was "a go." And in the messy manner in which history actually happens, that's quite possibly what took place. With a willing accomplice sitting right in the White House Oval Office, any so-called investigation would clearly be *in name only*.

Two of the men who were closest to President Kennedy get the "last word" here:

Dave Powers, Special Assistant to the President of the United States (in car behind President Kennedy):

> "Dave Powers, Special Assistant to the President, was riding only ten feet behind Kennedy's limousine in Dallas. He clearly saw at least two shots from the infamous grassy knoll in front of the motorcade—evidence of a conspiracy, since Oswald was allegedly firing from the rear, on the 6th floor of the Texas ok Depository building. Powers felt they were "riding into an ambush" and said that he was pressured to change his story by the Warren Commission."[329]

Kenny O'Donnell, Special Assistant to the President of the United States (in car behind President Kennedy):

The following is an excerpt from a book by former Speaker of the House, Tip O'Neill:

> I was having dinner with Kenny O'Donnell and a few other people at Jimmy's Harborside Restaurant in Boston, and we got to talking about the assassination.

> I was surprised to hear O'Donnell say that he was sure he had heard two shots that came from behind the fence.

> "That's not what you told the Warren Commission," I said. "You're right," he replied. "I told the FBI what I had heard but they said it couldn't have happened that way and that I must have been imagining things. So I testified the way they wanted me to. I just didn't want to stir up any more pain and trouble for the family."

---

[328] Dankbaar, *Files on JFK* (in "Interview of James Files by Robert G. Vernon, March 22, 1994").
[329] Waldron & Hartmann, *Ultimate Sacrifice*

"I can't believe it," I said. "I wouldn't have done that in a million years. I would have told the truth."

"Tip, you have to understand. The family—everybody wanted this thing behind them."

Dave Powers was with us at dinner that night, and his recollection of the shots was the same as O'Donnell's."[330]

BIBLIOGRAPHY

JFK Homicide: Forensic Reconstruction, Sherry Gutierrez Fiester, CSCSI (former Certified Senior Crime Scene Investigator), (dvd), 2010

JFK: The Analysis of a Shooting: The Ultimate Ballistics Truth Exposed, Orlando Martin, 2010

Head Shot: The Science Behind the JFK Assassination, G. Paul Chambers, 2010

Hear No Evil: Social Constructivism & the Forensic Evidence in the Kennedy Assassination, Donald Byron Thomas, 2010

American Conspiracies: Lies, Lies, and More Dirty Lies that the Government Tells Us, Jesse Ventura & Dick Russell, 2010

The Man Who Knew Too Much: Hired to Kill Oswald and Prevent the Assassination of JFK, Dick Russell, 2003

The Guns of Texas Are Upon You, Walt Brown, 2005

Harvey & Lee, John Armstrong, 2003

"Where Was Oswald From 11:50 to 12:35 P.M. on the Day of the Assassination?", Michael T. Griffith, 1998. http://www.mtgriffith.com/web_documents/wherewasoswald.htm

"The JFK Assassination: The Lunchroom Encounter", Gil Jesus, 2011. http://www.giljesus.com/jfk/lunchroom_encounter.htm

The Oswald Affair: An Examination of the Contradictions and Omissions of the Warren Report, Léo Sauvage, 1966

The Warren Omission: A Micro-study of the Methods and Failures of the Warren Commission, Walt Brown, 1996

"Defaming History or, Who Didn't Kill JFK", Richard Belzer, August 13, 2007, *Huff Post.* http://www.huffingtonpost.com/richard-belzer/defaming-history-or-who-d_b_60188.html

On the Trail of the JFK Assassins: A Groundbreaking Look at America's Most Infamous Conspiracy, Dick Russell, 2010

"'Harvey and Lee': Military Records-Soviet Union", John Armstrong, *JFK Deep Politics Quarterly,* July, 2011

---

[330] Thomas P. O'Neill & William Novak, *Man of the House: The Life and Political Memoirs of Speaker Tip O'Neill* (Random House, 1987).

"Case Closed: Stampede of the Apologists," Chauncey Holt (Karyn Holt Harcourt, 2005), *Assassination Research: Journal for the Advanced Study of the Death of JFK*: Vol. 3, No. 2; 2005. http://www.assassinationresearch.com/v3n2/v3n2holt/pdf

Files on JFK, Wim Dankbaar, 2003

"Toward a JFK Assassination Theory", Martin Shackelford, November 5, 1996 http://spot.acorn.net/JFKplace/09/fp.back_issues/15th_Issue/theory.html

Spooks, Hoods and the Hidden Elite, dir. by Wim Dankbaar, (dvd), 2008. http://www.jfkmurdersolved.com/spooks.htm

"The Last Testament of E. Howard Hunt," dir. by Saint John Hunt (Dreamland Productions, 2007, dvd). http://www.saintjohnhunt.com/testament.html

CHAPTER 6

The Reverend Dr. Martin Luther King, Jr. April 4, 1968

Civil Rights Leader, Nobel Peace Prize Laureate

VICTIM	**DR. MARTIN LUTHER KING, JR.**
Cause of Death	SINGLE GUNSHOT

James Earl Ray, acting alone, fired the rifle shot from the 2nd floor bathroom window (while standing on the ledge of the bathtub) in his rooming house, across the street from the motel where Dr. King was staying. He then (according to a state exhibit depicting the scene) came down the hallway into his room and carefully packed the rifle into a box along with other items that were easily identifiable as belonging to him, tied up the package, proceeded across the walkway (the entire length

Official Verdict	of the building), went out the back door, went down the stairs in back, placed the box right in a building entryway, then got into his car, a white Mustang, and drove that same car all the way from Memphis, Tennessee to Atlanta, Georgia, never challenged by police.
Actual Circumstances	Dr. King was killed by one bullet, traversing in a sharply downward direction, from right-to-left. The bullet entered his right cheek, then went down through the bottom of his throat where it severed the spinal cord, and then lodged, still lower, in his left shoulder. The trajectory was <u>not even close</u> to how the trajectory lines up from where the accused allegedly fired. A rifle was found across the street in a nice, convenient package of evidence that was just waiting for police, that clearly identified the alleged shooter. Two months later, James Earl Ray was arrested in London, extradited and charged with the murder. The murder of Dr. King has never been satisfactorily adjudicated. There was <u>no trial</u>. The defendant never received "his day in court"—after his arrest, he was threatened with the certainty of a death sentence and coerced into pleading guilty. To avoid the electric chair, he pleaded Guilty and was immediately sentenced to life in prison. He quickly attempted to withdraw the guilty plea. He spent the remainder of his life—over 29 years—attempting, through legal counsel, to withdraw his guilty plea and secure a jury trial; those attempts were universally unsuccessful. Since he was never granted a trial, there was never a fair or even impartial adjudication of the actual evidence.
Inconsistencies	1. The bullet taken from Dr. King's body <u>did not come</u> from the rifle of James Earl Ray. That <u>possibility was excluded</u> by the Judge who presided over the trial. 2. Ballistics testing on Ray's <u>bullets</u> determined that they did <u>not</u> match the crime. 3. Ballistics tests on Ray's rifle were never able to match it to the crime. 4. Ballistics tests confirmed that any bullet fired from Ray's rifle would have a very specific type of gauging on it, due to a manufacturing defect in that rifle. That gauging mark DOES NOT appear on the bullet that killed Dr. King. 5. Bullet trajectory clearly indicates that the gunshot was from a dramatically different location than the rooming house window from where the accused allegedly fired the rifle. The official version was that the shot came from-

directly across the street at a position that was virtually level with the victim. But:

- Autopsy findings prove the bullet path was sharply downward and extreme right-to-left, not straight;
- Ballistics evidence verifies a sharply right-to-left downward bullet trajectory;
- Photographic evidence from immediately after the gunshot confirms four witnesses with victim all looking and/or pointing <u>up and to the right</u> to a position also consistent with a sharply downward right-to-left trajectory.

6. It was <u>never proven</u> that the rifle shot came from the bathroom window of the rooming house, as alleged by the Government.
7. The design of the bathroom from which the Government states that the Defendant fired the rifle is laid out in a way that would have made it impossible to have effectively fired a rifle from the window. Aside from the fact that the shooter would have had to stand balanced on the ledge of the bathtub, even more ridiculous is the fact that there was a wall that was so close to the window that it would have made the shot with a Remington 30.06 rifle impossible because the rifle was actually <u>six inches too long</u> to position for a shot out that window.
8. Ray's rifle was not even "sighted"; the bullet would never have hit what was lined up in the sight.
9. New testimony has established evidence that there were two rifles at the crime scene: a "throw-down" rifle to set up the patsy and a "hot" rifle that was broken down and removed from the scene in conjunction with a coordinated plan of escape.
10. James Earl Ray consistently maintained that his rifle, the alleged murder weapon, was never fired at Martin Luther King, and he repeatedly requested advanced ballistics testing to prove it. Ballistics tests conducted by the FBI did <u>not</u> indicate that Ray's rifle was the murder weapon. Ballistics tests conducted at the behest of a Congressional Committee did <u>not</u> indicate the rifle was the murder weapon. Advanced tests undertaken in 1997 at the behest of Ray's counsel also could <u>not</u> link the rifle ballistically to the shot that was fired at Martin Luther King.
11. James Earl Ray, who served in the U.S. Army, was not known as being a very good shot with a rifle.

12. There was no eyewitness to the shooting. No eyewitness saw the shooter. There was only one eyewitness who placed James Earl Ray at the rooming house at the time of the shooting, and their reliability as a witness was seriously questioned (extremely inebriated and not in a position to have witnessed the exit). There is, however, a reliable witness (a manager of a gas station) who identified James Earl Ray as being in his car at the time of the shooting, which was several blocks away from the crime scene.

13. James Earl Ray did not have a motive. Prosecutors did not even bother to outline his motive for the killing or to accuse him of being a racist.

14. The defendant had no prior history of violent crime. He was basically just a petty thief. The murder of anyone, let alone a prominent figure, was dramatically out-of-character with his past history.

15. FBI Deputy Director William Sullivan, who led the FBI investigation of James Earl Ray, was convinced that an 8th grade dropout like Ray could not possibly have managed everything that was alleged. Sullivan wrote:

> "Someone, I feel sure, taught Ray how to get a false Canadian passport, how to get out of the country, and how to travel to Europe because he could never have managed it alone. And how did Ray pay for the passport and the airline tickets?"[331]

16. A package of evidence was intentionally left outside Ray's rooming house that *clearly* indicated it belonged to James Earl Ray. Ray was a professional criminal and would have known that leaving a bundle of incriminating evidence was like leaving a calling card that he had committed the crime. Judge Hanes cited "terrific evidence" that Ray was set up: A witness stated that "the package was dropped in his doorway by a man headed south down Main Street on foot and that this happened at about ten minutes before the shot was fired."[332]

17. The entire area of grass and bushes outside the alleged "sniper's nest" were immediately cut back by a landscaping crew soon after the shooting, obliterating evidence. At best, it was direct violation of standard crime scene procedures—at worst; it was actually criminal destruction of evidence at an active crime scene.

---

[331] William C. Sullivan & Bill Brown, *The Bureau: My Thirty Years in Hoover's FBI* (Norton, 1979).

[332] Jim Douglass, "Martin Luther King Conspiracy Exposed in Memphis," Spring 2000, *Probe Magazine*. http://www.ratical.org/ratville/JFK/MLKconExp.html

18. Ray alleged that he had been coerced into pleading guilty to avoid an imminent death sentence that he was being threatened with, and that he was told that the only way he could keep his brother and father out of prison was to plead guilty. He stated that he was framed as part of a larger plot (the existence of the man whose involvement he alleged, "Raul" from Montreal, has been acknowledged by authorities).

19. The family of Dr. Martin Luther King has consistently believed that James Earl Ray was not the killer and gregariously supported efforts to clear his name.

20. Ray appealed his conviction seven times, continually seeking an expansion of facts in evidence and the right to present evidence at trial.

21. Martin Luther King's family filed a wrongful death civil lawsuit, presenting ballistics evidence that Ray's rifle could not have fired the gunshot.

22. In a court decision that would be earth-shattering, but for the fact that few are aware of it, a jury returned a verdict that Martin Luther King was killed by a conspiracy "including governmental agencies."

"The jury was clearly convinced by the extensive evidence that was presented during the trial that, in addition to Mr. Jowers, the conspiracy of the Mafia, local, state and federal government agencies, were deeply involved in the assassination of my husband. The jury also affirmed overwhelming evidence that identified someone else, not James Earl Ray, as the shooter, and that Mr. Ray was set up to take the blame."

—Coretta Scott King

Most Americans are completely unaware that a Tennessee jury in 1999 reached the verdict that a conspiracy involving agencies of the U.S. government was responsible for the assassination of Dr. Martin Luther King. Circuit Court Judge James E. Swearengen read back the jury's verdict in open court:

"In answer to the question did Loyd Jowers participate in a conspiracy to do harm to Martin Luther King, your answer is yes. Do you also find that others, including governmental agencies, were parties to this conspiracy as alleged by the defendant? Your answer to that one is also yes."[333]

---

[333] *Verdict, King Family vs. Jowers and Other Unknown Co-Conspirators*, December 8, 1999, Circuit Court of Tennessee, Division 4, The Honorable James E. Swearengen presiding.

In some of the most important court testimony in contemporary American history (completely ignored by mainstream U.S. media), and in one of the most important trials in American history (also completely ignored by major media)—the extent of media manipulation in the United States was clearly laid out by an expert in that field.

William Schaap was a Professor of Criminal Justice, attorney, publisher of *Covert Action Quarterly* and Court-Certified Expert on intelligence matters and the governmental use of media, specifically the use of sophisticated disinformation techniques on the American public. He has testified as an expert witness on such matters in many proceedings, including in the civil trial brought by the family of Martin Luther King.

Mr. Schaap testified that, from analysis of the documentation, it was quite clear from a historical standpoint that the CIA and FBI had both intentionally attempted to destroy Martin Luther King, even to the point of trying to drive him to commit suicide—especially after he came out publicly against the Vietnam War. They also planted stories they knew were untrue, in newspapers across the country, in a vicious media campaign against him.

On November 18, 1964, FBI Director J. Edgar Hoover in a press conference, called Dr. King (a man who was about to receive the *Nobel Peace Prize)* "the most notorious liar in the country." Three weeks later, on December 10, 1964, Dr. King was awarded the *Peace Prize for 1964* with the praise that:

> **"He is the first person in the Western world to have shown us that a struggle can be waged without violence. He is the first to make the message of brotherly love a reality in the course of his struggle, and he has brought this message to all men, to all nations and races."[334]**

But that hadn't stopped the FBI from trying to destroy him:

> **"They—one of the most outrageous was a doctored tape recording that was prepared that purported to—to be a recording of Dr. King engaging in raucous and possibly sexual activities with various people. It turned out to be—most of it was totally fraudulent. And what wasn't fraudulent did not have to do with anything torrid going on. It was all put together. And the tape—in fact, the tape was originally used—and this is one of the things that the House Committee found the most outrageous—in an attempt to try and drive Dr. King to commit suicide. Shortly before he went to get the Nobel Prize, the tape was mailed to him with a long letter basically saying, if you don't kill yourself, we're going to make this public."[335]**

---

[334] *The Nobel Peace Prize 1964, Award Ceremony Speech*, Gunnar Jahn, Chairman, Nobel Committee, Oslo, Norway, December 10, 1964

[335] William Schaap, "Testimony of Mr. William Schaap on the role of the U.S. Government in the assassination of Martin Luther Ling," *The King Center*, 30 November, 1999, http://www.ratical.org/ratville/JFK/MLKv9Schaap.html (accessed 22 Oct. 2011)

Professor Schaap further testified that such U.S. governmental misuse of information was and *still is* prevalent in the United States and that Americans are particularly vulnerable to it as a result of the way that the notion of conspiracy has been publicly maligned by the press:

> "I mean, after all, "conspiracy" just means, you know, more than one person being involved in something. And if you stop and think about it, almost everything significant that happens anywhere involves more than one person. Yet here there is a—not a myth really, but there's just an underlying assumption that most things are not conspiracies. And when you have that, it enables a government which has a propaganda program, has a disinformation program, to be relatively successful in—in having its disinformation accepted."[336]

We are intentionally including a lot of this testimony for one very simple reason: until now, <u>very few Americans were aware of it</u>. Mr. Schaap also testified that:

- About a third of the CIA's budget is for its media operations, which includes <u>domestic use of propaganda</u>, such as solidifying and continuing the public perception that there were <u>no conspiracies</u> in the murders of President Kennedy, Senator Robert F. Kennedy, and Dr. Martin Luther King. Their budget is secret (it's kept "classified" because you don't *tell* people that they are being intentionally misinformed); but at least a *billion dollars* per year goes to media propaganda operations, much of that *in* the U.S.;
- There is still an *active focus* on media propaganda in the U.S. by Intelligence agencies to discredit conspiracy theories and solidify the official version of historical events;
- The reason that there was virtually no media coverage of the civil trial in 1999 resulting in a conspiracy verdict in the King assassination is directly linked to governmental control of the media in the United States.[337]

At this point, misinformation has been so imprinted in the minds of Americans that "James Earl Ray killed Martin Luther King"—that even certain proof to the contrary would not be accepted, because that's the way that disinformation works.

> "Disinformation is not only getting certain things to appear in print, it's also getting certain things not to appear in print. I mean, the first—the first thing I would say as a way of explanation is the incredibly powerful effect of disinformation over a long period of time that I mentioned before. For 30 years the official line has been that James Earl Ray killed Martin Luther King and he did it all by himself ... And when that is imprinted in the minds of the general public for 30 years, if somebody stood up and confessed and said: I did it. Ray didn't do it, I did it. Here's a movie. Here's a

---

[336] Schaap, *Testimony*
[337] Schaap, *Testimony*

video showing me do it. 99 percent of the people wouldn't believe him because it just—it just wouldn't click in the mind. It would just go right to—it couldn't be. It's just a powerful psychological effect over 30 years of disinformation that's been imprinted on the brains of the—the public."[338]

FORENSIC, BALLISTICS & MEDICAL EVIDENCE

There is a **total ballistics mismatch** with the evidence of this case. Judge Joe Brown was the main trial judge during proceedings where new evidence was introduced. After spending two years examining technical points about the murder weapon, Judge Brown concluded that:

The bullet that killed Dr. King **could not** have been fired from Ray's rifle; the scientific testing *excluded* it as having come from that cartridge case.[339]

The *entire* set of ballistics just doesn't match up. As Judge Brown put it:

- "What you've got in terms of the physical evidence relative to ballistics is frightening."

- "First, it's not the right type of rifle."
- The Remington Gamemaster 30.06 is a pump-action rifle and would be extremely difficult to fire from a position of resting it on a window sill;
- "It's never been sighted in."
- Test-firing the rifle verified that the alignment of the rifle was off, by several feet, at about 100 yards;
- "It's the wrong kind of scope."
- "With a 30.06, it makes a particularly difficult shot firing at a downward trajectory in that circumstance."
- "Metallurgical analysis excludes the bullet taken from the body of Dr. King from coming from the cartridge case they say was fired in that rifle."
- **The bullet that killed Dr. King <u>did not come</u> from the rifle found at the crime scene.**[340]

During the time period that he was presiding over James Earl Ray's appeal, Judge Brown informed the Black Congressional Caucus that it was <u>not possible</u> that Ray's rifle, the alleged murder weapon, had fired the shot that killed Dr. King. After that comment, Judge Brown was removed from presiding over that trial for alleged bias.

U.S. Congresswoman Cynthia McKinney wrote that Judge Brown told her and the rest of the Congressional Black Caucus that, unequivocally, Ray's rifle was *not* the weapon that killed Dr. Martin Luther King, Jr. Here are her words, exactly as she recorded them:

[338] Schaap, *Testimony*

[339] Dick Russell, "A King-Sized Conspiracy," 1999, *High Times*, http://www.dickrussell.org/articles/king.htm. Dick Russell, "Judge Brown Slams Memphis over the King Case," July-August, 1998, *Probe Magazine. http://www.ctka.net/pr798-judge.html*

[340] Russell, "A King-Sized Conspiracy". Russell, "Judge Brown Slams Memphis".

> "Yesterday, Judge Joe Brown told us unequivocally that the so-called murder rifle was NOT the weapon that killed Dr. King."[341]

As veteran researcher Michael Rivero noted:

> "Ballistics tests are an either/or situation. Either the bullet matches or it doesn't. Either the James Earl Ray rifle fired that bullet or it didn't. Legally, if it cannot be proven, it didn't happen. A report leaked from the court confirms that the second set of ballistics tests showed that there is a manufacturing defect in the James Earl Ray rifle that gouges any bullet it fires. That mark does NOT appear on the bullet that killed Martin Luther King. When the judge ordered one more set of tests to make sure, the Federal government, instead of complying with the court order, had the judge removed from the case March 7th, 1998!"[342]

In the case of Dr. Martin Luther King, Jr. he was shot only once. Therefore, the trajectory of that bullet is crucial evidence.

Bullet trajectories do not tell lies. They reveal clear indications of bullet paths. They telegraph to us exactly where gunshots originated.

Dr. King was shot at the Lorraine Motel in Memphis, Tennessee while standing on the balcony of Room 306 which was actually located on the second story of the building. The 2nd floor bathroom window of the rooming house across the street is the site from which James Earl Ray allegedly fired the shot.

The bullet entered Dr. King's right cheek and passed through from right-to-left in a sharp, downward trajectory, then severing the spinal column in his neck, continuing downward, and lodging, still lower, in his left shoulder.

Therefore, the trajectory tells us that the bullet was fired from a point high above the victim and to his right, which also happens to be precisely where three eyewitnesses on the balcony are pointing in the photographic evidence from immediately after the shot.

Dr. Jerry Thomas Francisco, the Medical Examiner, testified about the autopsy:

> "The examination revealed a gunshot wound to the right side of the face, passing through the body into the neck, through the spinal cord at the base of the neck, with the bullet lodging beneath the skin near the shoulder blade on the left."[343]

Yet we are told that the shot came from the bathroom window at Ray's rooming house which is *only slightly above* the balcony of Dr. King—in fact, it's almost what is called a *flat trajectory*.

---

[341] Rep. Cynthia McKinney, "Goodbye to All That," 18 September 2002, *Counterpunch*, Alexander Cockburn & Jeffrey St. Clair, eds. (emphasis in original), http://www.counterpunch.org/mckinney0918.html.

[342] Michael Rivero, "If James Earl Ray Did Not Kill Martin Luther King, Then Who Did," *WhatReallyHappened.com*. http://whatreallyhappened.com/RANCHO/POLITICS/MLK/mlk.html (accessed 12 Dec. 2011).

[343] Mark Lane & Dick Gregory, *Murder in Memphis: The FBI and the Assassination of Martin Luther King* (Thunder's Mouth, 1993).

In 1979, the U.S. Congress *House Select Committee on Assassinations* investigated the King assassination. They hired a review board headed by three noted forensic pathologists to examine the autopsy. One of the three was the famous Dr. Michael Baden, Chief Medical Examiner for New York City. Dr. Baden was the spokesperson for the panel. And they agreed with Dr. Francisco on the downward trajectory:

> **"Dr. Baden testified that Dr. King died as a result of a single gunshot wound caused by a bullet that entered the right side of the face approximately an inch to the right and a half inch below the mouth. The bullet fractured Dr. King's jaw, exited the lower part of the face and reentered the body in the neck area. It then severed numerous vital arteries and fractured the spine in several places, causing severe damage to the spinal column and coming to rest on the left side of the back. The bullet traveled in a downward, and rearward from a medial direction."[344]**

Therefore, the shooter was *above* the victim; not parallel in the rooming house across the street where the official U.S. government version of events places James Earl Ray. If Dr. King had been struck from a shot fired from where the government states that he fired, then the bullet pathway through Dr. King's body would, of scientific necessity, be almost level, parallel, or only slightly above, since Ray's rooming house was on a slope; it was on the second floor of a building just like Dr. King was, but a slope on the terrain placed it slightly higher than Dr. King's balcony. But the sharply downward trajectory of that bullet establishes unequivocally that the shot was fired from a point much higher than the victim. Therefore, it is physically impossible for the official version to be correct.

As author Michael Rivero states:

> **"If you go back to my article and look at the photo taken from the rooming house window, you will see it is almost a flat trajectory."[345]**

We also know that the rifle shot came from the victim's right, because the bullet traversed his body right-to-left. It was up-and-to-the-right from the 2nd floor balcony upon which Dr. King stood; from a position that was about "two-o'clock-high" from the target. That's not even close to the rooming house where the official version places the shot. The rooming house is directly across from the balcony; it's not to the right and it is most certainly not sufficiently higher to have caused the sharply downward trajectory.

So where *did* the rifle shot come from? It came from above the victim, precisely where a professional assassin prefers to position. The shot also came from precisely where the eyewitnesses are pointing in the photographic evidence.

Below are the official findings of the House Assassinations Committee, 1979. This is direct from their report in the National Archives. Frankly, it is

---

[344] U.S. House of Representatives, *Report of the Select Committee on Assassinations of the U.S. House of Representatives*, 1979. http://www.archives.gov/research/jfk/select-committee-report/part-2a.html
[345] Michael Rivero, email to author, 17 August 2010.

bureaucratic gobbledygook—but read it slowly and with the height and directional issues in mind and see if it makes any sense.

> "From extrinsic evidence, the autopsy panel accepted that at the moment the bullet entered his body, Dr. King was at the balcony railing talking to someone on the pavement one story below. Accordingly, the panel found that <u>the bullet pathway was consistent with the shot coming from his right and above</u>. The autopsy panel concluded that the single bullet that struck Dr. King must have come from across Mulberry Street, because Dr. King's body was <u>facing in that direction</u> and because a bullet coming from that direction would have traveled on a downward slope. The panel concluded, further, that the bullet was probably fired from the area of the rooming house at 422 1/2 South Main Street, but the panel could not determine, from the medical evidence alone, whether the shot was fired from the bathroom window on the second floor or from the shrubbery below the window."[346]

There are *big* problems with the would-be logic of the above statement. If the bullet came from where he was facing then it could not have traversed sharply right-to-left through his face. Ray's rooming house was directly across the street and only slightly to the right, from Dr. King's perspective; think of the face of a clock right in front of the victim and the rooming house would be at about 12:30. So if Dr. King "*was facing in that direction*" then there is quite obviously *no way* that a bullet shot from slightly to his right could enter his right cheek and then travel *right-to-left* through his body (unless he was leaning sharply downward and to his very extreme left, in which case he wouldn't be facing where they said he was!). *Also* above, they say that it may have been fired from street level, yet it somehow managed to go through someone on the second floor in a sharply downward direction! "The shrubbery below the window" is at street-level. So can somebody please tell us how a bullet from street level is going to have a *downward* trajectory when it goes through somebody on the second floor? The area *is* sloped a bit, but the second floor where Dr. King stood is *higher* than "the shrubbery below the window" not *lower*, as you can see in the photos below.

The fact is that the trajectory of the bullet contradicts the official version. That fact *necessarily* mandates that the shooter fired from a level substantially higher than the victim. Logic dictates that a shooting level lower, parallel, or slightly above Dr. King could not have resulted in the sharply downward trajectory of his wounds. Like we said: Trajectory does not tell lies … the government does.

Below is the actual photograph taken as Dr. King lay dying, seconds after the gunshot. The witnesses on the balcony are looking and pointing at where they thought it came from:

---

[346] U.S. House of Representatives, *Report of the Select Committee on Assassinations of the U.S. House of Representatives*, 1979. http://www.archives.gov/research/jfk/select-committee-report/part-2a.html

Seconds after the shooting, aides of Dr. King are obviously pointing up-and-over (to a position about "two o'clock-high") which was not even *near* the direction of the official version. Dr. King is laying shot, knees up, being comforted by a 4th aide, who is also looking up at approximately two o'clock-high.

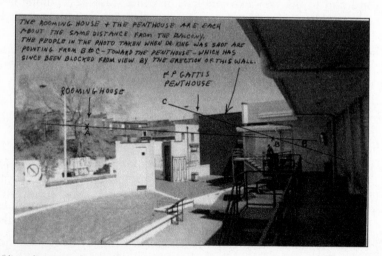

The "A-B" line diagrams the direct angle of Ray's rooming house, the "official" kill-angle. The "B-C" line diagrams where everyone on the balcony was looking and pointing, a dramatically different location. At the time of the assassination, it was a penthouse that provided the high-ground direct shot down at Martin Luther King, precisely what a professional shooter looks for: Positions are "2 o'clock-high" vs. "12:30-low."

Now here is what they were pointing at. At the time, prior to the erection of a wall that blocked it from view, at the position of "two o'clock high" was a tower which would have been the perfect "higher ground" selection of a professional shooter:

As a landmark, use the fire extinguisher on the balcony; the A-B line is to the window which was the alleged location of James Earl Ray, but is nowhere near the B-C line of where the witnesses were actually looking and pointing.

Now here are the witnesses pointing again in the real photograph, but with the same angles diagrammed in:

Therefore, something is clearly amiss "officially" folks:

The yellow line diagrams where they are actually pointing: 2 o'clock-high. The red line diagrams where they would have been pointing, 12:30-low, had they thought it came from Ray's rooming house across the street.

> **"The evidence in the photo taken just moments after the assassination is unequivocal. The claim that the witnesses are pointing to the rooming house where James Earl Ray was staying is a complete fabrication. The gunfire came from another direction high above the bathroom window."**[347]

The photographic evidence is day-one documentation from moments after the gunshot and it is unequivocal. In the newspapers that published that photo, the caption read that the men were pointing at the rooming house from where Ray allegedly fired. That was a bald-faced lie. That is *not* where they are pointing.

If you read the articles *"Martin Luther King: The Fatal Shot Came From a Different Direction"* and *"Overlooked Evidence in the Murder of Dr. Martin Luther King, Jr."* then you'll see the common sense in their findings. They're easily accesible at: http://whatreallyhappened.com/WRHARTICLES/ARTICLE1/overlooked.html.

Therefore, we have two direct substantiations that the gunshot—and there was only one—came not *not* from where the Official Version tells us it did, but from precisely where the autopsy report and the four witnesses in the photographic evidence were looking and/or pointing two o'clock-high. And it's a distinctly different location.

[347] Michael Rivero, "The Fatal Shot Came From a Different Direction," 2000, *WhatReallyHappened.com*. http://whatreallyhappened.com/WRHARTICLES/ARTICLE1/overlooked.php

Astoundingly, even though they were eyewitnesses to one of the most important crimes of the twentieth century, police *never* even interviewed Andrew Young and other key witnesses who were present:

> **"Young, Bevel, Jackson and Kiles told *TIME* that although they witnessed everything that happened, no authority from the Memphis Police, the Tennessee State Police or the FBI have ever asked them a single question."[348]**

Researcher Ted Wilburn took the matter a step further. He went *into* the second floor bathroom from where James Earl Ray supposedly shot, and photographed the second floor balcony where Dr. King had stood. He and fellow researcher Michael Rivero have diagrammed the supposed shot from that window:

> **"From this vantage point, we can confirm that the angle from the bathroom window to where Dr. King was killed is nearly level."[349]**

Therefore, the bullet could not have traversed its victim's body in a downward trajectory:

> **"The bathroom window where police officers claimed the bullet was fired from obviously does not support the eyewitnesses' pointing fingers or the doctor's autopsy report."[350]**

And *from* that bathroom window, at the *time* of the assassination, whoever would have been clumsily standing on the bathtub ledge in order to see out that window, as the Official Version still goes, <u>would not have had a clear shot</u> at Dr. King on the second floor balcony:

> **"In the original rooming house bathroom where James Earl Ray supposedly shot MLK from, there was a wall right by the window that actually made it impossible to take the shot. As I understand it, the wall was "removed for clarity" when the rooming house was taken over for the museum."[351]**

The idea of an expert assassin standing on the ledge of the bathtub and trying to line up a shot with a rifle that's too long to position there, is absolutely preposterous.

> **An "FBI ballistics expert testified that not even the most skilled gunman could have accurately fired a rifle in the manner claimed**

[348] Madison Gray, "The Witnesses," (in "Martin Luther King: An Assassination Remembered"), 31 March, 2008, *TIME Magazine.* http://www.time.com/time/specials/2007/article/0,28804,1726656_1726689_1726465,00.html

[349] Rivero, "The Fatal Shot"

[350] Ted Wilburn, "Overlooked Evidence in the Murder of Dr. Martin Luther King Jr.," 1999, *WhatReallyHappened.com.* http://whatreallyhappened.com/WRHARTICLES/ARTICLE1/overlooked.php

[351] Michael Rivero, email to author, 17 August 2010.

by the government prosecution. According to the expert, to effectively line up the rifle for such a shot, the butt of the rifle would have had to stick six inches into the wall. The prosecution countered that Ray had contorted himself into position around the bathtub in order to make the kill shot, which seems equally incredulous."[352]

Exculpatory Evidence in the Case of James Earl Ray

1. The bullet taken from Dr. King's body (and there was only one bullet) <u>did not come</u> from the rifle of the Defendant.
2. The bullets did not match. Metallurgical testing determined that the bullet that struck Dr. King <u>did not</u> match the bullets of the defendant.
3. Ray's rifle was <u>not the murder weapon</u>. It was <u>never matched</u> to the bullet that struck Dr. King. That was a crystal clear evidentiary finding: None of the many ballistics tests that were performed on the rifle that James Earl Ray allegedly used, were able to link that rifle to the bullet that struck Dr. Martin Luther King, Jr. Judge Joe Brown, who presided over two years of hearings on the rifle evidence, held up the defendant's rifle and told the jury: "It is my opinion that this is not the murder weapon."
4. Ray's rifle was not even "sighted in"; the scope had not been sighted properly, meaning that the shooter would not hit what he was looking at through the site (a mistake that an assassin would not and could not make). Judge Brown said: "This weapon literally could not have hit the broad side of a barn."
5. The trajectory of the bullet reveals that the shot did not come from where the prosecution said it did. It literally had to be from a dramatically different location.
6. The government prosecution team obviously tried everything within their substantial powers to prove that Ray's rifle was the murder weapon and to attempt to link the rifle ballistically with the bullet that hit MLK. They couldn't do it.
7. Ray (through his legal counsel) continuously sought advanced testing on the rifle, via the new methods that crime labs had developed and advances in ballistics, to prove conclusively that he could not have done the shooting. Those efforts were continuously denied. What was the government afraid of? Why wouldn't they allow advanced methods of testing? *

---

[352] Rivero, "The Fatal Shot"

8. New testimony has established evidence that there were two rifles at the crime scene: a "throw-down" rifle to set up the patsy and a "hot" rifle that was broken down and removed from the scene in conjunction with a coordinated plan of escape.

9. Ray could not have committed the crime. The man had an eighth-grade education. Even FBI Deputy Director William Sullivan, who led the FBI investigation of James Earl Ray, was convinced that an eighth-grade dropout like Ray could not possibly have managed everything that was alleged. Sullivan wrote:

"Someone, I feel sure, taught Ray how to get a false Canadian passport, how to get out of the country, and how to travel to Europe because he could never have managed it alone. And how did Ray pay for the passport and the airline tickets?"

10. The government was self-convinced that Ray should be convicted, but the victim's family certainly wasn't. They defended the accused killer straight down the line and even worked with attorneys for his release because they were that sure that he wasn't the man who killed Martin. "The Kings also presented evidence suggesting that Ray's gun could not have fired the fatal shot."

* Various reports substantiate years of efforts by the defendant's legal counsel to allow the rifle to be re-tested with advanced methods that had become available and scientifically acknowledged as more accurate. The fact that it was the defendant who actually sought the ballistics testing and it was the prosecution which forestalled those efforts speaks volumes about who was seeking the truth in this case and who wasn't (Ray appealed his conviction seven times, continually seeking the expansion of facts in evidence).

Source material for the above chart was derived primarily from the following:

A King-Sized Conspiracy, Dick Russell, 1999; *American Conspiracies*, Jesse Ventura & Dick Russell, 2010; "Overlooked evidence in the murder of Dr. Martin Luther King, Jr.", Ted Wilburn, 1999; "Martin Luther King – The Fatal Shot Came From a Different Direction", "The Martin Luther King Conspiracy Exposed in Memphis", Jim Douglass, Spring 2000, *Probe Magazine*; "Who Killed Martin Luther King?", Matt Alsdorf, *Slate Magazine*, December 15, 1999.

But even stronger exculpatory evidence exists that should have exonerated falsely accused James Earl Ray: His bullets *didn't match* the crime scene and *neither* did his rifle! That's right, folks; the top crime labs in the country were never able to match Ray's rifle to the murder evidence, and Ray's bullets were found to actually be different than the one that killed Dr. King.

Gary Revel was Special Investigator to the *House Select Committee on Assassinations* investigating the King assassination in 1977. He *immediately* realized that things were *dramatically* amiss:

> "OK, it's like this. Just pretend for a moment that you are an investigator and are asked to help investigate a high profile murder. You agree to take the assignment and begin your investigation. One of the first things you do is meet the convicted murderer. During your first interview you find he is far from being the cunning killer that the police and the press have made him out to be. This is exactly what happened in my attempt to investigate the killing of Martin Luther King Jr. After the interview and a few days of researching legal documents I was shocked to find the case had little merit. Still today very little evidence is available to convict the man if the case went to court, which it didn't- James Earl Ray was railroaded into a guilty plea."[353]

James Earl Ray was a habitual petty criminal. He went to jail for stealing a typewriter in Los Angeles. He tried to rob a taxicab in Chicago and botched it up and again got arrested. He was caught with postal money orders that were stolen, and he did three years in federal prison. Then he was caught robbing a grocery store in St. Louis. He was a small-time crook who was repeatedly caught at small-time crimes.

As Special Investigator Revel observed:

> "Is this the kind of man who could spend several months, single handedly, while being sought after as an escaped convict, travel throughout this country and internationally (Canada and Mexico), methodically, slowly and surely track down the high profile Nobel Peace Prize Winner and hero of the Civil Rights Movement, the Reverend and Dr. Martin Luther King Jr., then when finding him on April 4, 1968, shoot and kill him with one sure and certain pull of the trigger; he would then (again by himself) elude the entire Memphis Police Department (made easier earlier that day by the pullback of 4 tactical police units from the Lorraine Motel area- ordered by their Commander, Memphis Police Department Inspector Sam Evans) and most able Federal Bureau of Investigation directed by the infallible J. Edgar Hoover to escape to Canada and on to Europe."[354]

James Earl Ray was an eighth-grade dropout and it was evidenced in his unsuccessful "career" as a petty thief. *That* is one of the main reasons why most open-minded researchers, as well as the head of the FBI's team on the King murder case, concluded that there had to have been someone like the "Raoul" referred to by the defendant—a conspirator directing the actions of

---

[353] Gary Revel, "Investigating the Murder of MLK – People get Killed," 30 April 2010. http://garyrevel.wordpress.com/2010/04/30/investigating-the-murder-of-mlk-people-get-killed/

[354] Gary Revel, "Email to James Polk – CNN, CC: Soledad O'Brien and others," 8 April 2010. http://garyrevel.wordpress.com/2010/04/08/mlk-assassination-cnn-james-polk/

James Earl Ray—because he most certainly was *not* a master criminal and, acting alone, was clearly incapable of the sophisticated use of aliases (five were used), expertly forged passports and the finesse required for international escapes.

For example, Ray used the aliases of actual people living in Montreal, but he was using those aliases *prior* to his traveling there. Four of the five aliases he used during the nine-month period *prior* to the assassination, were the correct identities of real Canadians. *All four* lived in the same area of Toronto. And *three* of the aliases even bore a resemblance to James Earl Ray![355]

> **"Though Ray had used aliases throughout his criminal career, there is no evidence Ray had been to Toronto prior to fleeing there after the King murder, and no explanation for how he came to use these particular names."[356]**

As FBI Deputy Director William Sullivan, leader of the special FBI unit tracking James Earl Ray concluded:

> **"Ray was so stupid that I don't think he could have robbed a five-and-ten-cent store."[357]**

Therefore, the whole operation was far too complex for a petty criminal like James Earl Ray to have engineered it. That's why many serious researchers have "interpreted the evidence as a sophisticated operation which brought Ray into an assassination plot and then left him holding the bag at the scene of King's murder."[358]

That was essentially the scenario that the defendant himself detailed when he tried to withdraw his plea of guilty. He told investigators that a controller whom he knew only as "Raoul" had given him his instructions for purchasing and delivering the rifle and had also paid for the purchase of the rifle, the car and other items. Those instructions and cash had to have come from somewhere, that much is clear. Ray claimed that the gun had then been placed there to frame him and, therefore, it was not clear to him until later that he had been duped as part of a larger plot.

As Judge Joe Brown noted, the Defendant explained to the man at the gun shop that he was exchanging the rifle that he had originally purchased because "he was told by others" that the .243 caliber weapon he originally bought was "not a suitable weapon for the purpose."

- **Judge Brown**: "'Others,' o-t-h-e-r-s, I'm assuming that means the same to everyone else that it does to me."[359]

---

[355] Dr. Philip H. Melanson, *The Martin Luther King Assassination: New Revelations on the Conspiracy and Cover-Up* (S.P.I. Books, 1994).

[356] *Mary Ferrell Foundation,* "The Martin Luther King Assassination," http://www.maryferrell.org/wiki/index.php/Martin_Luther_King_Assassination (accessed 8 October 2011).

[357] Sullivan, *The Bureau*

[358] *Mary Ferrell Foundation,* "The Martin Luther King Assassination"

[359] Russell, "Judge Brown Slams Memphis"

There were a lot of other noteworthy irregularities about the crime in general and the crime scene in particular—and they are the types of irregularities which create genuine concern that the defendant was set up to take the fall for the crime, just as he claimed:

- There was not one eyewitness who saw the shooting;[360]
- There was not one eyewitness who claimed that the gunshot came from the bathroom window of the rooming house. And it has never been proven that the rifle shot actually came from there;[361]
- There were major credibility problems with the sole witness to Ray's allegedly fleeing the rooming house bathroom from which he is said to have fired the rifle;[362]
- Another witness, who actually *was* credible, testified that he remembered seeing James Earl Ray seated in his car, which was several blocks away, at the time of the shooting;[363]
- The rifle doesn't fit the crime scene—*literally*. The logistics of the bathroom at the rooming house at that time made firing from that bathroom window virtually impossible. It had a wall that prevented a weapon the size of the Remington Model 760 Gamemaster 30.06 caliber rifle from even *fitting* in the space between the window and a wall that was adjacent to it, at the time. And if the rifle had been positioned out the window so that it would actually fit into the small space, then the shooter would not have been able to look through the gunsight of the rifle to make the shot—there wasn't enough room! *And* that wall was later removed (which is suspicious) when the rooming house became part of the complex now known as the *National Civil Rights Museum*. With that wall there, it must have been pretty blinking obvious that no shooter would use it as their spot from which to take one of the most significant gunshots in history.[364]

Then go back and match all of those circumstantial inconsistencies with the brutally clear ballistics, and you've got a case that no Prosecutor in his or her right mind would take to trial; unless, of course, they were told that they *had* to by the Powers That Be. Remember, folks—The bullet that was removed from Martin Luther King's body **did not come from Ray's rifle**.

There were other things that bothered a lot of people. Andrew Young became Mayor of Atlanta, U.S. Ambassador to the United Nations, and a U.S. Congressman; but during the 1960s, he was a close supporter of Reverend King and had been right there at the motel in Memphis with him on the evening of the assassination. In addition to the obvious, several more obscure things *still* trouble Ambassador Young about the shooting.

---

[360] Jim Douglass, "Martin Luther King Conspiracy Exposed in Memphis," Spring 2000, *Probe Magazine. http://www.ratical.org/ratville/JFK/MLKconExp.html*

[361] Douglass, "Conspiracy Exposed"

[362] Douglass, "Conspiracy Exposed"

[363] Douglass, "Conspiracy Exposed"

[364] Revel, "Investigating the Murder"

- No member of any law enforcement agency investigating the shooting—Federal, State or local—<u>ever</u> bothered to interview him, even though he had obviously been positioned close to Dr. King at the moment of the shooting.
- In an obvious case of <u>destruction of a crime scene</u>, the City of Memphis had a large portion of the area of the shooting cut down by a landscaping crew the morning after the murder—evidence and all.

ANDREW YOUNG:

"One of the disturbing features about that day for us was that when we were pointing, we were pointing over across the street. There was a building there, but there was also a six-to-eight-foot pile of bushes and some people thought that the shot came from the bushes. The FBI said it came from a bathroom window. But when we got up the next morning, those bushes were gone."[365]

Also take note of a very important fact that the historical record conveniently ignores, sidesteps, obfuscates and otherwise attempts to obliterate from our collective memory on this case: James Earl Ray <u>never confessed to the murder</u> of Martin Luther King. From a legal standpoint, a guilty plea and a confession are two *entirely* different matters. Ray pleaded guilty in a manner that is known legally as taking the *Alford Plea*—based on the case law in *North Carolina vs. Alford, 1970*, which essentially states that a defendant can plead guilty if they believe that conviction is imminent, yet still maintain their innocence. So a defendant who believes that they are actually *not* guilty of a crime *still* submits a plea of guilty due to circumstances in which they believe that conviction is certain anyway—which is *exactly* what James Earl Ray's attorney had been *pounding* into him relentlessly.[366]

As James Earl Ray explained it to the investigator hired by his own attorney, he had been under the impression that he was only pleading "legally guilty" because he had been involved in the incident, not that he was actually admitting to himself having killed Dr. King. He also clearly believed that there was a conspiracy; in fact, he *knew* there was, because he had been directly involved in it—*he was the guy* that they'd framed.[367]

- "He never asked me either question. I would have answered that I did not shoot Dr. King but that I was unwittingly part of a conspiracy since I was hired to purchase a weapon of the type allegedly used in the killing and did bring it to Memphis."[368]
- "I signed the plea document but told Foreman I didn't intend to plead guilty. He went to work trying to persuade me to do so. He said I should cop a plea because the media had convicted me already."[369]

[365] Gray, "The Witnesses"

[366] USLegal.com: Definitions, "Alford Plea Law and Legal Definition," http://definitions.uslegal.com/a/alford-plea/ (accessed 11 October 2011).

[367] Gary Revel, "James Earl Ray Should Have Gotten a Trial," 16 April 2010. http://www.garyrevel.com/news/James%20Earl%20Ray%20Guilty%20Plea%20_%20Gary%20Revel_files/jamesearlrayshouldhavegottrial.htm

[368] James Earl Ray, *Who Killed Dr. Martin Luther King?: The True Story by the Alleged Assassin* (DaCapo Press, 1997) 120.

[369] James Earl Ray, *Who Killed Dr. King?*, 127.

The package conveniently left for police at the scene was so incriminating that it was virtually a "calling card" for the incrimination of James Earl Ray. It included:

- A Remington 30.06 rifle with serial number matching the rifle that James Earl Ray had purchased in Birmingham, Alabama;
- Ammunition for the rifle and a pair of surveillance binoculars that had James Earl Ray's fingerprints;
- A radio, upon which was Ray's inmate number from the Misssouri State Penitentiary;
- The FBI said they found several fingerprints on the items, including prints on the rifle, that matched James Earl Ray.[370]

Jesse Ventura and Dick Russell point out the obvious insanity of leaving that information for the police—*and* that he probably was <u>not</u> the one who left it:

> **"Later, Ray claimed that somebody else had left behind the bundle so as to incriminate him. In fact, one witness, Guy Canipe, said the package was actually dropped in the doorway to his store about ten minutes *before* the shot was fired. Makes a little more sense, doesn't it? Another witness, Olivia Catling, saw a fellow in a checkered shirt running out of the alley beside a building across from the Lorraine soon after the killing, who went screaming off in a green '65 Chevy."[371]**

So now ask yourself *this*: Would a *professional* assassin seriously take the <u>extra time</u> required to commit the singularly *insane* act of leaving behind very incriminating evidence before fleeing the scene? It just *does not make sense*.

And it apparently never even happened to begin with! Circuit Court Judge Arthur Hanes Jr. testified that the owner of the store was a credible witness—Guy Canipe. Mr. Canipe stated that the bundle of incriminating evidence was dropped off in front of his store before the assassination even took place. He remembered that and testified accordingly.[372]

Judge Hanes also testified that the firehouse near the assassination was already swarming with police prior to the shooting. Some were already watching Dr. King across the street. So "when they saw Dr. King go down, the fire house erupted like a beehive ... In addition to the time involved (if Ray had fired the weapon, returned to his room, boxed it, left the box in front, and then got into his car and drove away), it was circumstantially almost impossible to believe that somebody had been able to throw that (rifle) down and leave right in the face of that erupting fire station."[373] That's crucial evidence that's gone unreported, or at least *under*-reported, but speaks volumes about the impossibility of the official version.

Judge Hanes summarized how utterly preposterous the official version of events is, while referring to an official exhibit that depicted the crime:

[370] Melanson, *The King Asassination*, 87. James Earl Ray, *Who Killed Dr. King*, 100.
[371] Ventura & Russell, *American Conspiracies*
[372] Douglass, "Conspiracy Exposed"
[373] Douglass, "Conspiracy Exposed"

With police swarming all around like angry bees, "James Earl Ray had fired the shot from the bathroom on that second floor, come down that hallway into his room and carefully packed that box, tied it up, then had proceeded across the walkway the length of the building to the back where that stair from that door came up, had come down the stairs out the door, placed the Browning box containing the rifle and the radio there in the Canipe entryway."[374] He then simply got into his car and left, unassisted, and simply drove the same car from Memphis, Tennessee all the way to Atlanta, Georgia, never once challenged by a police officer. Yeah, *right*. *Sure* he did ...

Another witness stated "that right after the shot was fired he received a smoking rifle at the rear door of Jim's Grill from Clark. He broke the rifle down into two pieces and wrapped it in a tablecloth. Raul picked it up the next day."[375] That obviously has to be a *different* rifle than the *throw-down* weapon that incriminated the Defendant—there had to be *two rifles*; we know that Ray's rifle wasn't the murder weapon—and there had to be another rifle that was.

And another witness testified that he was in the rooming house at the exact time of the shooting, was in the hall near the bathroom that Ray supposedly shot from, and that at that time the door to the bathroom was open and there was no one in there. That fits with another testimony which places James Earl Ray sitting in his car at the time of the gunshot—a reliable eyewitness saw him there and he was several blocks away at the time.[376]

Ray was also known to be a rather lousy shot with a rifle, making the alleged feat—one perfect shot at a very high-profile target—additionally difficult to fathom. One thing that's crystal clear in all this is that there's *no way* that our Defendant, the eighth-grade dropout, masterminded this crime. It quite simply is just not even possible.

> **"Ray's skill with a rifle is dubious, and while he did commit armed robbery he had never harmed anyone previously during his criminal endeavors. And the man whose career one author described as "a record of bungled and ludicrously inept robberies and burglaries" purportedly managed to kill King with one perfect shot and then elude authorities for longer than any other American political assassin."[377]**

But we are told—instead of believing what is clear and obvious—to believe in our government's Official Version of events, that:

- Just like Lee Harvey Oswald—James Earl Ray was a "loner" and "lone nut" and there were no conspirators ...
- Just like they told us about Jack Ruby ...

[374] Douglass, "Conspiracy Exposed"
[375] Douglass, "Conspiracy Exposed"
[376] Douglass, "Conspiracy Exposed"
[377] *Mary Ferrell Foundation*, "The Martin Luther King Assassination,"

- And (a very short time later when Bobby Kennedy was murdered) just like they told us about Sirhan Bishara Sirhan …

- Even though the "Official Versions" are full of impossibilities and gaping holes so huge that you could drive a truck through them …
- And even though there was NO APPARENT MOTIVE for James Earl Ray, just like there was none for Oswald, none for Ruby, and none for Sirhan.

In Ray's case, he was clearly a small-time criminal, with *no* motive for murder:

> **"A petty criminal, Ray seems unlikely to have committed the crime purely out of racial hatred, and anecdotes of his racism are thin. The idea that he killed King in order to achieve notoriety is implausible given the lengths to which he went to avoid capture (nearly succeeding)."[378]**

He had no known motive for killing Martin Luther King, nor was one presented by the prosecution. To this day, there is no known motive and no motive has ever been given—its absence is very conspicuous:

> **"Prosecutors did not outline a motive for the killing or accuse Ray of being a racist. He repeatedly but unsuccessfully sought the trial that his guilty plea had forestalled."[379]**

Another huge factor is that James Earl Ray had *no* history of violence: His crimes were *thefts*—stealing money in order to *get* money—and he made a point of not hurting people in the process. His history backs that up. The defendant's brother spelled it out plain and simple for all to see. He said:

- "If my brother did kill King he did it for a lot of money—he never did anything if it wasn't for money …"[380]
- Ray's other brother echoed the same sentiment:

> **"I said if he had done it there had to be a lot of money involved because he wouldn't do it for hatred or just because he didn't like somebody, because that, is not his line of work."[381]**

But he *was* the perfect "patsy"; he was enough of a crook to follow the scent of making some money, but not smart enough to realize that he was in the process of being set up. *That* is why many serious researchers "have interpreted the evidence as a sophisticated operation which brought Ray into an assassination plot and then left him holding the bag at the scene of King's murder."[382] That scenario

---

[378] *Mary Ferrell Foundation*, "The Martin Luther King Assassination," (parenthetical comment in original)

[379] BBC News, "Questions left hanging by James Earl Ray death," 23 April 1998. http://news.bbc.co.uk/2/hi/americas/82893.stm

[380] *Report of the Select Committee on Assassinations*, 1979.

[381] *Report of the Select Committee on Assassinations*, 1979.

[382] *Mary Ferrell Foundation*, "The Martin Luther King Assassination"

certainly makes a *lot* more sense than the "official version" of events, which is not only preposterous, but literally impossible.

HISTORICAL PERSPECTIVE

Rioting in over 100 American cities was the immediate response to the assassination of Martin Luther King. A man of peace and reason had been gunned down in broad daylight and nothing less than rioting in the streets should have been expected.

The period of the 1960's was known for hippies and the politics of peace and love, but the hard realities of contemporary events sent it rapidly freefalling from the *Summer of Love* in 1967 to the upheaval, one year later, of tanks and armored personnel carriers moving National Guard soldiers in to "protect" American streets from their own people. We were a nation in turmoil toward the end of the decade. And it was the assassination of Martin Luther King that precipitated that social descent:

- The bloody *Battle of Khe Sanh* and then the relentless onslaught of the *Tet Offensive*, reveal the real horrors of the Vietnam War to a shocked American public closely following its hopelessness at home on their televisions;
- North Korea captures the crew of the *USS Pueblo*, a Naval Intelligence vessel, and holds the ship and its eighty-three-man crew hostage, for violating Korea's territorial waters;
- Anti-war protesters take over many of the nation's college campuses, openly defying police and National Guard soldiers who are called in to "maintain order";
- Huge Civil Rights protests take place in many major cities and universities;
- In response to his broad public disapproval, President Johnson announces that he will not seek re-election;

- Martin Luther King and his Civil Rights marches gain momentum in leading the nation in a new direction, away from the commitment to an un-winnable war;
- Then Dr. King is cut down in his prime;
- Burning cities are on the television news every night, as rioters react to their new sense of hopelessness and frustration;
- Senator Robert F. Kennedy declares his candidacy for President and quickly looks like he is on his way to winning the nomination and becoming President. And then *he too* is cut down in his prime on June 6 by what they officially tell us is *another* lone nut, in *another* non-conspiracy;
- It seems like every time you turn on your television and begin watching a T.V. show, you are suddenly hearing, "We interrupt this program for a *Special News Bulletin*";
- The Democratic Convention in August 1968 turns into a bloodbath right on the streets of Chicago, with police beating peaceful protesters and newscasters alike—filmed live and watched around the world;
- *ALL* of the above happened in an eight-month period between January-August 1968.

Martin Luther King had interrupted his plans and come to Memphis, Tennessee to lead a workers' strike by sanitation workers there. Martin had been worried that the strike was showing signs of violence, and his purpose in going was to lead a peaceful march and because he knew that his presence there would help to *keep* it peaceful.

James Earl Ray appealed his conviction seven times, continually seeking permission to introduce new evidence. Those requests were summarily denied.

Ray's last legal effort concentrated on tests he wanted conducted on the rifle that prosecutors say was the murder weapon. It had been purchased by Ray and was found near the murder scene moments after King was shot, with Ray's fingerprints on it. But Ray claimed it was placed there to frame him.

Martin Luther King's family filed a wrongful death civil lawsuit presenting ballistics evidence that the rifle of James Earl Ray could not have fired the gunshot.

In a 1999 court decision that would be earth-shattering but for the fact that few are aware of it, the jury found that Martin Luther King was killed by a conspiracy that involved Jowers and "others, including governmental agencies." James Earl Ray was not alive to hear that he; died in prison the year before.

As important as the arrest of James Earl Ray had supposedly been, it didn't stop politics from rearing its ugly head. Get a load of this little nugget, direct from the Deputy Director of the FBI:

> "Ray was in custody in London for two days before Hoover released the story to the press. He waited until the day of Bobby Kennedy's funeral to break the news so that the FBI could steal the headline from Kennedy one last time. I told Hoover that we

should give the credit for Ray's capture to the RCMP (Royal Canadian Mounted Police). Hoover said no and the FBI falsely got the credit."[383]

As horrible as the above fact is, it was nothing compared to what had already been done against Dr. King while he was alive. The United States government, through the FBI, employed a series of covert action programs in an attempt to destroy the Civil Rights Movement and the momentum it was gaining across the country. Those efforts even included blackmail. Dr. King was specifically targeted. The project was known under the acronym COINTELPRO (from "Counter Intelligence Program"). Other political activists were also specifically targeted, including Fred Hampton and Mark Clark (their deaths are detailed in Chapter 8 of this book), Dick Gregory, Stokely Carmichael, H. "Rap" Brown, Huey Newton, Eldridge Cleaver, Bobby Seale, David Hilliard, Geronimo Pratt, and Jeff Fort. For an excellent list of official documents related to COINTELPRO, see: http://www.icdc.com/~paulwolf/cointelpro/cointel.htmI

The following are *direct quotes* from the Final Report of a United States Senate study of intelligence activities:

- "From December 1963 until his death in 1968, Martin Luther King, Jr. was the target of an intensive campaign by the Federal Bureau of Investigation to 'neutralize' him as an effective civil rights leader. In the words of the man in charge of the FBI's 'war' against Dr. King:

  'No holds were barred. We have used [similar] techniques against Soviet agents. [The same methods were] brought home against any organization against which we were targeted. We did not differentiate. This is a rough, tough business.'

  The FBI collected information about Dr. King's plans and activities through an extensive surveillance program, employing nearly every intelligence-gathering technique at the Bureau's disposal."

- "The FBI's program to destroy Dr. King as the leader of the civil rights movement entailed attempts to discredit him with churches, universities, and the press. Steps were taken to attempt to convince the National Council of Churches, the Baptist World Alliance, and leading Protestant ministers to halt financial support of the Southern Christian Leadership Conference (SCLC), and to persuade them that "Negro leaders should completely isolate King and remove him from the role he is now occupying in civil rights activities."

- "The FBI responded to Dr. King's receipt of the Nobel Peace Prize by attempting to undermine his reception by foreign heads of state and American ambassadors in the countries that he planned to visit."

- "The FBI offered to play for reporters tape recordings allegedly made from microphone surveillance of Dr. King's hotel rooms. The FBI mailed Dr. King

[383] Sullivan, *The Bureau*

a tape recording made from its microphone coverage. According to the Chief of the FBI's Domestic Intelligence Division, the tape was intended to precipitate a separation between Dr. King and his wife in the belief that the separation would reduce Dr. King's stature. The tape recording was accompanied by a note which Dr. King and his advisers interpreted as a threat to release the tape recording unless Dr. King committed suicide."[384]

It's thought by many that Martin Luther King became a serious threat to "The Powers That Be" by moving into dangerous territory during the last two years of his life. The Nobel Peace Prize winner in 1964, a preacher and pacifist for much of his life, his reputation had typically been one of seeking the peaceful course of non-violent resistance to oppression. However, that changed dramatically in his last years.

He came to believe that the oppression—not only to Blacks, but to the poor under-classes all around the world—was deeply rooted in an economic system so unjust, that it needed to be corrected.

That change is well-documented in his speeches. King was one of the first U.S. leaders to strongly oppose the Vietnam War. He spoke in an eloquence that inspired and united millions of diverse people around the world in a common cause—to end the ongoing insanity of war:

> "Somehow this madness must cease. We must stop now. I speak as a child of God and brother to the suffering poor of Vietnam. I speak for those whose land is being laid waste, whose homes are being destroyed, whose culture is being subverted. I speak for the poor of America who are paying the double price of smashed hopes at home, and death and corruption in Vietnam. I speak as a citizen of the world, for the world as it stands aghast at the path we have taken. I speak as one who loves America, to the leaders of our own nation: The great initiative in this war is ours; the initiative to stop it must be ours."[385]

He humanized the "enemy"—which was a direct threat to the military authority of the United States:

> "They know they must move on or be destroyed by our bombs. So they go, primarily women and children and the aged. They watch as we poison their water, as we kill a million acres of their crops. They must weep as the bulldozers roar through their areas preparing to destroy the precious trees. They wander into the hospitals with at least twenty casualties from American firepower for one Vietcong-inflicted injury. So far we may have killed a million of them, mostly children. They wander into the towns and see thousands of the children, homeless, without clothes, running in packs

---

[384] United States Senate, *Final Report of the Select Committee to Study Governmental Operations with respect to Intelligence Activities: Supplementary Detailed Staff Reports on Intelligence Activities and the Rights of Americans*, 23 April 1976. http://www.icdc.com/~paulwolf/cointelpro/churchfinalreportIIIb.htm

[385] The Reverend Dr. Martin Luther King Jr., "Beyond Vietnam," 4 April 1967, New York, NY. http://brainz.org/martin-luther-king-speech-beyond-vietnam/

on the streets like animals. They see the children degraded by our soldiers as they beg for food. They see the children selling their sisters to our soldiers, soliciting for their mothers."[386]

These changes in his beliefs began to broaden his base: he was no longer a Black preacher rallying families of former slaves—he was a dynamic international leader spearheading an attack against the wealthiest economic powers on the planet on behalf of all who were poor and under-represented in that system. That was why he became perceived as a threat.

"True compassion is more than flinging a coin to a beggar. It comes to see that an edifice which produces beggars needs restructuring. A true revolution of values will soon look uneasily on the glaring contrast of poverty and wealth. With righteous indignation, it will look across the seas and see individual capitalists of the West investing huge sums of money in Asia, Africa, and South America, only to take the profits out with no concern for the social betterment of the countries, and say, "This is not just."[387]

And he didn't stop there, he went further:

"A true revolution of values will lay hand on the world order and say of war, "This way of settling differences is not just." This business of burning human beings with napalm, of filling our nation's homes with orphans and widows, of injecting poisonous drugs of hate into the veins of peoples normally humane, of sending men home from dark and bloody battlefields physically handicapped and psychologically deranged, cannot be reconciled with wisdom, justice, and love. A nation that continues year after year to spend more money on military defense than on programs of social uplift is approaching spiritual death."[388]

In his final year he was busy organizing a Poor People's March on Washington— it was expected by some to practically close down the nation's capitol. His words were their rallying cry:

"We are now faced with the fact, my friends, that tomorrow is today. We are confronted with the fierce urgency of now. In this unfolding conundrum of life and history, there is such a thing as being too late. Procrastination is still the thief of time ..."

"In 1957, a sensitive American official overseas said that it seemed to him that our nation was on the wrong side of a world revolution. During the past ten years, we have seen emerge a pattern of suppression which has now justified the presence of U.S. military

[386] Dr. King, "Beyond Vietnam"
[387] Dr. King, "Beyond Vietnam"
[388] Dr. King, "Beyond Vietnam"

advisors in Venezuela. This need to maintain social stability for our investments accounts for the counterrevolutionary action of American forces in Guatemala. It tells why American helicopters are being used against guerrillas in Cambodia and why American napalm and Green Beret forces have already been active against rebels in Peru. It is with such activity in mind that the words of the late John F. Kennedy come back to haunt us. Five years ago he said, "Those who make peaceful revolution impossible will make violent revolution inevitable."[389]

"We will be marching for these and a dozen other names and attending rallies without end, unless there is a significant and profound change in American life and policy."[390]

Therefore, he obviously and increasingly posed a major threat to the strongest business and political powers in the world. It's thought by some that those powers found it necessary to eliminate that threat.

Dr. King clearly knew that his days were numbered, and that the number was probably a pretty low one, at that:

"He was so preoccupied with his death, so obsessed with its likely occurrence, that in the last years, he could relax only in a room with no windows because he was tortured with worry about who might pull the trigger. His eyes fell on strangers, wondering if they were the messenger of death."[391]

And, contrary to the notions that honoring Dr. King in death somehow absolves and cleanses the historical conscience, White America is largely to blame for his murder:

"White Americans have long since forgotten just how much heat and hate the thought of King could whip up. They have absolved themselves of blame for producing, or failing to fight, the murderous passions that finally tracked King down in Memphis, Tenn. If one man held the gun, millions more propped him up and made it seem a good, even valiant idea. In exchange for collective guilt, whites have given King lesser victories, including a national holiday."[392]

It can be fairly said that—to a large extent—Dr. King knowingly sacrificed a great many years of his life, in a philosophical gamble to advance the civil and human rights movements. The final result of that wager has not yet been determined:

"In the end, King used the inevitability of a premature death to argue for social change and measure our commitment to truth."[393]

[389] Dr. King, "Beyond Vietnam"

[390] Dr. King, "Beyond Vietnam"

[391] Michael Eric Dyson, *April 4, 1968: Martin Luther King Jr.'s Death and How it Changed America* (Basic Civitas Books, 2008).

[392] Dyson, *April 4, 1968*

[393] Dyson, *April 4, 1968*

That commitment to truth, from a historical standpoint, is still in the process of being measured. One would think that the moral yardstick used to *take* that measurement should, in fairness, be one of which Dr. King would approve. And it can be fairly said that the social change for which he argued—economic equality in a nation which is striving for the progress of humanity, rather than simply competing for commercial dominance—has not yet been achieved. The man had a lot more in mind than just a national holiday.

BIBLIOGRAPHY

For a quick course in the amazing evidentiary history of the alleged murder weapon,see:

"Who Killed Martin Luther King?",

"Judge Brown Slams Memphis over the King Case", Dick Russell, *Probe Magazine*, July-August 1998. http://ctka.net/pr798-judge.html

"A King-Sized Conspiracy", Dick Russell, *1999, High Times*

American Conspiracies: Lies, Lies, and More Dirty Lies that the Government Tells Us, Jesse Ventura & Dick Russell, 2010

"Questions left hanging by James Earl Ray's death", BBC News,, April 23, 1998. http://news.bbc.co.uk/2/hi/americas/82893.stm

The Martin Luther King Assassination: New Revelations on the Conspiracy and Cover-Up, Philip H. Melanson, 1994

"The Martin Luther King Conspiracy Exposed in Memphis", Jim Douglass, Spring 2000, *Probe Magazine.*

Murder in Memphis: The FBI and the Assassination of Martin Luther King, Mark Lane & Dick Gregory, 1993

Who Killed Dr. Martin Luther King?: The True Story by the Alleged Assassin, James Earl Ray, James Earl Ray, 1997

The Bureau: My Thirty Years in Hoover's FBI, FBI Deputy Director William Sullivan; 1979

"Testimony of William Schaap, King Family vs. Jowers and Other Unknown Co-Conspirators", 1999, Circuit Court of Tennessee, Division 4, The Honorable James E. Swearingen presiding. http://www.ratical.org/ratville/JFK/MLKv9Schaap.html

"Report of the Select Committee on Assassinations of the U.S. House of Representatives, Washington, DC", United States Government Printing Office, 1979

"Overlooked Evidence in the Murder of Dr. Martin Luther King, Jr.", Ted Wilburn, Special Correspondent *to WhatReallyHappened.com, 1999.* http://whatreallyhappened.com/WRHARTICLES/ARTICLE1/overlooked.php

"Martin Luther King – The Fatal Shot Came From a Different Direction", Michael Rivero, 2000, *WhatReallyHappened.com* http://whatreallyhappened.com/WRHARTICLES/ARTICLE1/overlooked.php

"The Martin Luther King Assassination", Mary Ferrell Foundation http://www.maryferrell.org/wiki/index.php/Martin_Luther_King_Assassination

"James Earl Ray Should Have Gotten A Trial", Gary Revel, April 16, 2010, *Newsvine. com* http://gary-2.newsvine.com/_news/2010/04/16/4166623-why-james-earl-ray-should-have-gotten-a-trial

"The Witnesses", Madison Gray, March 31, 2008, in "Martin Luther King: An Assassination Remembered", TIME Magazine, March 31, 2008. http://www.time.com/time/specials/2007/article/0,28804,1726656_1726689_1726465,00. html

"Who Killed Martin Luther King?", Matt Alsdorf, *Slate Magazine*, December 15, 1999

April 4, 1968: Martin Luther King, Jr.'s Death and How It Changed America, Michael Eric Dyson, 2008

"FINAL REPORT OF THE SELECT COMMITTEE TO STUDY GOVERNMENTAL OPERATIONS WITH RESPECT TO INTELLIGENCE ACTIVITIES; UNITED STATES SENATE: SUPPLEMENTARY DETAILED STAFF REPORTS ON INTELLIGENCE ACTIVITIES AND THE RIGHTS OF AMERICANS", April 23, 1976. http://www.icdc.com/~paulwolf/cointelpro/churchfinalreportIIIb.htm

CHAPTER 7

Robert F. Kennedy –
June 6, 1968

*U.S. Senator/Attorney General of the
United States/Candidate for President of
the United States*

VICTIM	**SENATOR ROBERT F. KENNEDY**
Cause of Death	MULTIPLE GUNSHOTS
Official Verdict	Senator Kennedy was assassinated by a lone gunman, Sirhan Bishara Sirhan, who fired from a distance, not at point-blank range, in the kitchen of the Ambassador Hotel. Sirhan was found guilty "alone and not in concert with anyone else" of Murder in the First Degree.
Actual Circumstances	Shot three times from behind, bullets traversing body at an upward angle, back-to-front. Coroner determined that the kill shot came from directly behind the right ear and at

point-blank range. Defendant was never <u>anywhere near</u> enough to the victim to have fired the kill shot and, furthermore, shots from the Defendant could not have left a back-to-front bullet path, because Defendant was in front of the victim. Therefore, bullet trajectory would necessarily have been front-to-back.

Inconsistencies

1. Sirhan was not at any point close enough to Senator Kennedy to have fired the kill shot. Coroner determined that the shot was fired from within one to three inches away from left ear. About the only thing that everybody in that room agreed with was that Sirhan was never that close.

2. Bullet trajectories indicate that primary shooter was at close range, behind target, and to his right. Sirhan was in front of Senator Kennedy and to his left, walking towards him. So it is not possible for bullets fired from his gun to have entered Senator Kennedy from behind and then traversed back-to-front.

3. Sirhan held his gun parallel to Senator Kennedy, therefore the trajectories traversing upwards are also totally contradictory to his actual position.

4. Sirhan's gun held only eight bullets but fourteen bullets were fired, necessitating at least two shooters. *At least fourteen shots were identified.*

5. Psychiatrists determined that Sirhan was the most easily hypnotizable subject they'd ever seen; his notebooks contained repetitious entries such as "RFK must die" that were determined to have been written as post-hypnotic suggestion; conditions indicate that he was in a trance state during the murder.

6. Investigators from the Los Angeles Police Department acknowledged that they were completely unable to document any of Sirhan's actions during a six-week period prior to the assassination which they labeled his "White Fog" period. They also acknowledged that such a complete disappearance was extremely unusual.

7. Sirhan Bishara Sirhan has been imprisoned since 1968 for a crime he did not commit because he was convicted of "Murder in the First Degree" and did not meet the requirements of that charge; he did not possess conscious intent at the moment of the crime, therefore, the act was not premeditated; nor did he possess malice aforethought. The evidence proves conclusively that the defendant was never at any point close enough to the victim to have fired

the fatal shot. It has also been proven that the trajectories of the shots that hit Senator Kennedy could not have come from the defendant's gun. Those facts mandate a verdict of "Not Guilty" when a person is accused of "Murder in the First Degree." Therefore he should be a free man and, technically, never should have been convicted on that charge in the first place.

"There is no doubt in our minds that no fewer than 14 shots were fired in the pantry on that evening and that Sirhan did not in fact kill Senator Kennedy."

—Robert Joling, forensic scientist who examined the case for decades.

If you believe that an alleged assassin could have fired fourteen bullets from an eight-shot gun then the official version probably won't keep you up at night. … but it *has* kept a lot of other folks up at night—especially those who believe in concepts like innocent until proven guilty, fair trials, and a justice system that should at least have the appearance of actually being just.

In addition to the aforementioned impossibility, Sirhan Bishara Sirhan also allegedly fired the kill shot from point-blank range—even though in reality (confirmed by multiple eyewitnesses) he was never at any moment anywhere near enough the victim to have fired such a shot.[394]

In addition, the angles of the shots are all off … way off. The shots that struck Senator Kennedy traversed his body from back-to-front (per the experts).[395] If those shots had been fired from the alleged assassin, then they would have, by necessity, traversed the victim's body front-to-back; because one thing that everybody agrees upon is that Sirhan was in front of RFK.

The shots also traversed the body (also per the experts) in a downward direction, entering, for example, above the ear and then traveling downward.[396] Had they come from Sirhan's direction, they would have been, by necessity, traveling upward—his gun was not held in a location and angle from which the shots could have been going downward in the victim.

The bullets clearly traversed in directions and at angles that were not physically possible given the alleged assassin's location at the crime scene.[397] So if the shots that hit Senator Kennedy actually *had* come from Sirhan's gun, then they would have had to defy the laws of physics—and bullets don't do that.

"The four bullets which touched Kennedy all hit on his back right side and were traveling forward relative to his body. Kennedy

---

[394] Mary Ferrell Foundation, "The Robert Kennedy Assassination," http://www.maryferrell.org/wiki/index.php/Robert_Kennedy_Assassination (accessed 12 Feb 2012).

[395] Mary Ferrell Foundation, "The Robert Kennedy Assassination"

[396] William Klaber & Philip H. Melanson, Shadow Play: The Murder of Robert F. Kennedy, the Trial of Sirhan Sirhan, and the Failure of American Justice (St Martins Pres, 1997).

[397] Klaber & Melanson, Shadow Play

was walking towards Sirhan, his body was always facing Sirhan during the shots, and afterwards he even fell backwards before saying his last lucid words, ('Is everyone all right?')—at each and every moment facing toward Sirhan. It is impossible for bullets out of Sirhan's gun to have hit Kennedy's backside and been traveling forward unless Kennedy was almost entirely turned around."[398]

"The upward angle of every shot was so steep as to be much closer to straight up than horizontal (80 degrees). And yet, all witnesses claim Sirhan's gun was completely horizontal for his first two shots, after which

his gun hand was repeatedly slammed against a steam table (and now so far away from Kennedy that any errant shots of such upwardness would have been twenty feet high before reaching Kennedy, as opposed to entering Kennedy's backside as they did)."[399]

"According to the autopsy all the wound tracks were upward: the Kennedy head wound was at a mild 15 degrees off the horizontal, but the three back shots were described as at a steep 59, 67 and 80 degrees, as though a gun had been pressed to the senator's back and pointed up so as not to protrude. In contrast, Sirhan was said to have fired with his gun parallel to the floor."[400]

Forensic expert Dr. Robert J. Joling, J.D., was also a Professor of Medical Law, as well as a judge and attorney. He conducted extensive scientific testing of the evidence in this case. Accompanied by Forensic Acoustic Expert Phil Van Praag, they undertook a comprehensive study of all evidence. Their study determined that a total of *at least* fouteen gunshots were fired at the time of the murder. When the bullets taken from the various victims in the room are added to the bullets that lodged elsewhere in the room, guess what folks?—The total isn't the eight in Sirhan's eight-shot gun, the total is fourteen. The acoustic evidence confirms it:

"There is no doubt in our minds that no fewer than fourteen shots were fired in the pantry on that evening and that Sirhan did not, in fact, kill Senator Kennedy."[401]

They reach that conclusion for an extremely important reason; because it is **scientifically impossible** that Sirhan killed him:

---

[398] "Simple Facts about the Robert F. Kennedy Assassination," http://flag.blackened.net/daver/misc/rfk.html (accessed 2 May 2011).

[399] "Simple Facts about the Robert F. Kennedy Assassination," http://flag.blackened.net/daver/misc/rfk.html

[400] Klaber & Melanson, *Shadow Play*, 109.

[401] Robert Joling & Philip Van Prag, *An Open and Shut Case,* cited in James Randerson, "New evidence challenges official picture of Kennedy shooting," 22 February 2008, *theguardian.* http://www.guardian.co.uk/science/2008/feb/22/kennedy.assassination (accessed 1 Jan. 2011).

DR. JOLING:

"It can be established conclusively that Sirhan did not shoot Senator Kennedy. And in fact not only did he not do it, he <u>could not</u> have done it."[402]

Actor Robert Vaughn was a close friend of Senator Kennedy and has closely followed the development of evidence in the case, not briefly, but over a period of several decades. As Vaughn notes with importance:

> The results of the study **"present indisputable scientific data that leads to the inescapable conclusion that two guns were fired from two different locations and two different directions on that fatal night."[403]**

On top of all that, here's another very interesting point: the Defendant doesn't remember any of it. We don't mean he's a bit foggy from all the adrenaline and that there are a few little things that he can't remember—we mean he can't remember *any* of it.[404]

Then there was the alleged assassin's "White Fog" period: LAPD investigators were amazed to find a six-week period prior to the assassination of Senator Kennedy where the suspect could not be accounted for at all. He had simply disappeared from the face of the earth. Combine that with the fact that the man, even under hypnotism, cannot recall his own life during that period, and it's not too big a leap to get to *Manchurian Candidate* scenario, is it?

> **"Meanwhile, Special Unit Senator, the LAPD's assassination task force, had constructed a meticulous timetable of Sirhan's activities prior to the shooting. "We took him back for more than a year with some intensity—where he'd been, what he'd been doing, who he'd been seeing. But there was this ten—or twelve-week gap, like a blanket of white fog, we could never penetrate, and which Sirhan himself appeared to have a complete amnesia block about," says Bill Jordan, the night watch commander at Ramparts detectives who was Sirhan's first interrogator."[405]**

Chief Psychiatrist Bernard Diamond noted immediately that Sirhan had been previously programmed under hypnosis:

> **"Earlier, when Diamond saw how quickly Sirhan could be hypnotized, and realized that he had been hypnotized frequently before, Diamond put him into a light trance, gave him a yellow**

---

[402] Pierre Thomas, "Two Guns Used in RFK Shooting, Experts Say," 27 March, 2008, ABC News (emphasis added). http://abcnews.go.com/GMA/LegalCenter/story?id=4534689 (accessed 4 Jan. 2011).

[403] Robert Vaughn, Ph.D., "Commentary re: *An Open and Shut Case*," 2008. http://www.anopenandshutcase.com/commentary/ (accessed 4 Feb. 2011).

[404] Klaber & Melanson, *Shadow Play*

[405] Peter Evans, *Nemesis: The True Story of Aristotle Onassis, Jackie O, and the Love Triangle That Brought Down the Kennedys* (William Morrow: 2004) 213.

legal pad, and told him to write something about Kennedy. Sirhan wrote "RFK RFK RFK RFK RFK." Diamond asked him to write more than Kennedy's name, and Sirhan wrote, "Robert F. Kennedy. Robert F. Kennedy." What about Kennedy? Sirhan wrote. "RFK RFK RFK RFK RFK must die RFK must die RFK must die," nine times, until Diamond told him to stop.

The experiment, witnessed by Kaiser and Dr. Seymour Pollack, director of the University of Southern California's Institute of Psychiatry and Law, who represented the district attorney's office, had been continuing along these lines for a while when Diamond asked whether Sirhan thought he was "crazy."

"No no no no," wrote Sirhan, still in a trance. If he wasn't crazy, why was he writing in such a crazy fashion? "Practice practice practice practice practice," Sirhan wrote. Practice for what? "Mind control mind control mind control mind."[406]

A thorough study of Sirhan's notebooks, which it was professionally ascertained were clearly written while in a hypnotic trance, also made many suspect that money had changed hands at some point:

"The same question was also troubling defense team investigator Bob Kaiser, who suspected that the answer might be linked to the references to money in Sirhan's notebooks. The more he thought about it, the more it seemed to him that money had changed hands, or been promised, and Sirhan had been hypnotized to forget it. "You wrote certain things over and over and over again," he pressed Sirhan. "And when you wrote about killing Kennedy, you join it to the unexplainable phrase, 'I have never heard Please pay to the order of of of of.'" But Sirhan stonewalled: He couldn't remember writing it; he couldn't even remember the notebooks, he insisted."[407]

The chart that follows proves that there must have been a second gun. But prior to reading that, bear in mind that they never established linkage of the first gun.

The Firearms Panel that examined the evidence concluded as follows:

"The examiners found that the Sirhan gun cannot be identified with the bullets from the crime scene."[408]

Obviously, in a case where the U.S. government's official version is that there was *not* a conspiracy, proof that there had to be a second gun proves that there *was* a conspiracy and that the official version that it was a "lone nut" is the nuttiest thing out there.

"The specter of a second gun changes most everything."[409]

---

[406] Evans, *Nemesis*, 217.
[407] Evans, *Nemesis*, 214.
[408] Klaber & Melanson, *Shadow Play*, 123.
[409] Klaber & Melanson, *Shadow Play*, 101.

Findings of Prominent Ballistics Expert William W. Harper

A review of the ballistics evidence by noted Criminalist and Ballistics Expert, William W. Harper, was very revealing. Harper studied the bullets in evidence, the autopsy, and the police trajectory diagrams and then constructed an affidavit to serve as legally sworn testimony to his findings. His conclusions from that affidavit follow:

▶ **PRINCIPAL FINDING:**

"Robert Kennedy was fired upon from two distinct firing positions.

Firing Position A, the position of Sirhan, was located directly in front of the Senator, with Sirhan face to face with the Senator. This position is established by more than a dozen eyewitnesses. A second firing position, Firing Position B, is clearly established by the autopsy report. It was located in close proximity to the Senator, immediately to his right and rear. It was from this position that 4 (four) shots were fired, three of which entered the Senator's body ... It is extremely unlikely that any of the bullets fired by Sirhan's gun ever struck the body of Robert Kennedy."[410]

It should also be noted that after Sirhan was convicted and sentenced, Harper later proved to a scientific certainty that the bullets removed from Senator Kennedy and the bullet removed from newsman William Weisel were fired from two different guns.[411]

Harper's findings were later corroborated by an LAPD document, kept secret until its release in 1988 from LAPD to the California State Archives where the document can currently be viewed. The document confirms that LAPD ran its own independent analysis of the two bullets using a Hycon Balliscon camera. The following are the verbatim critical conclusions of LAPD Criminalist Larry Baggett:

▶ **"HYCON BALLISANIC CAMERA**

DIFF. OF 1/2 DEGREE IN RIFLING ANGLES KENNEDY BULLET FIRED FROM BARREL WITH SHARPER RIFLING THAN WEISEL

▶ **CONCLUSION**

1. KENNEDY AND WEISEL BULLETS NOT FIRED FROM SAME GUN.
2. KENNEDY BULLET NOT FIRED FROM SIRHAN'S REVOLVER."[412]

Later research has also revealed that LAPD used a substitute gun (not the gun that Sirhan had actually fired) in its test comparisons that were used as evidence at trial, apparently to attempt to establish linkage to the bullets which hit the Senator.[413]

---

[410] Klaber & Melanson, 1997, *Shadow Play*, page 108

[411] Simkin, Spartacus Educational, 2007

[412] *California State Archives*

[413] Rose Lynn Mangan, *SPECIAL EXHIBIT 10 REPORT: Ballistics Research in the Assassination of Senator Robert F. Kennedy*, 2001

Three audio tapes recorded that night were examined and tested by top forensics acoustics expert, Dr. Michael H.L. Hecker of the *Stanford Research Institute*. Dr. Hecker's study determined that a *minimum* of ten gunshots were fired (the gun of Sirhan was only capable of firing eight rounds):

> **"On the basis of auditory, oscillographic and spectrographic analyses of these three recordings, it is my opinion, to a reasonable degree of scientific certainty, that no fewer than ten gunshots are ascertainable following the conclusion of the Senator's victory speech until after the time Sirhan Bishara Sirhan was disarmed."[414]**

The LAPD adamantly maintained their official position that, other than Sirhan's, there were no guns fired in the pantry of the Ambassador Hotel during the shooting of Senator Kennedy. Clearly *there were* other guns fired, as we know that Sirhan's .22 only held eight shots and that more than that were fired.[415]

In addition, several eyewitnesses testified that they saw men in plainclothes with their weapons drawn at the time of the assassination. The obvious assumption is that they were Secret Service, but *there were no* Secret Service agents protecting Robert Kennedy in 1968. The next most obvious assumption is that they were LAPD or off-duty officers working security for the Senator. But Kennedy *did not have* any armed bodyguards and LAPD said they were not theirs either. Yet *there they were*: The terminology that one eyewitness used was that he was "absolutely positive" that there were other men in plainclothes with guns drawn at the time of the shooting.[416]

When Sirhan was arrested he appeared normal but his complete disorientation and disassociation with the events that had taken place were noted by authorities and the issue came up at his trial. The Prosecution asked:

> **"Do you remember later on in that same conversation you said to Mr. Howard, 'I have been before a magistrate, have I, or have I not?' Mr. Howard said 'No, you have not. You will be taken before a magistrate as soon as possible. Probably will be tried.' ... You didn't ask Mr. Howard at that time, 'Tried for what?' did you?"**
>
> **"I don't remember, sir, if I did or not."**
>
> **"Sirhan had not said, 'Tried for what?' to Mr. Howard, but his question as to whether or not he had been before a magistrate was a clear indication that he was disoriented. He appeared to be normal, yet he did not know if he had been before a judge. Had Grant Cooper been running an aggressive defense, Mr. Howard would have been on the witness stand explaining what in Sirhan's behavior just hours after the murder had caused the assistant DA to repeatedly ask the prisoner if he knew where he was."[417]**

---

[414] William Turner, *Rearview Mirror: Looking Back at the FBI, the CIA and Other Tails* (Penmarin, 2001).

[415] Klaber & Melanson, *Shadow Play*

[416] Klaber & Melanson, *Shadow Play*, 135-136.

[417] Klaber & Melanson, *Shadow Play*, 215-216.

No one has been more at a loss to describe Sirhan's motive for the act than has Sirhan himself:

> "If I had wanted to kill him," says Sirhan, again questioning whether he ever had planned to murder Robert Kennedy in the first place, "would I, sir, have been so stupid as to leave that notebook there, waiting for those cops, sir, to pick it up?"[418]

The *LAPD Summary Report* of the eyewitness statements to the RFK assassination contained blatant and total fabrications. Take the case of Booker Griffin, director of the *Negro Industrial and Educational Union*. Griffin, as he himself pointed out, was a perfect witness:

> "I am a trained newsperson and I had been taught to watch details … I was not there with a lay eye, I had covered, you know, shooting stories and others, and I was raised in a neighborhood situation where seeing people shot and being around bullets was something I was used to, and I was always taught to keep a kind of cool head. I'm not blind. I'm not a dishonest person. I know what I saw."[419]

Evidence Exonerating Sirhan Bishara Sirhan of Murder in the First Degree

1. Ballistics-testing by noted criminalist and ballistics expert, William W. Harper, determined that the bullets that hit Senator Kennedy did not come from Sirhan's gun.
2. The defendant was never at <u>any</u> point close enough to the victim to have fired the fatal shot. It was determined that the kill shot came from within <u>less than three inches</u> from the victim's head. Every witness places the defendant much farther away.
3. All the bullets that hit Senator Kennedy traversed his body in a back-to-front direction. All witnesses placed the defendant in front of the victim. Therefore shots from the defendant's gun hitting the Senator obviously would have traversed the victim's body in a front-to-back trajectory, not back-to-front.
4. The trajectories of the bullets hitting Senator Kennedy's body were all at downward angles. From the placement of the defendant by all witnesses, shots hitting the Senator would have necessarily had trajectories at upward angles.

---

[418] Klaber & Melanson, Shadow Play, 187.
[419] Melanson, Robert F. Kennedy Assassination

5. The crime was not premeditated because the accused did not possess conscious intent at the moment of the crime; he does not even remember the crime, even under sodium pentothal and intense psychiatric sessions involving hypnotic regression. The last thing in the defendant's memory is having coffee with a girl. His next memory—quite literally—is being in police custody.

6. The defendant did not possess malice aforethought and, indeed, how could he have? Through months of interrogation, hypnotic regression and even truth serum, no one was ever able to unearth a serious possible motive as to why he would shoot the Senator. The defendant has no memory whatsoever of planning to kill the Senator.

7. No motive existed or has ever been identified. The police and prosecution tried to assert that RFK's intention of providing fifty jets to Israel was what caused Sirhan to kill him. That is simply impossible because Sirhan started his programmed writing in his notebooks about killing RFK on May 18, prior to the press coverage and the first public statement by RFK supporting the sale of jets, which was on May 21.

8. No memory of crime. Police were baffled by the fact that, even after months of intensive and expert interrogation, Sirhan had no recollection whatsoever of committing the crime, nor had he any coherent explanation of why he would commit the crime. Zero motive. Zero memory.[420]

9. Police procedures determined that the defendant was clearly operating under the influence of a drug, of which the defendant had no recollection whatsoever. Police shined a flashlight into Sirhan's eyes after his arrest, which is standard procedure to determine if a suspect is under the influence of drugs. The officer who conducted that check, LAPD Officer Arthur Placencia, testified under oath that his pupils did not react to the light, "indicating that he was under the influence of something."[421]

10. Sirhan volunteered to undergo multiple psychiatric examinations, hypnosis, and even volunteered for "truth serum" which was administered to him. Testing and extensive interrogation revealed that he had been "programmed" without his own conscious knowledge of the event.

11. There are also other blatant signs that the defendant had been programmed. Under hypnosis, he could be instructed to climb the bars of his cell like a monkey, would perform the instruction by acting it out, and then, after being brought out of hypnosis, would have no recollection at all of what

[420] Klaber & Melanson, 1997, *Shadow Play*, page 65
[421] Klaber & Melanson, 1997, *Shadow Play*, page 87

had taken place. He was considered by experts to be the most easily hypnotizable subject they had ever encountered. The repetitious writing of "RFK must die!" in Sirhan's notebook was a clear example of what is termed "automatic writing": Under hypnosis, Sirhan would go into a deep trance and then would automatically begin writing "RFK must die! RFK must die!" over and over on the page of paper in front of him (and this is later, while in custody!).

Chief Psychiatrist Bernard Diamond:

> "Let me specifically state that it was immediately apparent that Sirhan had been programmed."[422]

12. The cover-up was blatant. For example, LAPD Criminalists denied claims that they had themselves clearly delineated in previous statements. They said they recovered bullets and then later denied having recovered them. They stated that there were bullet holes in the pantry walls and door. Then they later denied that there ever were any, after they were the ones who had originally claimed that there were![423]

Not true, according to an expert in such matters, who viewed the bullet holes with his own eyes. FBI Agent William Bailey, who was at the crime scene shortly after the shooting, investigating it in preparation for witness interviews, stated :

> "As I toured the pantry area I noticed in a wood door-frame, a center divider between the two swinging doors, two bullet holes. I've inspected quite a few crime scenes in my day. These were clearly bullet holes; the wood around them was freshly broken away and I could see the base of a bullet in each one."[424]

> "The arithmetic here is devastatingly simple: the gun taken from Sirhan Sirhan held a maximum of eight bullets; thus, with at least eight bullets already accounted for, there could be no bullets in the walls or doorframe, if only one gun was firing. Any bullets or bullet holes in the walls would be irrefutable proof of a second gun."[425]

> Crucial evidence, such as the doorframes cited above, promptly disappeared into LAPD's "evidentiary black hole" and was literally never seen again. They were later described as "accidentally destroyed." Photographs of the crime scene vanished. Testimonies were dramatically altered.

422 Klaber & Melanson, 1997, *Shadow Play*, page 237
423 Klaber & Melanson, 1997, Shadow Play, page 88
424 Klaber & Melanson, 1997, *Shadow Play*, page 91
425 Klaber & Melanson, 1997, *Shadow Play*, page 92

U.S. Congressman Allard Lowenstein summarized the obvious cover-up bluntly:

"I do not know why those responsible for law enforcement in Los Angeles decided to stonewall the RFK case. But once they had made that decision, the rest followed: facts had to be concealed or distorted and inconvenient evidence done away with, inoperative statements had to be replaced by new statements, until they in turn became inoperative; people raising awkward questions had to be discredited, preferably as self-seeking or flaky."[426]

13. Harassment of witnesses was commonplace. As one witness later summarized the effects of her "harassment" (her word) at the hands of LAPD:

" ... I was just twenty years old and I became unglued. I said what they wanted me to say."[427]

---

[426] Lowenstein, 1977
[427] Klaber & Melanson, 1997, *Shadow Play*, page 175

Griffin also told police that he saw Sirhan on three different occasions that night. On two of those occasions he saw him with an attractive woman who seemed to be his companion that evening. He noticed the two of them because they somehow seemed like they were "out of place."

"When the first shots were fired Griffin was standing just outside the pantry. He noticed the woman and another man whom he had seen earlier with Sirhan run out of the pantry. Something in their motion and demeanor made Griffin blurt out, 'They're getting away!'"[428]

Other eyewitnesses saw the same two individuals, an attractive well-built young woman and an Arab-looking man, running out of the pantry while everyone else was heading in, or toward Senator Kennedy. Their descriptions matched. Some noted that the Arab-looking man was perspiring profusely and held a gun visible beneath a newspaper. Other eyewitnesses reported that once outside, the same two individuals yelled "We got him! We shot him!" More than one witness saw and heard that. Again, their descriptions matched.[429]

For some reason, LAPD found it necessary to discredit Griffin and his statement.

"The *LAPD Summary Report* would dismiss Booker Griffin by stating that Griffin confessed "that the story of the male and female

---

[428] Melanson, *Robert F. Kennedy Assassination*
[429] Melanson, *Robert F. Kennedy Assassination*

escaping was a total fabrication on his part." This allegation has no basis whatsoever in any of the tapes, transcripts, or summaries of Griffin's law enforcement interviews. It is so transparent in its goal of discrediting a witness that it serves as further evidence of a hidden agenda on the part of those producing the final *Summary Report* alleging he had admitted he had lied."[430]

Griffin was furious and rightfully so. There was obviously an agenda, and people were going to great lengths to support that agenda.

It was against that backdrop that Sirhan was found guilty "alone and not in concert with anyone else" of Murder in the First Degree. Sirhan later told his attorney:

"Even Jesus Christ couldn't have saved me."[431]

From a standpoint of being framed by the "justice" system, he was apparently right. Incredibly, over forty years after the murder, Sirhan Bishara Sirhan still sits in prison for a crime he could not have committed: Murder in the First Degree requires willful, that is, conscious premeditation and, as we show above, he scientifically and literally could not have fired the shot that killed Senator Kennedy. Either no one has been able to find a federal judge who will look fairly at the exculpatory evidence, or the case is simply too hot to handle—probably the latter.

POSSIBLE SCENARIOS

Some very interesting evidence exists that Sirhan may have somehow been "mentally manipulated."

Those who saw Sirhan after the murder noted with great surprise that both his facial expression and his demeanor were *dramatically* opposite his actual situation.

> **"Writer George Plimpton, who had helped in the struggle to disarm him, was taken aback by his 'dark brown and enormously peaceful eyes.' Another witness recalled that he looked 'very tranquil.' His detachment seemed almost transcendal, as if he had an inner life that had no relation to the hysteria around him.'[432]**

The LAPD Night Watch Commander who had read Sirhan his legal rights, Sgt. William C. Jordan, was also shocked by the serenity of the defendant in such a hysterical situation. Jordan said:

---

430 Klaber & Melanson, *Shadow Play*, 147-150.
431 George Lardner Jr., "Jurors Decree Death for Sirhan in RFK Slaying," 23 April 1969, *Washington Post*, A1. http://jfk.hood.edu/Collection/Weisberg%20Subject%20Index%20Files/S%20Disk/Sirhan%20Sirhan%20Verdict/Item%2004.pdf
432 Evans, *Nemesis*

> "There was more than a touch of mob hysteria in the kitchen after the shooting." Yet the suspect remained less agitated than "individuals arrested for a traffic violation."[433]

Legal precedent *does* exist for murder-by-proxy via hypnosis.[434]

The linkage between powerful billionaire Aristotle Onassis, known simply as "The Greek," and the Kennedy family is one that is both curious and possibly very important. The animosity between the two was historically well-documented and extreme in nature:

> "When Franklin D. Roosevelt, Jr. ... asked Bobby what they proposed to do about Onassis's invitation, the Attorney General answered grimly,
>
> 'Sink the fucking yacht.'"[435]

As investigative journalist Peter Evans points out, the links can be made from Onassis all the way to Sirhan. The missing portion of Sirhan's history known as his "white fog" period, coincides exactly with the trips to California of a strong link to Onassis, Mahmoud Hamshari, who also had links to terrorist networks.

Onassis and Hamshari both also link up directly to the infamous hypnotist, Bill Bryan, whose work was even the basis of the film, *The Manchurian Candidate*, for which Bryan also served as technical consultant.

Bill Bryan was a "hypnosis superstar," possibly the best there ever was. He apparently worked on the CIA's MKULTRA and ARTICHOKE mind control programs and it was verified that, believe it or not, he could make patients "bleed on cue"; he actually did precisely that at a hypnosis seminar for trial lawyers in San Francisco in 1961; the event was witnessed by many and was not sleight-of-hand.[436]

Onassis was a patient of Dr. Bryan and often referred friends and associates to the famous hypnotist. Most of the records for the CIA behavioral research programs MKULTRA and ARTICHOKE were secretly destroyed and it is not officially known whether they succeeded in creating a successful *Manchurian Candidate* (programmed assassin) at the time of the projects' termination in 1964. However, Milton Kline, an expert who worked on the secret projects (and was President, American Society for Clinical and Experimental Hypnosis), summarizes the capability as follows:

> "It cannot be done by everyone, it cannot be done consistently, but it <u>can be done</u>."[437]

---

[433] Evans, *Nemesis*

[434] Evans, *Nemesis*, 218.

[435] Evans, *Nemesis*

[436] Evans, *Nemesis*, 219.

[437] Evans, *Nemesis* (emphasis added).

Therefore, the relationship between Jackie Kennedy and Aristotle Onassis is not only of historical importance, it also seems somehow linked to the murder of Robert Kennedy.

LBJ reportedly loved hearing news of the marriage because it gave him the revenge against Bobby Kennedy that he craved:

> *"Aristotle Onassis and Jackie Kennedy were going to be married.*
>
> This would have been raw meat to Johnson. Three days before, he had announced that he would not run for another term, and he was still seething at the Kennedy camp's slur that Bobby's challenge had driven him back to the ranch.
>
> When Johnson planned to play this card we shall probably never know. But shortly after Karr's visit to the Oval Office, Eugene McCarthy saw Johnson, and when he brought up the subject of Bobby's presidential run,
>
> *'The president said nothing; instead he drew a finger across his throat, silently, in a slitting motion.'"* [438]

The world was shocked when Jackie publicly announced her plans to marry Onassis, and everyone wondered the same thing: *Why?* It seemed such an odd alliance and, frankly, true love was about the last reason that came to anyone's mind. A friend and associate of Onassis noted a very revealing statement that Onassis had made once; one that he never forgot:

> "He then made this interesting remark: He said, 'A marriage of interests can solve many problems, my dear fellow.'
>
> I missed its significance at the time; it only struck a chord when he married Jackie Kennedy." [439]

Reactions to the marriage were predictably bleak. Consider the following newspaper headlines of the time:

Jack Kennedy Dies Today for a Second Time [440]

The Reaction Here is Anger, Shock and Dismay [441]

The pages of Sirhan's notebooks contained two other names written by Sirhan under a hypnotic trance that specifically linked to Aristotle Onassis: Fiona

---

[438] Evans, *Nemesis* (emphasis in original).

[439] Evans, *Nemesis*

[440] Karen Schneider, J.D. Reed, Shelley Levitt & Elizabeth Gleick, "Hour of Farewell," 6 June 1994, *People*. http://www.people.com/people/archive/article/0,,20108270,00.html

[441] Schneider et al., "Hour of Farewell"

Thyssen, the lover of Ari Onassis' son, whom Onassis had threatened to have killed; and Stavros Niarchos, Onassis' arch-enemy of many decades with a competing business empire.

> "On the first page, Sirhan had written at the center of a roundel, amid Arabic writing, the single name,
> *Fiona.*
> And on another page:
> *2 Niarkos!*
> On a third page, between the lines
> *One Hundred thousand dollars and Dollars-One Hundreds,*
> Sirhan had written in Arabic:
> *they should be killed.*
> And next to that, the number:
> *Three.*
> Fiona, Niarchos, and Kennedy: The names were startling by virtue of their very juxtaposition."[442]

Yannis Georgakis was Onassis's attorney, good friend, confidant, and closest business associate for many, many years—and he concluded that Onassis was behind Bobby Kennedy's murder:

> "The truth was, he was *shattered* by the very real possibility that Onassis had paid for the bullets that killed Bobby Kennedy, and not for the first time he wondered about the nature of Onassis's deal with Hamshari.
>
> 'Sometimes remarkable chains of circumstances can reasonably be ascribed to coincidence. But at some point the connection is so astonishing that one must assume that it could only have happened by design,' Georgakis would later muse. 'And when an Irish-American name, a Scottish name, and a Greek name—the names of Onassis's three most loathed and troublesome enemies—are found in a Palestinian killer's notebook written in Los Angeles shortly after Onassis had given more than a million dollars to a Palestinian terrorist in Paris (far more than that Palestinian had demanded), and the first name on that list has already been killed, you must seriously consider the possibility that you have reached that point.'"[443]

Onassis reportedly seemed to somehow have knowledge of Bobby's death before it happened:

"Onassis heard the news at about ten o'clock on the morning of Wednesday, June 5, 1968, while having breakfast in the middle of the Atlantic Ocean. Bobby wasn't dead but it looked bad. Meyer told him from New York.

---

[442] Evans, *Nemesis*, 231.
[443] Evans, *Nemesis*, 231-232.

'Somebody was going to fix the little bastard sooner or later,'

Onassis said. He wasn't a hypocrite, and the callousness of his reaction did not surprise Meyer. Onassis told him to call as soon as Kennedy was dead—'as if he wanted to know the result of the four o'clock race at Santa Anita,' Meyer later said:

> Thring (Onassis' lover who was on board the yacht with him at this time) remembers the impassiveness with which Onassis took the news. 'Hearing something like that when you are so removed from reality made it even more shocking for me. I didn't expect Ari to be upset; I knew that Bobby's death was vastly convenient for him; but his reaction was … it was **as if he'd been told something he already knew**."[444]

As a final note, Onassis actually confessed to his role in the murder. Onassis made the confession to his lover, Hélène Gaillet, who vividly recalls the event:

> "He stood looking at the ocean, the lights of his yacht glittering across the dark water. Because his back was turned to her, it took Gaillet several moments to realize that he was talking: 'like somebody praying, really … that is the only way I can describe it.' As she strained to catch his words, he turned around and said matter-of-factly,
>
> *You know, Hélène, I put up the money for Bobby Kennedy's murder."*
>
> Said as a simple statement of fact … 'I said something like, "Bobby Kennedy? Oh, Ari."
>
> He gave that little Levantine shrug of his, like *so what?* … Onassis had actually confessed his complicity in Bobby Kennedy's murder, and, in her heart of hearts, she feared that she believed him. 'In fact, the more I thought about it, the more I became convinced that he was speaking the truth,' she said. 'It was part of Ari's charm that he would trust you with an extreme confidence."[445]

Another close associate of Onassis, David Karr, who handled much of his dirty work, also claimed to know that "Onassis had been behind Bobby Kennedy's murder."[446]

Christina Onassis (who once demanded of Jackie Kennedy: *"If you want my father's fucking money, you keep his fucking name"*—and Jackie took both[447]) was

---

[444] Evans, *Nemesis*, (emphasis added).

[445] Evans, *Nemesis*

[446] Evans, *Nemesis*, 300.

[447] Evans, *Nemesis*

told of her father's complicity in the RFK assassination when she was twenty-one years old. She let it be known (to family confidants such as Georgakis) that she had always resented the weight of that burden. In what might best be described a sanitized version of events, she later told a journalist that:

> "Ari had paid an Arab terrorist protection money to keep his Olympic airline safe from skyjacking, and terrorist attack, which were a huge risk at that time. He later learned that the terrorist, a Palestinian named Mahmoud Hamshari, had used the money to finance the murder of Bobby Kennedy."[448]

Historical Perspective

By 1966, Robert Kennedy had clearly undergone a personal transformation. Many had considered him a power-focused and ruthless politician (in the vein of "Don't get mad, get even") who had been focused on bitter enemies such as Organized Crime. But tragedies that were both personal and historical had transformed him into a worldly, forward-thinking intellectual who suddenly seemed to have no less in mind than the personal well-being of every less fortunate individual on the planet and how their lot could be improved by strategic political leadership. Nothing evidenced this change more than his address to the students of Cape Town University in South Africa on June 6, 1966. Some students had already begun protesting the racist government policy of apartheid. Rather than avoid a hotly divisive political issue, Kennedy tackled it straight on, claiming the higher moral and philosophical ground:

> "Hand in hand with freedom of speech goes the power to be heard, to share in the decisions of government which shape men's lives. Everything that makes man's life worthwhile—family, work, education, a place to rear one's children and a place to rest one's head—all this depends on the decisions of government; all can be swept away by a government which does not heed the demands of its people, and I mean *all* of its people. Therefore, the essential humanity of man can be protected and preserved only where government must answer—not just to the wealthy, not just to those of a particular religion, not just to those of a particular race, but to all of the people."[449]

His words were stirringly reminiscent of the U.S. Declaration of Independence, almost as though he was invoking that document at a global level, as a call to international equality:

---

[448] Evans, *Nemesis*

[449] Robert F. Kennedy, "Day of Affirmation Address at Cape Town University," 6 June, 1966. http://www.americanrhetoric.com/speeches/rfkcapetown.htm

> "We must recognize the full human equality of all of our people before God, before the law, and in the councils of government. We must do this, not because it is economically advantageous, although it is; not because the laws of God command it, although they do; not because people in other lands wish it so. We must do it for the single and fundamental reason that it is the right thing to do."[450]

Kennedy evidenced that he had mastered the art of placing political movements in both historical and philosophical perspective, and even doing so in a manner that was up close and personal:

> "In a few hours, the plane that brought me to this country crossed over oceans and countries which have been a crucible of human history. In minutes we traced migrations of men over thousands of years; seconds, the briefest glimpse, and we passed battlefields on which millions of men once struggled and died. We could see no national boundaries, no vast gulfs or high walls dividing people from people; only nature and the works of man—homes and factories and farms—everywhere reflecting Man's common effort to enrich his life. Everywhere new technology and communications brings men and nations closer together, the concerns of one inevitably becomes the concerns of all. And our new closeness is stripping away the false masks, the illusion of differences which is the root of injustice and of hate and of war."[451]

The eloquent speech has become known as "The Ripple of Hope" address for the stirring words in one of the last passages:

> "Thousands of Peace Corps volunteers are making a difference in the isolated villages and the city slums of dozens of countries. Thousands of unknown men and women in Europe resisted the occupation of the Nazis and many died, but all added to the ultimate strength and freedom of their countries. It is from numberless diverse acts of courage such as these that human history is thus shaped. Each time a man stands up for an ideal, or acts to improve the lot of others, or strikes out against injustice, he sends forth a tiny ripple of hope, and crossing each other from a million different centers of energy and daring, those ripples build a current which can sweep down the mightiest walls of oppression and resistance
>
> ... There is a Chinese curse which says, 'May he live in interesting times.' Like it or not we live in interesting times. They are times of danger and uncertainty; but they are also the most creative of any time in the history of mankind. And everyone here will ultimately

---

[450] Robert Kennedy, "Cape Town"
[451] Robert Kennedy, "Cape Town"

be judged, will ultimately judge himself, on the effort he has contributed to building a new world society and the extent to which
his ideals and goals have shaped that effort."[452]

That candescent hope that seemed to materialize in millions of people as a
result of his inspired leadership, made his sudden loss on June 6, 1968 all the
more poignant. It had seemed that a man who had championed compassion
and equality was about to ascend to the presidency. And then he was gone.

When a train carried Robert Kennedy's body from Washington D.C. to New York
on the afternoon of June 8, 1968, thousands of people instinctively lined the
tracks over the entire route to pay him their final respects.

BIBLIOGRAPHY

American Conspiracies: Lies, Lies, and More Dirty Lies that the Government Tells Us,
  Jesse Ventura & Dick Russell, 2010

Shadow Play: The Untold Story of The Robert F. Kennedy Assassination, William Klaber
  & Philip H. Melanson, 1998

An Open and Shut Case, Dr. Robert Joling & Philip Van Praag , 2008

"Testimonial, An Open and Shut Case", Robert Vaughn, 2008. http://www.
  anopenandshutcase.com/?page_id=4

The Robert F. Kennedy Assassination: New Revelations on the Conspiracy and Cover-
  Up, 1968-1991, Philip H. Melanson, 1994

---

[452] Robert Kennedy, "Cape Town"

Rearview Mirror: Looking Back at the FBI, the CIA and Other Tails, William Turner, 2001

Who Killed Robert Kennedy? (The Real Story Series), Philip H. Melanson, 2002

Nemesis, Peter Evans, 2004

"Two Guns Used in RFK Assassination, Experts Say", Pierre Thomas, March 27, 2008, ABC News. http://abcnews.go.com/GMA/LegalCenter/story?id=4534689

"New Evidence Challenges Official Picture of Kennedy Shooting", James Randerson, February 22, 2008, guardian.co.uk http://www.guardian.co.uk/science/2008/feb/22/kennedy.assassination

"Simple Facts about the Robert F. Kennedy Assassination", http://flag.blackened.net/daver/ index.html

"Sirhan's Researcher", Rose Lynn Mangan (Sirhan Bishara Sirhan's authorized researcher for many years): http://www.sirhansresearcher.com/

"JFK and RFK: The Plots that Killed Them, The Patsies that Didn't", James Fetzer, June 13, 2010, Voltairenet.org; Non Aligned Press Network. http://www.voltairenet.org/article165721.html

"I know who was behind Bobby Kennedy's murder, by his actor friend Robert Vaughn", Robert Vaughn, 2009. www.dailymail.co.uk/news/article-1111444/I-know-Bobby-Kennedys-murder-actor-friend-Robert-Vaughn.html

CHAPTER 8 | Fred Hampton
December 4, 1969

*President, NAACP Youth Council/Chairman,
Illinois Chapter/Deputy National Chairman &
National Spokesman The Black Panther Party*

Photo excerpted from the DVD
release of *The Murder of Fred Hampton*
© Facets Multi-Media, 2007

VICTIM	FRED HAMPTON
Cause of Death	MULTIPLE GUNSHOT WOUNDS
Official Verdict	SHOT WHILE ASSAULTING POLICE OFFICERS DURING RAID Police said they attempted to peacefully serve a warrant and were met with massive gunfire from inside the apartment, so they fired back. Police testified that in excess of 200 shots were exchanged in a two-sided gun battle that lasted approximately ten to twelve minutes.

Actual Circumstances	The raid was actually a massive police assault by a special tactical unit of 15 plainclothes officers armed with everything from machine guns to sawed-off shotguns. Contrary to knocking on the door to serve a warrant, actually they stormed into the small apartment from both the front and back at 4:45 a.m. with weapons blazing. Ballistics evidence reveals that only one shot came from inside the apartment, which was fired directly into the door and did not wound anyone. All other gunfire was from police, directed at those inside. Victim was drugged by an FBI informant and was totally unconscious during the raid. Victim was shot in bed while unconscious, then dragged out of bed and, still alive, was then executed by a police officer with two shots to the head at point-blank range.
Inconsistencies	1. The victim was rendered completely unconscious prior to the police raid. Medical testing revealed he was drugged with a very high dose of a strong barbiturate. He was slipped the drugs by a confessed FBI informant and he remained unconscious from the time he went to bed. Witnesses confirmed that he never even woke up, let alone fired a weapon. 2. Forensic expert Dr. Cyril Wecht was shocked when he viewed Hampton's blood findings: "Hampton's blood samples contained incredibly high levels of Seconal, or secobarbital—4.5 milligrams per deciliter, in fact, or about four times the amount considered toxic and potentially lethal."[453] 3. As Dr. Wecht notes: "This Seconal level is very important evidence that's been overlooked. If this toxicology report is true, then Fred Hampton was in a very deep sleep or even in a stuporous state at the time the police raided his apartment. If that's the case, then there's no way he could have been shooting a gun, let alone initiating a gunfight. And if this is true, then the police have been lying from the beginning and this whole operation may have been nothing more than a political assassination."[454] 4. Dr. Wecht immediately recognized that the bullet trajectories tell a quite different story than the Official

---

[453] Cyril Wecht, M.D., J.D., Mark Curriden & Benjamin Wecht, *Grave Secrets: Leading Forensic Expert Reveals the Startling Truth About O.J. Simpson, David Koresh, Vincent Foster, and Other Sensational Cases*, Cyril Wecht, M.D., J.D. with Mark Curriden and Benjamin Wecht, 1998.

[454] Cyril Wecht, M.D., J.D., et al., *Grave Secrets*

Version: "If these trajectories were correct, then Hampton was not standing up facing the officers when he was shot; rather, he was lying on his back, and the officer who shot him was standing directly above him and slightly to his right."[455]

"We expected about twenty Panthers to be in the apartment when the police raided the place. Only two of those black nigger fuckers were killed, Fred Hampton and Mark Clark."

—FBI Special Agent Gregg York

"Fred understood he was a marked man … "

—Attorney Jeffrey Haas

"As the old law enforcement saying goes, even in the most carefully thought-out crimes, a criminal will make a mistake. I suppose it is no different when police officers become criminals."

—Dr. Cyril Wecht

Fred Hampton was a gifted student and athletic star who planned on becoming an attorney. He graduated with honors from his high school in Chicago and gradually became politically active. Hampton came to embrace the philosophy of self-defense as a legal and intelligent response to racism and overt political oppression. His murder by the police is perhaps the best example of the organized oppression he sought to socially overcome.

Hampton studied pre-Law in Junior College and used what he learned to employ justice in his own neighborhood. To combat police brutality in poor urban neighborhoods of Chicago, Hampton and his fellow group members followed police around in the city to let them know that their actions were being monitored by residents. So when the *Black Panther Party* came along, it was the perfect vehicle for Fred Hampton.

Much contrary to how it was intentionally maligned in the media, the *Black Panther Party* was actually a *political defense* organization—if *you didn't mess with them, they didn't mess with you*. Their complete name was actually the *Black Panther Party for Self-Defense*. They advocated and maintained a strict no-drugs policy (no personal use *or* trafficking) and stressed a Ten-Point Program that advocated strong educational principles, community health centers, political activism and education, a Free Breakfast Program and other assistance for those who needed it most. As Doc Satchel, founder of the *Chicago Black Panther Health Clinic* interpreted it:

---

[455] Cyril Wecht, M.D., J.D., et al., *Grave Secrets*

> **"The Panthers were an armed propaganda unit that raised the contradictions, set the example, and provided the vehicle that the people could ride to revolution. We do not say the Black Panther Party will be ovethrowing the government; we heighten the contradictions so the people can decide if they** *want* **to change the government."**[456]

Hampton galvanized national attention by engineering a strategically brilliant alliance between the *Panthers* and other groups. The first and most important was a Non-Aggression pact between the *Black Panthers* and the major gangs that controlled the streets of south and west Chicago, in neighborhoods so tough that the police were literally afraid to enter.

The truces with these huge groups—the *Blackstone Rangers* (over 5,000 members), and particularly with the *Black Disciples* (approximately 5,500 members) allowed the *Panthers* to recruit in the roughest neighborhoods of Chicago which contained the ripest audience for new members. This brilliant coup instantly supercharged *Panther* membership and solidified an incredible power base at the heart of the movement—the poorest of the inner city poor, composed of much disenfranchised minorities.

It was actually Fred Hampton, not Reverend Jesse Jackson, who first employed the term *Rainbow Coalition*. His coalition included not only the *Black Panthers* and the city's two largest street gangs, but a diverse network comprised of the *Young Lords,* the *Young Patriots,* the *Student Nonviolent Coordinating Committee, Students for a Democratic Society,* the *Brown Berets,* and the *Red Guard Party.*

Hampton's efforts also began visibly changing the most impoverished parts of the city. He changed the activities of these street gangs from just being criminal, to becoming *political.* Instead of expanding their drug dealing, gangs like the *D's* (the *Disciples)* began massive picketing campaigns protesting the lack of minority hirings at Chicago construction sites and were so successful in their socio-political efforts that they actually forced sites to shut down until they agreed to hire inner-city workers. The *Stones* street gang focused on political efforts against the well-known city political machine and actually got activists and other community members elected to posts in which they formally represented their inner-city neighborhoods. Hampton's achievements prompted the national leadership of the *Black Panther Party* to appoint him as the party's National Spokesman.

Hampton held a press conference in May, 1969 and publicly announced the truce among his *Rainbow Coalition*; it was a noteworthy advancement in both the unification of diverse socio-political interests and their ability to effect serious political change.

This progress, politically, brought Hampton to national attention—and not just in the *Black Panther Party* either. The threat to the power structure

---

[456] *The Murder of Fred Hampton*, dir. by Mike Gray & Howard Alk (Facets Multi-Media, 2007, dvd). http://www.amazon.com/Murder-Fred-Hampton/dp/B000O75GWQ

from Hampton's organizational brilliance was that it <u>united</u> white students with inner-city blacks, and Hispanics, and people of all classes.

The FBI targeted the *Black Panther Party* with its COINTELPRO Program, generally, and targeted Fred Hampton, *specifically*.

Hampton's eloquence further advanced his young career as he coined phrases still remembered today:

> **"You can kill the revolutionary, but you can't kill the revolution."**
>
> **"I know of no other intelligent way to act in an extreme situation other than extreme."**[457]

While Hampton's eloquence was gaining him followers, it was still his organizing brilliance that made a difference in the streets and politically. He was reportedly on the verge of pulling off a huge merger with the largest street gang on the south side of Chicago that literally would have doubled membership in the *Black Panther Party* overnight.

On the night of December 3, 1969, Fred Hampton taught a Political Education course at a local church.

That night, after returning home from teaching his course, he was murdered in his sleep, under the "official cover" of a police raid. To make matters worse, the entire event was witnessed by Hampton's girlfriend, who was 8-months pregnant with their child.

Forensic experts determined that the police version of a two-sided gunfight was an outright lie. It was scientifically determined that of the hundreds of gunshots in Hampton's apartment, all but one had been fired by police.

---

[457] *The Murder of Fred Hampton*, dir. by Mike Gray & Howard Alk

This is the bed on which Hampton was shot as he slept, before being dragged onto the floor and executed at point-blank range.

Forensics also determined that a wounded and completely unconscious Fred Hampton had been dragged out of his bed and into the hallway, then executed by police with two shots to the head at point-blank range.

According to eyewitness testimony at the scene, this is how the murder of Fred Hampton was set:

> "Automatic gunfire then converged at the head of the bedroom where Hampton slept, unable to wake up as a result of the barbiturates that the FBI infiltrator had slipped into his drink. He was lying on a mattress in the bedroom with his pregnant girlfriend. Two officers found him wounded in the shoulder, and fellow Black Panther Harold Bell reported that he heard the following exchange:
>
> "That's Fred Hampton."
>
> "Is he dead? ... Bring him out."
>
> "He's barely alive; he'll make it."

Deborah Johnson and Fred Jr.

Photo excerpted from the DVD release of *The Murder of Fred Hampton* © Facets Multi-Media, 2007

> Two shots were heard, which it was later discovered were fired point blank in Hampton's head. According to Deborah Johnson, one officer then said:
>
> "He's good and dead now."[458]

Their informant had provided the police with a map that diagrammed the exact layout of Hampton's apartment. They knew exactly where to go, and they burst through the door with guns blazing to get there.

Fred Hampton, Jr. was born twenty-five days later.

Here's the account that his mother gave of the pre-dawn murder of the boy's father—this is in her own words:

> I looked up and saw bullets coming from what seemed like the front of the apartment and the kitchen area in the back. Bullets were going into the mattress. The sparks of light, the bed vibrating—I just knew with all this going on, it was all over. At some point the shooting stopped. Fred didn't move anymore. I came out with my hands up. There were two lines of police I had to walk though. One of them grabbed my robe and pulled it open. I was eight and a half months pregnant then. "Well, what do you know. We have a pregnant broad." Another policeman grabbed me by the hair and slung me into the kitchen area. I looked around and saw Ron Satchel on the dining room floor. He had blood all over him. Verlina Brewer was in the kitchen, bleeding. She started to fall. They grabbed her and threw her against the refrigerator. Then more shooting. I heard a voice that wasn't familiar to me say, "He's barely alive. He'll barely make it." I assumed they were talking about Fred.

---

[458] Ward Churchill & Jim Vander Wall, *Agents of Repression: The FBI's Secret Wars Against the Black Panther Party and the American Indian Movement* (South End Press, 1988).

The shooting started again, just for a brief period. It stopped. Then another unfamiliar voice said, "He's good and dead now."[459]

BIBLIOGRAPHY

"The Murder of Fred Hampton," dir. by Mike Gray & Howard Alk (Facets Multi-Media, 2007, dvd). http://www.amazon.com/Murder-Fred-Hampton/dp/B000O75GWQ

The Assassination of Fred Hampton: How the FBI and the Chicago Police Murdered a Black Panther; Jeffrey Haas, 2009

We Are Not What We Seem: Black Nationalism and Class Struggle in the American Century, Rod Bush, 2000, NYU Press. (Panthers doubling in size through merger: p. 216)

Agents of Repression: The FBI's Secret Wars Against the Black Panther Party and the American Indian Movement; Ward Churchill & Jim Vander Wall, 1988

The COINTELPRO Papers: Documents from the FBI's Secret Wars Against Dissent in the United States; Ward Churchill & Jim Vander Wall, 1990

"COINTELPRO from the Church Committee Reports" and "FBI COINTELPRO Documents", Paul Wolf, 1996-2004, ICDC.com. http://www.icdc.com/~paulwolf/cointelpro/cointel.htm

"Akua Njeri (Deborah Johnson)", *Human Constitutional Rights.org.* http://www.hrcr.org/ccr/njeri.html

"Interview with Deborah Johnson, Eyes on the Prize II Interviews", Terry Rockefeller, October 19, 1988. http://digital.wustl.edu/e/eii/eiiweb/joh5427.0255.082marc_record_interviewee_process.html

"Fred Hampton", John Simkin, *Spartacus Educational,* http://www.spartacus.schoolnet.co.uk/USAhamptonF.htm

---

[459] HumanConstitutionalRights.org, Akua Njeri (Deborah Johnson), http://www.hrcr.org/ccr/njeri.html (accessed 12 Jan 2012).

CHAPTER 9 | Vincent Foster —
July 20, 1993
White House Counsel

VICTIM	VINCE FOSTER, WHITE HOUSE COUNSEL
Cause of Death	GUNSHOT
Official Verdict	SUICIDE
Actual Circumstances	Victim found in public park on a Tuesday afternoon. The evidence indicates he was murdered with a low-velocity weapon such as a .22, producing no exit wound. Evidence is not consistent with the official version which purports that he shot himself with a Colt .38 at point-blank range (directly into his own mouth) with high-velocity ammunition.

1. The person who first found Foster in the park examined his body closely because he was very curious as to what had happened. He swore under oath that no gun was present at that time in either hand of the victim, and that he was certain of that fact. The FBI pressured the witness to alter his story, but he refused.

2. A gun was found in victim's hand according to the official version, but it was a .38 caliber revolver. A .38 produces a powerful recoil after discharge and that recoil typically "throws" the gun several feet from a suicide victim.

3. No blowback of blood or tissue was found on the gun or on Foster's hand or on his sleeve. That is literally impossible from a .38 caliber Army Colt Special expending a high-velocity round into his head at very close range.

4. The powder burn patterns on Foster's hand indicate they were discharged from the FRONT of a gun cylinder. If Foster had been holding the gun himself when he was shot, then the pattern burns would have indicated that they were discharged from the REAR of the gun cylinder.

5. Foster's fingerprints were not on the gun. The FBI identified two prints on the weapon, but they did not belong to Foster.

Inconsistencies

6. The gunpowder residue that was found on Foster's clothing and eyeglasses DID NOT COME from the gun found in his hand.

7. The forensic evidence clearly indicates that the body was moved after the death of the victim. Witness testimony is consistent that there was very little blood at the scene. A .38 caliber high-velocity round produces a huge exit wound and a large pool of blood due to the fact that the heart keeps pumping after a gunshot to the head; an action that lasts until the heart runs out of blood to pump, thereby producing a massive pool at the scene of the gunshot. Its absence is a forensic indication that either the victim was killed somewhere else and then moved, or the gunshot took place after the victim was already dead.

8. The blood evidence also indicates that the body was moved post-mortem. Blood does not run uphill, it runs in accordance with gravity. Yet a dried trickle of blood on Foster's face did run uphill in defiance of gravity, indicating that the corpse was originally in a much different position. The corpse was not checked for lividity marks at the crime scene (standard police procedure), which would have indicated whether or not the victim had actually died in that position.

9. No soil samples were obtainable from Foster's shoes, according to the FBI report. However, in two re-enactments, walking from the parking lot to the crime scene in similar shoes, both tests accumulated very detectable soil samples on the exact same type of shoes that Foster was wearing. This fact is yet another indication that the body was moved post-mortem.

10. The "suicide note" supposedly found later in Foster's office at the White House has been determined to be a forgery by three handwriting experts who analyzed it independently.

11. The "suicide note" contained no fingerprints of Foster's, even though he supposedly had torn it into twenty-eight pieces.

12. A report from the Medical Examiner uncovered at the National Archives reveals that Foster had an ADDITIONAL GUNSHOT WOUND in his neck that was not reported.

13. There is no evidence that the gun found in his hand belonged to Foster. Nor is there any evidence that the gun fired the fatal shot.

14. The gun reportedly found in Foster's hand was not his own gun, but was a "drop gun" of the type that is used by professional killers because it is pieced together from various guns and is therefore impossible to trace.

15. The gun in Foster's hand was a .38, yet he was apparently shot with a .22, a smaller caliber wound which explains why it was not at first disclosed that there was no exit wound. The medical examiner viewing the damage at the scene stated that "it was consistent with a low-velocity weapon." A higher caliber .38 creates an exit wound with a gaping hole because of its much higher velocity. The much more powerful explosion taking place from a .38 also produces a strong "blowback," discharging blood and tissue out the mouth of the victim. Yet no blood or tissue was found on the gun.

16. Although the official version is that the bullet exited the rear of Foster's skull, the bullet was never located. Furthermore, autopsy doctor clearly states that there was no exit wound and there is substantial eyewitness testimony corroborating the absence of an exit wound.

17. The supposed crime scene weapon contained two .38 cartridges, one of which had been expended and one which had not. They were high-velocity .38 rounds of ammunition, which is dramatically inconsistent with

the evidence at the crime scene, which displayed the absence of a large pool of blood and the absence of a large exit wound on the victim.

18. One of the first witnesses to arrive at the crime scene was a medical technician who emphatically describes the weapon as an automatic not as a revolver and his detailed description of it is highly consistent with that of an automatic.

19. The gun in Foster's hand is clearly shown in an ABC color photo and its color is black. Foster's family members all concur that Vince Foster's gun was silver in color. Yet when the FBI showed Foster's widow the gun supposedly from the crime scene, the gun that they showed her was a silver one.

20. When Foster's widow went to look for her husband's gun where it was normally stored, she found a different gun there that no one in the family recognized as being Vince Foster's.

21. The only ammunition found at Foster's home was of .22 caliber, not .38. The FBI will not reveal the caliber of the silver handgun in their possession.

22. Eyewitness testimony indicates that Foster's car was not present at the park at the time that his body was first found. Two other cars were. Foster's car was found in the parking lot AFTER the corpse had been found, and the two other cars were then gone.

23. Foster was a very tall man, nearly 6'5". Yet the driver's seat of his car found at the park was pushed so far forward that it was in a position which was appropriate for a person about 5'8" tall. It would have been needlessly difficult for Foster to have driven his car with the seat that far forward. That fact implies that Foster's car was driven to the park later by someone other than he.

24. X-rays of Foster's skull have either disappeared or were never taken in the first place. They do not officially exist. Original crime scene photos have also "disappeared"; they do not officially exist.

25. The death was immediately labeled a suicide, precluding a homicide investigation. Standard operating procedure in the case of a violent death is to assume, investigate, and exhaust all possibilities of homicide first.

26. Foster was, by all accounts, a loving family man and very devoted father of three. On the morning of his death, he mailed a letter to his mother which stated nothing at all out of the ordinary. Nor did he make any mention

to his wife or children, or leave any explanation of any type. His sister had just traveled 1,000 miles to visit him on the day of his death, and Foster was upbeat about it and had promised her an exciting tour including lunch at the White House. Therefore, it defies credulity that he was even remotely considering suicide.

Bullets don't magically vanish;
Blood doesn't run uphill, or disappear;
Dead bodies don't move themselves;
And good parents don't blow their brains out
on their lunch hour.

"Hubbell said if you really want to understand Foster, to take a look at his recent speech at the University of Arkansas."[460]

"The class of 1971 had many distinguished members who also went on to achieve high public office. But it also had several who forfeited their license to practice law. Blinded by greed, some served time in prison."

"Sometimes doing the right thing will be very unpopular ... When the heat of controversy swarms around you, the conviction that you did the right thing will be the best salve and the best sleeping medicine ... The reputation you develop for intellectual and ethical integrity will be your great asset, or your worst enemy ... I cannot make this point to you too strongly. There is *no* victory— *no* advantage— *no* fee— *no* favor— which is worth even a blemish on your reputation for intellect and integrity."[461]

"Don't believe a word you hear. It was not suicide. It couldn't have been."[462]

When the personal attorney and lifelong friend of the *President of the United States* turns up dead on his lunch hour on a work day afternoon, you can say it's a security breach of the highest level. In fact, you don't even need to *wonder* if that's a national security issue—it's the very definition of one. That's why, *right* from the start, and even *before* they officially acknowledged being aware of Foster's death—the Clinton Administration controlled the *would-be* investigation by exerting considerable influence upon both the FBI and the U.S. Park Police, and ensuring that the death would quickly be officially labeled "suicide"—and if that was in direct violation of long-established protocol, then *so be it.* It's what Presidents call stonewalling and they're very good at it.

---

[460] FBI Interview of Associate Attorney General Webster Hubbell
[461] Vincent Foster speech at the University of Arkansas, shortly prior to his death and personally written by Vince Foster.
[462] Associate Attorney General Webster Hubbell, July 20, 1993, quoted in *Esquire Magazine*, 11/93

Vincent Foster was quite obviously a man of extremely high integrity, as evidenced in the words of the above address which was personally written by him and given only days prior to Foster's death. His "conviction to do the right thing" may very well be what got him killed.

The laws of our nation and of each state clearly proscribe that any violent death is to be treated as a potential homicide and investigated as such, even in cases that appear to be suicide (suicide is a legal determination made later). In the case of Vince Foster, less investigation was made than would have been mandated in any typically occurring violent death—the violent death of the highest ranking government official killed since President Kennedy was actually given less investigation than a common death.

Vince was a long and trusted friend of President Bill Clinton—they went all the way back to boyhood, growing up as close friends in Arkansas. He became a partner in the same firm as Hilary Clinton and worked closely with the Clintons for decades. When Clinton was elected President, Vince went with him, becoming personal attorney to the President and First Lady with an office right in the White House, a trusted member of the innermost circle of power in Washington. So he certainly "knew where all the bodies were buried," as the old expression goes.

Foster's very suspicious death also occurred at a very auspicious moment. The Whitewater investigation was official, on the front page every single day and dramatically threatening the very Presidency with which Foster was charged to protect.

Kindergarten class photo in Hope, Arkansas, 1950. Bill Clinton is at the far left. Vince Foster is the taller boy to Clinton's left.

The official version of the United States government, published in the 1994 Fiske Report, is that on July 20, 1993, White House Counsel Vince Foster, depressed about his work, drove to Fort Marcy Park in suburban Virginia after having lunch in his White House office on a Tuesday afternoon, parked his family's Honda automobile in the park's parking lot, walked 700 feet through the park to a very remote area, and then pressed a 1913 Colt .38 caliber revolver deep against the back of his mouth and pulled the trigger.

However, a *proper* police investigation would have revealed that story was <u>not possible</u> because a plethora of forensic evidence clearly indicates otherwise.

Vince left the White House one afternoon after eating lunch in his office on what everyone described as a normal work day for him. Prior to leaving,

Courtesy of *Reuters/ABC/Archive Photos*

The gun pictured in the crime scene photo above is obviously very dark. The gun that the FBI showed Foster's wife and got her to identify as his, was <u>silver</u>. The gun in the photo is a .38 with high-velocity ammo. The forensic evidence is dramatically inconsistent with this weapon. Note the absence of blood on hand, shirt and gun. A .38 with a high-velocity load splatters "blowback" all over everything. The wounds are only consistent with a low-velocity weapon such as a .22 caliber. The gun above is pieced together with parts from different guns to make it impossible to trace; it's the type used by professional killers—known as a "drop-gun" for hits.

he offered some candy to a co-worker and then told his secretary "I'll be right back" on his way out. Everything was normal—a typical work day—he wasn't suicidal. A few hours later—before you could say "Presidential privilege," Foster was dead, his body discovered that afternoon in a park in Virginia. They said he stuck a .38 in his mouth and pulled the trigger.

If a person places a .38 caliber revolver in their mouth and pulls the trigger, the blowback is incredible. It splatters blood and tissue all over, drenching the hand in it, as well as the wrist, the gun itself, the clothing nearest by, and obviously the wound in the mouth and nasal cavity which literally pour out huge amounts of blood from the residual blood pressure in the body and because the heart keeps pumping and sending more and more blood which escapes through the wound and the nasal cavity. The heart itself is fine. That's why donor hearts for transplants often come from head-trauma deaths. The heart keeps pumping blood for up to two full minutes after a gunshot wound to the head. So you can imagine how much blood keeps pouring out of those gaping wounds.[463]

But that didn't happen to Vince Foster. His hand was clean; the gun was free of blood; the white cuff of his shirt was still white; witnesses stated that they saw almost no blood at all on the white dress shirt; there wasn't oozing blood from his mouth and nasal wound; or a large pool of blood beneath him. It wasn't until his body was moved to take it to the morgue that the blood poured out of his wounds and bloodied his white shirt—the way that forensics tells us that it should have been bloodied to begin with, right at the crime scene.

And the incongruities go on and on. The gun that belonged to Vincent Foster was silver. The gun that was photographed underneath Foster's hand at the crime scene was black.[464]

It gets worse. There are, in point of fact, so many inconsistencies that it becomes difficult to prioritize them. And we're not talking here about things such as differing witness opinions that can be argued about like "He said—She said"; these are straight forensic facts, folks. So let's tackle a few, right here:

DEFENSIVE POWDER BURNS:

The powder burn patterns of a gunshot, known as GSR—for gunshot residue, paint a vivid picture about the violence that occurred. The powder burn patterns on Foster's hands were on the *inside* of *both index fingers*, i.e., towards his thumbs. The long GSR burns indicate he had his hands in *front* of a gun barrel, in a *defensive* manner, and further indicate that his hands were not actually touching the gun when it was fired—because the length of the GSR burn is determined by the distance from the gun (details follow in this chapter).

GUNPOWDER EVIDENCE:

GSR staining from a *different* gun was found on Foster's clothing and on his eyeglasses—not the gun found in the victim's hand. That has a dramatic evidentiary indication—that the victim was exposed to gunfire from a gun that

---

[463] Christopher Ruddy, *The Strange Death of Vincent Foster: An Investigation* (Free Press, 1997)
[464] Ruddy, *The Strange Death of Vincent Foster*

was <u>not present</u> at the official crime scene. The powder burns clearly indicate that Foster's hands were *not* on the gun grip when the gun was fired. Simple translation: Foul play clearly involved. Furthermore, even though he supposedly stuck the gun *inside* his mouth and fired it, there was <u>no gunpowder on his tongue</u>. If a .38 is fired directly into the mouth, it leaves certain gunpowder markings.[465]

FINGERPRINT EVIDENCE:

Foster's prints were <u>nowhere</u> on the gun, even though we would expect a person seriously contemplating suicide to be perspiring, which would facilitate the adherence of fingerprints to a gun; and it was a hot and humid July day, which would **further facilitate** it. That's a clear forensic indication that the gun was placed in his hand in the hours <u>after</u> his death, at which time his fingerprints would no longer adhere to the gun. **Someone *else's* prints *were* on the gun** (but we do not know whose).[466]

BLOOD POOLING EVIDENCE:

A .38 caliber at point-blank range with high—velocity ammo obviously leaves a *lot* of blood. However, the first doctor on the scene, as well as the EMTs (Emergency Medical Technicians), were very surprised by the dramatically insufficient amount of blood and tissue evidence on or around the body. Based on substantial experience with gunshot wounds, for a wound of that type they would have expected to find a bloodbath, but did not.[467]

BLOOD SPATTER EVIDENCE:

A .38 (even *without* the high-velocity ammo that was in the crime scene gun) fired at point-blank range into a human skull <u>always</u> leaves a large amount of blowback, i.e., it splatters blood and tissue all over the victim, all over their clothing, and all over the gun. Yet when the crime scene photo is examined (of Foster with a dark gun in his hand), virtually *no* blood is visible on victim, victim's clothing or gun. Even *the cuff* of his white dress shirt corresponding to the hand with which he supposedly fired, is in practically pristine condition. That is simply <u>not possible</u>.[468]

ABCENSE OF BULLET:

After a bullet traverses through a human skull, it loses its velocity and does not travel very much further. A huge team of FBI agents scoured every inch of the area where the body was supposedly found, figuring trajectories and bullet angles and using hi-tech gear to locate the bullet. They couldn't find it.[469]

---

[465] Ruddy, *The Strange Death of Vincent Foster*
[466] Ruddy, *The Strange Death of Vincent Foster*
[467] Ruddy, *The Strange Death of Vincent Foster*
[468] Ruddy, *The Strange Death of Vincent Foster*
[469] Ruddy, *The Strange Death of Vincent Foster*

ABCENSE OF CHIPPED TEETH:

If a .38 is fired directly into the mouth, it breaks teeth. That's especially true of the Army Colt. 38 Special, the type of gun found in Foster's hand, because it is a very bulky weapon with a high sight. At the impact of a huge explosion and resulting recoil of a .38 inside one's mouth, especially one firing a high-velocity round, teeth are broken and nearby tissue is practically destroyed. But the victim had no chipped teeth, insufficient tissue destruction and not even gunpowder on the tongue.[470]

ABCENSE OF BONE FRAGMENTATION:

Bone fragmentation is also what usually happens from the above-described explosion. But, you guessed it— *not* in Vince Foster.

VICTIM'S CAR KEYS:

If the victim drove to the park, as the official version purports, he obviously would have needed his car keys. Yet they were not there. The crime scene was thoroughly searched, as well as the victim and victim's car. There were no car keys. They turned up later, very "mysteriously" at the morgue, in Foster's pockets, which had already been checked.[471]

VICTIM'S EYEGLASSES:

Even though the Government maintains the position that the gun stayed in Foster's hand because there was no dramatic recoil (and you can't have it both ways), it *also* purports that the recoil of the gun was so dramatic that it knocked Foster's eyeglasses off his head and drove them up a steep hill, over and down the other side of that hill at a distance of approximately 15 feet from the victim, where they were found deep inside heavy underbrush. That's not to mention the facts that the ballistics indicate that the glasses should have been thrown in the *opposite* direction, and that the eyeglasses contained gunpowder from a gun *other* than the crime scene gun![472]

ABCENSE OF SOIL ON SHOES:

The virtually complete absence of soil or dirt on the bottom of Foster's shoes clearly reveals that he never took that 700-foot walk through the park trail that afternoon. Independent investigators test-walked the same path in the same type shoes and, quite unlike Foster's shoes, picked up considerable dirt and soil on their shoes.[473]

---

[470] Ruddy, *The Strange Death of Vincent Foster*
[471] Ruddy, *The Strange Death of Vincent Foster*
[472] Ruddy, *The Strange Death of Vincent Foster*
[473] Ruddy, *The Strange Death of Vincent Foster*

BALLISTICS MISMATCH:

The gun in Foster's hand was <u>not</u> the gun that killed him. The ballistics *did not* match.[474]

"FOREIGN" WEAPON:

No link was ever established between the victim and the weapon. It was <u>not</u> his gun.

PROFESSIONAL WEAPON:

The weapon was what is known as a "drop-gun"—a gun favored by professional killers because it is hard to trace. Drop-guns are pieced together from parts of different guns. They are so-named because the shooter drops it without fear because it is untraceable, or places it in a victim's hand to stage a suicide.[475]

EYEWITNESS ACCOUNTS:

Most of the eyewitness testimony dramatically contradicts the official version of events. For example, the first person to find Foster's body, swore under oath repeatedly that he was absolutely certain that there was no gun in either of his hands, and that he was laying with his palms up, which is not at all how officials claim.[476]

Solid eyewitnesses have repeatedly verified that Foster's car <u>was not in the parking lot</u> at the time that the body was found. It arrived later. One police officer reportedly even felt the hood of Foster's car after it arrived—long after Foster's body was found— and noticed that the hood of the car was still warm. As Brett Kavanaugh conceded (he followed Miguel Rodriguez as Lead Prosecutor after Rodriguez resigned), all of the police, medical emergency personnel, and others—<u>twenty-four witnesses</u> in total—<u>all</u> identified the Honda in the park's parking lot at the time of their arrival as being "brown"—not silver-gray, which was the color of Foster's Honda.

PROSECUTOR RODRIGUEZ:

> "Well, it all comes down to that brown car issue, right? All the police and medical personnel who were in the park also described it as brown."[477]

The witnesses were all consistent that the car was brown. Therefore, the car was not the Foster family's grey Honda. But, through semantic gamesmanship, that car magically became Foster's car in the official version of events, by

[474] Richard L. Franklin, "101 Peculiarities Surrounding the Death of Vincent Foster," http://prorev.com/foster.htm (accessed 1 May 2011).
[475] Franklin, "101 Peculiarities"
[476] John Clarke, Patrick Knowlton & Hugh Turley, *Failure of the Public Trust* (P.J. Knowlton, 1999).
[477] Clarke et al., *Failure of the Public Trust*

misrepresentation of witness testimony, preposterously implying that they had somehow all gotten the color wrong.

RECAP:

Those dramatic inconsistencies lead to some startling, but very logical conclusions. We know from the above facts that:

- The gun photographed in Foster's hand was <u>not</u> the murder weapon;
- Foster did <u>not</u> die at the official crime scene but must have been transported there <u>after</u> he was shot;
- A cover-up distorted the true facts;
- Most in major media played right along with the scripted show, apparently either because they lacked the time to investigate, or because they were "in somebody's pocket" from the start.

And silly us, we still believed in a "free press" back then, right? Keep on reading, my friends.

So we know that the gun in Foster's hand was not the murder weapon, and that he was killed elsewhere and dumped at the official crime scene <u>after</u> he was already dead.

There's even *more* (not that more is even necessary in this case!):

No one in the park saw him alive;

The person who found the body, and had someone call it in to 9-1-1, was absolutely certain that there was no gun in either of Vince's hands— he was curious, so he looked closely. Imagine yourself in his position. You're not sure what's going on—you approach suspiciously—your senses are heightened from the danger—you look closely and you <u>remember</u> it too, probably for the rest of your days. Well he looked, he inspected, he remembered—he swore repeatedly that there was no gun in either hand (the FBI pressured him to change his testimony and he resisted);

That crucial first witness <u>also</u> stated with certainty that Vince's palms were *face up*. The official version states that they were just the opposite and that one hand was under his leg;

Another early witness who saw the body a bit later stated with certainty that there *was* a gun in Vince's hand, but guess what? It was an *automatic*. The witness was a "gun guy" who knew his weapons too. He described it repeatedly as an automatic, which differs dramatically from the 1913 Colt .38 revolver that was found in his hand later. They pressured *him* to change his testimony too; he refused, reiterating that he knows what an automatic looks like, and an automatic is what he saw in the victim's hand. (Then, everyone *after* these early witnesses, states that they saw the .38 revolver in his hand);[478]

Foster's wife could not identify the gun;

Patrick Knowlton was another extremely credible witness. Guess what he saw? The cars that were in the parking lot at the time that the body was discovered. And guess what? Vince Foster's Honda <u>was not one of them</u>—it arrived later!;

---

[478] Ruddy, *The Strange Death of Vincent Foster*

Blood tracking on his face and shoulders indicated that his head had been moved in several different positions *after* the gun had been fired;

Blood trails from Vince's nose and mouth "defied gravity"— the tracks were hard forensic evidence that the blood had traveled *upward* on his face— but the body was laying on a steep slope, so blood should have traveled *downward*;

Both of the EMTs on the scene (Emergency Medical Technicians who are trained in life support, and trauma identification, and treatment) stated that they definitely observed gunshot trauma in Foster's <u>neck</u>; they observed <u>no</u> entry or exit wound in the head (one of the EMTs even reinforced this in testimony— when he was questioned about the exit wound, he countered "Was there one? I didn't know there was one." Here's how he actually testified:

<u>EMS Technician Richard Arthur:</u>

Q: "Where was the blood coming from?"

A: "To me it looked like there was a bullet hole right here."

Q: "In the neck?"

A: "Yes, right around the jaw line."

Q: "The neck and jaw line underneath the right ear?"

A: "Somewhere there. I would have to see a picture to point it out exactly where, but there was a little bit of blood coming out of the mouth too, and a little out of the nose, but the main was right here. I didn't see any on the left side. I didn't see any on the chest or anything."[479]

And again later, more testimony from the same EMT:

Q: "With respect to the bullet wound you think you saw in the—at the scene could you describe in some detail exactly what you thought you saw?"

A: "I saw what appeared to be a bullet hole, which was right around the jaw line on the right side of the neck."

Q: "About how big?"

A: "It looked like a small-caliber entrance wound, something with—I don't want to say a .22 or whatever, but it was a small caliber. It appeared to be a smaller caliber than the gun I saw."

Q: "How close to the body were you when you saw this?"

A: "Two to three feet."[480]

There was also a doctor at the scene, a Dr. Haut, who also saw the neck wound (which varies dramatically from how the wound was later officially described, as entering the mouth and exiting the back of Vince's head). Dr. Haut wrote in his report:

"Gunshot wound mouth-neck"

---

[479] Michael Rivero, "The Death of Vincent Foster: Vince Foster's wounds were not as reported," WhatReallyHappenned.com, http://whatreallyhappened.com/RANCHO/POLITICS/FOSTER_COVERUP/NECK/neck.html (accessed 14 May 2012).

[480] Rivero, "The Death of Vincent Foster"

Dr. Haut's *sworn* **report (the form actually reads "I hereby certify and affirm under the laws of the Commonwealth of Virginia") reads:**

"U.S. Park Police found a gunshot victim, mouth to neck."[481]

The paramedics from the local fire station were used to seeing dead bodies and knew what to expect from a death scene, be it a suicide or a murder. They assumed it was a murder because the body was lying perfectly straight and you don't see that in a suicide. They said it looked staged, like somebody had laid the body out—one of them even originally wrote it up as "murder" in his report for that reason. Here's how he testified:

> **"He was just perfectly straight. It just seemed weird, how the gun got underneath the leg and he was off the beaten path over a hill. I mean, most people wouldn't go back into shrubbery and sit down in all this shrubbery and everything around him, and shoot himself. I mean, maybe he would, but I don't know. I didn't know the man, so I'm just saying it just doesn't seem like a normal suicide that I would have run into."**[482]

The lead prosecutor <u>quit</u> because he said he wasn't being allowed to actually investigate the crime!

Critical crime scene photos are "missing"—officers *know* that they exist because they *saw* them being taken. But guess what?—nobody knows where they are, or at least that's what they told everybody, including Prosecutor Miguel Rodriguez. But Rodriguez got a peek at some enhanced crime scene photos, and guess what he says?—that there **_was_ a neck wound**, folks!

Law enforcement officers were also pressured to *stay in line* with the official version. Here's how one of *them* testified:

> **"Lieutenant Bianchi told me from orders higher up, said that I'm not allowed to talk to anybody about this, if I value my job. I said 'Well, what about the CIA, FBI and all that stuff?' He said you are not allowed to talk to anybody if you value your job."**[483]

That's some very explosive evidence. It reveals that Foster didn't die with the gun in his hand, *and* that he didn't die in the location in the park where they said he did. But bear in mind that there is also forensic evidence which actually proves that Foster didn't shoot himself with *any* gun, and that he was definitely murdered. That's arguably the most important forensic finding. The powder burn patterns reveal that he was acting in a <u>defensive</u> manner, and that his hands could not have actually been on the weapon that killed him.

---

[481] Rivero, "The Death of Vincent Foster"
[482] Rivero, "The Death of Vincent Foster"
[483] Clarke et al., *Failure of the Public Trust*

The work of Washington D.C. attorney John Clarke has proven that Vince Foster <u>literally</u> *could not* have fired the gun:

> "The only possible way to have gunshot residue deposited on the right index finger and web area and left index finger, a sufficient distance from the barrel-cylinder gap to provide the five-inch length of the residue pattern, is if the weapon was fired by the hand of another. The gunshot residue patterns found were made when Mr. Foster held his hands with the palms facing the revolver's cylinder, consistent with his hands being in a defensive posture."[484]

Clarke explains that in simpler language:

> "Foster couldn't have fired the weapon with the gunshot residue the way it was left on his hands. The residue was caused by Foster holding his hands consistent with a defensive posture. His hands were spread open; he wasn't touching the gun, though he seems to have been pushing the barrel away when the gunman pulled the trigger."[485]

Clarke also determined that the Remington Company, manufacturer of the bullets that were found in the gun that is the "official" vehicle of Foster's death, has never used the ball smokeless powder that was found all over the victim:

> "Ball smokeless powder is what was found on Vince Foster's body and clothing. We think that's significant because it's used for reloads. But professional hit men also use it to get particular firing characteristics out of a gun. That would be consistent with there being no exit wound. They'd put a light powder charge in the gun so that it wouldn't blow the back of his head off as it would, had it been stock ammunition. That's why I think it was a professional hit."[486]

Therefore:

- Foster did <u>not</u> fire the crime scene gun into his mouth as officially alleged, nor <u>any other</u> gun, for that matter.
- The gun that was photographed in his hand was <u>placed</u> there, at least one hour post-mortem.
- <u>Another</u> gun was involved in the crime and it was not present at the official crime scene, which is *also* highly indicative of murder.
- The victim acted in a <u>defensive manner</u>, ***resisting* a gun that was being pointed at him**, also highly indicative of murder.[487]

---

[484] Clarke et al., *Failure of the Public Trust*
[485] Clarke et al., *Failure of the Public Trust*
[486] Clarke et al., *Failure of the Public Trust*
[487] Clarke et al., *Failure of the Public Trust*

Criminals don't seem to understand a few things about crime scenes. If you move a body *after* death, then the evidence shows that. And that's what it clearly shows in this case.

Vince Foster's killers made other mistakes too. For example, his body was placed in the park before his car was—and it's pretty difficult to drive after a gunshot to the head. And whoever *did* drive Foster's car to the park forgot to move the seat back to where Foster always kept it when he drove—the seat position was dramatically different, which would have made it ridiculously uncomfortable for the tall (just under 6'5") Vince Foster to operate.[488]

Foster's car keys were <u>not found</u> at the crime scene—so how could he *possibly* have driven there?[489]

There's also this long-established factor known as *gravity*—blood doesn't run uphill. Yet the dried blood stains on Foster had trickled down in the direction that was *against* gravity in the position they say he was found in.[490]

So let's see what we have here: Blood doesn't run uphill, dead bodies don't move themselves, and good parents don't blow their brains out on their lunch hour.

The Clinton White House was accused of intentionally weakening the FBI and using it as a political tool. The FBI's Director, William Sessions, apparently refused to play along and was eventually fired as a result. He is the <u>*only*</u> <u>FBI Director in history</u> ever to be dismissed by a President.

It seems that more was going on there than appearances indicate. The reasons given for investigating and firing William Sessions as FBI Director were very flimsy— "improprieties" such as that he had used an FBI airplane to visit his daughter; changing the security system at his home, for which the government may have been billed. Sessions denied that he had acted improperly. Nonetheless, he was told by the President to step down. He defied the President, refusing to resign his position. President Clinton then fired Sessions as Director, on the day before Vince Foster's death. On Monday, July 19, 1993, President Clinton telephoned Director Sessions and ordered him to vacate his office immediately. So on the following day, Tuesday, when Vince Foster died, the FBI did <u>not have</u> a Director.

Compare the investigation and removal from office of Director Sessions—stemming from very weak evidence—with the *absence* of a serious investigation into the extremely suspicious death of Vince Foster; the contrast is startling. Sessions was eventually cleared of any wrongdoing—there was obviously little there, to begin with—and the "ethics" charges pursued against him are widely perceived as having been <u>politically motivated</u>. Sessions later explained what he considers to be the *real* reason for his firing to a reporter, saying that "at the time I left the Bureau, (I stated) that I would not be part of politicizing the FBI from within or without." That'll apparently cost one their job in a place like Washington. It certainly cost Sessions his.[491] He cited his refusal to buckle under to pressure from the White House,

---

[488] Clarke et al., *Failure of the Public Trust*

[489] Clarke et al., *Failure of the Public Trust*

[490] Clarke et al., *Failure of the Public Trust*

[491] Phil Brennan, "The Disintegration of the FBI," *31 May 2002, NewsMax.com*; http://archive.newsmax.com/archives/articles/2002/5/30/183028.shtml

and the Justice Department, and their political interference with running the FBI—that was the *actual* reason that he was fired as Director. Any would-be investigation into the very mysterious death of Vince Foster was therefore the victim of Washington politics. As Sessions put it, "the decision about the investigative role of the FBI in the Foster death was therefore compromised from the beginning."[492]

Veteran Homicide Investigator Mark Fuhrman examined the evidence and concluded that the body was obviously moved, the crime scene was staged, and the reason the Park Police were given jurisdiction was because then the investigation could be controlled. "Someone tried to stage a crime scene that is not believable in the least, and to make it work they gave it to an investigative body like the Park Police who can be ordered around and bullied," said Fuhrman.[493]

Detective Fuhrman cited <u>obvious signs of foul play</u>: "There was no brain matter, no skull fragments, not anything behind his head or blood on the vegetation around it. It was a sunny day, the light was good, yet there was nothing noted, nothing photographed." The conclusions from that evidence are obvious: "If he killed himself, he didn't do it there," stated Fuhrman. "If he committed suicide, then someone moved him to Fort Marcy Park."[494]

Or—someone may have moved him *in* Fort Marcy Park. Investigator Hugh Turley agrees with an observation shared by U.S. Attorney and Lead Prosecutor, Miguel Rodriguez: The evidence clearly indicates that Foster's body was at first found—and even *photographed*—at a different location *within* Fort Marcy Park, and then, for some inexplicable reason, moved to the location in the park where it is officially stated that the body was found (and which ignores any possibility that it was first found elsewhere). U.S. Attorney Rodriguez states that he saw the *original* crime scene photos, which confirm that the body was initially in a *different* location inside Fort Marcy.[495]

But what *is* evident is that the scenario officially embraced by the Government's version of events clearly *did not happen*—Foster did not die in the location or in the position in which we are officially told, despite attempts by Washington attorneys using their lawyerly ways to try to force square pegs into round holes. Saying it simply does not make it so. The body was either moved *to* the park or the body was moved *at* the park, and to posit that it wasn't defies the preponderance of forensic evidence.

Famed forensic scientist Dr. Henry Lee became a national personality during the O.J. Simpson trial, but he made a name for himself in criminal investigations in the decades prior. Dr. Lee points out that an accurate "reconstruction of the circumstances of Mr. Foster's death was not possible at the time of the OIC's (Office of Independent Counsel) investigation." He cited "the lack of complete documentation," "the lack of x-rays of Mr. Foster's body," "the lack of close-up photographs," and "the unknown location of the fatal bullet" as being obvious problems with doing a complete and proper reconstruction of

---

[492] Brennan, "Disintegration of FBI"
[493] Brennan, "Disintegration of FBI"
[494] Ruddy, The Strange Death of Vincent Foster, 170.
[495] Clarke et al., *Failure of the Public Trust*

the crime. The crime scene was corrupted long before the experts could get to it. Standard criminology procedures were blatantly violated. That never became a huge issue because, Dr. Lee continues, "In the Foster case, the death was not publicized enough to generate a firestorm ... " Had the case been scrutinized in the media to anywhere *near* the extent the O.J. case was, the facts *would* have generated a firestorm from the massive irregularities and inconsistencies clearly identifiable in the factual evidence. Dr. Henry Lee makes particular note of the immediate and most obvious discrepancies in the evidence:

> **"There were conflicting reports of where his body was found in the park, its position on a steep slope and whether or not his right hand clutched a .38 Colt handgun ... In consideration of powder burns found on both his hands, it was a feat that some believed could only have been performed by a contortionist ... It was alleged that within 24 hours of the crime, Foster's White House office had been stripped of documents, and U.S. Park Police investigators were prevented from entering the office or conducting routine interviews.** *Five days later*, **a torn suicide note was supposedly found in his office briefcase."[496]**

It's interesting to note that crime scene expert Dr. Henry Lee and Homicide Detective Mark Fuhrman were bitter enemies about the evidence interpretations in the O.J. Simpson murder trial and took dramatically different positions; yet they apparently share the same disdain for some of the striking disparities of evidence in the Vince Foster case.

EVIDENTIARY OVERVIEW

Primary Indications that Official Version of Vince Foster's Death is Incorrect

Official Version: On the afternoon of July 20, 1993, Vince Foster left his White House office shortly after lunch, without his briefcase, met with no one, drove to Fort Marcy Park in Virginia, walked to a desolate area of the park, placed a Colt .38 revolver directly inside his mouth and fired the weapon.

1. Powder Burns Were Defensive

The powder burn patterns found on both of Foster's hands came from the front of a gun cylinder. If he had shot himself, then his hands

---

[496] Dr. Henry Lee & Dr. Jerry Labriola, *Famous Crime Revisited: A Forensic Scientist Reexamines the Evidence* (Berkley, 2004).

would have had stains consistent with powder discharged from the rear of the cylinder. Heavy gunpowder deposits were found on the inside area of both his index fingers, meaning that they were both wrapped around the front of the gun. Forensic experts determined that such a grip is simply not consistent with a suicide and is, in fact, consistent with the actions of a person acting defensively. Ballistics experts conclude this is an indication of foul play.

2. No Fingerprints

No prints of the victim were anywhere on the gun. Two fingerprints were identified on the weapon—both prints belonging to an individual other than Foster.

According to the FBI, the lack of sweat on Foster's hand was responsible for the absence of fingerprints. However, the temperature that afternoon was over ninety-five degrees Fahrenheit, it was very humid, and common sense tells us that a man seriously planning on firing a weapon into his mouth is probably going to be sweating even if he's in Antarctica. The temperature, the humidity, and the drama of the moment are not indicative of a situation in which perspiration would be completely absent.

3. No Ballistics Match

There is <u>no</u> evidence that the gun found in Foster's hand fired the shot. There is also <u>no</u> evidence that the gun belonged to Foster.

4. No Gunpowder Match

GSR (gunshot residue) was found on Foster's clothing and eyeglasses but it did <u>not match</u> the gunpowder from the gun found in his hand—it was from a different gun. Let's make that very clear—the gunpowder residue on his clothing and eyeglasses did not come from the gun that was in his hand.

5. No Blowback

There should have been substantial blowback of blood and tissue from a .38 at point-blank range with high-velocity ammunition, which was found in the gun. Yet the official crime scene photograph clearly shows Foster's hand, shirt, and the gun in his hand, all in virtually pristine condition. Homicide experts agree that there should have been a "jet stream" shooting out of the back of the head that drenched vegetation in the area with huge amounts of blood and body matter, especially near the victim's head. Yet the Park Police report clearly states "there was no blood spatter on the plants or trees surrounding the decedent's head."

6. No Blood Pooling

A .38 caliber gunshot at point-blank range obviously leaves a gaping wound and a lot of blood. Trained personnel observed dramatically insufficient amounts of blood and tissue on the victim, underneath him, or anywhere at crime scene. During one search:

> At least "sixteen FBI agents used high-tech equipment to search the park for the missing bullet, bone fragments from Foster's skull, and the presence of blood beneath the soil." (Crime Lab investigative reports, cited in The Mysterious Death of Vincent Foster, Dr. Cyril Wecht, 1998)

7. No Bullet

A .38 caliber bullet was supposedly fired at the crime scene. But no bullet or bullet fragments of that slug were ever recovered. The bullet is typically found because, after traveling through a human skull, it loses most of its velocity.

The level of importance of the above fact is demonstrated by the level of the search that it mandated. An army of FBI agents combed the entire area methodically using the latest hi-tech equipment. There were three separate FBI searches utilizing dozens of agents and spanning several months of efforts. The searches came up with <u>nothing that could be linked to the supposed murder weapon</u>:

> "The FBI even developed a map showing the likely path and direction of the bullet after it exited Foster's skull." (Crime Lab investigative reports, cited in The Mysterious Death of Vincent Foster, Dr. Cyril Wecht, 1998)

8. No Witnesses

The park is tiny— less than a quarter of a mile wide— and a Colt .38 is loud. The embassy of Saudi Arabia, with guards on duty, was very near the crime scene and five homes were also located within a few hundred yards. It's a very quiet area. Yet no one at those locations, or anywhere in a public park, reported hearing a gunshot. Emergency personnel encountered two witnesses who were a few hundred feet away from where the body was found. They reported that they had heard nothing.

9. No Car Keys

How exactly does a person drive their car with no car keys? They searched the victim; no car keys. They searched the vehicle; no car keys. They searched the park; no car keys. They were not there. Later that evening at the morgue, a "re-check" was made of Foster's pockets by White House officials and—you guessed it, folks—the car keys magically appeared. However, it is quite logical to conclude that the professional investigators, who made a thorough search of Foster and were specifically looking for those same car keys, would not have missed them had they originally been in Foster's pockets. They were not there. So can somebody please explain how he drove his car to this remote park with no car keys?

10. No Dirt On Shoes

If the victim had actually walked hundreds of yards (as alleged) through the park to reach the location where the body was found, he would have picked up large amounts of dirt on his shoes and clothing. Witnesses saw no dirt on his clothing and the amount of dirt on his shoes was dramatically insufficient for that scenario.

11. No Chipped Teeth

The Colt .38 found in the victim's hand (an Army Colt .38 Special) is a large weapon. It has a high gun sight and a very bulky ejector rod head (the metal extension beneath the barrel of the gun) that, if placed inside a person's mouth and fired, would inevitably produce chipped teeth and damaged lips at discharge. Foster had no chipped teeth and his lips were undamaged. That simply isn't possible if that weapon had gone off inside his mouth, especially with a high velocity round, as was present in the revolver.

12. No Exit Wound

According to the U.S. Government's story, the only gunshot wounds on Vince Foster were a .38 caliber entry wound in the mouth and its wound of exit at the back of his head. The medical experts who initially handled Foster's body did not see an exit wound anywhere in the victim's head, even though they looked for one. The paramedics at the scene handled the body and moved it into a body bag. They knew it was extremely rare to not have an exit wound in a high-velocity shot into the head at point blank range. So they looked for an exit wound, and their testimony confirms that there was not one. The doctor who certified Foster's death also said that he did not see an exit wound in Foster's head.

13. No Skull Fragments

A Colt .38 fired directly into the mouth explodes with such force that it blows out the back of the brain casing and, inevitably, knocks out skull fragments in the process. But there were no skull fragments found. An officer at the scene stated:

> **"There was no blowout. There weren't brains running all over the place ... I initially thought the bullet might still be in his head."**
> (Richard L. Franklin, *101 Peculiarities*)

14. Small-Caliber Gunshot Wound In Neck

Two paramedics who were at the scene clearly saw what they identified as a gunshot wound in the victim's neck and they testified accordingly. The doctor, who was also at the scene, also saw a neck wound and described it as such in his official report. Lead Prosecutor Miguel Rodriguez stated that he also saw evidence of the gunshot wound in Vince's throat, but that evidence was suppressed, and he was unable to obtain documentation of the original crime scene photos that he had earlier viewed.

15. "Gravity-Defying" Blood — Sign Body Was Moved

If the body was not moved, then the blood stains on Foster's cheek defied gravity by running uphill instead of downhill. One or the other is true, so the smart money would have to bet that the body was moved after death when the blood had already dried.

16. Other Signs That Body Was Moved:

Independent homicide experts concluded there is "overwhelming evidence" that Foster's body was moved to the park, and that he did not die in the location he was found. The fact that there was a gun in his hand on a hot day and no fingerprints under circumstances ideal for leaving prints, is a forensic indicator that the gun was placed in his hand in the hours after his death, when the prints would no longer adhere.

His car arrived at the crime scene after Foster was already dead.

His car keys were not located after a thorough search of his person and the scene.

The body was lain out straight and neat as though it had been placed in such a position, a fact which caught the eye of the Emergency Medical Tech on the scene.

The same EMT wrote "Homicide" under cause of death in his official report.

A gun found in the hand of the victim is an automatic red flag of possible foul play (the gun is usually thrown out of the hand of the victim when firing, especially with a high-velocity weapon like a 38).

The underbrush near the area where the body lay was very trampled, unlike the rest of that very remote area of the park— the indication being that several people had been busy in the area.

17. Wine Stain

A large purplish wine stain was very visible on the front of Foster's shirt, and a witness also observed vomit on his shirt and a wine cooler bottle two and a half feet from the body. That's inconsistent with our victim— Foster was not an afternoon drinker— we know that he had a Coke that day with his lunch. He was also very neat and orderly, always professional. Therefore the large wine stain is suggestive of a struggle, or of a staged crime scene. The stain was never analyzed.

18. Semen Stain

Laboratory testing also could have determined if the large semen stain on the inside of Foster's underwear was the result of a natural spontaneous post-mortem emission (which occasionally happens) or evidence of sexual activity just prior to death. Even if the stain had simply been photographed (standard procedure), comparative testing of the drying of fresh semen on similar fabric could have established the approximate time of ejaculation. That's the way you properly investigate a violent crime.

19. Blonde Hairs

Blonde hairs were found on the victim, which were inconsistent with the victim's hair or that of his wife. Incredibly, no testing of those hairs was ever conducted. By the time that The Starr Report was released—September 11, 1998, over five years after Foster's death—the government attempted to diffuse this issue by implying that it was a moot point because the people who would have been asked to provide hair samples, were people with whom it was already known that Foster had been in contact. So we still do not know who the hair samples matched.

20. Carpet Fibers

Multi-colored carpet fibers (six different colors) were found all over the victim, even on his underwear. No investigation was initially made to match the carpet fibers to the victim's car (for example, the trunk, to see if he had been transported in it), home or office, which is standard investigatory procedure. The police later claimed that the carpet fibers must have gotten all over his clothing from cross-contamination when his clothes were all thrown together in an evidence bag—but that possibility has been thoroughly disproven. The Starr Report, five years later, amid growing controversy that Foster's body may have been moved, attempted to diffuse this issue by stating that most of the carpet fibers were white and the white carpet fibers were consistent with the carpet in Foster's home back in 1993. Pink wool fibers were also found on the victim's undershirt, socks and shoes. Apparently, no testing was done upon those either.

21. Gun Anomolies

   a) The official crime scene photograph clearly shows a black or very dark blue gun lodged in Foster's hand. The gun that the FBI showed Foster's wife and got her to identify as the gun that Foster owned, was silver, not black.
   b) The witness who first found the body in the park examined the scene very closely and swore that he was positive that there was no gun in Foster's hand. The FBI bullied the witness in an attempt to get him to change his testimony, but he would not budge.
   c) Another witness who saw the gun at the crime scene described it as an automatic, describing it with correct precision. Richard Arthur, an experienced Paramedic who was also experienced

with handguns, was one of the first people to view Foster's body. He swore emphatically that he saw an automatic weapon in the victim's hand. He described the weapon in extreme detail, matching the profile of an automatic and not that of a revolver. His FBI Statement reads: "100% sure automatic weapon (was in Army, looks at magazines, knows difference between automatic and revolver). Appeared like .45 automatic."

d) A gun still in the hand of a supposed suicide victim is another standard red flag of crime scene investigation. The explosive action or "kick" of the gun, combined with the reflexive actions of the victim, ordinarily "throws" the gun many feet away. A gun still in the hand is rare; added to this is the fact that the kick of the Colt .38 is very strong and usually throws the gun many feet away. Foster's eyeglasses were found many yards away from the body. Yet the gun was said to still be in hand.

e) According to a U.S. Park Police report and an initial report from the White House to the media, two different guns were used in the shooting; a .22 and a 38.

f) The only bullets that could be linked to Foster were some of .22 caliber found at his home. The crimes scene gun was a 38.

g) Foster's eyeglasses were found nineteen feet away from his head in dense underbrush— knee-high vegetation. The kick of the Colt .38 should have thrown his glasses in precisely the opposite direction.

h) And if the kick of the gun was sufficient to send the eyeglasses hurling nineteen feet away, then it clearly should have also kicked the weapon out of the victim's hand, which was much nearer to the explosive discharge than were the eyeglasses. The kick should have either thrown both the glasses and the gun, or neither.

22. Car Anomalies

a) Four witnesses reported seeing a car other than Foster's parked in the spot where Foster's car later appeared. Their sightings of the other car were at the time that Foster's body was found in the park.

b) Foster's car was later found in the same spot after the crime scene was identified; it was apparently placed there at a later time. An officer reportedly felt the hood of the car and noticed that it was still warm—long after Foster's body had been found.

c) Car seat was in a ridiculously awkward position for 6'5" driver.

d) Foster's pager was reportedly at the crime scene, but its memory had been erased. Rather than preserving the evidence, the Park Police immediately returned Foster's pager to the White House. It is not only illegal to give away primary evidence, but since associates of the victim are automatically considered pro forma suspects in the case of a violent death, it amounted to giving away the evidence to the very people whom they should have been investigating!

e) Four eyewitnesses reported seeing a briefcase on the front seat of Foster's car and described it in detail. The briefcase disappeared. Like Foster's pager, it was probably turned over to the White House, in direct violation of proper procedure.

23. Blatant Forensic Errors

Standard Forensic Procedures were blatantly ignored. Imperative forensic evidence was never obtained because police failed to examine the victim's body for lividity markings (settling of blood near the skin) which would have told a precise story of exactly how the body had been moved. Failure to check for lividity is such a sophomoric mistake that it must have been done intentionally, in deference to the White House. The victim's fingernails were not scraped for samples, which is also standard procedure. The four-inch semen stain on the inside of the underwear was not tested or even photographed. Nor was the urine stain of the victim tested (it is common to urinate upon death and Foster apparently did). The blonde hairs and multi-color carpet fibers that were found recurringly all over the victim's body were not initially tested. The Starr Report, over five years after Foster's death, skirted these issues and attempted to diffuse them by stating that there was no need to check the hairs because it was already known that Foster had contact with the very people who would have been asked for hair samples, and the white carpet fibers were consistent with the carpet in his home in 1993. The crime scene gun was never tested during the initial investigation for a standard check on firing capability. There was no attempt to identify recent tire tracks at the extremely remote rear access road of the park.

24. Rush To Suicide Verdict

In the case of any death with violence, like a gunshot, there are standard investigatory procedures to be followed. One of those procedures is that Homicide is never ruled out until the all the evidence has been gathered and it is certain that Homicide can be ruled out. The determination of Suicide is a legal ruling to be given at a much later date. Yet, in the case of Vince Foster, within minutes of his death, it was deemed Suicide, thereby closing off standard investigatory avenues. It is also noteworthy, that the Park Police who made the determination of Suicide were also aware that Foster worked at the White House, due to Foster's White House ID.

25. No Note

Foster was known far and wide as a good family man and devoted father. The notion that he would not leave a note of explanation if he planned to take his own life is simply beyond comprehension.

26. Forged Suicide Note

A note of Foster's, deemed to be "the suicide note"— was said to be found five days later by top Clinton White House attorney Bernie Nussbaum, in a briefcase that had <u>already been searched</u> under police supervision. However, the note never even mentioned suicide and appeared, rather, to be a list of the things with which Foster was dissatisfied and was planning to resign over. The contents of the note, torn into many pieces and <u>absent</u> of Foster's fingerprints, were categorically unsuicidal: they relate to Foster's disdain for the dishonesty he saw evident in Washington politics ("The FBI lied in their report to the Attorney General."); in the media ("The Wall Street Journal editors lie without consequence."); and his dissatisfaction at the level of immorality at the national political level in general ("Here ruining people is considered sport.") They appear, therefore, to be a list of his <u>reasons for resigning</u>, in accordance with his stated intentions; he had explained that intention to his wife and had scheduled a private meeting with President Clinton for Wednesday morning at which he quite apparently intended to inform the President of his decision to resign. And he was apparently killed less than 24 hours prior to that scheduled private meeting.

Three handwriting experts independently determined that the note supposedly written by Foster was an "obvious forgery" that was apparently pieced together from samples of things that Foster had actually written.

27. No Warning Sign

Suicides have warning signs. As personal attorney to the President of the United States, Foster was certainly no stranger to stress. Yet the last day of his life was one of his least stressful. He spent the morning at his desk, paying bills and taking care of some family matters, which were child's play in comparison to the legal concerns with which he typically dealt, such as the emerging scandals of his lifelong friend and client, President Bill Clinton.

He wrote a letter to his mother, with whom he was close—he was known as quite the "Southern gentleman"— he mentioned nothing out of the ordinary in the letter. He had been looking forward to the Washington visit of his sister, Sharon, with whom he was very close and who had just come to town with her daughter— Vince had promised to show her a great time in Washington and one of his plans was to take his niece to have lunch at the White House.

For lunch, he sat on the couch in his office, calmly opened up a newspaper, and ate a hamburger and french fries. He asked a co-worker if she wanted some of his M & Ms candy. He then left his White House office, calmly telling Executive Assistant Betsy Pond: "I'll be back." Linda Tripp, the Executive Assistant to whom Foster had given the candy prior to his departure, told the FBI that there "was nothing unusual about his demeanor and he did not seem distressed." Foster's personal Executive Assistant Deborah Gorham said that Foster had been "relaxed and normal," and that he had left a couple of letters and a memo for her to type, which were nothing out of the ordinary. Foster then walked by guard post E-4 of the west wing of the White House; Uniformed Secret Service Officer John Skyles remembered Foster passing by— he was his usual friendly self. Skyles "distinctly recalled that Foster did not appear to be at all depressed or preoccupied as he walked by." Skyles said "How are you doing sir?" and Foster smiled and responded "Hello-fine." And that was the last time he was officially seen alive.

28. No Log Entry

The White House is the most secure residence in the world— video and log entries record each entry and exit. There is no Security log or White House Gate Record entry known to exist anywhere showing Vince Foster leaving the White House complex that day, under his own power, or otherwise.

29. No Surveillance Tapes

The tapes from surveillance cameras that would have shown Foster's car leaving the parking lot are said to have disappeared— they were stored in a safe in the White House and they were apparently taken from that safe. No one from the Clinton Administration was willing to address what happened to the missing surveillance tapes which, as standard security measures, obviously once existed.

30. Violation Of Crime Scene

Police requested that Foster's office in the White House be sealed off. Technically, his office was part of a crime scene. The White House blatantly failed to comply with that request. The President's top lawyer (Foster's boss) ordered the immediate removal of sensitive files from Foster's office. Files and papers of Foster's were removed and brought to Hilary Clinton's Chief of Staff— and that was documented by a uniformed Secret Service Officer.

31. Vince's Safe Was Broken Into

The White House made sure that Foster's safe was "cleaned out" before any official investigation of his office. Even before Foster went missing, high-level White House action was trying to gain access. Only the White House Security Office, and Foster himself, had the combination to his safe. An aide told the Security Office that "Bill Kennedy (another lawyer to President Clinton) needed to get into Mr. Foster's safe." The Security Office checked their records and, seeing that Foster had only authorized himself to have the combination, correctly denied the request for the combination. The safe in Foster's office was later broken into on the night of his death by a security team who knew how to get into it, and items known to be in it then disappeared. Foster's personal secretary, Deborah Gorham, verified that documents and letters that she knew to be in that safe had vanished, as well as Foster's file index which was a complete master list of everything contained in his files.

32. Witness Intimidation By FBI

FBI agents clearly employed intimidation tactics against witnesses. For example, Patrick Knowlton was a crucial witness because of his certainty that Foster's car was not present in the parking lot at the time when the body was already in the park. Knowlton said the FBI falsified his official witness statement, and he brought a lawsuit against the FBI. He also states that he was targeted and harassed, that when he would leave his home he would be followed by several different men who would make a point of glaring at him in an intimidating manner. When a reporter expressed doubt about the veracity of that claim, he was invited to accompany Knowlton for a walk, witnessed the intimidation firsthand and was certain that it was clearly intentional (it was very intimidating). He was followed by teams of agents, when on foot and when driving, he was given threatening gestures, awoken in the middle of night, etc., in a vivid pattern of harassment that was witnessed and confirmed by other people. In addition to suing the FBI, Knowlton co-authored the book Failure of the Public Trust, with his attorney and an investigator. The FBI pressured this and other witnesses to change testimony that did not fit the official version of events.

33. White House Lied

The White House (using the term collectively) lied about their search of Foster's office, saying it was only for about 10 minutes— in reality, it was for about 2 hours, and that was just during the first search of it.

President Clinton stated that he did not learn of Foster's death immediately because at 9:00 pm he began filming a Larry King interview. The interview went so well that they continued past the scheduled conclusion. He reportedly only learned of Foster's death when an aide later interrupted him during a commercial break.

However— at 8:30 p.m. that evening, President Clinton was having his makeup professionally done for that 9:00 p.m. Larry King interview. The makeup artist who was present there testified that the President was chatting with his aide, Mack McLarty, when another aide to the President entered the room and told President Clinton:

"They found a note in Foster's office."

The sworn statement of the makeup artist was conspicuously absent from the Fiske Report.

The sworn testimony of three police officers (under penalty of perjury) attests to the fact that the White House knew of Foster's death by 6:15 p.m. (the White House officially claimed that it did not learn of the death until 8:30 p.m., which simply does not concur with how events unfolded). The phone logs would have ordinarily documented the phone call which took place from White House aide Helen Dickey to the Governor's Mansion in Little Rock, Arkansas at 6:15 (informing the Governor that Foster was dead), but the phone log— like Foster's files, file index and appointment book— apparently vanished (the White House denied a Freedom of Information request for the phone log for that evening, without explanation). The corresponding phone logs for the recipient of the same phone call, the office of the Governor of Arkansas, also coincidentally vanished. But the White House's claim that "no call to the Governor's mansion was made … on July 20, 1993" is simply untrue. Helen Dickey also testified under oath that the phone call took place.

White House aide David Watkins learned of Foster's death when he was paged by the White House military communications office on the day of Foster's death, at slightly after 7:00 pm. Watkins testified to the U.S. Senate in 1995 that at 10:30 p.m. he contacted the White House's Patsy Thomasson and asked her to search Foster's White House office: "I asked her to look for a note … I also knew that the Park Police had been in touch with the Secret Service for some five hours prior to making that request … ": That testimony places the informing of the Secret Service prior to the official time of the body's discovery in the park. It's simple common sense that the White House would be notified immediately when a top White House official is found dead.

34. Contradictory Toxicology Reports

The original and official toxicology report on Vince Foster was conducted by Dr. Hyunh. It states very clearly that no Trazodone (an antidepressant) or derivatives of Valium were found in Foster's blood. Yet the FBI's report to the U.S. Senate's Committee on Whitewater stated that both Trazodone and Valium-derivatives were found in Foster's blood; information that supported the very weak claims of the Fiske Investigation that Foster had been depressed.

35. Obvious Obfuscations; Cover-Up

- The White House blatantly ignored police instruction to seal off Foster's White House office. U.S. Secret Service agents confirmed that files were being removed from Foster's office and taken to Hilary Clinton's Chief of Staff;

- The White House denied that Foster even had a safe, making the preposterous statement that "I don't think there was a safe, as I understand it. To the best of my knowledge, there was not." (Mack McLarty, White House Chief of Staff). Apparently, having learned (after they had cracked Vince's safe!) that it had several drawer compartments, they re-classified the safe as a "file cabinet." Also note that the "official search" of Vince's office did not take place until Thursday, two days after he had gone missing, and after his office had been thoroughly sanitized;

- Foster's missing car keys (his body, his clothing, his car, and the crime scene were thoroughly checked for them, and they were not found) mysteriously appeared right after two top White House aides had urgently rushed to the morgue for the stated purpose of identifying Foster's body (which had already been identified— he even had his White House ID with him). And hey, guess what, folks? — it turns out they were right in Vince's pockets all along. Two large and bulky key rings that everybody at the crime scene somehow missed— gee, what a miracle! Investigators sarcastically refer to it as The Magic Keys Incident;

- Despite the fact that the supposed murder weapon found in Foster's hand was a vintage <u>80-year old weapon</u>, the Government never even tested it during the time of the initial investigation to verify that it could <u>actually even fire;</u>

- The FBI never even tested the blonde hairs, carpet fiber, and wine stain evidence that were found on the victim's body;

- Not only did crucial evidence disappear from Foster's safe, but the video surveillance tapes that would have shown who removed them from Foster's safe, lo and behold, have also conveniently vanished;

- Important crime scene photographs "disappeared";

- Important x-rays of Foster also disappeared;

- Medical records contradict the official claim that Foster had experienced recent weight loss as a result of stress;

- Witnesses have sued the FBI about outright lies they have made, as well as attempting to badger witnesses into changing their stories and attempting to discredit witnesses whose testimony was not in line with the official version of events, rather than actually investigating the leads that their testimony provided. In the case of Patrick Knowlton, they even <u>harassed a witness</u> who was simply attempting to help;

- Investigators badgered the Arkansas State Troopers who testified under oath (subjecting them to criminal perjury charges if they lied), to try to get them to change their testimony about the phone call from the White House to the Governor of Arkansas which occurred prior to the time the White House stated it was aware of Foster's death;

- FBI Director William Sessions was fired by President Clinton on the day before Foster's mysterious death. Sessions later remarked that the result of that was that any serious investigation into Foster's death had been "compromised from the beginning";

- Lead Prosecutor Rodriguez concluded that the official claims regarding the time that the White House and Secret Service were made aware of Foster's death are simply <u>not plausible;</u>

- The White House was clearly "calling the shots" in the quick rush to a "suicide" determination and in limiting the scope of the investigation. President Clinton immediately went public with the preemptive determination that the death was a mystery that would not be solved: "No one can know why things like this happen";

- High-level White House aides had incredibly convenient and recurring "memory lapses" during their testimony regarding what had taken place in matters related to Foster's death. For example, Susan Thomases was a close aide to First Lady Hillary Clinton. Although Ms. Thomases was logged in at the White House for six hours on the day that Foster's documents were being moved and was in phone communication with Ms. Clinton, she could not satisfactorily explain what had taken place during those six hours and invoked her "poor memory" 178 times during four days of Senate testimony";

- Meanwhile, back in Arkansas— the Rose Law Firm was busily shredding all the Vince Foster files it could find before they could be officially requested by investigators. The "Independent" Counsel (Fiske) assured the press that he would investigate the matter, but apparently he never got around to that;

Source material for the above chart was derived primarily from the following:

"Independent Report in Re: The Death of Vincent Foster, Jr.", Vincent J. Scalice Associates, April 27, 1995, *Western Journalism Center*.

"Forensic Experts Doubt Foster Suicide Finding", Christoper Ruddy, January 18, 1995, *Pittsburgh Tribune-Review*

"The Mysterious Death of Vincent Foster", in *Grave Secrets: A Leading Forensic Expert Reveals the Startling Truth About O.J. Simpson, David Koresh, Vincent Foster, and Other Sensational Cases*, Cyril Wecht, M.D., J.D. with Mark Curriden and Benjamin Wecht, 1998.

The Strange Death of Vincent Foster, Christopher Ruddy, 1997

Citizen's Independent Report, Hugh H. Sprunt; 1995

The Secret Life of Bill Clinton: The Unreported Stories, Ambrose Evans-Pritchard, 1997

The Murder of Vince Foster, Michael Kellett, 1995

"White House Lying on Foster's Death", John Crudele, February 7, 1996, *New York Post*

"New Evidence Exposes Vince Foster Murder: Victim Not Shot With .38 Caliber Revolver", Wesley Phelan, *The Washington Weekly*, October 26, 1998.http://www.bigeye.com/vfoster.htm

"101 Peculiarities Surrounding the Death of Vincent Foster", Richard L. Franklin, http://prorev.com/foster.htm

"The Death of Vincent Foster", Michael Rivero, *WhatReallyHappened.com*, http://whatreallyhappened.com/RANCHO/POLITICS/FOSTER_COVERUP/foster.php

Let's now go back to the beginning: On the last day of his life, Vincent Foster spent a less than typically stressful morning in his White House office, dealing with a variety of matters that were not of crucial importance.

It also seems prudent to examine a few of the things that were going on in his mind at this particular time. He had been very disturbed by the Justice Department's handling of the Waco disaster and what seemed like the completely unnecessary loss of life there due, quite simply, to a failure of patience and negotiation. Foster's wife recalled that Vince had been "horrified" by the FBI's assault on the Waco compound that resulted in seventy-five civilian deaths, twenty-five of whom were children.

As observed earlier, Vince Foster clearly considered himself a man of high integrity with a strong moral compass to guide him, which was well-evidenced in his choice of words for the Commencement Address he gave at the University of Arkansas just prior to his death. When that mental composition was combined with the fact that he was also old friends, close confidant, and personal attorney to both the President of the United States and First Lady—sharing all their secrets; it's easy to imagine a situation in which that morality and integrity are compromised and pushed beyond the limits of endurance. That's quite possibly what was going on during Vince's last days.

Contrary to the "official version," Foster's actions in those final days were not at all typical a person suffering severe depression and contemplating suicide. They were typical of a man who was wrestling a moral lion and attempting to do what he considered right, in the face of immense opposition.

Another point of note is that strange things were brewing at this particular time, and not only was Vincent Foster right in the thick of things, but he also seemed to be the one who was up to something. This was right after several smaller scandals had struck the Clinton Administration, for example, issues of impropriety in the White House travel office, which garnered much attention in the media. But bigger things were now afoot. What was soon to become a huge national scandal involving all the Clinton cronies from Arkansas, high among them the senior partners of the Rose Law Firm which was the Clinton's power base in Arkansas. Therefore, Foster's action in regard to this newly brewing tempest are particularly noteworthy.

- What Foster seemed to be doing was circumventing that regular Arkansas power base that he was a part of and had always, in the past, been allegiant to and protected.
- The week before his death, Vince called a close and trusted advisor, James Lyons of the Lyons Law Firm in Denver; known as a "Super-Lawyer" in conflict resolution, Lyons was instrumental in successfully bringing the peace process to Northern Ireland. It's clear that Lyons was a man whom Vince thought he could trust.
- Vince contacted Lyons the week prior to Vince's death with a rather strange request. He asked Lyons if he could be sure to make himself available soon for a trip to Washington on very short notice. Lyons agreed to be available.

- On the following Sunday night, less than two days before Foster's death, Foster again called Lyons and set up a special meeting with him in Washington for that Wednesday. Lyons agreed to be there.
- Foster was dead on Tuesday afternoon so their meeting never took place. But it obviously raises the question why a man who had any thoughts of committing suicide prior to it, would be taking very certain steps to set up a very important meeting with an old friend whom he knew he could trust; especially when the old friend is a specialist in extreme conflict resolution. Those would obviously seem to be the actions of a man who was not suicidal and was seeking counsel on an important matter from *outside* the Rose Law Firm and Arkansas power center.
- We know too that Vince had also scheduled a rare personal audience meeting with President Clinton—a *face-to-face* where he could have the total attention of the President—and that the topic of the meeting was reportedly Foster's resignation and the reasons for it. That meeting was scheduled for the following day, what turned out to be the day after his death. Vince never made it to that meeting.
- At 9:00—9:30 AM on the *same day* that Foster dies, the FBI raids the Little Rock office of former Arkansas Judge David Hale, a powerful political supporter of the Clintons. This is the move that breaks the dam wide open on a series of corrupt political deals that were operating in Arkansas while Clinton was Governor. It is David Hale who implicates the Clintons. Indicted and convicted in what will become known as the *Whitewater Scandal* are Arkansas Governor Jim Tucker (Clinton's successor), who is removed from office; Clinton's Assistant Attorney General Webster Hubbell (a fellow law partner of Foster's at the powerful Rose Law Firm); and Judge Hale; a total of fifteen persons convicted of over forty crimes.
- It's also very noteworthy that, rather than the reaction that you would expect from close colleagues of a man who dies a violent sudden death—one of shock and investigation—the collective reaction of those who worked closely with Foster at the White House—Bernie Nussbaum, William Kennedy and Hilary Clinton—instead appeared to be one of immediately <u>closing ranks</u> after Foster's death and attempting to seal the gaping holes in the so-called *suicide scenario*. The appearance was one of "circling the wagons" to protect the White House at any cost. For example, they played roles in "finding" Foster's missing car keys (in a ludicrously convenient set-up) and "needed to get into Foster's safe" immediately after his death, according to White House security records; Nussbaum (Chief Counsel to the President and, therefore, Foster's immediate superior) was involved in the search of Vince's office—which was technically part of a crime scene—prior to the arrival of police investigators. Uniformed Secret Service Officer Henry P. O'Neill testified that he was certain that items were removed from Foster's office and that he saw folders being carried out of the

office by Margaret Williams, Hilary Clinton's Chief of Staff, prior to the arrival of police. It didn't matter if Foster's car keys had to magically and implausibly appear in his pants at the morgue after police had already thoroughly searched him and the crime scene and not found his car keys. It didn't matter if Foster hadn't been acting suicidal or that his office was technically part of a crime scene that should be preserved rather than invaded. And it didn't matter that any violent death is supposed to be fully investigated and any ruling of suicide a determination that is to be made much, much later. It was officially labeled a suicide within *minutes*. Files left Vince's office *immediately*. His car keys *magically materialized* in his pockets at the morgue. The White House had to be protected. So the White House took control.

Now let's get back to that Tuesday, Vince's last day. He worked all morning in his office, nothing at all unusual. He continued making arrangements for the forthcoming next-day visit of his sister's family, a visit they were all looking forward to (he planned a lunch right at the White House to impress them and give them the "royal tour"). He wrote a letter to his mother to complete some family business and, although Foster was known far and wide as a loving family man, especially dear to his mother with whom he still remained very close, his last letter to her mentioned nothing out of the ordinary and was not particularly serious or otherwise noteworthy in any way— certainly not what one would expect had he known they would be his last words to her.

Vince typically worked hard and he would often ask a co-worker on their way to lunch if they could bring him back something in order to save time and be more productive. On his last day, a Tuesday at lunchtime, a co-worker *did* bring Vince his lunch from the White House cafeteria and she remembered it specifically— a cheeseburger, french fries, a *Coke*, and *M&Ms* candy. She remembered that right after she brought it to him, he had casually opened up a newspaper to read, as he took the onions off the cheeseburger. She then left and he ate it alone, seated on the sofa in his office. He left the *M&Ms* candy uneaten. He took his briefcase, mentioned to a co-worker (Linda Tripp) that she could have his *M&Ms* if she wanted them, and left the office, telling his secretary "I'll be back."

Those certainly don't sound like the actions of a man about to commit suicide, do they? This is a guy who— shortly prior to his death and in his *last known actions*— takes the onions off his cheeseburger, offers some candy to a co-worker, and tells his secretary he'll be right back.

WITNESS STATEMENTS:

If Vince Foster was Depressed, Why Does the Evidence Indicate Otherwise?

The later reports that Vince had been depressed simply do not hold up to serious scrutiny. Consider the initial reactions of those who worked closely with Vince (some later changed their stories to align with the official version, but below are their original statements):

- WEBSTER HUBBELL, ASSOCIATE ATTORNEY GENERAL OF THE UNITED STATES (3rd-RANKING MEMBER OF JUSTICE DEPT.), PARTNER AT ROSE LAW FIRM, FRIEND AND ASSOCIATE OF FOSTER'S FOR MANY YEARS:

(FBI Interview) **He had not "observed any noticeable behavioral or emotional changes ... prior to his death." He noted no changes in Foster's "personal appearance, physical ailments, headaches, loss of appetite, or any kind of stomach trouble." As far as the brewing scandals, "Foster was upset, but not terribly so, about the criticism."**

- DR. LARRY WATKINS (VINCE FOSTER'S PERSONAL PHYSICIAN):

(FBI Interview) **He "did not think that Foster was significantly depressed nor had Foster given the impression that he was 'in crisis.'"**

- DEBORAH GORHAM, PERSONAL SECRETARY TO VINCENT FOSTER

(FBI Interview) **"She viewed (Foster) as reserved, not depressed or unhappy ... He had a very long fuse so it was relatively rare for him to show agitation ... Foster had not ever made any statements or comments to Gorham indicating despondency and she had not noticed any physical changes in Foster from the time she started as his secretary to his death. (On his final day) he appeared relaxed and normal. ... Even with hindsight, Gorham did not see anything in Foster's behavior which would indicate a distressed state of mind."**

- DAVID WATKINS, WHITE HOUSE ADMINISTRATOR:

(FBI Interview) **Unaware of any "internal hostility"; "Watkins never heard directly or indirectly that Foster was distressed about (office issues), or about anything else for that matter."**

- BERNIE NUSSBAUM, COUNSEL TO THE PRESIDENT OF THE UNITED STATES (Foster's immediate superior):

(U.S. PARK POLICE interview) **Foster "had not exhibited any unusual behavior" on the day of his death.**

- BETSY POND, SECRETARY TO BERNARD NUSSBAUM

(U.S. PARK POLICE interview) **"There was nothing unusual about his emotional state. In fact, over the last several weeks she did not notice any changes, either physically or emotionally."**

- FISKE REPORT:

Even the FISKE REPORT **concedes that the victim had a very enjoyable and relaxing weekend only two days before his death:**

"Foster jogged, went boating, hit some golf balls, read the newspaper and ate fresh crab for the first time."

- DEE DEE MYERS, WHITE HOUSE PRESS SECRETARY:

(On national television) **"Okay. Let me just try to say what I think— what I said certainly on Thursday, which was that people— there was absolutely no reason to believe that Vince was despondent, that he was in any way considering doing what happened. Nobody believed that."**

- FORMER U.S. CONGRESSMAN BERYL ANTHONY

(Vince's brother-in-law, with whom he was close and even lived with when he came to Washington, all the time until early June, when Foster's wife and children arrived)

(Asked on Thursday, July 22, if Vince had been depressed during the two weeks prior to his death—as other witnesses, Anthony later does a full "180"—but this was original response:)

"There is not a damn thing to it. That's a bunch of crap."

- TIMOTHY J. KEATING, SPECIAL ASSISTANT TO THE PRESIDENT

(FBI Interview) **"He described Foster as being 'very professional and a strong individual ... together and on top of his game ... '"**

- PHILLIP CARROLL, SENIOR LITIGATOR, ROSE LAW FIRM (Foster's mentor, friend, neighbor, and godfather to Vince's first son):

(FBI Interview) **"Foster handled stress wonderfully."**

(Interview, *Esquire* Magazine) **"He was so competent. He was a very strong individual. I keep coming back to foul play. There had to be foul play involved." "Webb (mutual friend and Associate Attorney General Webster Hubbell) called me at midnight the night it happened. He said 'Don't believe a word you hear. It was not suicide. It couldn't have been.'"**

Source material for the above chart was derived primarily from the following:

The Strange Death of Vincent Foster, Christopher Ruddy, 1997

Failure of the Public Trust, John Clarke, Patrick Knowlton & Hugh Turley, 1999

"*A Washington Tragedy* by Dan Moldea: A Review by Hugh Sprunt", Hugh Sprunt, April, 1998.

A Washington Tragedy by Dan Moldea: A Review by Hugh Sprunt, Hugh Sprunt, April, 1998.

Certainly no death in recent years has had more incongruities in the official version of events than the death of Vince Foster. The only thing that can be said with certainty is that the official death verdict is severely flawed in every aspect. In everything from the supposed murder weapon to a fake suicide note, from the eyewitness testimony to the forensic evidence, the facts simply cannot be reconciled with the purported version of events. The facts do not fit, and no stretch of the imagination can make them fit.

No one has adequately addressed a disturbingly obvious question: If Vince Foster had actually intended to commit suicide by shooting himself, why would he need to drive to a very remote area of a public park to do it? He *wouldn't*, is the simple answer to that question—they have parking places all over Washington, D.C., the last time we checked. So the exact same effect could have been achieved by much simpler means. A successful White House attorney, Vince Foster was clearly the very picture of intellectual efficiency; a man of methodical means. Yet his death was *diametrically opposed* to efficiency—instead of a scientific mind reasoning methodically, he reportedly goes to a very remote area of an unattractive park for the purpose of killing himself in a distasteful location on a very hot, humid day, and one offering no view of anything pleasant (certainly not of the Potomac River, which was posted at one point, but which cannot be seen from where Foster's body was found). Why would he do something so stupid? He wouldn't.

Evidence like the absence of blood pooling is very important, yet it doesn't tell us *when* the victim died. But something else does, and it's one of those marvels of forensic science that surprise even the experts: it's *the summer flies*. The flies in a hot and humid Washington summer behave in a very established and predictable manner—and that combined with another factor, clearly establishes the incongruity between the estimated time of death versus the time that the victim was in the park.

Believe it or not, it's a well established fact (to biologists, at least) that the summer flies in a hot humid park on an afternoon in July will behave in a manner that is entirely predictable. Insect experts know it, and Emergency Medical Technicians know it too—because they're called out to emergencies and they know that the flies begin to swarm around a dead body. They *even* know that it's a process that takes an hour or two. They don't begin to swarm immediately. But after two hours, or a bit less, the flies will inevitably begin swarming around a dead body and then, like clockwork, they will, after a certain period, begin laying eggs. As Professor Carl Jones, an expert on insects at the College of Veterinary Medicine determined, based on the date, the location, the temperature and the approximate time of day at Fort Marcy Park, the flies would have began laying eggs in "no more than one and a half hours."[497]

But the flies *hadn't* begun laying eggs when Vince Foster was found in the park, and the EMTs and first officers on the scene not only noticed it, they knew what it meant—that Foster's body could not have been in the park for very long. Their testimony was clear—one of the officers on the scene, on *three* occasions,

---

[497] Michael Kellett, *The Murder of Vince Foster* (CLS Publishers, 1995), 155.

made specific reference to the presence of the flies on the body but the absence of fly eggs, because he was aware of its significance:

> **"Flies were buzzing around his face, starting to—no eggs were laid yet."**

> **"Again, the flies, I just—he hadn't been there long because they are pretty fast workers."[498]**

"The blood was starting to clot—the flies work pretty fast once they start, but I would say they won't go immediately."[499]

Digestion stops at death. So a common forensic method that doctors use to get an accurate estimated time of death is examining the contents of the stomach. We know what Vince Foster had for lunch that day: cheeseburger, french fries, and a Coke. We also know when he ate it: approximately 12:45 PM, because after he finished his lunch in his office, he passed by his secretary and then a Secret Service agent, both of whom recall the time as approximately 1:00 PM.

As a result of examining the stomach contents, doctors concluded that Foster had eaten a large meal between two to three hours prior to the moment of death. Therefore, we can estimate death as occurring in a time window of 2:45 PM to 3:45 PM (12:45 PM, plus two to three hours).

But the officers in the park observed Foster's corpse—absent of fly eggs—at 6:40 PM. Allowing a period of up to one and half hours—because fly eggs had not been lain—the earliest that Foster could have been dead in the park is 5:10 PM. The point is crucial because of what it proves— Foster's body could not have been in the park prior to 5:00 PM, but we know that he was already dead by 4:00 PM. Therefore, in accordance with other evidence, Foster did not die at the location where his body was found. He died earlier, and his body was moved to the park![500]

The semen stain found on the inside front portion of Foster's underwear provides us with another important forensic clue. The stain was approximately four inches in size.[501]

The government maintains that the stain was the result of spontaneous ejaculation, which does sometimes occur at the moment of death. However, we researched this further and found that spontaneous ejaculation is somewhat rare and generally only occurs from two possible scenarios. Rigor mortis, the hardening process that begins in the body after death, can cause spontaneous ejaculation. It occurs as the result of increasing pressure upon the scrotum which forces out the release of semen. The implication is a relatively small amount, whereas the stain in the victim's shorts was apparently rather large

---

[498] Kellett, *The Murder of Vince Foster*
[499] *The Murder of Vince Foster*
[500] *The Murder of Vince Foster*
[501] Ruddy, *The Strange Death of Vincent Foster*

(a stain of four inches is indicative of a *lot* of semen, especially considering that if it occurred spontaneously at death as the government alleges, then the victim would have been laying supine at the time, not standing).

However, the rigor mortis process begins at two to four hours after death yet does not begin to *manifest* (become active) until at least six hours post-mortem (six to twelve hours after death). Therefore, we can logically deduce that the 4-inch semen stain observed less than six hours after the victim had been dead was in all likelihood <u>not</u> the result of spontaneous ejaculation caused by rigor mortis.

Spontaneous ejaculation can also occur at the moment of death as the result of trauma to the spinal cord. For example, a person who suffers a broken neck, such as in a death by hanging, can experience spontaneous ejaculation. However, that is usually accompanied by bowel and bladder incontinence, meaning they lose control of all bodily functions and release contents at death. Other than a small urine stain, Foster apparently did not suffer bowel and urinary incontinence, nor was his death the result of extreme trauma to the spinal cord.

Therefore, we can conclude with a high degree of probability, that the victim had sexual activity shortly prior to his death which resulted in the four inch semen stain. The obvious question is "With whom?" and the answer is that we do not know. But it does lend a further degree of suspicion to an already extremely suspicious death.

Blonde hairs were also found on the victim—blonde hairs that do not match the victim *or* his wife. No attempt was made to ascertain their origin.

A large purplish wine stain was apparent on the upper front of the victim's white dress shirt. No official attempt was made to ascertain its origin either. The large stain is dramatically out of keeping with Foster's history and with the last known image we have of the typical Vince Foster leaving his White House office after a typical morning and lunch. He was very neat—even *fussy* neat—and was certainly not an afternoon drinker, by any stretch of the imagination. Therefore, the stain is highly incongruous with his personal history and yet another indication of possible foul play. Why wasn't it investigated?

The multi-colored carpet fibers found from head-to-toe on Foster—of <u>six different colors</u>—provide an indication that he was somehow immersed in that carpeting; either laying on it, rolling it, or having had his body *wrapped* in it. No search was made for a match. Normally, investigators would search his trunk and car for a match, as well as his home, his office, and surrounding areas. The fact that this was <u>not</u> done is highly suspicious because it would be standard investigatory procedure in a gunshot death. The fact that the fibers recurrently showed six colors should have made it an easy match.

One investigative journalist found evidence that rooms of the White House (bear in mind that Foster's office was *in* the White House, and no log entry or video recording shows him actually leaving the White House that day, even though it is one of the most secure buildings in the world) were totally re-carpeted in the days following Foster's death, even though they had been virtually new carpets.

"The Clintons had ordered that one of the White House offices be completely re-carpeted shortly before the death of Vince Foster. The day following his death, a crew of workmen arrived at the White House and completely ripped up and removed what was a nearly brand new carpet. They hastily piled the carpeting into a van and quickly left. The final destination of that carpet and why it was so hastily removed during the chaos and trauma following the death of Foster are mysteries I've never been able to solve. However, it strikes me as entirely possible this carpeting was evidence of a crime committed within the White House. Was the carpet bloodstained? Did it contain other forensic clues? In short, is it possible Vince Foster was actually murdered within the White House? The fact that two key videotapes, which would have shown Foster leaving the White House on the day of his death, are both missing. What did they show?"[502]

[502] Franklin, "101 Peculiarities"

The intrigue thickens when we consider that Foster was planning to resign his position as White House Counsel and even had a private audience appointment scheduled with the President for the following day:

"**Vincent Foster's intention to resign is from his wife's interview in the New Yorker Magazine. Life After Vince by Peter J. Boyer confirms that Vincent told his wife numerous times he had made a mistake coming to the White House and planned to resign.**

That Vince has a private appointment scheduled with Bill Clinton the day after his murder is established White House record.

The unavailability of any logs or videos showing Vince Foster leaving under his own power that day is from the Robert Fiske Investigation into the matter. Ken Starr's Whitewater probe also confirmed there was no security record of Foster's departure."[503]

SIGNS OF HOMICIDE

As Crime Scene Investigators know, a "neat" crime scene for a gunshot wound is an indication that either the victim did not die as a result of the gunshot wound, or that the body was moved after death, i.e., what is known as a staged crime scene. Everything about the Vince Foster crime scene hints at staging:

- Blood pooling is the first thing that investigators look for at a gunshot crime scene. The absence of sufficient blood is a huge red

[503] Michael Rivero, email to author, 22 January, 2011.

flag that the body may have been moved and a murder staged as a suicide. At the site of Foster's body, there was very little blood when there should have been a massive blood pool, especially from a .38, especially at point-blank range, and especially with high-velocity rounds. It should have poured out in large quantities from both the entrance and exit wounds. Yet even the Fiske Report concedes that "relatively little blood was visible."

- Homicide experts know it's physically impossible that a gun as powerful as the Colt Army Special .38 fired into the mouth at point blank range does not splatter blowback of blood and tissue on the victim's body, clothing, and on the gun itself. The fact that they are all virtually pristine is vivid evidence that it simply did not happen.

- Body was found in a very neat, symmetrical position, face up, arms extended neatly at both sides The first EMT (Emergency Medical Technician) at the scene noticed that it was just too neat to be natural and testified that it was "coffin-like" as though it had been "placed" like that and that he had "just never seen a body lying so perfectly straight after shooting a bullet in his head." Another officer at the scene also confirmed that the body looked like it had been laid out "ready for a coffin."

- No fingerprints on the gun is a standard indicator of the obvious possibility that the gun was placed in the victim's hand by his killers, to stage it as a suicide. A suicide victim would have to handle the weapon several times, transporting it, checking and/or loading it, then firing it. Had he actually shot himself with the gun found in his hand, then his prints should have been all over the weapon, especially on such a hot, humid day. The fact that they were not is an indication that the gun may have been placed in his hand after he was already dead, when the prints would no longer adhere to the gun.

- Gun still in victim's hand is another standard red flag. The gun is ordinarily "thrown" by the shot, and especially so with a high-velocity weapon like the .38. The first EMT on the scene also testified that the gun just seemed too neatly positioned in the hand next to the body. Note that this fact cannot be explained away by a spasmodic reflex known as "cadaveric spasm" because the officer who removed the gun from Foster's hand stated that the hand was still pliable, therefore, rigor mortis had not even begun, and cadaveric spasm could not have taken place. Two New York Homicide veterans who examined the evidence stated in their report that in their "combined experience of fifty years of investigating homicides, never seen a ... gun positioned in a suicide's hand in such an orderly position."

- Dried blood stains traveled in opposite direction, i.e., they would have had to defy gravity to travel that way in the position the body was ultimately found (a sure sign that they dried while the body was in a different position earlier in time).

- Even though the body was found in a very remote area of the park, the underbrush in that area had been trampled, as though several men had busied themselves with something there.

- Whenever a gunshot victim turns up in a remote location, it is a source of investigative concern. The fact that the location is a remote area of a remote park is not consistent with suicide—there are much easier ways to kill one's self. There's no need for a suicide to go to a remote location. It is consistent with the modus operandi of professional hits because they need to make sure that they are unseen when transporting a body.

- The absence of an exit wound (confirmed by the treating EMT at the scene) is simply totally incongruent with a wound from a .38 directly into the victim's mouth.

- The fact that two EMTs and the doctor at the scene identified a gunshot wound in the <u>neck</u> is inconsistent with suicide and is evidence that Homicide Investigators would consider indicative of foul play. Lead Prosecutor Miguel Rodriguez also confirms a neck wound—Rodriguez saw the original crime scene photos (before they conveniently disappeared) that showed a very evident large gash with black gunpowder marks on the right side of Vince Foster's neck.

- Ballistics angles indicate that the victim's eyeglasses actually should have been thrown in the opposite direction from where they were found.

- The summer flies hadn't laid eggs at the crime scene which, on a hot and humid summer day, is a scientific indication that the body had been there for only a very short time.

- Other evidence also indicates the victim had not been dead long: Blood was still draining from the wounds when police arrived at the scene.

- The victim's car arrived in the parking lot after the victim was already dead in the park.

- The victim's car keys were not found on the victim or anywhere else at the crime scene (there was a thorough search for them).

- Vince had recently expressed his suspicion that his phones were tapped, had also recently installed an expensive alarm system in his home, and reportedly kept a gun in the house; leading some investigators to suspect that the mild-mannered Foster may have been afraid of something.

- The autopsy was able to establish a time of death by checking the level of digestion, because Foster had eaten a large lunch. Doctors concluded that Foster died between 3:00 and 4:00 PM. But he left the White House at 1:00 PM, and no one knows what happened after that, which is highly unusual when you consider the prominence of his position and the fact that he was a very busy man on every single work day. Yet, there is a huge block of unaccounted time—almost five hours—that is a source of obvious investigatory concern. It is "official" that Foster left his White House office about 1:00 PM and then no one knows what transpired between then and late afternoon when his body is finally found at a park in suburban Virginia. No one has come forward, no one saw him anywhere, doing anything, at any point during that long gap of several hours. Even the police conceded that: "It is unusual that, so far, we haven't heard from one person who can tell us anything about his activities after 1:00 p.m." The fact that no one saw him means he was apparently in a situation in which he would not be seen and is therefore a sign of possible foul play.

Homicide Investigators would be <u>extremely</u> interested in:

- Weapon was a drop-gun, with no link to victim and no prints of victim, but did have prints of individual other than victim.

- Gunpowder patterns on victim were defensive, consistent with his two hands being near the front of the gun barrel and not consistent with them being on the trigger.

- Fact that everything at crime scene is consistent with low-velocity weapon like a .22, and not the weapon found in victim's hand (high-velocity .38).

- Fact that victim's shoes had almost no dirt on them even though he supposedly walked hundreds of yards in a remote park.

- Fact that victim's car keys could not be found at scene.

- Source of the blonde hairs on the victim that do not match victim or his wife.

- Multi-color carpet fibers (of six-colors, that do not match victim's home or office) found from head-to-toe on victim (including on his underwear).

- Semen-stained underwear.

- Source of wine stain on victim's shirt.

- The FBI Report indicates that the victim's head was moved while the blood was still wet—that's an indicator that the body was moved prior to the arrival of investigators.

- One of the trickles of blood on victim's face had dried when the body had to have been in a much different position for it to travel that way. That's huge sign that the body was moved.

- The fact that the fatal bullet was never located is highly unusual because if a bullet traverses all the way through a human skull, then it loses its force, does not traverse far, and is ordinarily found nearby.

- Huge block of totally unaccounted time—no one ever came forward to fill in the many missing hours of what happened to victim after his 1:00 p.m. lunch when everything was fine until about 6:00 p.m. when body was found.

- A tow truck driver stated that the same evening that Foster's body was found, he was called to remove a car from the same park. The car had blood on the seats, and dashboard, and also had a broken driver's side window.

- The contradictory witness statements:

  - First witness is sure there was <u>no gun</u> in either of victim's hands or anywhere near him (and he was looking for one).

  - Paramedic is positive there was an <u>automatic</u> in victim's hand, not a revolver, and described it in precise detail.

  - Revolver (<u>non-</u> automatic) is officially found in victim's hand.

  The above seem to reveal bungled crime scene staging, rather than poor witness recall.

The preponderance of evidence indicates that the victim was killed with a gun different than the .38 found in his hand, probably a .22 or other low-velocity weapon, in a different location, then dumped at the park with a different gun placed in his hand for a plausible suicide. Crime scene also indicates multiple perpetrators due to the extent of trampled underbrush in the remote location near the body.

KILLERS INEVITABLY MAKE MISTAKES: The victim's car arrived later, <u>after</u> Foster's body was already in the park.

The car seat was in a dramatically different position— Foster was very tall, almost 6'5"— but the driver's seat was pulled so far forward that it would have been extremely awkward for a tall person to sit in it (indicating a shorter person probably drove the car to the park).

Consider that his car keys were <u>not</u> found at the crime scene, which included a search of his person— so how could he possibly have driven there?

NO SUICIDE NOTE: It was well-known that Foster was an excellent father and dedicated family man, therefore, it is dubious that he would do something as devastating as shooting himself without leaving behind some explanation. He wrote a note to his mother, with whom he was still very close, only a few hours before his death. In that letter there was nothing at all out of the ordinary. His morning was normal work, followed by a normal lunch in his office. He casually offered a co-worker some candy, then left his office, telling his secretary "I'll be back soon." Nothing was wrong. So something dramatic happened shortly thereafter.

VICTIM'S BRIEFCASE DISAPPEARED: Four eyewitnesses saw Foster's briefcase sitting on the front seat of his car in the parking lot. One witness was medical technician George Gonzalez who remembered it in detail: It was "a black briefcase-attache case." It vanished.

VICTIM'S PAGER WAS ERASED: Foster's pager was found at the crime scene, but the memory had been erased from it. Rather than preserving it and analyzing it, it was immediately turned over to the White House. Why? That's a blatant flaw as far as proper crime scene investigation. Foster was attorney to the President of the United States and had a very busy schedule—it's logical to infer that he would have several messages on his pager, at any given time. A person committing suicide would have very little reason to erase the memory in their pager. However, persons covering tracks at a murder would have logical reasons to erase the memory. The fact that his messages were erased at death certainly points to individuals other than Foster.

FOSTER'S OFFICE SEARCHED: Victim's office was ransacked and items known to have been there disappeared, including Foster's files, other items from his office safe, and his file index that listed all of his files. That took place even though the police asked the White House to seal off Foster's office and treat it as a crime scene, i.e., stay out of it. So who took what, and why? Foster's appointment book also vanished (it was either in his briefcase or his office). Obviously, Homicide Investigators would want to look at that appointment book for the day of his death, since the victim's whereabouts for the last five hours preceding his death are completely unknown.

FAKE SUICIDE NOTE APPARENTLY PLANTED: A highly suspicious note turned up in one of Foster's briefcases four days after an official search had been conducted— the briefcase had actually already been searched twice and in the presence of police— on those two occasions, there was nothing in the briefcase. Be that as it may, a torn up note eventually appeared in the very same briefcase and, lo and behold, was quickly called a "suicide note." In reality, it was nothing of the sort; the note indicated nothing about suicide, it was simply a list of reasons for leaving Washington, D.C. and its power games. Three handwriting experts (one of whom is considered the foremost expert in the world) concluded independently of each other that the "suicide" note was a forgery. In fact, it was so obvious a forgery that it was deemed to be the clumsy work of an amateur.

Source material for the above chart was derived primarily from the following:

Citizen's Independent Report, Hugh H. Sprunt; 1995

Source material for the above chart was derived primarily from the following: '

Failure of the Public Trust, John Clarke, Patrick Knowlton & Hugh Turley, 1999

The Strange Death of Vincent Foster, Christopher Ruddy, 1997

Citizen's Independent Report, Hugh H. Sprunt; 1995

The Secret Life of Bill Clinton: The Unreported Stories, Ambrose Evans-Pritchard, 1997

The Murder of Vince Foster, Michael Kellett, 1995

"New Evidence Exposes Vince Foster Murder: Victim Not Shot With .38 Caliber Revolver", Wesley Phelan, *The Washington Weekly*, October 26, 1998.http://www.bigeye.com/vfoster.htm

"101 Peculiarities Surrounding the Death of Vincent Foster", Richard L. Franklin, http://prorev.com/foster.htm

"The Death of Vincent Foster", Michael Rivero, *WhatReallyHappened. com*, http://whatreallyhappened.com/ RANCHO/POLITICS/FOSTER_ COVERUP/foster.php

The government wishes that the whole Vince Foster controversy would just go away. The holes in the official version aren't explainable, nor are they small. They are gaping wounds; much like the one that Vincent Foster should have had, had he actually been shot with a .38 caliber gun like the government says he was.

The Vince Foster murder is recognized as the ultimate potential political consequence of not playing politics with *The Powers That Be*. In fact, it's even recognized as such "within the industry." For example, when a high-ranking political aide who was a longtime insider and trusted friend of the leading contender for President recently resigned amid a cover-up of a sex scandal involving that candidate, fears of becoming the "next Vince Foster" were openly voiced:

"Young also told *Good Morning America* today that after he broke with Edwards, tensions over the cover-up got so heated that he feared for his family's safety."

"For several months, I used to get up at 3:00 AM and walk around the house with a baseball bat and a knife," he said.

During that time, Young said he had his three young children sleep with him and his wife.

That fear, he said, peaked during a car ride "out in the middle of nowhere" with Edwards. During that ride, "all I could think about was Vince Foster."[504]

---

[504] Sarah Netter, "John Edwards Scandal: Andrew Young Offered 'Gigantic' Sum for Sex Tape," 1 February 2010, *ABC Good Morning America*. http://abcnews.go.com/GMA/John_Edwards_Scandal/john-edwards-sex-tape-andrew-young-offered-gigantic-money-video/story?id=9715445

BIBLIOGRAPHY

"For a comprehensive resource list," consult: http://scribblguy.50megs.com/vincefoster.htm

Failure of the Public Trust, John Clarke, Patrick Knowlton & Hugh Turley, 1999 http://www.fbicover-up.com/order/index.htm

"The Knowlton Addendum" (attached to the Starr report by the three panel judges: The Honorable David B. Sentelle, The Honorable John C. Butzner, the Honorable Peter T. Fay; UNITED STATES COURT OF APPEALS FOR THE DISTRICT OF COLUMBIA CIRCUIT, Division 94–1 for the Purpose of Appointing Independent Counsels Re: In re: Madison Guaranty Savings & Loan Association, Patrick James Knowlton, Request to include comments and factual information, pursuant to the Ethics in Government Act of 1978, As Amended, to the Report on the Death of Vincent Foster, Jr.). http://www.mega.nu/ampp/knowlton.html

The Strange Death of Vincent Foster, Christopher Ruddy, 1997

"The Mysterious Death of Vincent Foster", in *Grave Secrets: A Leading Forensic Expert Reveals the Startling Truth About O.J. Simpson, David Koresh, Vincent Foster, and Other Sensational Cases,* Cyril Wecht, M.D., J.D. with Mark Curriden and Benjamin Wecht, 1998

"Citizen's Independent Report," Hugh H. Sprunt; 1995. http://whatreallyhappened.com/RANCHO/POLITICS/FOSTER_COVERUP/TEXTS/vwfhs75a.html

The Secret Life of Bill Clinton: The Unreported Stories, Ambrose Evans-Pritchard, 1997

A Washington Tragedy: How the Death of Vincent Foster Ignited a Political Firestorm, Dan E. Moldea, 1998

The Murder of Vince Foster, Michael Kellett, 1995

Failure of the Public Trust, John Clarke, Patrick Knowlton & Hugh Turley, 1999

"Independent Report in Re: The Death of Vincent Foster, Jr.", Vincent J. Scalice Associates, April 27, 1995, *Western Journalism Center*

"Forensic Experts Doubt Foster Suicide Finding", Christoper Ruddy, January 18, 1995, *Pittsburgh Tribune-Review*

"White House Lying on Foster's Death", John Crudele, February 7, 1996, *New York Post*

"New Evidence Exposes Vince Foster Murder: Victim Not Shot With .38 Caliber Revolver", Wesley Phelan, *The Washington Weekly,* October 26, 1998.http://www.bigeye.com/vfoster.htm

"101 Peculiarities Surrounding the Death of Vincent Foster," Richard L. Franklin, accessed January 24, 2011. http://www.prorev.com/foster.htm

"The Death of Vincent Foster: Vincent Foster's Wounds Were Not as Reported," Michael Rivero, WhatReallyHappened.com http://hatreallyhappened.com/RANCHO/POLITICS/FOSTER_COVERUP/NECK/neck.html

"Vincent Foster Scenario: A Possible Scenario for the Murder of Vincent Foster," Michael Rivero, WhatReallyHappened.com http://whatreallyhappened.com/RANCHO/POLITICS/ARTICLES/SCENARIO.html

| # Dr. David C. Kelly CMG — July 17, 2003

(CMG- Most Distinguished Order of Saint Michael and Saint George- is a British title bestowed to honor contributions of extraordinary significance in matters of State. Some in the British military and intelligence field refer to CMG as "just Call Me God")

Senior United Nations Weapons Inspector, Iraq/ World's Premier Biological Weapons Expert

VICTIM	**DAVID KELLY**
Cause of Death	BLOOD LOSS (cause of death is contested)
Official Verdict	SUICIDE; "self-inflicted wound to left wrist" Also "may have" ingested "up to twenty-nine" tablets of co-proxamol (an analgesic for mild to moderate pain relief, it is a mixture of paracetamol and dextropropoxyphene and is commonly prescribed for arthritis pain, mild backache, or cramps)

Actual Circumstances	Dr. Kelly was named as the source of a media leak that accused Prime Minister Tony Blair of lying to justify war with Iraq. When asked what would happen if Iraq was to be invaded, Dr. Kelly responded (on more than one occasion): "I will probably be found dead in the woods."[500] Iraq was invaded and Dr. Kelly was found dead in the woods. A "public inquiry" was immediately appointed by Prime Minister Blair (before his airplane had even landed), thus precluding an official inquest. No inquest into the death has ever been held.[501]
Inconsistencies	A special Independent Forensic Panel consisting of three doctors who were specialists in their respected fields examined the crime scene and forensic details and determined that: 1. "As specialist medical professionals, we do not consider the evidence given at the Hutton inquiry has demonstrated that Dr. David Kelly committed suicide."[502] 2. Regarding the finding that Dr. Kelly bled to death from a slashed wrist, the Independent Forensic Panel concluded, "We view this as highly improbable. Arteries in the wrist are of matchstick thickness and severing them does not lead to life-threatening blood loss."[503] The ulnar artery is also an extremely unnatural place to slash one's wrist. It is located at the far inner portion of the wrist, in line with the little finger. If, however, someone else had been facing the victim and slashing their wrist, it then would be the logical place to expect a cut. 3. The only artery that was cut, the ulnar artery, had been completely transected. As the Independent Forensic Team Panel stated: "Complete transection causes the artery to quickly retract and close down, and this promotes clotting of the blood."[504] 4. Blood loss would have been insufficient to cause death. The conclusion of the Independent Forensic Panel was that "The ambulance team reported that the quantity of blood at the scene was minimal and surprisingly small. It is extremely difficult to lose significant amounts of blood at a pressure below 50-60 systolic in a subject who is compensating by

---

[500] Norman Baker, *The Strange Death of David Kelly* (London: Methuen, 2007).

[501] Baker, *The Strange Death of David Kelly*

[502] "Letter forwarded to national British newspapers," Dr. David Halpin, MB, BS, FRCS & Dr. C. Stephen Frost BsC, MBChB & Dr. Searle Sennett, BSc, MBChB, FFARCS, in Rowena Thursby, "Our doubts about Dr. Kelly's suicide," *theguardian*, http://www.guardian.co.uk/theguardian/2004/jan/27/guardianletters4

[503] "Letter forwarded," Dr. Halpin, et al.

[504] "Letter forwarded," Dr. Halpin, et al.

vasoconstriction. To have died from hemorrhage, Dr. Kelly would have had to lose about five pints of blood. It is unlikely that he lost more than a pint."[505]

5. The paramedics who were on the scene, Dave Bartlett and Vanessa Hunt, have testified that there was not nearly enough blood at the scene to justify the belief that he died from blood loss. They inspected the entire area. They located a small amount of blood on some plants near Dr. Kelly's body and a small patch of blood on his trousers that was about the size of a coin.[506]

6. The victim's body was outside on a cold afternoon. Cold weather exposure causes further vasoconstriction, dramatically slowing blood loss.[507]

7. Only a fifth of one tablet of co-proxamol was found in Dr. Kelly's stomach. Although levels of the drug's two components in his bloodstream were higher than therapeutic levels, they were less than a third of the level considered fatal. Therefore, the Independent Forensic Panel concluded:

> "We dispute that Dr. Kelly could have died from hemorrhage or from co-proxamol or from both."[508]

8. A group of thirteen highly respected British physicians has officially contested the official findings and are still locked in a legal battle to overturn what they know to be false. Their conclusions are blunt:

> "You couldn't commit suicide like that."

> "'The idea that a man like Dr. Kelly would choose to end his life like that is preposterous. This was a scientist, an expert on drugs.'"[509]

9. The knife that he allegedly used to commit suicide was blunt and did not have any fingerprints on it whatsoever (a fact not released until late 2007 when it was obtained via a Freedom of Information request from Member of Parliament Norman Baker). Dr. Kelly was not wearing gloves, so there should have been fingerprints. [510] Norman Baker, MP:

---

[505] "Letter forwarded," Dr. Halpin, et al.

[506] "Letter forwarded," Dr. Halpin, et al.

[507] "Letter forwarded," Dr. Halpin, et al.

[508] "Letter forwarded," Dr. Halpin, et al.

[509] Glen Owen & Miles Goslett, "Thirteen doctors demand inquest into Dr. David Kelly's death," 13 July, 2009, *dailymail*, http://www.dailymail.co.uk/news/article-1199109/13-doctors-demand-inquest-Dr-David-Kellys-death.html

[510] Baker, *Strange Death of David Kelly*

"Someone who wanted to kill themselves wouldn't go to the lengths of wiping the knife clean of fingerprints. It is just very suspicious. It is one of the things that makes me think Dr. Kelly was murdered."[511]

10. No fingerprints or DNA were found on any of Dr. Kelly's personal items at the death scene.[512] Police tested his personal items three times, and all tests came back negative for both DNA and prints.[513] Forensic experts note that it is now routine to examine crime scene objects for DNA because it is logical to expect the owner's microscopic cells on personal items they have handled, such as cell phones or eyeglasses. Since Dr. Kelly was not wearing gloves, forensic experts say it is difficult to explain the abcense of DNA and fingerprints on: his mobile phone, the knife that he allegedly used, the packages of pills he allegedly took, the water bottle he allegedly took the pills with, and his wristwatch. [514]

11. Dr. Kelly had a weak right arm which would have made it exceedingly difficult to make the already awkward motion of cutting one's left ulnar artery. He also had a strong aversion to swallowing tablets. Close friend & co-worker Mai Pederson:

    " … Kelly's weak right arm and inability to swallow pills make it impossible"[515]

12. Dr. Kelly was reportedly not wearing a jacket when he left his house, which was logical, as it was not yet that cold outside, and he planned on being right back. However, his jacket was found near him at the crime scene.[516]

13. Also found at the crime scene were a pruning knife with blood on it, right next to the body, as well as three foil packets (packets holding ten each) of the mild pain reliever copraxamol. But none of the items were near the body when the searchers first discovered it. It's quite logical to think that they

[511] Baker, *Strange Death of David Kelly*

[512] Miles Goslett, "Police admit they could not find trace of fingerprints on Dr. David Kelly's glasses after 'suicide'," 14 March, 2011, dailymail, http://www.*dailymail*.co.uk/news/article-1366301/David-Kelly-inquest-Police-admit-fingerprints-DNA-glasses.htmll

[513] Miles Goslett, "David Kelly death riddle grows as it emerges personal items found on his body did not have fingerprints on them," 27 January, 2011, *dailymail*, http://www.dailymail.co.uk/news/article-1350898/David-Kelly-death-Personal-items-fingerprints.html

[514] *The Truth is Hotter than a Pile of Curry*, "Dr. David Kelly No DNA or Fingerprints Found on Personal Possessions – Murdered Because He Knew Too Much?," http://hotterthanapileofcurry.wordpress.com/2011/03/16/dr-david-kelly-no-dna-or-fingerprints-found-on-personal-possessions-murdered-because-he-knew-too-much/ (accessed 1 Mar 2012).

[515] Baker, *Strange Death of David Kelly*. Andrew Malone, "Why I'm certain my friend Dr. Kelly was murdered," 3 August 2010, *dailymail*. http://www.dailymail.co.uk/news/article-1293568/Why-Im-certain-friend-Dr-Kelly-murdered.html

[516] Baker, *Strange Death of David Kelly*

would have seen and noticed a knife and a water bottle, both with blood on them, both right next to the body. But they did not observe them. [517]

14. Several reports were made to police by local residents who had independently of each other witnessed several men in black clothing wandering in the woods in the hours prior to his body being located and in the areas near where the body was found.[518]

15. Dr. Kelly's body was moved post-mortem on at least two occasions. The two search volunteers who first located the body, both swore that it was leaning up against a tree. The body was later said to be found laying flat upon the ground. Additionally, the searcher who found the body is also positive that his right arm was at the side his body. But by the time that the two paramedics arrived, they both clearly remember having to move his right arm off his chest in order to check for vital signs. [519]

16. Contrary to the attempts of the "clean-up" efforts after his death, Dr. Kelly actually made the statement "I will probably be found dead in the woods" on several different occasions and, moreover, he made it clear that it was a serious statement regarding concrete fear for his life if the promises made to Iraq were betrayed (Iraq was told that it would *not* be invaded if it cooperated with inspections, which it did). [520]

17. Many sources close to Dr. Kelly confirm the fact that he was not a man who was even remotely contemplating taking his own life.[521]

18. All official medical reports concerning the death were sealed confidential for seventy years.[522]

19. Remarkably, forensic testing that is considered standard, was never done on Dr. Kelly's body. For example, a test to measure residual blood (blood left in the body) would have revealed the exact extent of blood loss. The testing was never conducted. [523]

[517] Baker, *Strange Death of David Kelly*

[518] Baker, *Strange Death of David Kelly*

[519] Baker, *Strange Death of David Kelly*

[520] Baker, *Strange Death of David Kelly*

[521] Baker, *Strange Death of David Kelly*

[522] Miles Goslett, "David Kelly post mortem to be kept secret for 70 years as doctors accuse Lord Hutton of concealing vital information," 25 January, 2010, *dailymail*, http://www.dailymail.co.uk/news/article-1245599/David-Kelly-post-mortem-kept-secret-70-years-doctors-accuse-Lord-Hutton-concealing-vital-information.html

[523] Haroon Sidique, "Experts call for David Kelly inquest: Official cause of David Kelly's death is 'extremely unlikely', say group of legal and medical experts," 13 August 2010, *theguardian*. http://www.guardian.co.uk/politics/2010/aug/13/experts-call-david-kelly-inquest

20. Dr. Kelly was at work on an unauthorized book that he said was going to expose the lies of the Bush and Blair Governments. He shared that information with intelligence expert and historian Gordon Thomas:

"I visited Dr. Kelly as part of research into a book I was writing. But he told me that he was writing his own book, which intended to show that Tony Blair had lied about his reasons for going to war with Iraq. He had told the Prime Minister categorically that there were no weapons of mass destruction."

"Dr. Kelly was not a man given to exaggeration or showing off; he was the absolute expert in his field and if he said there no weapons of mass destruction, then there were none.

I told Dr. Kelly he would never be allowed to publish his book in Britain. I told him he would put himself into immense danger."[524]

21. Agents of MI5 arrived at Dr. Kelly's house and seized the hard drive to his computer (containing his book) thirty minutes before Kelly's body was found. All signs of Kelly's book vanished along with it.[525]

22. One of the items found in the Kelly home was an unopened letter from the Ministry of Defence formally reiterating earlier warnings that had taken place verbally, telling Dr. Kelly to refrain from writing or divulging any further state secrets. Kelly never opened the letter, although he surely could guess its contents after the warnings he had recently received.[526]

23. Concerted efforts have taken place to minimize the effects of irreconcilable facts in the death of Dr. Kelly and to thwart efforts aimed at opening a sincere investigation of his murder.[527]

---

[524] Sue Reid, "Did MI5 kill Dr. David Kelly? Just another crazy conspiracy theory? But, amid claims he wrote tell-all book that vanished after his death, it's one that refuses to go away," 27 July, 2009, *dailymail*. http://www.dailymail.co.uk/news/article-1200004/Did-MI5-kill-Dr-David-Kelly-Another-crazy-conspiracy-theory-amid-claims-wrote-tell-book-vanished-death.html

[525] Reid, "Did MI5 kill Kelly?"

[526] Baker, *Strange Death of David Kelly*

[527] Baker, *Strange Death of David Kelly*

Dr. David C. Kelly was Britain's premier expert on BW/CW (Biological Warfare/Chemical Warfare) and senior Weapons Inspector for the United Nations charged with inspecting Iraq at precisely the moment in history that the U.S. and U.K. were attempting to justify an invasion of Iraq. He was an accomplished scientist at the top of his field and was respected internationally for his proven professionalism. His credentials are officially described as "the senior adviser on biological warfare to the MoD (Britain's Ministry of Defence) … the West's leading biological warfare inspector" with "world-recognized expertise in every aspect of biological warfare [whose] knowledge cannot be overtrumped."[528]

Dr. Kelly had inspected Iraq's chemical and biological facilities on many occasions and knew that Iraq possessed no WMD (weapons of mass destruction). He also knew, with absolute certainty, that Iraq possessed no capability of delivering WMD.

As the pounding of the war drums increased in intensity, the claim was officially made in Western media that Iraq's weapons programs effectively placed the Allies "forty-five minutes from doom." That claim was a lie, and David Kelly knew it.

Dr. Kelly was also a man of great integrity:

> "Dr. Kelly became senior adviser on biological warfare for the UN in Iraq in 1994, holding the post until 1999. He was sufficiently well respected to have been nominated for a Nobel peace prize by the man who led the Iraq weapons inspections for much of the 1990s."[529]

The same integrity that led to Dr. Kelly's nomination for the Nobel Peace Prize for uncovering biological weapons in Iraq during the 1990s caused his refusal to go along in complete silence with a claim that he knew to be false about Iraq's weapons capabilities in 2003.

The above combination of events cost Dr. Kelly his life.

Dr. Kelly liked to say that his loyalty is to what

"I believe is right or wrong, true or false."[530]

And he had sound reason for believing it too—

"This discussion of the past is also about the future. As David Kay, the American weapons-hunter who found no weapons, told the Guardian:

---

[528] *The Hutton Report*, Chapter Four, 2003

[529] *BBC News*, "Profile: Dr. David Kelly," 27 January 2004. http://news.bbc.co.uk/2/hi/uk_news/politics/3076869.stm (accessed 2 December 2011).

[530] Gordon Thomas, "The Secret World of Dr. David Kelly," 18 August, 2003, http://www.apfn.net/messageboard/8-18-03/discussion.cgi.32.html

'The next time you have to go and shout there's fire in the theatre people are going to doubt it.'"[531]

Dr. Kelly's background took him deeper into the secret world of Intelligence than most people are aware. Consider that he:

- Was directly responsible for and directly involved in the defection of Russia's leading microbiologist, which thwarted attempts at a bio-weapon capable of wiping out a third of the world's population;

- Worked for *MOSSAD* (the elite Israeli intelligence corps) since 1995, with the approval of MI6 (British Intelligence);

- Played a key role in defining the Ames-strain of anthrax for the FBI in the U.S. anthrax attacks;

- Consulted frequently for the CIA, MI6, and MOSSAD on matters of the highest security level imaginable;

- Was the only civilian that the CIA allowed to question a top-level Chinese defector.

His actual role in the Intel community then was as a *major player*. He was considered the "go-to guy" for the world's greatest threats of a biological nature. He "consulted" confidentially on matters of world-class importance in this role, like a James Bond of the academic world, a "scientist spy" of the highest caliber in existence. He was even more than that:

"It is no exaggeration to say that between 1990 and his death in 2003, Dr. Kelly probably did more to make the world a more secure place than anyone else on the planet."[532]

So let's not insult this man's intelligence. Dr. Kelly possessed a *brilliant* mind— he was a world-renowned, top-of-his-field scientist— which is further demonstrated by the fact that he even predicted his own murder.

Yet we are asked to believe, by the Official Version, that this extremely intelligent individual—armed only with an old pruning knife with a dull blade— inexplicably wandered off into the woods to do away with himself.

Britain's leading vascular surgeon, John Scurr, confirmed the nonsensicalness of the notion that Kelly slashed his ulnar artery:

"Cutting the wrist, it's a sort of cry for help—it's not generally regarded as a reliable way of committing suicide ... It would have been necessary to use the knife, really the wrong way round, and go up. It's an unusual way of trying to cut yourself to start with."

—John Scurr, Vascular Surgeon[533]

[531] Timothy Garton Ash, *We were duped: We need to confront the men who led us astray over Saddam's non-existent arsenal*, 4 March 2004. http://www.guardian.co.uk/politics/2004/mar/04/iraq.iraq

[532] Baker, *Strange Death of David Kelly*

[533] *Anthrax War – Dead Silence: The untold story of the 2001 U.S. Anthrax Attacks, dead scientists and the dark secret of germ war research*, dir. by Bob Coen & Eric Nadler (2009, dvd). http://www.anthraxwar.com/1/?page_id=134

The suicide explanation that was advanced by the authorities was that David Kelly was human and that he had an increasingly difficult time in dealing with the publicity arising from the media exposure over his professional disagreement with the claim about Iraq's WMD program, and that it was that discomfort which led him to suicide.

That version of his death has been proven false by the known facts. While not pleased by that turn of events, Dr. Kelly was quite clearly not suicidal over it or, for that matter, over anything else. His mood and attitude at the time have been clearly characterized as "tired, subdued but not depressed."[534] Dr. Kelly had a very tough reputation as a professional who was as solid as they come. Colleagues and friends described him as the least potentially suicidal person they knew. He's the man who, during a tense interrogation, broke down the infamous "Dr. Germ"—when interrogating Dr. Rihab Taha, a ruthless expert in the weaponization of biological agents, he literally brought her to tears. So let's not fall for any of the nonsense that he was suicidal over some media coverage because a man of Dr. Kelly's personality would have batted that off like a flea, and there is substantial evidence that he had.

Therefore, in any fair assessment, he was far from suicidal over the press coverage, but he was embroiled in a controversy brought about by his professional integrity causing resentment of the overwhelmingly apparent fact: Intelligence material that he had developed was being dramatically misrepresented in order to justify the illegal invasion of another nation.

The Bush and Blair Administrations falsified "intel" that Iraq had WMD (weapons of mass destruction) to justify going to war in the Middle East. That was a lie. The Administration did *not* have that intel and Iraq did not have WMD.

They had an agenda to go to war and off to war they went. The West (the Bush/Cheney Administration in the U.S. and the Tony Blair Administration in the U.K.) were intent upon an invasion of Iraq and were not about to be stopped. Officials within the Bush Administration have stated that from the moment that Bush took office there was never really any doubt that Iraq was going to be invaded, the only question was when. Therefore, a justification, real or imagined, was a top priority.

> **"Except a desire for regime change is an illegal basis in international law for invading a country. So we had the hyped up dossiers and the pretence that, if only Saddam would cooperate with the UN and its inspectors, invasion could be avoided."[535]**

Well folks, Iraq *did* cooperate with the UN weapons inspectors. Dr. David Kelly inspected Iraq's WMD potential and came to the conclusion that it had none. On June 15 (approximately one month prior to his death), Dr. Kelly clearly struck down the West's claim that Iraq possessed WMD.[536]

But that didn't stop the Blair and Bush Administrations from disregarding the inspection team's hard intel, barring the *real* intel from public, and pushing

---

[534] Baker, *Strange Death of David Kelly*
[535] Baker, *Strange Death of David Kelly*, 139.
[536] Baker, *Strange Death of David Kelly*, 279.

forth its own phony claims about Iraq's true WMD potential, as well as its having sought enriched uranium for nuclear weaponry from Africa.

The specific claims that The West used in its false justification for the illegal invasion of Iraq are below—and bear in mind that Dr. Kelly's mysterious death occurred right in the middle of this sadly false scenario. Two completely false claims were made about:

1. Iraq possessed the ability to possess and deliver WMD;
2. Iraq's attempts to obtain weapons-grade uranium from Africa were indicative that it was a nuclear threat.

And make no mistake about it, for the facts are now crystal clear—they not only lied about the above two claims, they *then* even lied about having falsified them.

That was their case for an invasion. Therefore, the WMD lie needed to be maintained at any cost.

Some, in the face of such adversity, simply crumble in humility and go quietly along with the Powers That Be. Others—and Dr. Kelly was clearly one—are of such serious integrity and professionalism that they do not shrink from the challenge of speaking the truth. David Kelly did not go quietly; he put up a fight.

Kelly contacted a BBC news journalist and gave him his appraisal of the real on-the-ground intelligence. A political explosion took place in Great Britain as a result of that action.

Britain's Ministry of Defense became aware of a high-level security leak—an official was disclosing to the press that WMD estimates in Iraq were being grossly overstated. Dr. Kelly had been revealed as the source of the leak. He died shortly thereafter just as he predicted: "found dead in the woods."

The focus on WMD as the reason for going to war was not an accident, but a decision that was carefully planned. As U.S. Deputy Defense Secretary Paul Wolfowitz admitted in a 2003 interview:

> **"The truth is that for reasons that have a lot to do with the U.S. government bureaucracy, we settled on the one issue that everyone could agree on which was weapons of mass destruction as the core reason."**[537]

The paper trail proves that it was no accident either—our leaders intentionally overstated the threat through "systematical" misrepresentations to justify their march to war:

> **"Bush administration officials exaggerated the threats from Iraq's weapons of mass destruction and failed to uncover any links between President Saddam Hussein and Al Qaeda leader Osama bin Laden, a private nonpartisan research organization concluded in a report released yesterday. The study by the Carnegie Endowment for International Peace states that 'administration officials systematically misrepresented the threat from Iraq's WMD and ballistic missile program' by treating possibilities as fact and 'mis-**

537 *USA Today*, "Wolfowitz comments revive doubts over Iraq's WMD," 30 May, 2003, http://www.usatoday.com/news/world/iraq/2003-05-30-wolfowitz-iraq_x.htm (accessed 20 Feb. 2012)

representing inspectors' findings in ways that turned threats from
minor to dire.'"[538]

As an example of the result of this gross misrepresentation, in every sense of the
phrase, consider that the headline of Britain's widely-read *Sun* newspaper soon
blasted the following (and we cite it precisely) in huge bold print letters at the
top of its front page:

BRITS 45mins
FROM DOOM [539]

During and after the invasion, no chemical, biological, or nuclear weapons
were found in Iraq— no WMDs—even though that was the stated reason to the
world for the launching of the invasion into another country that was clearly
in violation of international law. Dr. Kelly and his team had been absolutely
correct. Pre-invasion, the reality was that there was *no* evidence of WMD, just
as Dr. Kelly had said. And *that* was the intelligence assessment that Kelly and
his team had provided. Kelly maintained that the true facts were being "sexed
up" for political purposes, to justify an invasion that was unjustifiable.[540]

Dr. Kelly's group had concluded that there were no weapons of mass destruction in Iraq, and that Saddam hadn't even had a program for any such weapons
since way back in 1991. The response to the report from Dr. Kelly's group was
to *prevent it from being published.* These were the people to whom the West
was looking for the true facts surrounding the reasons of whether or not to go
forward to a horrific war, and the forces of British leadership were marshaled to
prevent that very truth from reaching the public! Changing the report to make it
incredibly—and quite intentionally—misleading, they simply made up a claim.
Iraq had no WMD and everybody knew it. But the U.S. and U.K., clearly acting
in concert, created self-supporting circular evidence. It was unquestionably the
subversion and perversion of raw intelligence to conform with a pre-determined
march to war. British Intelligence, as the Blair Government, knew that Saddam
Hussein did not possess WMD capabilities. So they deliberately chose to use
language and semantic subterfuge to intentionally create the contrary impression and thereby fortify their false justification for war.[541]

And it wasn't just Dr. Kelly who became a victim of that false path to an
illegal invasion—anyone who got in the way of it became a victim. During this
exact same time period, another component of the falsification of rationale for
invasion of Iraq was a claim just as weak as Iraq's WMD—supposed intelligence
showing that Iraq had sought enriched uranium, known as "yellow cake," from
the African nation of Niger. The conclusion was dramatically drawn that *with*
this weapons-grade uranium, Iraq's nuclear capabilities would pose a dire threat
to the world. But the reality of that situation was starkly different.

---

[538] Farah Stockman, "Carnegie study calls arms threat overstated," *The Boston Globe,* 9 Januray, 2004, http://www.boston.com/news/
nation/articles/2004/01/09/carnegie_study_calls_arms_threat_overstated/ (accessed 20 Feb. 2012)

[539] *The Sun,* "BRITS 45mins FROM DOOM," 25 September, 2002, page 1.

[540] Baker, *Strange Death of David Kelly,* 105-106.

[541] Baker, *Strange Death of David Kelly,* 110, 124, 132, 134.

In February, 2002, the CIA had sent Joseph Wilson, former Ambassador, to Niger for the specific purpose of investigating if Iraq had sought weapons-grade uranium. Wilson had spent over a week there, speaking with dozens of contacts, including present and former government officials who had been connected with Niger's uranium business. Wilson's investigation concluded that, given his discussions, as well as the restrictions, scrutiny and difficulties associated with uranium, it was extremely unlikely that international oversight had failed in the matter. He expressed his extreme doubt that uranium had been passed from Niger to Iraq and conveyed his opinion of same to the appropriate U.S. authorities.

Therefore, former Ambassador Wilson was quite astonished to see that the Bush Administration had gone full-forward with the claim as though it were accepted intelligence. He voiced his concerns about the matter in an article that appeared in *The New York Times* on July 6, 2003. The article revealed that Wilson found the claim "highly doubtful" and that, furthermore, there was no evidence that Saddam Hussein had even *attempted* to buy uranium from the country.

The White House responded quickly and lethally, revealing its true colors for all to see. On July 14, only three days prior to Dr. Kelly's death, information was leaked and printed by a journalist on good terms with the Bush Administration, that Wilson's wife, Valerie Plame, was an active CIA agent. Obviously, its intention was retribution at Wilson. In the process, it blew Plame's cover, effectively ending her very honorable intelligence career. But it also did something else—it compromised the relationships and even the lives of dozens of contacts she had, both covert and overt, through a career spanning many years all over the globe. If one checks the *United States Intelligence Identification Act* of 1982, one finds that it is a felony to disclose the name and details of a covert agent. But hey, no problem there, folks—when you have the U.S. Presidency at your disposal, those sorts of problems can be effectively dealt with. When President Bush's close advisor, "Scooter" Libby, was found to have lied to investigators about mentioning Ms. Plame, quicker than you can say "Get out of jail free-card," he was the immediate recipient of a Presidential Pardon. It's a lot like President Lyndon Johnson supposedly investigating the assassination of President Kennedy—it has the effect of getting the real point pushed aside, rather rudely at that, and usually for "national security." It was a clear shot by the Bush Administration at Ambassador Wilson and a clear warning to anyone else that they were risking everything if they got in the way of this Administration's march to war. However, Dr. Kelly was a man of much integrity and, although he clearly saw what had taken place with Ambassador Wilson, he was not about to see a major war fought over what he knew to be false intelligence.[542]

Colin Powell's contention before the United Nations that Iraq possessed mobile bio-weapons labs had also been investigated by Dr. Kelly and his team. They concluded that Iraq possessed nothing of the sort—the "mobile bio-terror labs" were established by the weapons inspectors to be simply for the purpose of helium—they posed no threat whatsoever.

---

[542] Baker, *Strange Death of David Kelly*, 113-114.

Dr. Kelly spoke his conscience, because he *knew* that the information was fraudulent. So he contacted a British source at the *Observer* and spoke candidly and clearly. His comments appeared in a Sunday edition on June 15, 2003, a month before his death. Dr. Kelly is referred to as "a British scientist and biological weapons expert, who has examined the trailers in Iraq." Here are his exact words:

"They are not mobile germ warfare laboratories. You could not use them for making biological weapons. They do not even look like them. They are exactly what the Iraqis said they were — facilities for the production of hydrogen gas to fill balloons."[543]

But that hadn't stopped U.S. Secretary of State Colin Powell from doing his major media show at the United Nations in which he laid out the need for war. He stated that it was reliable information from a known informant and had three corroborating sources. The "reliable informant" was none other than a man codenamed "Curveball" because that's exactly what he usually threw. All three of those corroborating sources, by the way, were also thoroughly discredited— they turned out to be "fraudulent," just as Curveball also was. In fact, *even the* CIA itself, and its chief of European Intelligence, openly questioned Curveball's credibility.

"Here were the foundations of sand on which were built Mr. Powell's authoritative call to war at the UN."[544]

Colin Powell, before the world at his highly publicized UN presentation, presented the information as "firsthand descriptions" and confidently stated that an "eyewitness account of these mobile production facilities has been corroborated by other sources."[545]

That public relations campaign paid off big-time too; albeit with massive misinformation. But that wasn't important at the time to the Administration. Only the "case for war" was important. To convey an idea of the success of that misinformation, just consider this: A 2003 poll showed that an astounding *seventy-two percent of Americans* believed that Saddam Hussein was personally involved in the attacks of 9-11. Like the old saying goes: Don't let the facts get in the way of a good story.

Great Britain and the U.S. could certainly breathe a lot easier after the "convenient" death of Dr. Kelly: Their WMD lie would then remain unchallenged because its biggest critic was gone—the one man who could prove it was a lie. That reality alone mandates a very close look at any role those groups may have played in his death.

---

[543] Peter Beaumont, "Iraq Mobil Labs Nothing to do with Germ Warfare, Report Finds," 15 June 2003, theguardian – The Observer. http://www.guardian.co.uk/world/2003/jun/15/iraq

[544] Baker, *Strange Death of David Kelly*, 315.

[545] Baker, *Strange Death of David Kelly*, 312-316.

Dr. Kelly was questioned intensely regarding reports from within the Government that he was the source of the security leak concerning the West's exaggerations on the true state of Iraq's bioweapons capabilities, as a false case to go to war.

As we look at Dr. Kelly's disappearance, it bears noting that there is no evidence that police or anyone else attempted to track Dr. Kelly's location after he went missing by use of cell phone technology—or that they even attempted calling his phone number to see if it was turned on. Dr. Kelly had his cell phone with him.[546]

Cellphone tracking technology was available at the time of his disappearance. If his phone was on, they could have pinpointed the location via triangulation. Even if his phone was turned off, it would have revealed the last reported location, which certainly would have been critical information under the circumstances. Why, nowhere in evidence, is that point even addressed? Even more disturbingly, why, nowhere in evidence, does anyone state that they at least attempted to call him on his cellphone? Are we expected to believe that the police never thought about that point? Isn't that the first and most logical step that could've been taken? Most disturbingly of all, why were these questions never asked? It appears nowhere in the testimony that Kelly's family tried calling him on his cellphone— or that the police ever asked them if they had—or that the official inquiry ever asked if someone had tried tracking his cellphone or at least calling him on it? That's a huge red flag, quite preposterous, and a sign that something is dreadfully wrong.

---

[546] Andy Bloxham, "Police 'ignored' Dr. David Kelly's mobile phone records: Police investigating the death of the Government weapons inspector Dr. David Kelly ignored mobile phone records which could have shed light on his movements before he died, it has been claimed," 7 January 2011, *The Telegraph*.

Dr. Kelly had completed 40,000 words of a book which he said would prove that the West had lied about its claims to go to war with Iraq. On the day that he disappeared, MI5 intelligence agents raided his house and seized the computer containing his book. The raid took place thirty minutes <u>before</u> his body was found dead in the woods. The book disappeared and no traces of it have ever surfaced.

TIMELINE

Disappearance of Dr. David Kelly

Dr. Kelly is at the center of a firestorm because he has recently been identified as the source ("mole" or "leak") of highly controversial information. He was immediately hauled before a House of Commons committee and grilled on the matter, then taken to a "safe house" where he was "interviewed" intensely for several days by British Intelligence services. Liaising with the media had been part of Kelly's job, however, revealing the knowledge that Iraq does not actually possess WMD (weapons of mass destruction) stands in direct opposition to the false claims being made by the U.S. and Great Britain in their fraudulent justification for war.

There are known threats against Dr. Kelly's life (he is on the Iraqi "hit list") and he is reportedly under protection of MoD (Ministry of Defence), MI5 (roughly the equivalent of the FBI) and/or MI6 (International Intelligence). In his own words, Dr.

and Britain's intelligence agencies with whom he had often sparred over interpretations of intelligence reports."

Dr. Kelly had reportedly been threatened with criminal prosecution and the loss of his pension if he did not cooperate with the Ministry of Defence inquiry.

- 11:00 AM–12:00 PM Various Emails

In addition to his several communications throughout this morning with Wing Commander Clark and his email to Judith Miller of The New York Times, Dr. Kelly also sends seven other emails, returning correspondence from several colleagues and other well-wishers, in a manner that is typically very upbeat.

He answers an email from Professor Alistair Hay, a colleague, who had stated he was concerned that the Ministry of Defence would "not enable" email contact between he and Dr. Kelly, and that he hoped he was holding up under what must be immense pressure. Dr. Kelly responded:

"Dear Alistair, Many thanks for your support. Hopefully it will soon pass and I can get to Baghdad and get on with the real job. Best Wishes, David"

Dr. Kelly responds to a sensitive email—the sender's name has been redacted for national security—the subject (with only the word "Media" in quotations) is "Media" presentation. The sender states "hope to see you abroad in a few weeks time." Kelly responds:

"(Recipient's name redacted for security purposes), Quite a week. If all blows over I will be in Baghdad next Friday (sic). Hope to see you shortly after that. All the best, David"

To Ron Manley, who has written "Sorry about your latest run in with the media" and sends his best wishes, Kelly responds:

"Ron, Many thanks for your thoughts. It has been difficult. Hopefully it will all blow over by the end of the week and I can travel to Baghdad and get on with the real work. Best wishes, David"

Dr. Kelly was a relatively new and enthusiastic member of the Baha'i faith and, as an example, sends an email to Geeta Kingdon, a fellow Baha'i member:

Kelly's response references the fact that he has been under sufficient threat that he even had to leave home for a week, possibly at an Intelligence "safe house":

"Geeta, Many thanks for your thoughts and prayers. It has been a remarkably tough time. Should all blow over by early next week then I will travel to Baghdad a week Friday (sic).

I have had to keep a low profile which meant leaving home for a week! Back now. With best wishes and thanks for your support. David"

He also responds to Debra Krikorian's email, many portions of which have been deleted for security purposes, but she stated that she is "in town" and would like to meet with him when possible. Kelly's response further confirms his "cloak-and-dagger" intrigue, again indicating that he has been under the protection of the Ministry of Defence for his own security:

"Deb, Many thanks for the email. GKW let me know that you had been trying to contact me but I have been keeping low on MOD advice. If all blows over by the beginning of next week I will get to Baghdad soon. Regards, David"

He responds to an email from colleague Philippe Michel who has stated "We are confident where is the truth and this one must be revealed rapidly"

"Philippe, Many thanks for your email. I know that I have a lot of good friends who are providing support at a difficult time. Hope to see you soon. Regards, David"

He also takes the time to respond courteously to colleague Malfrid Braut, who expresses his empathy for the situation Dr. Kelly finds himself in and also wants to send Kelly a draft of a report:

"Malfrid, Thanks. It has been difficult. I hope to get to Baghdad soon to really work. I will then probably be out of email contact but send me whatever you wish and I will respond as soon as I can.

I am sure that Cairo remains absorbing.   Best wishes, David"

Analysis: The Hutton Inquiry lists the above eight emails (including Miller) as all being sent by Dr. Kelly at exactly 11:18 AM—that doesn't seem very likely, given their length, thoughtfulness, and the sheer number of them. In any event, as with all his communications this morning, Dr. Kelly sounds very upbeat about returning to Iraq and getting on with "the real work" of weapons inspections even though he has been "laying low" and was away from home for a week due to security precautions implemented by the Ministry of Defence. His correspondence clearly attests to his mood on his final morning. He conducts his affairs in his typical manner: all-business, efficient, professional, polite, and quite obviously not behaving in a suicidal manner.

- 12:15 PM
Mrs. Kelly returns home (she had gone out to pick up some photographs). She tells her husband about the photos.
- 12:30 PM
Dr. Kelly leaves his study and joins her in the sitting room. In addition to talking about the photos, they also share some lunch, sitting opposite the table from each other, but do not speak a great deal (she feels he is very absorbed in his work).

Dr. Kelly eats the sandwich that she made and also has a glass of water.

Mrs. Kelly was later asked how she would describe her husband at 12:30 pm that day and she replied:

"Oh, I just thought he had a broken heart. He really was very, very—he had shrunk into himself ... I had no idea at that stage what he might do later, absolutely no idea at all."

As Norman Baker points out, this is what attorneys refer to as reinterpretation after-the-fact with benefit of subsequent knowledge. What that statement actually tells us is that—at that precise moment—nothing out of the ordinary had taken place to even remotely suggest that her husband was suicidal.

- 1:30–1:45 PM

  As she often does, Mrs. Kelly goes upstairs to rest after lunch. She suffers from arthritis and it is flaring up today. Dr. Kelly returns to his study to continue working.

  Analysis: Note that it is actually Mrs. Kelly who is very bothered by the recent media storm and is the one who is in pain. The Copraxamol tablets that are later ascribed to being Dr. Kelly's are not his. He has not been prescribed that medication and also has a very strong aversion to swallowing tablets. He walks for his back pain and that seems to work. The Copraxomol, which is a mild analgesic commonly prescribed for arthritis sufferers, probably belonged to his wife. And there is later a wide window of opportunity for items to be taken from the Kelly home to stage the crime scene.

- Slightly prior to 2:00 PM

  Dr. Kelly goes upstairs to check on his wife who is lying down a bit because he knows that she hasn't been feeling well today. She states: "Then shortly after I had lay down, he came to ask me if I was okay. I said: yes, I will be fine."

  At this point it bears noting that if he was sympathetic enough to go upstairs and check on his wife, he'd certainly be sympathetic enough not to make matters dramatically worse by killing himself.

- 2:00 PM

  Dr. Kelly gets ready for his afternoon walk. His wife states: "And then he went to change into his jeans. He would be around the house in a tracksuit or tracksuit bottoms during the day. So he went to change and put on his shoes."

- 2:30 PM

  Operation Mason officially begins (technically an investigation into Dr. Kelly's death, by the Thames Valley Police).

  Analysis: Since the operation clearly began half an hour prior to Dr. Kelly even leaving his house for his afternoon walk, it has been quite logically suggested that other forces were at play, and that Operation Mason, in reality, was a police response to a newly known and active threat upon the life of Dr. Kelly.

- 2:53–2:54 PM Phone Call

    Mrs. Kelly hears the phone ring and, not having the cordless with her upstairs, goes downstairs to answer it because she had believed her husband had already left for his walk. She then hears Dr. Kelly talking on the phone and is fairly sure he is speaking to someone at MoD again (which was almost certainly Wing Commander Clark who testified that it was he who again called Dr. Kelly shortly before 3:00 PM, and that was the last time that they had spoken).

- Slightly after 3:00 PM

    Dr. Kelly leaves the house for his afternoon walk. He took regular walks for his bad back. They were typically twenty-five minutes or less. He had told his wife earlier that he was going for his walk and would be back soon.

    His wife knew, in the way that spouses know specifically what to infer from the use of certain words, that he therefore planned on taking his regular brief walk (she testified as such), which would always put him back home in something under half an hour (as opposed to his longer ones, which were usually to Harrowdown Hill and took closer to an hour). If he was taking one of his longer walks, he always specifically mentioned that and would have taken his coat. He did not take his coat that afternoon.

    It would also be logical to infer that if he had actually packed away his pruning knife and pills and planned to do away with himself on his walk, he most probably would have made a more memorable gesture to his wife of many years. Instead, he simply told her that he was going out for his afternoon walk, as he normally did, and that he would be back soon, as he normally was.

- 3:20 PM

    Wing Commander Clark phones the Kelly home again. Mrs. Kelly answers and, sure this time that her husband is gone, she informs Clark that he's not at home, having left for his walk a few minutes after 3:00.

- 3:20 pm–3:25 PM

    Ruth Absalom, a neighbor who has known him many years, sees Dr. Kelly and the two chat a bit. She places the time at somewhere around 3:00 but is not at all sure, but it obviously had to be a little later than that if he left his house shortly after 3:00 and then walked to where they meet, at Harris's Lane, which is slightly less than a mile from Kelly's home (at a brisk pace that would take at least 15 minutes). They talk for about 5 minutes. As they part, Dr. Kelly says "See you again then,

Ruth." The witness later describes Dr. Kelly's demeanor during this conversation as perfectly normal, nothing at all out of the ordinary:

"Just his normal self, no different to any other time when I have met him.""We parted and he said 'Cheerio Ruth.'"

Since Dr. Kelly has been under the security watch of MoD, and/or MI5, and MI6 due to the known threats upon his life, it stands to reason that he would not be allowed to leave his home at this time unaccompanied or unsurveilled, to meander dangerously alone through the British country-side; especially considering that his afternoon walk was an established routine, thereby making it the most vulnerable point in his day. Yet, the above witness notes no other persons accompanying or surveilling Dr. Kelly at the time of his arrival, during their talk, or as he departs. The MoD has not produced documentation on the specific security procedures taken for Dr. Kelly, therefore, little is known except for the existence of Operation Mason. Operation Mason was a security program designed for the specific case of Dr. Kelly and it officially began at least thirty minutes prior to the time he left his home for his daily walk. So where was his security?

The above witness also verifies that Dr. Kelly was not carrying anything. He did not have a bottle of water, or a pruning knife, or three ten-sheet-packs of Copraxomol, or a heavy jacket to conceal them in—yet, later, he was supposedly found with all of these.

- 3:25 PM

Dr. Kelly continues on his walk, to Ruth's right, down Appleton Road, in the direction of Kingston Bagpuize.

Analysis: The direction in which Dr. Kelly continued walking was consistent with his regular short walks, and was not the walking route that he would have taken had he intended going to Harrowdown Hill (the location his body was later found).

- 3:25 –10:00 PM or later (Over seven hours missing)

Note that there are approximately seven missing hours between the time that neighbor Ruth Absolom bid goodbye to her friend (the last witness to see him alive), and the approximate time of Dr. Kelly's death. We know from forensics that Dr. Kelly was alive during this time period. When the body was discovered on the following morning, the pathologist ignored standard procedure and failed to take the victim's body temperature, with which an accurate time of death could be estimated. However, we know that the rigor mortis process generally takes six hours to begin and takes approximately twelve hours to become vivid. We know that Dr. Kelly's body did not evidence the full effect of rigor mortis when it was eventually found at 10:00 AM on Friday morning. Therefore, working backwards, the time of death can be established—and the earliest time Dr. Kelly could have died— was 10:00 PM, Thursday night; and it could very well have been later. So he was alive for many hours after he had gone missing.

- 4:30–5:00 PM
  Mrs. Kelly states that when it was getting close to a couple of hours that he'd been gone, she realized that her husband had been gone too long and she "began to get rather worried."
  The fact that she knew that his walks typically took less than thirty minutes, but did not begin to worry until almost two hours later, again suggests that—at the time in question— there was no reason for her to consider anything like suicide. There is also no mention anywhere in the record that Mrs. Kelly (or anyone else, for that matter) tried calling her husband on his cell phone, which would have clearly been the logical thing to do. He had his cell phone with him.

- 5:00–5:10 PM
  Mrs. Kelly speaks to her daughter, Rachel, on the phone and apparently informs her of the situation.

- 5:10–5:30 PM
  Rachel takes the twenty-minute drive to her parent's home.

- 5:30–6:00 PM
  Rachel arrives at the home of her parents and talks to her mother. She then retraces the route of her father's normal walk, a route that she knows.

- 5:00–6:00 PM
  A colleague of Dr. Kelly's from the British Ministry of Defence attempts to reach him on his cell, but Dr. Kelly's mobile phone is switched off.
  Analysis: We know that his cell phone was turned off during this time period which, in itself, is extremely suspicious—Dr. Kelly was in the midst of very fluidly-changing events and had been in constant contact with colleagues in the Ministry of Defence. Therefore, it is virtually unthinkable that he would have shut off his cell phone voluntarily. He had specifically informed friends that his mobile was always on.

- 6:30 PM
  Rachel returns to the Kelly home, not having found her father.

- Throughout the evening hours
  Rachel is joined by her sister, Sian, who has arrived at the Kelly home with her partner, Richard. The sisters search around town looking for their father, with no success.

Analysis: It was well known to all concerned that Dr. Kelly was in an extremely high profile position and in a very dangerous business—this was at the height of his controversy in the British press. Note that a man in that dangerous position went for his methodical half-hour walk many, many hours ago and yet, even in a small village, there is no trace of him having been anywhere. But, reportedly, the police still have not been called.

Note, also, that which is absent. At no time is it mentioned, anywhere in the official evidence, that anyone attempted to call him on his cell phone.

- 11:00 PM

The sisters finally return to the home, unsuccessful in tracking their father. Harrowdown Hill was checked as a possible location, because it was known that Dr. Kelly did sometimes go there on his longer walks.

- 11:40 PM – Police are finally called (Missing for over eight hours)
- 11:50–11:55 PM

Police arrive at the Kelly home

- 11:55 PM–1:00 AM Friday

Three police officers take down the information with a missing-persons form. Sergeant Simon Morris told the Hutton Inquiry that, at that time, he arranged "a reasonably thorough search of Dr. Kelly's house and the surrounding grounds to be carried out."The apparent reason for searching the area was in case Dr. Kelly had had a heart attack or was unconscious due to a medical emergency.

- 1:00 AM Friday

Sgt. Morris puts out an order for an aerial search, which Mrs. Kelly states began at about 1:00 AM. However, there is an exact record of the aerial searches made, and they were apparently much later. Records indicate that a police helicopter was dispatched from Luton and was airborne in search of Dr. Kelly from 2:50 to 4:05 AM. The police helicopter then refueled at RAF Benson, and a second search sortie then took place from 4:30 to 5:10 AM, for a total aerial search of one hour and fifty-five minutes.

- Sometime during the early am hours

A large vehicle with a 110-foot communication tower with a huge antenna, arrives by truck and is set up in the yard of the Kelly home. It has been deployed by Thames Valley Police.

Analysis: Norman Baker, Member of Parliament, checked with some experts about this item. They told him that, even in an area with poor reception, they would expect a communications mast no higher than fifteen feet to be used because it would be more than sufficient for all anticipated communication necessary. Therefore, the only discernible explanation for the huge tower would have been to enable hi-tech communication to someone very far away or perhaps airborne, for example. It is known that, at the time this took place, Prime Minister Tony Blair was airborne, en route from Washington to Japan.

- 2:00–4:00 AM: Search on foot
  "Half a dozen" officers search outside for Dr. Kelly, although the search is largely in the area very near his home.
- 2:50–4:05 AM
  Actual time of first aerial search
  Analysis: Note that the helicopter was reportedly equipped with high-tech heat-seeking equipment which should have been able to locate Dr. Kelly's body had the body actually been present at the time of the search. His body temperature still registered twenty-four degrees Celsius at 7:15 PM the following day, therefore, it would have been high enough to register on the heat-seeking equipment at the time of this search. It was also only four days after Full Moon which would have further facilitated said search.
- 4:30–5:10 AM
  Actual time of second aerial search
- 5:30 AM
  Meeting takes place at Abingdon Police Station, attended by Assistant Chief Constable Page, Sergeant Paul Wood (a police search advisor, the Detective Inspector for the area, and the local head of Special Branch (British equivalent to Intelligence/Security). ACC Page testified that at this time: "My concerns were that Dr. Kelly had gone out for a walk, perhaps become ill, perhaps had an accident befall him, possibly had been abducted against his will, possibly was being detained."
  Analysis: Note that, although the police have had substantial input from family members, etc., and have brainstormed together about the case, still, at this late hour, suicide was not even mentioned as a possibility.
- 6:00 AM
  Police forces are marshaled and sent out to what are now considered the five or six most likely locations Dr. Kelly could have disappeared (Harrowdown Hill is at number two on that list). Other constables are also called in from surrounding areas to assist and a call also goes out to the South East Berkshire Emergency Volunteers and search dogs. Detective Constable Graham Coe begins conducting door-to-door inquiries.
- 6:30–7:30 AM
  During this period, a force of thirty to forty officers are on outward search from the Kelly home.

- 7:15 AM
  The South East Berkshire Emergency Volunteers arrive at the Abingdon Police Station, are briefed on the situation and set out on their search with scent dogs.
- 8:00–8:25 AM
  Dog picks up scent
  Two volunteer searchers, Louise Holmes and Paul Chapman, and their search dog Brock, a highly-trained Collie, are searching the area to which they had been assigned—the woods between Harrowdown Hill and the Thames River.
  Brock the Collie picks up a scent and then indicates that he has found something, by returning and barking to Louise Holmes. Typically, responding as trained, he always takes his handler directly to what he has found. On this occasion, however, the search dog would not do so. Oddly, he refused, and would only direct his handler to what he had found, declining to approach the area himself.
- 8:30 AM—Dr. Kelly's body is found in the woods
  Louise Holmes locates a body in the woods at Harrowdown Hill. She shouts to fellow volunteer Paul Chapman to call the police. Chapman calls emergency 999 and soon gets a callback from Abingdon Police Station. The volunteers are told to wait in their car for police. On their way back to their car, they encounter three police intelligence detectives (C.I.D.) who had been walking towards the river. They were not aware that a body had been found. Two were identified as District Constable Graham Coe and District Constable Shields—the third man has never been identified. DC Coe told volunteer Chapman to show him the body and Chapman led him there. Coe then told Chapman to return to his car and wait for additional police.
- 8:30–9:00 AM
  DC Coe is then alone with the body for about half an hour and there have been numerous inconsistencies in the evidence ever since:
  "The volunteer searchers who first came across Dr. Kelly both described him as sitting upright. Mr. Chapman, from a distance of some fifteen to twenty meters, told the inquiry that Dr. Kelly's body was 'sitting with his back up against a tree'. Ms Holmes concurred, saying that Dr. Kelly's head and shoulders were 'just slumped back against the tree.'"
  DC Coe, however, testified to what has become the official version, which is that Dr. Kelly was laying out flat on the ground.
  Analysis: The two searchers do not even note the small cut on Dr. Kelly's wrist because there is actually very little blood. Quite a long period of time passes, under the circumstances, before paramedics are summoned. The apparent reason that it was

untenable for the body to be in an upright position becomes quite clear when we examine the forensic evidence below regarding the directional trail of dried vomit stains.

- 9:40 AM—Emergency call finally received at Abingdon Ambulance Station

An emergency call is received that a body has been found at Harrowdown Hill and an ambulance is dispatched there.

- 9:55 AM—Emergency Paramedics Arrive

Two paramedics, Dave Bartlett and Vanessa Hunt, arrive at the scene. They are struck by the large number of all types of law enforcement personnel present: police from the "special armed response units" and others, some in civilian clothing, "others in black jackets and army fatigues." They park their ambulance and are led into the woods by two armed-response officers, walking about one mile and carrying their resuscitation equipment. They locate the body and assess the status of the victim: Hunt checks for a pulse and Bartlett shines a flashlight in the eye looking for a pupil reaction. They place four electrodes on the chest and try to detect any heart activity. There is none.

Analysis: There is now evidence that the body has been moved. The two paramedics both note that the body is laying flat on the ground, as opposed to sitting up against a tree as the two search team members found it. Observe that the fact that the body was moved post-mortem means that a cover-up was already operational during the search. Had the investigation been an authentic one, they would not have moved the body to conform to other evidence. There would have been no reason to move it.

- 10:07 AM—David Christopher Kelly is Declared Dead

The paramedics are clinically trained emergency medical personnel who are well experienced in death scenes, having been paramedics in ambulance crews for over fifteen years each. Assessing the victim and the crime scene, the first thing that strikes them is the virtual absence of blood. They have witnessed "successful" wrist-slashing crime scenes: Vanessa Hunt described that as "like a slaughterhouse." And they note that the differences were dramatic. They do not see anything close to adequate evidence of a suicide. Paramedic Vanessa Hunt testified:

"The amount of blood that was around the scene seemed relatively minimal … no obvious arterial bleeding. There was no spraying of blood or huge blood loss or any obvious loss on the clothing."

"There wasn't a puddle of blood around. There was a little bit of blood on the nettles to the left of his left arm. But there was no real blood on the body of the shirt. The only other bit of blood I saw was on his clothing. It was the size of a 50p piece, above the right knee on his trousers … When somebody cuts an artery, whether accidentally or intentionally, the blood pumps everywhere. I just think it is incredibly unlikely that he died from the wrist wound we saw."

Paramedic Bartlett was in complete agreement with his partner. He recalled being at one attempted suicide where the blood actually shot all the way up to the ceiling and recalled the details of it:

"Even in this incident, the victim survived. It looked like The Texas Chainsaw Massacre and the guy walked out alive. We have been to a vast amount of incidents where people who have slashed their wrists, intentionally or not, most of them are taken down to the hospital and given a few stitches, then sent straight back home. But there is a lot of blood. It's all over them."

Bartlett even commented on the weakness of the wrist wound while at the crime scene:

"I remember saying to one of the policeman, it didn't look like he died from that … "

The paramedics also document clearly visible dried vomit stains running from the corners of the victim's mouth, directly downwards to his ears on both sides.

Analysis: Note that the dried stains running to both ears are consistent with the body position because it is now laying flat on the ground. Had the victim been leaning up against a tree—as he indeed quite obviously was—gravity would have made the trails come down the victim's front, not back to his ears. The logical inference is that the body was moved postmortem to rectify the inconsistency.

- 10:55 AM— Helicopter lands at Harrowdown Hill

Information finally released in 2011, only as a result of requirements related to a Freedom of Information Act request, revealed that a helicopter landed at the site where Dr. Kelly's body was found, approximately ninety minutes after his body was discovered. However, the document is so redacted (blacked out for "national security" reasons) that it is not even possible to discern the purpose of the helicopter, who was on board, or who requested it. Thames Police refused to comment.

Analysis: As with just about everything else with this case, there seems to be no sense of responsibility to explain actions reasonably, conduct affairs logically and in a trustworthy manner or, for that matter, to even lend the appearance of actually trying to ascertain the truth about these matters. As

Dr. Andrew Watt, one of the doctors who has brought the official version under much-deserving pressure, puts it: "If the purpose of the helicopter flight was innocent, one has to ask why it was kept secret."
Timeline constructed from:
"The Lord Hutton Inquiry—Evidence", August 27- September 2, 2003, Hearing transcripts; Report of the Inquiry into the Circumstances Surrounding the Death of Dr David Kelly C.M.G., Lord Hutton, January 28, 2004; http://www.the-hutton-inquiry. org.uk/content/report The Hutton Inquiry—Evidence, Ministry of Justice, United Kingdom. http://www.the-hutton- inquiry. org.uk/content/ evidence-lists/evidence030903.htm
The Strange Death of David Kelly, Norman Baker MP (Member of Parliament), 2007;
"Did Two Hired Assassins Snatch Weapons Inspector David Kelly?", Norman Baker, October 22, 2007, Daily Mail. http:// www.globalresearch.ca/index.php?context=viewArticle&cod e=BAK20071022&articleId=7155
"Kelly Death Paramedics Query Verdict", Antony Barnett, December 12, 2004, The Observer. http://www.guardian. co.uk/uk/2004/dec/12/politics.davidkelly
"Dr. Kelly's Final Email to a Friend: Dark Actors Playing Games", Jamie Macaskill, July 20, 2003, The Sunday Mail. http://www. rense.com/general39/kellyy.htm
"Police 'Ignored' Dr David Kelly's Mobile Phone Records: Police investigating the death of the Government weapons inspector Dr David Kelly ignored mobile phone records which could have shed light on his movements before he died, it has been claimed"; Andy Bloxham, January 7, 2011, The Telegraph
"Mystery Helicopter Claim Over Dr. David Kelly Death: Police have refused to comment on reports that a helicopter mysteriously landed at the scene of weapons expert Dr. David Kelly's death shortly after his body was discovered," May 25, 2011, The Telegraph.

With Dr. Kelly, we must ask the same question we asked regarding Vince Foster: The scientist clearly possessed a highly gifted intellect and a methodical mind, and with certainty, there were much more efficient methods of committing suicide than dashing off into the woods equipped only with a very dull gardening knife. Therefore, we must ask ourselves why a methodical scientist would select a most inefficient method of suicide. The identical effect could have been achieved much more efficiently; and surely, a scientist would have selected *methodically* the most efficient method.

It has been established that there was <u>official foreknowledge</u> of the impending death of Dr. Kelly: The Thames Police Department set up its *Operation Mason* thirty minutes prior to the time Dr. Kelly even left his home for his afternoon walk. We are told that *Operation Mason* was a "tactical support operation" on Kelly's behalf. An intelligence source in the U.K. has explained that its security services obtained intelligence on an assassination attempt against Dr. Kelly and *Operation Mason* was to deal with that threat. Well, assuming that's true, here's a question for them: Why didn't they just call him on his cell and tell him to sit tight until some uniforms got there and, in the meantime, don't do anything dangerous, <u>like taking a long walk in the woods by yourself?</u>[547]

Member of Parliament Norman Baker took a year off from his duties as Chair of the Environment, Food and Rural Affairs Committee for the express purpose of researching Dr. Kelly's highly suspicious death, resulting in his well-researched and thoroughly documented book, *The Strange Death of David Kelly*. In that work, he dissects the wrongful ruling of "Suicide" in a manner much the same as seen here. He concluded that, at the time of Dr. Kelly's death, everything in the Administrations of the U.S. and Great Britain were acutely geared toward "justification for a pre-emptive strike on Iraq" and that "the death of Dr. Kelly was central" to that issue and took place within that "highly charged atmosphere."[548]

CONCLUSION

As one British newspaper summed it all up, Dr. Kelly's highly suspicious death occurred "shortly after he was exposed as the source of a BBC news report questioning the Government's claims that Saddam Hussein had an arsenal of weapons of mass destruction which could be deployed within 45 minutes. Lord Hutton's 2004 report, commissioned by Mr Blair, concluded that Dr. Kelly killed himself with a blunt gardening knife. It was dismissed by many experts as a whitewash for clearing the Government of any culpability, despite evidence that it had leaked Dr. Kelly's name in an attempt to smear him."[549]

There are some very disturbing similarities in the deaths of Dr. Kelly and Vince Foster:

- Both were operating right in the eye of a political hurricane;
- The political firestorm had recently reached *critical mass*;
- Both were men of notably high integrity, who may have refused to "play ball" when it was expected of them;
- Both were very strong-willed, highly intelligent, and dedicated professionals, with no inclination toward suicide;
- Both died under extremely suspicious circumstances, with mountains of conflicting evidence, in "official" suicides that had all the characteristics of murder;
- Both cases *still* have a plethora of unanswered and even *unaddressed*—questions.

---

[547] Baker, *Strange Death of David Kelly*, 49, 68, 304, 307.

[548] Baker, *Strange Death of David Kelly*, vii, 281.

[549] Goslett, "David Kelly post mortem to be kept secret for 70 years"

At a certain point, there are so many anomalies that they begin to take a major role in determining what actually took place. That is clearly the case with the death of David Kelly.

However, with every great mystery, there is often one thing that holds the key to deciphering it: A matrix which, when applied over the evidence, correctly matches up all the factors in the equation which had previously not added up correctly.

In the case of the JFK assassination, that realization comes by asking the question *What if there were* two *conspiracies?—One that killed the President and another that, for whatever reason, covered up the crime.* Then the previously anomalous actions of the players suddenly are easily explainable. Then we understand how Attorney General Robert Kennedy acted in the aftermath, covering the tracks of the crime even though he obviously didn't participate in the crime itself. *Then* we know the right question to ask: *What could cause him to act in such a manner?* And when we look under that microscope it all fits—the disclosure of Oswald's name, which RFK immediately recognized from the anti-Castro black ops, seriously compromised U.S. Intelligence; and the secondary intent of the assassination was to force an invasion of Cuba, which the cover-up subverted. Then the contradictions disappear and darkness is illuminated.

This leads us to what is overwhelmingly the most commonly proposed explanation of what actually took place in the death of Dr. Kelly. Because it's the one matrix with which all the different variables of the puzzle suddenly fit precisely together and the many anomalies suddenly sing in harmony.

POSSIBLE SCENARIOS

One scenario illuminatingly explains the death of David Kelly, and it turns out to be the one that they don't want us to talk about: politically-based assassination. If Dr. Kelly was murdered, the crime scene staged as a suicide and those facts covered up by the government, then all the anomalies are magically explained:

- It would explain the inability to track Dr. Kelly's location via cell phone technology, and the complete absence of information regarding what should have been those attempts, as well as the absence of information on attempts to call him on his cellphone which would have been the first logical thing to do;
- It would explain the inability to locate Dr. Kelly's body with heat-seeking technology which was conducted over a wide area via helicopter searches with hi-tech equipment—because the body *wasn't there* at the time;
- It would explain the presence of the huge 110-foot communications towers placed in the yard of Dr. Kelly's home (there was no earthly reason for them to be there except to communicate with someone who was airborne, as PM Tony Blair was at the time);
- It would explain all the contradictory witness reports;
- It would explain the fact that he left his house without his jacket, yet it was found next to his body in the woods.

It should be noted that the term **political assassination** encompasses several possibilities:

- Assassination (sometimes referred to as "extermination") by an intelligence agency of one's own nation (in this case, *MI5* or *MI6*);
- Assassination that is *farmed out* (brokered) through another nation's security force or through private resources such as the Mafia;
- Enemy action: in this case, a Mid-eastern security force (Kelly was on Saddam Hussein's official "hit list") or China (he was also reportedly on the hit list of CSIC, Chinese Secret Intelligence Service.

One has to be very cautious about forming simplistic conclusions in the complex world of Intelligence. At first glance, Western Intelligence agencies (MI5, MI6 & CIA) seem to at blame for covering up the true facts concerning the death of Dr. Kelly. But just as with the JFK assassination, those who cover up a crime aren't necessarily those who committed it.

We checked with some intel sources, and it turns out it's a bit more complicated. We found out that MI6 (SIS, the Secret Intelligence Service of James Bond lore) was actively attempting to *protect* Dr. Kelly from known threats at the time of his death. For example, it was known that Kelly was on the notorious "hit list" of Saddam Hussein and also on the hit list of the lesser known but even more sophisticated CSIS . Kelly reportedly sought low-profile protection so as not to draw unwanted attention about the matter.[550]

It should also be noted that Dr. Kelly's death occurred against the backdrop of many other very mysterious deaths of microbiologists, in much the same time frame.

IRAQI HIT SQUAD

After a year and one half of work, Norman Baker's systematic research had eliminated the potential suspects of South Africa, Israel, and Russia as being not responsible for the death of David Kelly. For a time, he examined the possibility the Blair or Bush Administrations were behind the murder, but settled on the conclusion that Kelly was murdered by a London-based anti-Saddam Hussein group; one of the opposition groups that was created and funded by the West, in much the same manner as anti-Castro Cubans were trained and funded during the 1960s.

---

[550] Baker, "Strange Death of David Kelly"

He then theorizes that the group's links to a murder of Dr. Kelly was unacceptable politically for the Blair government, because it would create even greater focus on Dr. Kelly's views, which were that there was no case for war, from the standpoint of a weapons inspector. Those realizations made a cover-up necessary and, it was decided, to make the death out to be suicide.[551]

The counter to that argument, however, would be what purpose would there have been for his killers to take the extra time and risk to kill him in such a surreptitious manner?; especially due to the fact that it was known that Dr. Kelly was under the protection from MI5 because there were threats on his life (it was even suggested that he live in a "safe house," but Kelly refused); *and* that anyone planning to try to kill him would therefore assume that their window of opportunity would be a very tight one indeed. So why would they not simply shoot him and run? Why would they kidnap him and hold him for seven-to-twelve hours with the logical assumption that every security team within a thousand miles would be looking for them?

The key to solving these puzzles is in asking the right questions through a process of logical deduction. So if an Iraqi opposition group in London was seriously planning to attempt to assassinate a high-profile asset like Dr. Kelly, they would certainly have to operate on the assumption that their time-window of opportunity would be a very narrow one. Under those circumstances, why would they kidnap him and detain him, kill him in a surreptitious manner, and go to all the trouble of carting his body off to a remote part of Harrowdown Hill, all the time risking failure. Wouldn't it make a lot more sense just to have shot him and disappeared? And here's an even more pertinent question: *Why would they have been able to?*

The above reasons may, by the process of elimination, lead one back to looking at Western intelligence agencies as being responsible for his death.

WESTERN INTELLIGENCE AGENCIES (OR "ROGUE OPERATIVES" FROM SAME)

We have seen that the Bush and Tony Blair Administrations were both very keenly making a case for an illegal invasion of Iraq based on entirely fraudulent data. Dr. Kelly was in the process of exposing the weaknesses in their data, and became, officially or otherwise, an enemy of the State.

However, we have also seen how the U.S. and British governments were extremely adept at putting their spin on the news. Therefore, in the context of contemporaneous events, if they had been able to hold up any evidence of the fact that Iraq was in any way to blame for Dr. Kelly's death, logic demands that they would have done so. They certainly did so with the minimal evidence of Iraq's alleged possession of WMD and the manufactured evidence, falsely reported, that Iraq had sought enriched uranium from Africa. The fact that they did not seize upon such a golden opportunity is highly indicative that they couldn't.

---

[551] Norman Baker, "Did Two Hired Assassins Snatch Weapons Inspector David Kelly?," 22 October 2007, *dailymail.* http://www.globalresearch.ca/index.php?context=viewArticle&code=BAK20071022&articleId=7155

However, Norman Baker points out, there may exist a very good reason why they couldn't. If the killers came from the opposition group in London that was supported by the West, he argues that the blame would look bad and cause unacceptable political damage.

That argument could also be countered, however, by the observation that going to all of the trouble for a faked suicide and a cover-up is probably a lot more work than simply diverting blame from one Iraqi group to another Iraqi group via media spin, which certainly became a specialty of both the Blair and Bush Administrations in their false claims to justify and launch an invasion that was clearly in violation of accepted international law.

Dr. Kelly was what is known in Intelligence as a "high-value target" and, furthermore, everyone was well aware of that fact. At one point, just prior to his death, it was even recommended that he stay at a "safe house"—Kelly declined. But that means that he certainly should have been under surveillance for his own protection, and no one would be more aware of that need than MI5, the British equivalent of the FBI.

So where was his protection on the day that he went missing? Are we really expected to believe that MI5, under the circumstances of known death threats against a high-value target who is a national priority with the most top-secret intelligence of bioweapons research imaginable—just let Dr. Kelly wander off into the woods, all by himself, no protection, no surveillance? It doesn't seem very likely. And we know that the intelligence mission to protect Dr. Kelly, *Operation Mason,* went operational thirty minutes before he even left his house on that fateful afternoon. Whoever did pick up Dr. Kelly that afternoon would have been very hard-pressed to do it, unless some of his would-be protectors had been looking the other way.

Yet the last person to officially see Dr. Kelly alive testified that he was totally alone; unaccompanied, unobserved, unarmed, and completely vulnerable. *Why?*

Michael Shrimpton is a national security expert and prominent attorney in the U.K. with strong ties to MI5 and MI6. Shrimpton was informed, and apparently believes, that Kelly was injected in a high-tech, very professional assassination. His contacts informed him that the shoddy job at wrist-slashing was actually a technique to ensure they covered all traces of the needle mark where Dr. Kelly was injected.[552]

But wait— there's still one more suspect.

INTERNATIONAL BIOWARFARE MAFIA

Another theory on Dr. Kelly's death is that he was murdered by an international mafia operating in biochemical weapons. Though complicated, there is a great deal of evidence suggesting that such a network exists. Furthermore, the murder of Dr. Kelly by this network may have politically necessitated the cover-up and the suicide staging, in much the same way that the assassination of JFK necessitated a government cover-up for security purposes.

[552] Simon Aronowitz, "'Kelly was Murdered' Says U.K. Intelligence Insider," 25 February 2004, *ThoughtCrimeNews.com/PrisonPlanet. com,* http://www.prisonplanet.com/022304kellywasmurdered.html

The reader is directed to an excellent documentary, *Anthrax War*, accessible on YouTube, as well as the book of the same name: http://www.anthraxwar.com/1/?page_id=132

In any event, last word on the topic rightfully goes to House of Commons veteran Norman Baker MP:

"I am convinced beyond a reasonable doubt— *more* than that, in fact— that David Kelly was murdered."[536]

—**Norman Baker,** MP

BIBLIOGRAPHY:

"The Hutton Report", 2003;http://www.the-hutton-inquiry.org.uk/content/report/ *The Strange Death of David Kelly*, Norman Baker MP, 2007

"Dr David Kelly's Death 'was NOT caused by an overdose': Drugs Expert Dismisses Theory on Weapons Inspector", Miles Goslett, October 31, 2010, Daily Mail. http://www.dailymail.co.uk/news/article-1325024/Dr-David-Kelly-s-death-NOT-caused-overdose.html

"Doubts Grow in Whistle-blower Suicide", Alex Newman, June 30, 2010, The New American. http://www.thenewamerican.com/index.php/world-mainmenu-26/europe-mainmenu-35/3905-doubts-grow-in-whistle-blower-suicide

"Three Doctors Dispute How David Kelly Died: Letters Forwarded to National British Newspapers", David Halpin, MB, BS, FRCS, Trauma & Orthopaedic Surgeon & Dr C Stephen Frost, BSc, MB, ChB, Specialist in Diagnostic Radiology (Stockholm, Sweden)& Dr Searle Sennett, BSc, MBChB, FFARCS, Specialist Anaesthesiologist, January 27, 2004. http://www.propagandamatrix.com/260104doctorsdispute.html

"Why I'm certain my friend Dr Kelly was murdered", Andrew Malone, 3 August 2010, Daily Mail. http://www.dailymail.co.uk/news/article-1293568/Why-Im-certain-friend-Dr-Kelly-murdered.html

"Our Doubts About Dr Kelly's Suicide", David Halpin, Specialist in trauma and orthopaedic surgery & C Stephen Frost, Specialist in diagnostic radiology & Searle Sennett Specialist in anaesthesiology, The Guardian, January 27, 2004. http://www.guardian.co.uk/theguardian/2004/jan/27/guardianletters4

"Dr. Kelly's Final Email to a Friend: Dark Actors Playing Games", Jamie Macaskill, July 20, 2003, The Sunday Mail. http://www.rense.com/general39/kellyy.htm

"Kelly Death Paramedics Query Verdict", Antony Barnett, December 12, 2004, The Observer. http://www.guardian.co.uk/uk/2004/dec/12/politics.davidkelly

"Manipulating Pathologic Evidence: The David Kelly Story: Turning Murder into Suicide", Rowena Thursby, November 28, 2003. http://globalresearch.ca/articles/THU311A. html

---

[553] *Anthrax War*, dir. by Bob Coen & Eric Nadler

"Dr Kelly's Final Hours Did Not Indicate Suicide", The Scoop Editor, July 21, 2003 Scoop. co.nz.http://www.scoop.co.nz/stories/HL0307/S00165.htm

"The Murder of Dr. David Kelly, Part One & Part Two", Jim Rarey, October 19, 2003, Medium Rare. http://www.rense.com/general43/kelly.htm and http://www.rense. com/general43/helly2.htm

"Iraq Mobile Labs Nothing to do with Germ Warfare, Report Finds", Peter Beaumont, Observer, June 15, 2003

"Dr. Kelly and Victoria's Secret", November 12, 2003, Jim Rarey, Medium Rare. http:// www.rense.com/general44/jelly.htm

"'Kelly was Murdered' Says UK Intelligence Insider", Simon Aronowitz, February 24, 2004, ThoughtCrimeNews.com/PrisonPlanet.com. http://www.prisonplanet. com/022304kellywasmurdered.html

"Kelly 'Taken Out' By Assassination Team Says British National Security Lawyer", Alex Jones, February 24, 2004, The Alex Jones Show. http://www.rense.com/general49/ kelll.htm

"Alex Jones Interviews Michael Shrimpton: The Murder of Dr. David Kelly-Transcript", Alex Jones, February 24, 2004, The Alex Jones Show. http://www.prisonplanet. com/022504shrimptontranscript.html

"David Kelly's Closest Female Confidante On Why He COULDN'T Have Killed Himself", Sharon Churcher, August 31, 2008, Daily Mail. http://www.dailymail. co.uk/news/article-1050919/David-Kellys-closest-female-confidante-COULDNT-killed-himself.html

"Did Two Hired Assassins Snatch Weapons Inspector David Kelly?", Norman Baker, October 22, 2007, Daily Mail. http://www.globalresearch.ca/index.php?context=vi ewArticle&code=BAK20071022&articleId=7155

"Police admit they could not find trace of fingerprints on Dr David Kelly's glasses after 'suicide'", Miles Goslett, March 14, 2011. http://www.dailymail.co.uk/news/ article-1366301/David-Kelly-inquest-Police-admit-fingerprints-DNA-glasses.html

"Dr David Kelly Post-Mortem Ordered Buried for 70 Years", January 24, 2010, Daily Mail.

"Anthrax War", Bob Coen & Eric Nadler, 2009

"Did MI5 Kill Dr David Kelly?", Sue Reid, July 27, 2009, Daily Mail. http://www. dailymail.co.uk/news/article-1200004/Did-MI5-kill-Dr-David-Kelly-Another-crazy-conspiracy-theory-amid-claims-wrote-tell-book-vanished-death.html

"Police 'Ignored' Dr David Kelly's Mobile Phone Records: Police investigating the death of the Government weapons inspector Dr David Kelly ignored mobile phone records which could have shed light on his movements before he died, it has been claimed"; Andy Bloxham, January 7, 2011, The Telegraph

"Mystery Helicopter Claim Over Dr David Kelly Death: Police have refused to comment on reports that a helicopter mysteriously landed at the scene of weapons expert Dr David Kelly's death shortly after his body was discovered"; May 25, 2011, The Telegraph.

Afterword
By Jesse Ventura

I wanted to say a few words about this book because I consider it very patriotic—and I will explain why.

We, as Americans, would be well advised to take a closer look at our history and our definition of patriotism. With the passing of the insidiously-named *Patriot Act* which profoundly diminishes the civil liberties that veterans like myself and millions of others have fought to protect, we are now officially encouraged to *not* question authority. But, I ask you, is that patriotism? I don't think so. I think patriotism is exactly the opposite. Patriotism isn't blindly following whatever your leaders preach. Patriotism is questioning the government and seeking the truth wherever it leads. That's what real patriotism is in a country that calls itself a Democracy. Blindly following our so-called leaders is *not* patriotism. Behaving like a flock of docile sheep that go wherever they are led is *not* patriotic.

There is a famous movie quote that most people are familiar with where, during a trial, a Marine Corps Colonel is pressed on revealing the truth to a questioning attorney, until it gets to the point where the Colonel has finally had enough and he screams:

You can't handle the truth!

That's a good metaphor for the place that we're in right now because apparently—based on their actions—our so-called leaders don't seem to think that the American people are actually capable of handling the truth.

Isn't it ridiculous that documents related to the JFK assassination are *still sealed* by order of our own government? For what reasons are they still sealed? To protect us? To protect us from *whom* exactly? From *them*, apparently. Why are we being treated like babies who can't handle the truth? I've traveled this land far and wide, and I've come to quite a different conclusion: Americans *can* handle the truth.

This book is a perfect example of how Americans have not been trusted with the truth; it profiles case after case where we have often been intentionally misled and even clearly lied to on the most *basic* points of important events that changed history. The fact that we have been lied to about the JFK assassination is so obvious that it's outrageous. The government cover-up was— and still *is*— so transparent that it's ridiculous.

The assassination of Senator Robert Kennedy is another clear case of a cover-up because it has now been established unequivocally that the defendant, Sirhan Bishara Sirhan, was never *at any point* close enough to have fired the fatal shot.

Most Americans are *still* unaware that a jury in 1999 returned a verdict that Dr. Martin Luther King Jr. was assassinated by a conspiracy that *included agencies of the United States Government.*

That pattern of lying to us has continued. As this book has also documented, the U.S. and British governments lied about Iraq's ability to deliver "weapons of mass destruction." *There was no WMD.* They made it up. Those lies led directly to the war in Iraq, the death of Dr. David Kelly, and the "outing" of CIA agent Valerie Plame as revenge for the attempts of her husband, Ambassador Joe Wilson, to try to get the truth out to the people that there *was* no mass threat from Iraq. But that was a truth that The Powers That Be did not want to hear because it interfered with their plans for war in the oil-rich Middle East. As a veteran who proudly served this country and as an American who cares about his country's future, I think it is *absolutely disgraceful* that the office of the President of the United States was used to intentionally reveal a loyal covert Intelligence Operative and did so simply as a method of political revenge. That's not the definition of a leader—that's the definition of a *traitor.*

Another disturbing trend in recent events is what I see as the very intentional manipulation of the word "conspiracy." They would have us believe that any person who believes that something might possibly be a conspiracy has to be a demented individual. They make it sound like one would have to be crazy to even *suspect* that members of our government could take part in a conspiracy. I suggest that the truth of the matter is quite the contrary. As this book has clearly established, conspiracies are not some rare occurrence in history. They are *common.* They can and do happen all the time.

As we approach the fiftieth anniversary of the JFK assassination, it would seem well time that we, as Americans, come to terms with some very simple truths. I will offer a couple, just to get us started. Beyond the slightest doubt, John F. Kennedy was killed by a conspiracy involving many individuals. That isn't some *theory*—that's the only way it could have happened. Here's another one. Beyond a doubt, the American government in the years following the JFK assassination has intentionally clouded the issue with intentional obfuscations of the true facts of the matter.

So why are we still being lied to about these cases? They seem to be missing a basic point about Democracy—they are *our employees.* They're employed by us— We, The People. How *dare* they withhold the truth from us! Can you imagine if an employee in an office intentionally withheld pertinent information from her or his boss? With what justification? Because she or he didn't think that their boss could *handle* it? That employee would rightfully be thrown out of that office on their ear, and that's what should happen to a lot of people in Washington too. Somehow things have been twisted backwards, and we need to get them back the way that the founders of our country originally intended.

But remember something very important here. Our elected officials are officially *servants* of The People. Technically, they're our *employees*. That's the way this government was set up by its founders. I'd say that the time has now come when We, The People, need to oversee our employees quite a bit more carefully. We need to demand the truth.

There is one thing that is more powerful than all the armies in the world and that is an idea whose time has come. Mahatma Gandhi once said *The truth is far more powerful than any weapon of mass destruction.* Gandhi saw change coming; and it came. So did Martin Luther King; and again, change did come. It is also apparent today when we see the Occupy movements in almost every city in the country. It's a time of change.

In my opinion, it should be a peaceful revolution, and one which starts and continues from a very simple and basic foundation—demanding the truth from our elected representatives.

Some Americans are so demoralized that they may think that the truth doesn't even really matter anymore. I respectfully disagree. I think that we, as Americans, have an obligation to the great foundations of this Democracy, as well as a debt to those who have literally laid down their lives to protect it. As the pages of this book have revealed, we have not been told the truth. So now it's up to us to demand it. We can start with the JFK assassination. We want *all* the records released and we want them *now.* Our elected officials need to be reminded of who their real employers are.

I've said it before and I'll say it again. Americans *can handle* the truth.

And frankly, it's time that we are allowed the opportunity.

A responsible citizen is one who participates in the formation of what is and is not acceptable behavior from their representatives in a Democratic form of government. Our elected officials need to be held responsible for their actions— that's a basic principle of this Republic. And those same representatives have proved over and over again that they have their own agenda— such as the last few *wars*, for example— which are *not* the actual wishes of We, The People, whom they supposedly represent.

America has not officially declared war against any nation since December 8, 1941— yet we are now at war on a virtually continuous basis because, as Major General Smedley Butler cogently observed: "War is a racket." It's great for business and not just for weapons manufacturers either. It's also great for *Halliburton,* and for *Bechtel,* and *General Electric,* and dozens of multibillion-dollar mega-corporations who basically run this country now by buying influence on Capitol Hill. Because corporations know what Will Rogers knew long ago; this country has the best politicians that money can buy.

What's happening in our country? The First Amendment clearly states that "Congress shall make no law abridging the freedom of speech." But it was recently abridged anyway. It wasn't covered much in the media but a new bill, HR 347, was recently passed by Congress and quietly signed into law by President Obama that gives federal agents sweeping powers and now makes it a felony offense for the crime of standing and protesting, determined at the discretion of the Secret Service. As Judge Andrew Napolitano put it, "it is a part of American history since Day One that we have a right to speak freely to, about and against those in the government." But we no longer have it.

Lets' speak plainly. We are talking here about would-be leaders who "rescue" the same bankers who are the very cause of our economic problems, instead of helping the people who have suffered as a result of Wall Street's contemptuous actions. They even use public resources— *our money*— to fund the bailout of the same ruthless financiers, who planned, executed, and caused the whole mess that we find ourselves in. That's not Democracy in action; that's a gang of thieves feasting on the fat of this Republic. They are pigs at the trough, gorging themselves at our expense. We cannot and should not allow it to continue unchecked. It's not what the founders of this great country intended. In fact, it's *exactly* what they were trying to keep from happening.

I've had enough, and I suspect that if you are holding this book in your hands right now that you also have had enough of their lies and encroachment upon our civil liberties. Join me at my website: WeAintGotTimeToBleed.com

It's a place where your comments and opinions are always welcome and also one where we can mobilize our outrage into effective action.

Commit yourself to the process of reclaiming our Democracy. We outnumber them and we have the power of truth and history on our side. We can turn this great Republic of ours back into the Democracy it was intended to be. It won't be easy— but it can be done. And we have to do it, because no one else will.

So stand beside me. And take heart in these words, as I have:

My name is Jesse Ventura and I want my *country* back.

Jesse Ventura
May, 2012